Pro Wrestling
FAQ

Pro Wrestling FAQ

All That's Left to Know About the World's Most Entertaining Spectacle

Brian Solomon

Backbeat
Books

An Imprint of Hal Leonard Corporation

Published in 2015 by Backbeat Books
An Imprint of Hal Leonard Corporation
7777 West Bluemound Road
Milwaukee, WI 53213

Trade Book Division Editorial Offices
33 Plymouth St., Montclair, NJ 07042

The FAQ series was conceived by Robert Rodriguez and developed with Stuart Shea.

Printed in the United States of America

Book design by Snow Creative Services

Library of Congress Cataloging-in-Publication Data is available upon request.

ISBN 978-1-6171-3599-6

www.backbeatbooks.com

For my children, Layla and Jack.
Just when I thought I was out, they pulled me back in.

Contents

Foreword

Pro wrestling, at its very core, is a world of make-believe. What happens inside the ring and on television is just a small part of it.

Like every aspect of the business of pro wrestling, its history is a hotly debated subject. Questions such as the ones discussed in this book (like when pro wrestling went from sport to entertainment) are disputed. And they probably always will be. Those who knew the answers were the type of people who would never limit their telling of a good story by inconvenient things like the truth. And even if there were exceptions to that rule, everyone who was around is long gone.

Thanks to modern researchers, far more is known about the history of wrestling today than at any point in history, at least the basic knowledge of who was wrestling in what city on what day, who won, and when championships changed hands. There are certainly accounts of what happened, and why, that have come out—but the *real* stories, the machinations behind the scenes, the true inner tales, were taken to the grave by the power brokers of eras past. This has left researchers with their own theories and limited knowledge to reconstruct what may have been happening all those decades ago.

At its core, pro wrestling is, and has always been, an entertainment business borne out of both a sport and a world of slick (and sometimes not-so-slick) con men. It has had rises and falls of cultural significance throughout the globe, usually based around charismatic performers, clever promoters, and exposure often stemming from technology. In North America, it has been around in some form or another for more than a century. In some places, at certain times, it reached levels of such ridiculous popularity that few in the U.S. today could possibly conceive. At other times, it struggled just to stay afloat. These highs and lows were often only a short time apart.

Its heroes come in different shapes and sizes, from five-foot-two-inch Oscar Gutierrez (better known as Rey Mysterio) to men who were more than seven feet tall and others who weighed more than seven hundred pounds. Some were the types who had a natural charisma, turning heads wherever they went; others could walk into a room and nobody would pay attention to them. But all were able to perform magic under the lights.

To the fans, pro wrestling scenarios are often morality plays, featuring larger-than-life characters, good vs. evil, simulated sport, wacky comedy, incredible physical drama, good acting, and bad acting. It can be an exciting spectacle that raises your emotions to an almost euphoric state, and it can just as easily be an embarrassing sideshow that leaves its own fan base wondering why they spend time watching it.

It can be a fascinating spectacle both inside, and out, of the ring. Its standout performers are constantly in a quest for that perfect mix of slowing down, speeding up, going up and down, flying and staying grounded to create the most compelling performance. Those in charge behind the scenes are always trying to come up with ideas that are novel enough to captivate existing fans and create new ones. These processes are part of a never-ending evolution. Nobody ever gets it perfect, although on certain days, some come close.

But in pro wrestling, for the performer and the promoter, things are always changing. What worked five years ago, or even five days ago, may not work today, and probably won't work tomorrow. But other elements are timeless: the basic framework of creating a scenario of two or more people who don't like each other, who the public can relate to, and who are convincing and charismatic enough to make you care. That was certainly the case with Gotch and Hackenschmidt in 1911, with Rogers and O'Connor in 1961, and with Rock and Cena in 2011. But a pat hand, if it stays around for any length of time, turns into a losing hand. And the wrong kind of creativity is usually more dangerous than a pat hand.

If you look at a baseball game or a football game from your childhood, you will see that, while strategies certainly change, the basic foundations are there. The pro wrestling of one's childhood, however, never looks the same from an adult perspective. The presentation evolves outside the ring and inside the ring. The heroes of yesteryear, when viewed today, wouldn't fit into the modern product. And the reverse is also true.

It's a business all about a time and a place, and an ability to tap into something that interests enough people to keep everything moving forward.

It started out, more than a century ago, with personalities trying to tap into something similar to what boxing and mixed martial arts do today— establishing people who capture the public's interest and create a sports platform to determine which wrestler is the best. What wrestling always had that real sports didn't is that the people in charge were in far more control over who the best was, because they could manipulate stories and outcomes for maximum impact.

Today, pro wrestling is very different. It's an arena spectacle and television product constantly looking to find or create the characters that will catch on to make the business more popular. It's a constant quest to find—and, more often, luck into—that personality (or mix of personalities), and to create scenarios to keep them as popular as possible, while constantly creating new rivals and preparing successors. It sounds easy, although it's anything but. There's also the human element of the people involved, and the unpredictability of the audience. Today, it's both harder *and* easier than ever before. It's harder in that the audience has far more of an understanding of what the product is, creating a unique love/hate relationship among fans, performers, and their managers, all of whom want to be the ones making the decisions. It's easier, because wrestling companies in the past needed to create constantly successful scenarios and matches or they would cease to exist. Today, with far more revenue streams, the dominant promotion has the ability to make a profit in so many different places that there isn't the constant struggle to stay alive. That said, the barriers of entry are so huge that there are fewer successful companies than ever before.

With this book, Brian Solomon went back to pro wrestling's beginnings, in the different corners of the world, and explains every era, the biggest stars, and the evolution of this unique form of entertainment. All the key figures are represented, from the great manipulators to the great performers, from cultural icons like Hogan, Londos, Rikidozan, Inoki, and El Santo, to characters that represent a time and a place in local cultures, including Rhodes, Von Erich, Blassie, Sammartino, Lawler, Stevens, Crusher, Bruiser, and Flair, to those who started out in wrestling and became far bigger when they left, like Rock and Ventura. From the days when society romanticized their sports heroes in the '20s, to the heroes of the depression in the '30s, the explosion of television in the '50s, the proliferation of UHF stations in the '70s, and the cable explosion of the '80s, the wrestling business changed and mutated based on the technology of the time.

At its core, it is make-believe. But at its zenith, it leaves memories that are very real.

Dave Meltzer

Dave Meltzer is the world' foremost professional wrestling journalist. Since 1983, his Wrestling Observer *newsletter has been the most respected and widely read trade publication in the industry.*

Acknowledgments

This book has been a dream project for me, which is why I'm eternally grateful to those who have helped make it possible.

First and foremost, I wouldn't have been able to pull it off without the love and support of my family. That includes my amazing parents, Robert and Janice Solomon, who've tolerated my wrestling obsession since I was twelve years old; my wonderful children, Layla and Jack Solomon, who have been the best unpaid research assistants and transcribers an author can hope for; and my beleagured and beautiful fiancée Jaimee Moxham, who has put up with more 24/7 wrestling over the past few months than any non-fan should ever have to endure, and yet still was a good enough sport to read over the manuscript. Also deserving mention is my late uncle, Peter Purpura, who taught me that one can be both a cultured intellectual and an unapologetic wrestling fan.

The entire project never would have gotten off the ground if a fateful introduction hadn't been made between Hal Leonard Books and me by "Mean" Mike Edison. My editor Bernadette Malavarca has been nothing but helpful and patient in answering every question and working with me on every detail. Credit also goes to Wes Seeley in publicity and marketing.

In preparation for writing the book, I had the honor of picking the brains of a number of insightful individuals within the business: historians, writers, and talent who were generous with their time and knowledge. These include Bill Apter, Brian Heffron (a.k.a. The Blue Meanie), Charlie Thesz, Dave Meltzer, David Shoemaker, Dr. Tom Prichard, Greg Oliver, Kevin Kelly, Mike Chapman, Scott Teal, Norman Keitzer, Stu Saks, Steve Yohe, and Tim Hornbaker. That also includes Evan Ginzburg, who even invited me to be on *Legends TV* to promote the book, and my old colleague and mentor Keith Elliot Greenberg, who was kind enough to provide invaluable insight on the manuscript.

Even more challenging than the actual writing of the book was amassing the photographs, and there were several sources that provided crucial assistance in that regard. These include the folks at Kappa Publishing Group/*Pro Wrestling Illustrated*; George Rugg and Sara Weber, curators of the magnificent Jack Pfefer Collection at the University of Notre Dame; as well as longtime Canadian wrestling photographer Terry Dart.

Finally, I'd be remiss if I didn't thank those individuals from my days working for WWE who helped direct my career and provided inspiration for me to find my foothold in the wrestling business, especially Barry Werner, Mike Fazioli, Shane McMahon, and Howard Finkel.

Introduction
Before the Bell

There is no more a problem of truth in wrestling than in the theater. In both, what is expected is the intelligible representation of moral situations, which are usually private. This emptying out of interiority to the benefit of its exterior signs, this exhaustion of the content by the form, is the very principle of triumphant classical art.

—Roland Barthes, *Mythologies* (1957)

Whether you like or you don't like it, learn to love it—'cause it's the best thing going today!

—"Nature Boy" Ric Flair

Entertainment? Sport? Performance art? However you classify it, there's one thing professional wrestling definitely is: Big business. From its origins as a nineteenth century carnival attraction, right up to the multi-million-dollar pay-per-view and streaming extravaganzas of today, pro wrestling has captivated the attention of legions of enthusiasts. Drawing on an athletic endeavor with ancient origins, with a distinctly American spin that helped turn it into a worldwide cultural phenomenon, pro wrestling is something completely unique, defying all attempts at categorization or explanation. Is it "real" or "fake"? Those who "get it" will tell you that's a completely irrelevant question.

Pro Wrestling FAQ will delve into this bizarre and fascinating world, and the many aspects that define it. There's a rich history to explore: After all, professional wrestling was once presented as a legit contest, emerging from the Civil War era to become one of the nation's most popular sports, eventually evolving into the outrageous, soap-opera–like spectacle we have today, with its colorful cast of characters and over-the-top storylines. From the move toward overt theatricality in the 1920s, through the post-World War II TV wrestling craze now known as the "Golden Age," through Vince McMahon's reinvention of the genre in the 1980s and beyond, each era will be given its due.

Such a wild and woolly business would be nothing without the unforgettable personalities that have intrigued fans and insiders over the years. This

The Wrestlers (1905) by George Luks. Museum of Fine Arts, Boston.

The Hayden Collection—Charles Henry Hayden Fund

book will shine the light on notables such as Frank Gotch, possibly America's first major sports superstar; the Gold Dust Trio, who helped redefine the nature of the business; Gorgeous George, one of the first TV celebrities; Hulk Hogan, the larger-than-life superhero who became the most famous wrestler of all time; Vince McMahon, the visionary whose WWE megalith has dominated the business for the past three decades; and many, many more.

In addition, you'll find in-depth analysis on the nature of this crazy thing we call pro wrestling, as well as an exhaustive glossary of insider terminology, the greatest matches ever witnessed, and much more. If you've ever called yourself a fan of the most popular form of sports/entertainment/performance art that's ever existed, then this book probably has something in it for you.

As for me, I've been a fan for close to thirty years, and through an unusual series of life occurrences, I've managed to become even *more* than a fan. From 2000 to 2007, I was a writer and editor in WWE's Publications Department, contributing each month to periodicals like *RAW Magazine* and *WWE Magazine,* and even serving as editor-in-chief for the well-intentioned but ill-fated *SmackDown! Magazine.* It's not everyone who gets to write and edit a magazine he used to read as a kid, and in the end, my seven years in the Tower left me with a slew of stories I can tell my grandkids, and a slew of stories I *can't* tell my grandkids.

For a lifelong pro wrestling nut who got hooked on the business when Andre the Giant ripped off Hulk Hogan's crucifix on Piper's Pit ("You're bleedin', man.") and subsequently became an obsessive student of the history of the game stretching back to the storied days of Gotch and Hackenschmidt, the opportunity to work for WWE was a literal dream come true, and gave me a coveted glimpse into a world that fascinates me and so many others. It was also during this time that I conceptualized and wrote the book *WWE Legends* (a look at the company's major stars of the '50s, '60s, and '70s), and contributed to the boldly named *Ultimate WWE Trivia Book*. I traveled to twenty-three states and one foreign country; hung out in "Classy" Freddy Blassie's basement while wearing his house slippers; toasted champagne cocktails with Ric Flair all night in Manchester, England; was a guest at the Hulkster's Clearwater, Florida, compound; and once got stuck in a limo with Vince McMahon for three hours and lived to tell the tale.

No matter where life may take me, my great love will always be the squared circle, and all the insane things that take place both inside of it, and perhaps even more intriguingly, outside of it. For years, people have been telling me I should write a book on professional wrestling. Well, here it is.

Kayfabe

Wrestling's Time-Honored Code of Secrecy

Each culture has its own form of staged combat, evolved from its particular method of street fighting and cleaned up for presentation as a spectacle.
—David Mamet

Any in-depth study of the phenomenon of professional wrestling must begin with a very simple question: What exactly is it? This may, on the surface, seem like a superfluous or obvious question, but it is worth asking. Just what *is* professional wrestling, anyway?

In its purest form, it takes the appearance of a physical, competitive sport—although over the passage of time, this resemblance has become less and less apparent. However, it's worth pointing out the single greatest paradox of them all: professional wrestling is not, in fact, professional wrestling. That is to say, the very name of the endeavor itself is a euphemism designed to support the illusion. It implies that professional wrestling is the pro counterpart of amateur wrestling, in the same way as in sports such as basketball, football, or boxing. But nothing could be further from the truth. Not only are professional wrestling and amateur wrestling two completely different and unrelated pursuits, but one of the greatest misconceptions perpetuated in the early days of the business was that the former grew out of the latter.

The entertainment genre known as "professional wrestling" is, in reality, not a competitive sport in the mainstream sense at all, but a rehearsed and choreographed performance presented for the diversion of its fans. This is not meant to denigrate the pursuit in any way; it remains to this day one of the most popular forms of entertainment on the entire planet, and requires great athletic skill on the part of its participants. One could even argue that the athletic skills required are even greater than those required in some competitive sports, since the athletes must coordinate their performance in such a way as to simulate combat without actually harming each other (although injuries are inevitably common).

The key word here is "simulation." At its core, pro wrestling is the simulation of one-on-one physical competition. Since its earliest beginning as a business, the nagging question of whether it is "real" or "fake" has never truly gone away—which is surprising given its current manifestation and the very open secret under which it currently operates. Professional "wrestlers" (known inside the business as "workers") are not literally wrestlers, in the sense that they are not actually wrestling with one another in the ring; rather, they are generating the illusion that they are wrestling, employing a time-honored and highly impressive form of performance art to create an entertainment spectacle that is difficult to compare to anything else. This is why the fan-favorite question of "who is the greatest wrestler of all time?" is futile at best, and one that misses the entire point: when it comes to actual combat-style wrestling, the vast majority of modern performers require very little fundamental knowledge to be successful. The question of "who would win?" is irrelevant, because "who would win?" isn't decided between the ropes, but in the front office.

And so, to those who truly love and follow the wrestling business, the whole issue of real vs. fake is completely meaningless. Revealing to the average wrestling aficionado that pro wrestling is scripted and that his favorite wrestlers are not actually trying to defeat one another would be the equivalent of revealing to fans of *The Walking Dead* TV series that those zombies they see every week are actually actors wearing makeup. Which is to say, the fact that pro wrestling is scripted entertainment is—to those who understand it—not the knock that wrestling-bashers see it as; rather, it is exactly what pro wrestling is *supposed* to be. Especially in this era when mixed martial arts (MMA) provides sports fans with authentic grappling combat in a competitive sense, the role of pro wrestling as entertainment is more pronounced and obvious than ever before. People don't watch wrestling in the same way as they watch boxing or UFC, but more like they might watch an action movie, or stand-up comedy.

Hurry, Hurry, Step Right Up . . .

That isn't to say that it was always so. In order for professional wrestling to be a simulation of true combat, then that simulation must have been originally based on some kernel of reality. In short, pro wrestling currently exists as an exaggerated simulation of what it once was. In a business based in deception and misinformation, one of the greatest bits of misinformation was the often-stated claim that the pro wrestling business developed out of the ancient wrestling traditions dating back to Roman and Greek times, and even earlier. Promoters and well-intentioned historians often pointed to the practices of the Egyptians, the venerated Grecian champion Milo, and even the Biblical tale of Jacob and the angel (the first ladder match?).

Nevertheless, despite such bold claims, the origins of the professional wrestling business are not to be found there. The actual practice of wrestling may be one of the world's oldest sports, but the business we know and love today actually has its origins in the shady world of carnivals and sideshows. During the nineteenth and even into the early twentieth century, touring carnivals presented professional wrestling exhibitions as a way to entertain local crowds, and to separate them

So how did professional wrestling go from this . . .
George Grantham Bain Collection (Library of Congress)

from their cash. Several scenarios were popular. The carnival would often have a troupe of legitimately skilled wrestlers who would "work" matches with each other, in which the outcome was pre-planned. Unsuspecting onlookers would place wagers on the affair, and by controlling the result, the promoters and competitors could usually walk away with a tidy sum in side-bets alone. Sometimes, the wrestlers would challenge spectators from the crowd. In some situations, these "spectators" were actually plants, often meant to make the challenging wrestler appear beatable. Then, when an actual spectator made a challenge, he found himself twisted in knots, and he and his supporters bilked of their dough. Sometimes, the challenges made to the crowd were legitimate, which is why it was all-important in those days that the wrestlers actually knew how to wrestle.

Wrestlers were expected to be "straight shooters," or just "shooters," for short. An expression taken from the carnival practice of bending pellet guns so that "marks," or naïve spectators, could be prevented from actually winning at the shooting games, a "straight shooter" was a wrestler who could really take care of himself. A notch above shooters were the

... to *this?*   *Marty555/Wikimedia*

hookers—wrestlers who had been taught to "hook" their opponents in crippling ways, if necessary. These men were needed to ensure that the carnies always stayed a step ahead of the marks and never found themselves the victims of a double-cross.

This world of supreme con artistry and rigged athleticism is where the modern professional wrestling business was born, and where its fundamental philosophy and purpose for existing took shape. The debate still rages as to whether professional wrestling was ever actually a competitive sport, and to what degree it was ever really "real." Some claim that it started out as a legit competition and was later transformed into a show. Others will tell you that it was always a show, and promoters have been conning fans since the whole thing began. Given the hazy and often inscrutable nature of pro wrestling history, it's next to impossible to get to the bottom of it, but the truth probably lies, as it often does, somewhere in between.

Spectacle over Sport

It's safe to say that professional wrestling once involved a lot more actual competitive wrestling, and that a percentage of the matches presented were genuine contests. In the ensuing century and a half, that has changed dramatically, to the point that today the pretense is all but gone, and the business is presented as what it is: an athletic spectacle termed by its most prominent purveyor, Vince McMahon, as "sports-entertainment." Breaking more and more from its sporting origins as time goes by, what constitutes pro wrestling has come to include increasingly outlandish stunts and outrageous characters, to the point that the resemblance to how it all started becomes more tenuous with each passing decade.

"Pro wrestling has changed over the years, for sure," says respected author and historian Greg Oliver. "And it's not just the product itself; it's society. We expect things to be quicker, we expect things to be more complex, and there are so many more options for people to watch that you have to hook people with things that may be a little flashier than they would've been, say, thirty years ago. Pro wrestling had to evolve over the years."

Over the course of its evolution, professional wrestling came to be about so much more than the mere simulation of a competitive sport. Performers must be gifted in more than just athleticism; they must have the ability to project their personalities, to deliver a speech (or "cut a promo") on the mic. A good wrestler is also a good actor, and charisma goes a long way. More than just simple matches, the professional wrestling product is built around ongoing storylines, or "angles," designed to build interest in the show and the performers involved. Athletes take on specific character personas, or "gimmicks," which, in the surreal world of wrestling, can often become conflated with their real-life personas. Promoters and bookers craft these ongoing angles, and determine who will feud with whom, who will win and lose, and why. These people—both the ones in the ring, and behind the curtain—are storytellers, and pro wrestling, more than a mere pseudo-sport, is nothing short of a broad form of theater.

"The way that half of Shakespeare's jokes were directly addressed to the rabble of the front rows, and the way that ancient Greek theater had players with these giant masks so the guys in the twentieth row could understand— that's something that wrestling has never lost," explains David Shoemaker, Internet wrestling pundit and author of the 2013 book *Squared Circle: Life, Death and Professional Wrestling*. "A good guy isn't a good guy unless the crowd's cheering for him, and that's something that's almost completely lost in Hollywood or professional sports. It's one part fake sport, and one part modern mythology."

A Time-Honored Tradition

From the beginning, the business was protected by a code of secrecy known as "kayfabe." Thought by some to be a bastardization of the words "be fake" spoken backwards, the term started out as a catch-word used by those within the business to warn each other to dummy up when outsiders were present, so that the true nature of the business wouldn't be revealed. Back then, it was all-important to those within the business that their paying audience believed that what they were seeing was on the up-and-up. Even in later years, when the theatrics of the show became obvious to all but a naïve and sheltered few, the practice of maintaining "kayfabe" remained of major importance. The thinking was that if the fans understood the true nature of what they were watching, the business would die. And even later, when fans started to become more and more "in on the act," the practice remained—partly out of tradition, and partly due to the recognition that willing suspension of disbelief is a big part of what made wrestling work. It was an unspoken agreement between the business and its fans: you present a product that is reasonably convincing and entertainingly believable, and we'll happily play along. For unlike other forms of entertainment, pro wrestling is unique in that it has traditionally worked hard to convince viewers that what they are watching is "real."

"When I was growing up, I never thought [kayfabe] was that important because I thought people, at the end of the day, watched wrestling for entertainment, and I think Vince [McMahon] thought the same thing," says Dave Meltzer, creator of the iconic *Wrestling Observer* newsletter and the business's most prolific journalist. "Before TV, maybe it was really important. Once you're getting an audience on TV, I don't think real vs. fake was that big of a deal. It's the same thing as marketing a movie: if you have big stars, and you have good action, and it's exciting, people will gravitate towards it. I think that maintaining the illusion of reality while the show is going [on] is very important. But as far as maintaining the illusion twenty-four hours a day, was it that important? I don't think so. . . . You have to believe the guys are real stars. If you don't believe they're real stars, it doesn't matter if you think that what they're doing is real or not."

Kayfabe became much more than a word; it was an entire way of life, designed to protect the business and maintain the illusion. And although it still exists, these days it is more a method of enhancing the entertainment value than protecting any secrets. A combination of events, including Vince and Linda McMahon's 1989 legal declaration that wrestling was not a sport (in order to avoid taxation by state athletic commissions); Paul Heyman's ECW and its deconstruction of popular wrestling tropes; the rise of that exposer of all secret information, the Internet; and McMahon's on-air admission in 1997 that his WWF was meant to be taken as entertainment (commonly called the "Death of Kayfabe" speech) have resulted in an ongoing deterioration of kayfabe. The idea of a performer appearing on a TV talk show out of character, or of discussing storylines in a public venue, would once have been unthinkable.

"When you think about the fans today, WWE has spent the last quarter-century cultivating a different breed of fan," explains Keith Elliot Greenberg, longtime WWE magazine writer and author of biographies of such grappling luminaries as "Classy" Freddy Blassie, Superstar Billy Graham, and Ric Flair. "A fan who looks at it as entertainment, who is able to acknowledge, hey, these guys are great athletes, but who recognize this isn't like watching the Super Bowl. Maybe in the old days, people like my grandparents, if they had discovered that what they were vesting their passions in was anything but legit, they would feel betrayed and hurt and angry."

But in our postmodern, ironic world, pro wrestling has finally been embraced for what it really is. Nevertheless, during the show itself, kayfabe is still the name of the game, and fans continue to debate what is a "shoot" and what is a "work." Even after a century-and-a-half, and despite kayfabe's current status as an open secret, the carnies continue to find ways to work the marks. And the marks continue to enjoy every minute of it.

A Secret Language

In order to properly keep things from their intended marks, carnival workers (or "carnies") long ago came up with their own coded form of communication. Usually known as "carny," but sometimes as "ciazarn," it survives in large part today thanks to the wrestling business, which grew out of the carnival circuit.

Similar in some respect to other forms such as pig Latin, speaking carny involves twisting words a certain way so as to obscure their meaning to the uninitiated. Specifically, one inserts an "iz" sound prior to every syllable (a variant form instead calls for the insertion of an "ee-az" sound). For example, if one wanted to say, "Watch out for this mark," in carny that would sound something like, "Wizatch izout fizor thizis mizark." When spoken quickly and fluently, it is usually impenetrable to those not in the know.

Traditionally, carny might be used among performers and referees in the ring, for example, in order to prevent ringside fans from catching on to what was being said regarding the performance of the match, or any other guarded topic. Although it has somewhat fallen out of favor, this pseudo-language, sometimes called "Izzle" by linguists, is still used, and has even made its way into popular culture through its adoption by hip-hop culture. What led to this adoption remains unclear.

Let There Be Tights

Wrestling's Carny Origins

Everything being a constant carnival, there is no carnival left.
—Victor Hugo

The birth of professional wrestling is tied directly to the birth of professional sports. Owing in large part to the industrial revolution of the late-eighteenth century which allowed the average man to be less physically active than was previously required, a culture of exercise and fitness arose that emphasized physical activity and sports in particular, as a means of maintaining good health. Needless to say, as one of the most basic and fundamental of all sports, wrestling was an easy sell in this regard, and became a very common form of leisure activity for workingmen of the late eighteenth and early nineteenth centuries. Evidence shows that early American colonists enjoyed practicing a specific form of wrestling known as "collar-and-elbow," a style that begins with opponents locked up with one hand at the other's elbow and the other at his collar (which survives today in the traditional opening hold still often used in pro wrestling bouts).

"Wrestling was a very popular sport in those days, not just to prove how tough you were, but it also was a great way to get and stay in condition," explains Steve Yohe, one of the game's most accomplished and diligent historians. "It was the sport of America's farmland and rural areas, where dirt roads were muddy and hard to run on, and weight rooms were rare. Wrestling is a sport that builds up all the body's systems. It was something they could play with using little equipment at night or on breaks during work. With so many people involved, a lot of the guys gained reputations as major wrestlers. Very few could handle a true pro, but the best of them were picked to be trained in the skill of hooking."

A Carnival Attraction

With the rise of an athletic culture in Europe and the newborn United States, wrestling soon became adopted as a regular attraction in traveling circuses and carnivals on both sides of the Atlantic. As early as the late eighteenth century, one can find records of popular carnival wrestlers such as one William Richardson touring the countryside taking on all comers in local towns. Even going back this far, the legitimacy of the contests is difficult to determine for sure, but it is safe to say that these early carnival wrestlers were formidable grapplers who needed to take care of themselves, whether or not their selected opponents were a part of the show. Carnival wrestling would explode in popularity as the nineteenth century arrived, and would persist even into the twentieth century. Nevertheless, the future of professional wrestling lay along a different path that would take it far beyond the circus tent.

In those days there were several different forms of wrestling that were being taken up by the very earliest professionals. In addition to collar-and-elbow, there was also Greco-Roman, a version first popularized in France during the 1830s that harkened back (or so they claimed) to the wrestling of ancient Greece and Rome, with its prohibition of any holds below the waist. Then there was the much more dangerous catch-as-catch-can style, or simply "catch" for short, which allowed holds of any kind (with the usual exception of strangleholds). The most violent of forms, it often resulted in grievous injury, and sometimes even death. Ironically, this most "real" of all styles would be the one that would most directly develop into the modern professional style, and also flourishes today thanks to the mixed martial arts (MMA) craze.

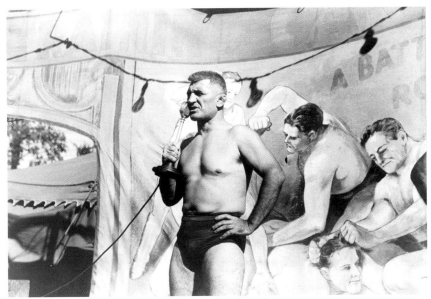

A carnival wrestler issues a challenge to the local marks.
Office of War Information Photograph Collection (Library of Congress)

With the influx of early immigrants to the U.S. from England, Ireland, France, and other parts of Western Europe came also an influx of these different wrestling styles. Whether settling down as migrant workers, farmers, or other forms of laborers, these newly minted Americans helped spread the popularity of wrestling, and also helped carry the carnival phenomenon over from the old country. A specific type of traveling entertainment, known as the athletic show (or "at show" for short) arose, which ostensibly served to entertain and edify backwoods locals with exhibitions of sporting skill, but were really more about conning them out of their hard-earned cash through the practice of wagering on highly questionable matchups.

"Pro wrestling was always a work in one way or another," offers Yohe. "The outcome of the match was always known before the athletes stepped into the ring. . . . Sport in the nineteenth century, and into the twentieth, was really about gambling. Americans loved gambling more than anything. So that's why sports like running, biking and rowing were popular at that time. "

A Wartime Pastime

For the first time since antiquity, wrestlers were able to make a regular living plying their trade, but things were only going to get more lucrative. By the mid-nineteenth century, the sporting culture was more popular than ever, and professional sport in particular was on the verge of taking hold of the American consciousness in a big way. During the 1860s, the Civil War served as something of a crucible for the development of American sports. Bringing together men of disparate backgrounds and nationalities, it allowed for a great deal of cross-pollination and helped popularize certain physical endeavors that would experience a renaissance following Robert E. Lee's surrender at the Appomattox Court House. Among these was baseball, which would soon see the creation of its first major league; and wrestling, which emerged for the first time as a sport people would be willing to pay money to see on its own, divorced from the carnivals.

The earliest successful professional wrestlers, men like Col. James Hiram McLaughlin and George William Flagg, would first come to prominence during their time serving in the war. McLaughlin was the wrestling champion of the 26th New York Infantry, while Flagg enjoyed the title of Grand Champion of the Army of the Potomac. Before long, wrestlers like McLaughlin, Flagg, and others such as John McMahon (no relation to the later sports-entertainment dynasty), Homer Lane, and Henry Moses "H. M." Dufur were calling the shots, challenging each other to matches that would be advertised in local (and sometimes national) newspapers, and would attract sizeable crowds of interested spectators. Before long they could expect significant purses from such encounters. One 1873 bout between McLaughlin and McMahon earned the winner four-thousand dollars, at a time when the average worker's yearly salary was roughly one-thousand dollars.

The locations of these bouts varied. With the professional sports phenomenon only just beginning, there were not yet many large arena-like venues, and so most matches transpired in saloons, at railway stations, in outdoor fields, or anywhere else large groups of working-class men might easily gather. If you were lucky, a bout might be held on the stage of a music hall, which was a dicey proposition since the use of a ring had not yet come into fashion and matches were typically held on a mat with nothing to keep the participants from spilling into the crowd. As much as the popularity of wrestling grew out of a desire for physical fitness and clean living, there can be no denying that the earliest professional wrestling events were most likely pretty unsavory happenings populated by some very rough-around-the-edges individuals. Given the alarmingly high rate of serious injury and fatality in these early encounters, it's reasonable to assume that many of them were completely on the level. However, given the large amounts of money at stake and the sport's carny mentality, it's easy to understand why this wouldn't last for very long.

"A true pro wrestler, and the major ones were few in number, were in the business to make money," says Yohe. "So they worked matches in a way to get the most money for their efforts. Pro wrestlers knew there was very little money to be made by just beating people who had very little chance to win. So they worked matches to make others look like equals and not show their superiority until the end. It became entertaining, and the marks would return for more. The money was always more important than anyone's ego. Many times the local was in on the work, and got a cut. Either way, the pro and his management knew who was going to win and who to put their money on."

From the Saloon Hall to the Arena

The stakes kept getting higher and higher, with newspapers feeding into the ballyhoo, as well as fledgling periodicals like the *National Police Gazette*, which even promoted its own championship. And speaking of championships, once newspapers and promoters realized that matches would have more allure if titles were on the line, they began to introduce them, with the earliest being the American Collar and Elbow Championship, first won by Col. McLaughlin in 1867 with a win over Louis Ainsworth in Newark, New Jersey. Later would come such titles as the American Greco-Roman Championship, the American Catch-As-Catch-Can Championship, and even the European Catch-As-Catch-Can Championships. All the more reason for the first generations of wrestling fans to pay money to watch the top grapplers of the era do battle.

Still, the majority of the money to be made in those days came not from ticket sales, but from wagering. And just as with many sports of the day, this would inevitably lead to fixing. For long before professional wrestling was scripted entertainment, it was quite simply a dirty sport. Baseball had its fair share of chicanery too, but it was boxing and wrestling, with far fewer participating parties to get in on the fix, that became ripe for corruption. By the 1880s it was already becoming common for spectators and sportswriters alike to suspect that certain matches may not have been entirely honest.

"It is almost impossible to say definitively when it crossed over from being legit to being a performance," says Tom Hornbaker, author of the definitive historical tome, *National Wrestling Alliance*. "This is one of the biggest mysteries of wrestling history. Pro wrestling was certainly genuine at times, even occasionally into the 1930s. But promoters learned in the latter stages of the 1800s that it was better to work a carefully crafted match full of excitement to make the crowd happy and set up a rematch."

As wrestling's popularity as a spectator sport grew, the "hippodrome match" became the order of the day. As opposed to the smaller traveling shows and backroom brawls that were still prevalent, hippodrome matches were the future: matches contested in large arenas, with the purpose of not only earning revenue from gambling, but of drawing as large a paying crowd as possible, with the attendance of several thousand fans becoming a common occurrence. The era of the modern live sporting event was at hand, but for wrestling, this only further edged the sport away from honest competition. While the competitors of the day were indeed highly skilled grapplers, and their matches no doubt very legitimate in appearance, the belief is that outcomes came to be fixed in advance, in order to not only reap the rewards via gambling, but also to increase interest in future matches and to protect the physical well-being of the participants, if possible.

"It's hard to say, because none of us were around then," says wrestling journalist Dave Meltzer. "My impression is that there were a little bit of both. If you watch a real match and a fake match, no matter how good the guys are, you have to be good to pull it off. Usually you can tell by the intensity level in it. I can't imagine in the 1880s the people were so good to be able to fool a trained eye. . . . But as far as pro wrestling as a 100 percent legitimate sport, I suppose that back in the 1860s, for whatever existed then, at the very first, perhaps. But it didn't last long, if it even ever existed. In the 1880s I know that worked matches existed and shoot matches existed. Shoot matches probably existed very sparingly."

A major impetus for wrestling's graduation from the pool halls to the arenas was the rise of one William Muldoon, a New York City policeman who would become the sport's first major star. After debuting in 1876, he quickly rose to prominence due to his dedication to physical fitness and level of near-unbeatability that led him to be nicknamed "The Solid Man," thanks to a popular song written about him. Muldoon defeated Prof. Thiebaud Bauer on January 18, 1880, to win the American Greco-Roman Championship in what was the first wrestling event held at the original Madison Square Garden (then known as Gilmore Garden). From there, he would embark on a nationwide tour in which he would meet and defeat all challengers, including such top competitors of the day as England's Edwin Bibby, Germany's Carl Abs, Japan's Sorakichi Matsuda, Evan "Strangler" Lewis (the first grappler to bear that moniker), and his greatest rival of all, "The Kansas Demon" Clarence Whistler.

Big-money purses and packed arenas were starting to become the norm, as wrestling became, alongside baseball, cycling, and boxing, one of America's first popular professional sports. And once boxing was eventually banned for a time due to excessive violence, wrestling's caché only grew. The style became more streamlined, as the archaic collar-and-elbow version fell out of favor, and catch (or "freestyle") wrestling became the standard of the day. Incorporating all manner of holds, as well as certain types of striking, it would be the form that would develop into the modern style of professional wrestling. As opposed to previous versions in which merely throwing your opponent was counted as a fall, under the new catch rules, wrestlers had to pin their opponent's shoulders to

"The Kansas Demon," Clarence Whistler, archrival of William Muldoon, who died in 1885 after swallowing broken glass for a carnival trick.
Carroll County Historical Museum (Public domain)

the mat in order to gain the fall. Much as in boxing, rings were introduced and elevated off the floor for easier viewing, with ropes to keep the combatants in (and the fans out, as the case may be).

Streamlining the Sport

In 1893, Evan "Strangler" Lewis solidified the emerging style by defeating Muldoon's protégé Ernst Roeber in a best-of-five-falls match in New Orleans to unify the American Greco-Roman and Catch-As-Catch-Can Championships into the American Heavyweight Championship. It would instantly become the most coveted title in the land, and the first time the sport was built around one major title. And yet Lewis would eventually lose it to an archrival that had dogged him for years and would become the most dominant American wrestler since Muldoon.

In addition to beating Lewis for the American Championship in 1895, Martin Burns helped popularize the new pinning method of achieving falls thanks to his dedication to developing such pinfall and submission holds as the full nelson, hammerlock, toe hold, and other maneuvers that would later become a part of nearly every wrestler's arsenal. Burns had competed against Lewis before; in 1889, when the full-time farmer arrived unannounced to challenge Lewis in Chicago while still in his overalls (legend has it he had forgotten his wrestling gear that day), the announcer introduced him as Farmer Burns, and the name stuck.

Although he would be perhaps the top American grappler of the 1890s, Burns's title victory over Lewis is also known for being one of the earliest examples of wrestling being ridiculed by the press and the public, as observers seemed to suspect that the two participants may have actually been cooperating rather than competing. The authenticity of the match notwithstanding, the toughness and raw ability of Farmer Burns was never in question. The man had trained his body to the peak of its ability, and despite his smaller size, his conditioning usually allowed him to outlast any opponent. It would also lead him to open a wrestling school in 1893 that would go on to become an even greater legacy for him than anything he accomplished in the ring.

By the end of the nineteenth century, the sport of professional wrestling was big business, and change was certainly in the air. Farmer Burns would be responsible for training a whole new generation of wrestlers that would help to transform the business, most notably a fellow farm boy from Humboldt, Iowa, whom he would discover in 1899 and help to become not only the most successful wrestler the sport had ever seen, but also America's first true sports celebrity.

Major Stars of the Era

The late nineteenth century produced some of America's original star athletes—including the men who first helped to put pro wrestling on the map.

- Benjamin F. Roller
- Carl Abs
- Clarence Whistler
- Dan McLeod
- Edwin Bibby
- Ernst Roeber
- Evan "Strangler" Lewis
- Farmer Burns
- George W. Flagg
- H. M. Dufur
- Jack Carkeek
- James Hiram McLaughlin
- Joe Acton
- John McMahon
- Sorakichi Matsuda
- The Terrible Turk
- Thiebaud Bauer
- Tom Cannon
- Viro Small
- William Muldoon

The Solid Man

Perhaps more than any of his peers, William Muldoon exemplified the ascent of professional wrestling from the pool halls to the arenas. With a foot in both worlds, he was one of the first major athletic figures in America, and a force in the New York sports landscape for half a century.

Born to Irish immigrants on May 25, 1852, in the tiny town of Caneadea in the western corner of New York State, Muldoon eventually chose to enter the profession in the tradition of so many sons of Erin in those days, becoming a New York City police officer after relocating to the Big Apple in his twenties. He would eventually rise to the rank of detective before the lure of the mat proved too much and he became a full-time pro in 1881.

A farmer in his earlier years, his impeccable physical condition from a tender age made him a natural in any sports he put his mind to. As a youth, he was also driven by an insatiable need for respect, which manifested itself in an unusually hot temper. It seemed he was suited to combat from the beginning.

But prior to mixing it up as a pro grappler, Muldoon would first prove his mettle after enlisting as a drummer boy with the Sixth Cavalry during the Civil War, and would later serve with the Sixth during the Indian Wars of the Great Plains. While in the service, he was exposed to the burgeoning sport of wrestling then en vogue among the soldiers. He'd put those skills to good use when he volunteered to serve on the side of France in the Franco-Prussian War of 1870–71. Strong proponents of the Greco-Roman style Muldoon preferred, French wrestling enthusiasts convinced Muldoon to pursue the sport as a profession.

The wrestling cop made quite a splash on the scene in the late 1870s, and by the time he captured the American Greco-Roman title from Prof. Thiebaud

Bauer in Madison Square Garden, he had become the toast of the sporting world. (Muldoon and Bauer were no strangers, having already competed in a nine-and-a-half-hour match, believed to be the longest in history.) Muldoon's efforts to take on all comers became legendary, earning him his lifelong nickname, The Solid Man. Chief among his rivals was "The Kansas Demon" Clarence Whistler, whom he faced in not one but two epic encounters renowned for their brutality and intensity. He would hold on to the prize for the remainder of his career, going undefeated until his retirement in 1890, when he passed the title along to his protégé Ernst Roeber.

But Muldoon was also smart enough to "do business." He famously took his act on the road, touring the country with a troupe of other wrestlers and taking on challengers everywhere he went. The press and the fans ate it up, even though most historians believe that these touring matches were among the sports' earliest examples of "worked" performance matches.

"He was smart enough to have a stable of wrestlers traveling around the country," says Steve Yohe. "He helped develop a booking system to get matches over. He understood it was better to draw a feud out over two or three cards, instead of one. He created some of the booking foundation of the sport."

During his years on top, his fame allowed him to appear on Broadway, including an 1889 appearance as Charles the Wrestler alongside old friend Maurice Barrymore (patriarch of the Barrymore acting family) in a high-profile production of Shakespeare's *As You Like It*. He also became a trainer to fabled bare-knuckle boxing champion John L. Sullivan, who respected him for his dedication to fitness and clean living.

This same dedication would ensure that Muldoon remained a sports icon long after his retirement. In 1900, he opened the Olympia health institute in Purchase, New York, becoming a fitness guru for luminaries that included Ralph Pulitzer, Theodore Dreiser, Nellie Bly, and Secretary of State Elihu Root. In 1921, the revered Muldoon was named the first chairman of the New York State Athletic Commission, and his unwavering ethics and integrity in that role earned him another nickname: "The Iron Duke." He served as commissioner for twelve years, until his death from cancer in 1933 at the age of eighty-one. In Muldoon's *New York Times* obituary, former Heavyweight Boxing Champion Gene Tunney stated, "All I know about training I learned from him. . . . His patience, intellectual courage and wisdom were inspirational."

The Farmer

For well over a century, the state of Iowa has enjoyed a reputation as the heart of amateur wrestling in America. That reputation can be traced directly back to the efforts of one man who competed during a time when the lines between amateur and professional were blurred, and became an inspiration to generations of athletes.

Martin Burns was born in a log cabin in Cedar County, Iowa, on February 15, 1861, and from as early as age eleven, following the death of his father, he was supporting his family as a farmhand earning twelve dollars per month. The grueling lifestyle resulted in a fierce level of physical conditioning that he would maintain for his entire life. In fact, even before he started working, the young Burns was already becoming known for vanquishing other kids in impromptu wrestling matches from as early as age eight.

The wrestling craze was in full swing following the Civil War, and as soon as Burns was old enough, he put his formidable skills to use on the carnival circuit, something he would continue to do even after his professional career took off in the early 1880s. An early loss to chokehold proponent Evan "Strangler" Lewis led him to develop the immense neck strength for which he'd become legendary; growing it to an eventual twenty inches around, he'd reportedly take a full hangman's drop, noose and all, without suffering harm (legend has it he'd whistle "Yankee Doodle" the whole time). And he became an overnight sensation in

Farmer Burns (right) spars with "Great White Hope" James J. Jeffries in preparation for Jeffries's upcoming match with heavyweight boxing champion Jack Johnson.
George Grantham Bain Collection (Library of Congress)

1889 after besting Jack Carkeek and old foe the Strangler in one afternoon in Chicago (the very same appearance that earned him the nickname "Farmer").

His winning ways continued, both in the arenas and at the carnivals, culminating in another victory over Lewis in 1895 that earned him the American Heavyweight Championship. He would hold on to it for two years, cementing his reputation as the dominant grappler of the 1890s along the way. All in all, in a career that reportedly included over six thousand matches, Burns claimed to have lost only seven.

His greatest influence would come as a trainer. The popularity of professional wrestling was resulting in a great interest in grappling among young boys, and Burns's efforts are credited with helping establish amateur wrestling as a sport in schools across the nation—with Iowa as its unofficial birthplace. Burns himself opened a series of gyms and wrestling schools, training a generation of new competitors that included the likes of Joseph "Toots" Mondt, "Panther" Joe Malcewicz, Rudy Dusek, and, of course, his prized pupil and future World Heavyweight Champion, Frank Gotch. The mail-order training course he published in 1914, *Lessons in Wrestling and Physical Culture*, became the bible of the sport for a generation of wrestlers, and is still consulted today by supporters of the catch style.

"I had the privilege of meeting Farmer Burns in Omaha, Nebraska, in 1936," Lou Thesz, one of the twentieth century's most gifted professional wrestlers, told me in his final interview in 2001. "He died not too long after that. He was one of the greatest coaches in the world. I think he was very innovative—the first guy who really knew how to handle somebody's professional career. He was a tough old dude. 'Young man,' he said, 'All I can tell you is train, train, train, train.' He plowed the fields and planted everything, and the rest of us went along and followed."

The Original Strangler

Although grown from wholesome and healthy beginnings, wrestling's professional incarnation in the late-nineteenth century could be especially brutal and barbaric. And no one epitomized that violent brutality like Evan "Strangler" Lewis, and his devastating stranglehold, the first of many feared finishers to be seen throughout wrestling history.

Although some reports indicate his real name was actually Henry Clayton, dependable records indicate he was indeed born Evan Lewis on May 24, 1861, in Ridgeway, Wisconsin. The son of a butcher and farmer, he burst onto the wrestling scene in a major way in 1882 when he emerged victorious from a sixty-four-man tournament held in Montana. Within three years he had relocated to the big city of Madison, Wisconsin, and picked up his deadly finishing maneuver from an opponent, Frank Whitmore.

Unlike the grappler who would copy his name a generation later while using a simple headlock as his pet hold, Evan Lewis's finisher of choice was a literal chokehold, in which he applied forearm pressure to his opponent's throat until he blacked out. Known today as MMA's rear naked choke, it was then still perfectly legal in catch wrestling. Thanks to the ruthless way in which Lewis utilized the hold, however, by the 1890s it would be banned from the sport forever.

He was "a cruel and really dangerous athlete," according to historian Nat Fleischer in his coveted 1936 book, *From Milo to Londos*. "[He] made no bones about his method," a writer once recalled in Fleischer's venerated publication, *Ring Magazine*, "which was to get an arm about the throat of an opponent and choke him until he whispered 'enough' or was unable to whisper anything."

This was a time when many wrestling matches were still competitive affairs, and it wasn't uncommon for bones to be broken, limbs to be dislocated, and much worse. Although remembered as mild-mannered and even-tempered in everyday life, Evan Lewis was anything but once on the wrestling mat, and his techniques were emblematic of the anything-goes style that proliferated in those days. When his favorite move was eventually banned, he found a way to continue torturing opponents with a crushing leghold.

But before the hold was barred, Lewis would use it to great effect in an encounter with Japanese sumo import Sorakichi Matsuda in two of the most high-profile matches of the nineteenth century. In their first bout, on January 27, 1886, at Chicago's Central Music Hall, Lewis strangled Sorakichi so badly that he could be seen spitting up blood as he very vocally surrendered the match. When they met again three weeks later in a lauded rematch that became the only wrestling match to be covered on the front page of the *New York Times*, Lewis—by then barred from strangling—won again, this time by savagely mangling his adversary's leg.

On March 2, 1893, Lewis, then the American Catch-As-Catch-Can Champion, made wrestling history by defeating American Greco-Roman Champion and heir to the Muldoon legacy Ernst Roeber, thereby becoming the first American Heavyweight Champion. This title is pointed to as the beginning of a unified style in professional wrestling, and is the antecedent to the first widely recognized World Heavyweight Championship that would come along a decade later.

By the end of the century, with fakery becoming more the norm in professional wrestling, the Strangler walked away from his sport and settled down in his home town of Ridgeway. Already the proprietor of a major Wisconsin hotel for years, he became a pillar of the community, serving on the town board as a game warden and sergeant-at-arms. He died of cancer in 1919 at age fifty-nine, his star already completely eclipsed by the fellow Wisconsan who had adopted his name, Ed "Strangler" Lewis (born Robert Friedrich). The violent origins of pro wrestling that Evan Lewis stood for had receded to a distant memory, as had the man himself.

Legit Tough Guys

Wrestling's Heyday as an Actual Sport

If I wasn't president of the United States, I would like to be George Hackenschmidt.

—Teddy Roosevelt

By the turn of the twentieth century, professional wrestling had more or less completely graduated from its carnival origins, and was swiftly becoming very big business. Instead of open fields, music halls and barrooms, big matches were held in the new arenas and stadiums that were being constructed, and playing to very large crowds. It was the Golden Age of American sport, and wrestling was right there at the very top in terms of popularity.

Due to this exploding popularity, it was inevitable that there would also be an explosion in the popularity of its top competitors. In the old days, guys like William Muldoon had become major figures in sports culture. But with the new century would come the rise of true professional wrestling superstars—athletes who would become major names not just in sports culture, but in popular culture. It would begin with two gentlemen from opposite sides of the Atlantic, who would captivate the attention of millions in their scramble for worldwide superiority.

A Rivalry for the Ages

Beginning in 1901, a charismatic, cultured and immensely strong Russian by the name of George Hackenschmidt made his way west, where, under the guidance of early impresario C. B. Cochran, he would go on to become the toast of Europe. Winning tournaments in Vienna, Paris, and throughout England, he quickly earned the nickname "The Russian Lion" and captured the attention of men and the adoration of women with his impressively chiseled physique—a rarity for the time. Before long, he had settled in England and staked his claim as the unquestioned champion of the entire continent.

At roughly the same time, a onetime plowboy from Humboldt, Iowa, Frank Gotch, was beginning his ascension to the role of America's first true pro sports idol. Wrestling folklorists recount the incident in which a young, unknown Gotch faced off against Dan McLeod, who hustled the youngster and everyone else who had bet on the impromptu outdoor match by pretending to be an anonymous traveling salesman when he was, in fact, the American Heavyweight Champion. Even though he beat the kid, McLeod was impressed enough to leave his calling card behind, and would soon introduce Gotch to the man he had beaten for the title and the preeminent wrestling coach of the day, Farmer Burns.

As Gotch embarked on a barnstorming tour, venturing to places like the Pacific Northwest and the Yukon, earning victory after victory, the Russian Lion turned his attentions toward America. Regardless of the nature of the sport at the time, which despite some romanticizing to the contrary, had already turned largely to match-fixing, virtually all historians agree that Gotch and Hackenschmidt (as well as many other top wrestlers of the day) were nevertheless formidable grapplers of great talent. This was to be the standard of the day, when wrestling had not yet become a performance, but was no longer a pure competition. Rather than seeking to openly entertain, these wrestlers were intent on making their sport appear as legitimate as possible, and, in rare cases, it may still have been.

"Frank Gotch and Farmer Burns ran their own troupe in the early 1900s," explains prominent wrestling historian Tim Hornbaker, "wherein Gotch was routinely facing members of his syndicate—nonthreatening opponents—in matches that were good financially."

In 1904, the same year that Gotch won the American Heavyweight Championship from the tough-as-nails Tom Jenkins, future wrestling coach of West Point, Hackenschmidt would also defeat Jenkins in their first encounter in England. Because of this victory, when Jenkins regained his title in the spring of 1905, the time seemed right for a rematch with Hackenschmidt. Billed as a de facto "European Heavyweight Champion," Hack finally set foot on American soil to show the Yanks just what the Old World had been up in arms over for years. And true to form, he bested Jenkins in New York's Madison Square Garden on May 4, 1905.

By triumphing over the American champion, Europe's heralded muscleman established something the ramifications of which continue to be felt in the pro wrestling business today: he became recognized as professional wrestling's very first universally acknowledged World Heavyweight Champion. This is the very same title that, through the various manipulations of history and reality that are the wrestling promoter's stock and trade, is seen as the origin point for virtually all major World titles since, including the NWA World Heavyweight Championship, and even WWE's current World Heavyweight Championship.

Now acknowledged as the best in the world, it would fall to Hackenschmidt to defend his crown against all comers. Being by all accounts a sporting gentleman of honor, it would have been important to him to face the most worthy of opponents. And it soon became apparent that the worthiest of them all was indeed Frank Gotch, who had attained the title of American Heavyweight Champion and was already viewed by U.S. fans as the most skilled competitor the sport had ever seen—dubbed "peerless" by his supporters.

Matches of the Century

The world champion had been completely undefeated as titleholder for three years when he stepped into the ring for the first time against Frank Gotch on April 3, 1908, in Chicago's Dexter Park Pavilion, a ramshackle outdoor arena that housed close to ten thousand people. As with all matches pre-1920, only photos and news reports of the encounter still exist, but many believe that this bout may have been a "shoot," in other words, an actual contest. Stories circulate—many of them from a bitter Hack himself—of Gotch's dirty tactics, and how he fouled the champ repeatedly, drawing blood and openly taunting him. Hackenschmidt even claimed that his challenger had bathed himself in oil to gain an unfair advantage, although critics pointed to Gotch's exceptional conditioning as his advantage, and the fact that the champion had visibly let himself go during his years with the title.

Whatever the cause, it seems fair to assume that Hackenschmidt had hoped for a quick win, as was usual for him, as opposed to the grueling marathon he got from Gotch. Once caught in the Peerless One's feared toehold, the titleholder verbally conceded the match to avoid serious injury. Despite the fact that most matches in those days were best two-out-of-three-falls, there would be no second fall. Hackenschmidt refused to continue, and Frank Gotch became the undisputed Heavyweight Champion of the World.

Just like that, Gotch cemented his status as one of the country's most beloved and well-known sports celebrities. With Farmer Burns at his side, he had reached the pinnacle of the business, doing so through a combination of legitimate skill and cagey business savvy. And for a number of years, pro wrestling experienced a popularity boom the likes of which it hadn't yet seen—and never would again in its original form. This period would be the high point of wrestling's existence as a competitive sport (or at least during its *perception* as a competitive sport).

One wrestling historian who adamantly believes in the legitimacy of the sport during the era of Gotch and Hackenschmidt and is firmly convinced that their matches were shoots is Mike Chapman, director of the George Tragos/Lou Thesz Pro Wrestling Hall of Fame in Newton, Iowa, and the world's foremost authority on Gotch. "There are writers and historians who desperately want to be on the inside," he says. "And so they'll claim it was all a work, even back in the Gotch days. But Gotch, along with guys like Joe Stecher and Earl Caddock, they had fierce pride in what they could accomplish. It saddens me to see people wanting to attack Gotch's character. As the years went by and everybody started beating up on pro wrestling, it was just natural to say it's always been fixed. That even the great Gotch worked matches. Baloney."

But in one of wrestling's earliest examples of hyped grudges and trash-talking, things turned ugly between the two giants of the mat. While Gotch basked in the glory of his title run, Hack (or perhaps his publicists) began to run down the champion—and American fans in general—in the press. He pointed to Gotch's many supposed fouls, and the general lack of good sportsmanship upon which he prided himself. Before long, fans were clamoring for a rematch; it would be three years in the making, and the first to earn the grandiose title of "Match of the Century." Perhaps it was. But it would also start the long process of opening the eyes of the public to the true nature of the wrestling business.

The Russian Lion had called for the match to take place in his native Europe, but it wound up being signed for September 4, 1911, in Chicago's newly constructed White Sox Park (soon to be renamed Comiskey Park in honor of the baseball team's owner). The day before, Gotch visited the town's other park, Wrigley Field, and watched the Chicago Cubs split a doubleheader with the St. Louis Cardinals. The challenger enjoyed no such leisure, however—he had suffered a knee injury during training. Renowned shooter Ad Santel would, in later years, claim that he had damaged the knee on orders from Gotch's camp, but the facts reveal that it was Hack's sparring partner Dr. Benjamin Roller who had accidentally caused the injury. Whatever the cause, Hack refused to postpone the match.

"Roller said he heard it pop," recounts historian Mike Chapman. "But Hack's knee wasn't injured that bad, and even if it had been, he would've suffered through it. But it ate at him mentally. Roller said the night before the match he went looking for Hackenschmidt and found him sitting on a bench staring out by Lake Michigan, trembling. He knew right then he was just terrified. He had badmouthed Gotch for three years, and knew he had no chance. He was mentally defeated. . . . Gotch had a huge ego. You have to, to be champion of the world. He wanted to demolish Hackenschmidt, and he knew he could. His training for that match was obsessive. He wanted to prove something once and for all."

The facts are hazy at best, as it is with so much wrestling history from this period, but it is reasonable to believe that this second Gotch/Hackenschmidt encounter was a classic double-cross—a "worked" match gone wrong. It seems likely that Hack believed he was to win the match, only to have the opportunistic Gotch "shoot" on him, rewriting the prearranged plans and winning the match by brute force. Using his toehold to vanquish his injured opponent in under twenty minutes, the Peerless One retained the gold that sunny day in the Windy City, and the Lion would remain bitter about it for the rest of his very long life. As for the public's perception, all bets were called off shortly before the match—a clear indication that "the fix was in" and everybody knew it. The shady double-dealing that occurred both before and during the match itself, on such a high-profile stage, did much to sully the reputation of the then well-respected and popular sport. One might say that this was the beginning of the mainstream culture's loss of innocence when it came to wrestling, as they started to suspect what sports writers and insiders had assumed for years.

"The way I heard it was that it was supposed to be a worked match, but Gotch shot on him because he knew he could," says Dave Meltzer, editor of the *Wrestling Observer* newsletter. "Hackenschmidt lived a long life and Gotch died very young. Hack was a popular guy for many years, and was very bitter. I think there was some reality to that, because Hack stayed so bitter about it. Whether he was double crossed I don't know, but if he had lost a worked match that was a business deal, where everything was worked out between the two of them, years later when he got old one would think that he'd have a soft spot for Gotch because he was most famous for those matches; but he didn't. That always made me think that there was some form of double cross in his mind that he never forgot."

Chapman, with access to many of Gotch's personal documents, including letters and scrapbooks, insists the rematch was a shoot, and finds no evidence that it damaged the sport's credibility: "I know more about the personalities of Frank Gotch and George Hackenschmidt than anybody alive. Sometimes, the better guy loses. It didn't destroy wrestling. Everywhere else Gotch wrestled for the next three years there were huge crowds. I'm tired of reading that that match killed pro wrestling. It did nothing of the sort."

But it would turn out to be George Hackenschmidt's final match. Gotch would hold on to the World Heavyweight title until 1913, before he finally retired (after threatening to do so for years). By walking away from the game, he left not only a vacant championship, but a vacancy as far as major star power is concerned. Unlike any other era in the history of the business, this particular time was utterly dominated by two men, and they had both hung up their boots.

The Rise of the Wrestling Promoter

In the ensuing years, several men would step up to try and claim legitimacy as World Heavyweight Champion, and the inheritor of Gotch's mantle. Some, like Charlie "Kid" Cutler, Fred Beell, Henry Ordeman and Jess Westegaard, would even gain the blessing of Gotch himself. But it wasn't until a twenty-two-year-old former high school wrestling star from Nebraska named Joe Stecher beat Cutler, then the American champion, on July 5, 1915, with Gotch in attendance, that the title picture was finally cleared up and a decisive new World Heavyweight Champion emerged.

During this murky in-between period, something new happened to help further transform the sport in a very crucial way. Whereas in the past the wrestlers themselves (along with their managers) largely controlled their destinies, using the press to make their own matches while the promoter played a supporting role, starting in the 1910s the power and role of the wrestling promoter grew dramatically. Most agree that the first modern wrestling promoter was Jack Curley, who had masterminded the second Gotch/Hackenschmidt match, and later became Stecher's handler. Curley helped establish New York City and Madison Square Garden as a hotbed for wrestling, something that, with the exception of the 1940s, has remained true ever since.

"The small-time carnival promoters were a different breed than arena promoters," says Hornbaker, "and when the likes of Jack Curley and his peers in the 1910s were establishing themselves in various venues, they capitalized on the void of competition and established wrestling as a local/ national attraction. . . . Money was the bottom line."

Curley and his ilk were helping to take professional wrestling from a rural, Midwestern pastime to a major attraction in America's urban centers. With promoters controlling the game, matches could be presented on a more regular basis; local promoters were no longer at the mercy of the caprices of traveling wrestlers who would set their own schedules while making matches wherever they happened to stop on their national tours. The pro wrestling impresario had arrived, and, inevitably, with such profit-minded ballyhoo artists in control, wrestling became more than ever about showmanship and predetermined outcomes rather than genuine in-ring competition.

"When two major pros met, the match was just about always worked," states Steve Yohe, a historian specializing in wrestling's earliest period. "The bigger star, the one who grew the gate, was the one who booked the finish. . . . Since both were actual wrestlers, the match could be a contest, but just the finish predetermined. Worked matches had to look real because people were betting on them. . . . Once the match was made, everyone knew what was going to happen and those involved had an edge in the gambling. That's where the money was made. There was a lot of ways developed to work a finish. It became an art form."

The Business Unmasked

Wrestling's popularity ebbed in the wake of Gotch's retirement, and try as he might, Stecher just couldn't get out of his predecessor's shadow. Also in the years following the second Gotch/Hack match, questions about the sport's "legitimacy" began to be raised more and more in the public sphere. A notorious month-long tournament in late 1915 and early 1916 at the Manhattan Opera House (a building that remains steeped in wrestling tradition a full century later) brought unwanted attention when a hooded grappler known as The Masked Marvel attracted journalists eager to expose him—and the business. Newspapers such as the *Brooklyn Daily Eagle* relished reporting the Marvel's true identity (railway worker Mort Henderson of Pennsylvania), and eventually lambasted the entire month-long proceedings, reporting that professional wrestling "has for so many years been tainted with open or covert fraud that it is a wonder the 'tournament' was ever taken seriously."

"In the 1900s, I've read stuff indicating that 95 percent of matches were worked, and 5 percent were shoots," says Meltzer. "But who knows if that's even real? From 1915 on, the number was very tiny. When it came out that the tournament was worked . . . that was one of the first big exposés."

Despite the beating it took in the media, the tournament helped elevate two participants in particular who would go on to help redefine the course of the business and what it meant to be a pro wrestler. One was Nekoosa, Wisconsin's Robert Friedrich, whose ring name, Ed "Strangler" Lewis, had been inspired by that of the previous generation's Strangler (more on him in the next chapter). The other was a hulking Pole named Stanislaus Zbyszko, who, along with his brother Wladek, had earned a reputation as one of the toughest, most dangerous wrestlers around. Zbyszko had been making waves in international competition for years, and the Manhattan tournament helped establish him strongly with American fans. In the late teens, both Lewis and Stan's brother Wladek would claim controversial, disputed versions of the World Championship, despite the greater recognition accorded to Stecher and the man who eventually beat him on April 9, 1917, Earl Caddock.

When Caddock let the title go temporarily dormant in order to serve overseas in World War I, it gave Lewis and the Zbyszkos even more leverage to raise their respective profiles and establish their questionable claims to world champion status. (Stanislaus and the Strangler would eventually legitimize this status, but that wouldn't happen until the following decade.)

The Great Gama

Lewis and Zbyszko represented the new breed of wrestler: part shoot fighter and part performer, willing to play into the hype machine with bombast and gimmickry, but also extremely formidable and more than able to take care of themselves on the mat if need be. And they did occasionally need to, as the sport's murky waters were still filled with their fair share of sharks, such as India's Ghulam Muhammad, a.k.a. The Great Gama; considered by some to be the greatest pure wrestler who ever lived, Gama competed for half a century and is believed never to have lost a match. Ducked by both Gotch and Hackenschmidt, among many other Western competitors, Gama finally found competition in the form of Zbyszko, who first accepted the Punjabi's challenge in 1910. The two wrestled to a three-hour draw, with Zbyszko spending almost the entire match on the mat in a defensive position. After many years of semi-retirement due to lack of willing opponents, Gama would finally meet Zbyszko a second time, in 1928. This time, Gama bested his archrival in a mere forty-two seconds.

A true professional *wrestler* who preferred competition that was not of the pre-arranged variety, Gama was something of an anomaly during a time when the sport was on the verge of becoming a full-blown performance art. It was precisely because of men like him that real, credible in-ring skill was still of paramount importance. Yet it would be Ed Lewis, along with a couple of noteworthy associates, who would soon have a hand in radically transforming the business and making sure that dinosaurs like Gama continued on the path to extinction.

Major Stars of the Era

At the beginning of the twentieth century, these legitimately skilled competitors made pro wrestling into one of America's most popular sports.

- Americus
- Charlie "Kid" Cutler
- Earl Caddock
- Emil Klank
- Frank Gotch
- Fred Beell
- George Bothner
- George Hackenschmidt
- The Great Gama
- Henry Ordeman

- Ivan "Bigfoot" Poddubny
- Jess Westegaard
- Joe Stecher
- John Olin
- The Masked Marvel

- Paul Pons
- Stanislaus Zbyszko
- Tom Jenkins
- William Demetral
- Wladek Zbyszko

The Peerless One

Was he an inspirational, All-American boy? Or was he a bully with little respect for the rules? The answer may be partially lost to the mists of time, but one thing is certain: Frank Gotch was a bona fide wrestling superstar, and an American sports hero. During his heyday, he was one of the most beloved figures in the nation, and although his legend has faded, in the entire history of the business perhaps only Gorgeous George and Hulk Hogan enjoyed comparable levels of mainstream fame.

Born Frank Alvin Gotch to German parents on April 27, 1878, on a small farm three miles south of Humboldt, Iowa, he was working as a farm boy when he first began wrestling as a teenager, using the strength and conditioning he developed in the fields to throw every local kid put in front of him. Particularly, his devastating toehold (which he used to pin his opponents, not as a submission maneuver) was the most effective weapon in his arsenal.

Shortly after turning pro in 1899, his fortuitous encounter with American champion Dan McLeod on an Iowa cinder track soon led to a meeting with another major star of the era, Martin "Farmer" Burns. The Farmer was always credited with "discovering" Gotch, and it's true that he became the Mick to Gotch's Rocky Balboa. Under his tutelage, Gotch started on the path to becoming the dominant American wrestler of his era.

After a tour of the Yukon, during which he temporarily took on the ring name of "Frank Kennedy," Gotch returned to Iowa with a great deal of momentum, as the wrestling world began to buzz about the toughness of the young Midwesterner. Following an initial defeat at the hands of new American champion Tom Jenkins, Gotch later rebounded on January 27, 1904, winning the title for the first time. He would lose it on December 1, 1906, in a freak upset to future policeman Fred Beell, who tossed Gotch from the ring and knocked him out. But Gotch regained the gold mere days later. That Beell defeat would be the last of only six losses Gotch would suffer in his 160-match career.

Soon after, his 1908 triumph over "The Russian Lion," George Hackenschmidt, made him the first American-born Heavyweight Champion of the World. In the entire history of wrestling, only Lou Thesz, Bruno Sammartino, Verne Gagne, and Bob Backlund can claim world-title reigns that lasted longer than Frank Gotch's five-year stretch at the top. In the process, Gotch became America's golden boy and the idol of millions. His matches outdrew heavyweight boxing championships.

He appeared in a Broadway play, and wrestled an exhibition match in the White House for President Theodore Roosevelt. In an era when most wrestling matches were still at least partially competitive, Gotch was an unparalleled ring technician. Although, unfortunately, there are no extant moving pictures of him, he was, by all accounts, a virtually unbeatable competitor with a head for ring strategy that was unmatched. Before long, the press had dubbed him "peerless" and a "nonpareil." On February 11, 1911, he married his Humboldt sweetheart, Gladys Oestrich.

"He was the first wrestler to be a big enough star to base his income on gates and not gambling," says Steve Yohe. "In 1908, after proving American superiority over Europe by beating George Hackenschmidt, he was the most popular sports star in America. Ty Cobb was a rookie and Jack Johnson hadn't won the title. For a year, he was God."

But there was another side to Gotch. In later years, several contemporaries, both wrestlers and referees, reported that he could be cruel, even sadistic, in the ring, never reluctant to take advantage of an injured opponent. This side was especially evident in an infamous title defense against fellow superstar Stanislaus Zbyszko on June 1, 1910, in which the champion brutally dominated his Polish challenger, taking the first fall in mere seconds when he caught Zbyszko when he wasn't ready, mercilessly crushing him in under a half hour (short for the day) to take the deciding fall.

"I don't think there's any doubt that Gotch was a top-of-the-line wrestler," says Dave Meltzer. "Or at least he had enough of a rep as one that people didn't try to cross him too much, because there are not examples of it."

Hackenschmidt, the man he had defeated for the title, wasn't afraid to point out his rival's apparent unsportsmanlike behavior, and his desire for satisfaction led to the historic match in Chicago's Comiskey Park, in which Gotch would retain his title and reaffirm his role as wrestling's top dog, retiring the Russian Lion in the process. A record thirty thousand fans would pay eighty-seven-thousand dollars to see the match, setting an attendance/gate record that would stand for a quarter–century.

"[Gotch] was a country boy who could be dirty," Yohe says. "Hackenschmidt was a gentleman who believed in sportsmanship. Hack got double-crossed and roughed up, so he quit. He thought it was a sports contest and Gotch thought he was in a fight. His toehold was considered brutal in its time, because Gotch would break a leg to win. But he was idolized in America and the press always presented him as a hero."

But the grueling schedule and hard-nosed wrestling of the era was taking its toll, and after teasing retirement for years, Gotch finally did so in 1913, walking away from the sport and vacating the world championship that had earned him such acclaim. And although he would occasionally wrestle over the next couple of years, he was content to enjoy the rewards of his amazing career. Unfortunately, he would not have long to enjoy them, as a mysterious illness took his life abruptly on December 16, 1917. Reports of the time state the cause of death as uremic poisoning, although some have since suggested that he may have died from the effects of syphilis. He left behind his wife, Gladys, and their four-year-old son, Robert.

"Was he the greatest wrestler?" asks Yohe. "I think he could claim that. As champion, he was never close to being beat. And he got sick before he could put over the next great champion, Joe Stecher. His big negative is that he destroyed all his contenders, and by the time of his retirement had also destroyed the business for a few years. He booked everything for himself."

It's been over a century since the passing of "Peerless" Frank Gotch, but to this day he remains a revered figure in the history of catch-as-catch-can wrestling. Thanks to his immense popularity and the efforts of his mentor Farmer Burns, amateur wrestling became a staple in high schools and colleges across America. And although we may never know the "real" Frank Gotch, one thing we know was real was his skill as a wrestler.

"I think he was the greatest who ever lived, and nobody could've ever beaten him in a shoot," says Mike Chapman. "He was lightning quick, he was farm-strong, and he had a mean streak, just like [Jack] Dempsey. He was the best."

The Russian Lion

He was a European sensation who became wrestling's first World Heavyweight Champion. A philosopher and intellectual whose gentleness and soft-spoken civility belied his heavily muscled physique, George Hackenschmidt was an early proponent of natural bodybuilding and clean living. His matches with Gotch would define him, but there was much more to the Russian Lion.

He was born Georg Karl Julius Hackenschmidt on August 1, 1877, in Dorpat (now Tartu), Estonia, in the Russian Empire, to parents of German and Swedish descent. As a young student, his feats of strength—which included lifting a small horse—drew much attention, and he put his talents to use in every sport available, including swimming, cycling, running, and, of course, weightlifting. While working as a blacksmith's apprentice, he was discovered by traveling champion wrestler George Lurich, who helped to train the young Hack for a career in wrestling. Hack also came under the training of Dr. Vladislav von Krajewski, whom he would later refer to as "The Father of Modern Athletics." It was Krajewski who helped Hackenschmidt become one of the strongest men in the world.

Shortly after debuting in 1898, he beat renowned French grappler Paul Pons. After a short stint as guard to Tsar Nicholas II, he dove full bore into the wrestling business. In later years, his triumphant tour of European music halls would become the stuff of legend. The powerful Estonian was known to take on upwards of five or ten opponents in a single evening, and also dazzle the crowds with his awe-inspiring weight-lifting abilities. His gentlemanly demeanor and Adonis-like looks made him the toast of the continent, and before long, he had found a second home in Great Britain, where he would spend most of his life.

He bested any and all comers, including the second "Terrible Turk," Ahmed Madrali, whose January 1904 match with Hack drew such interest that traffic was packed through the heart of London. In July, he defeated an American named Tom Jenkins, in England's Royal Albert Hall. When Jenkins later captured the American championship it only made sense for Hackenschmidt to finally cross the Atlantic. His victory over Jenkins at Madison Square Garden, in New York City, made him a star on two continents, and the first World Heavyweight Champion.

The Russian Lion models for Reinhold Begas's statue of Prometheus.   *Public domain*

But it would be for his two matches against Frank Gotch for which Hackenschmidt would best be remembered. They were the only two known losses of his career; the first lost him the title, and the second ended his career. Reports indicate that the Russian Lion didn't train properly for his first match with Gotch in 1908. Chronic depression was the reason behind his refusal of an invitation to train publicly at the Chicago Athletic Club; he chose instead to confine his training to morning jogs along Lake Michigan. Hack was visibly out of shape when he entered the ring at Dexter Park Pavilion, and was taken easily by his Iowan opponent.

Although at first he praised Gotch after the loss, Hack later reversed his opinion and complained to the press of the American's bullying tactics. When the rematch finally happened, the already injured former champ was easy pickings for his opportunistic adversary. Although he planned to continue wrestling when he got back to Europe, his badly damaged knee prevented it, and Hack instead ended his career on a disappointing note.

Although his in-ring time was done, the Russian Lion remained in peak physical shape, and continued his rigorous exercise routine well into his eighties. He also wrote extensively on philosophy and physical culture, including his most famous book, *The Way to Live*, which continues to be used to this day. On February 19, 1968, he died in the London suburb of Dulwich at the age of ninety. A true sportsman in a sport that has never been known for sportsmanship, he remains one of wrestling's class acts.

The Polish Powerhouse

Bridging the eras of pro wrestling as a fixed competition and pro wrestling as out-and-out performance, the name Stanislaus Zbyszko was once synonymous with the grappling sport. A stocky mass of muscle with consummate wrestling skill and the strength of a bull, he was also a pragmatist who understood that professional

Zbyszko shows off his prodigious strength in this posed studio shot.

George Grantham Bain Collection (Library of Congress)

wrestling was, first and foremost, a business. And although in his old age he would bemoan the spectacle his sport had become, one cannot deny his role in sending it in that direction.

He was born Stanislaw Jan Cyganiewicz on April 1, 1879, in the Austria-Hungarian village of Jodłowa, near modern-day Kraków, Poland. Raised in the high culture of Vienna, Austria, he gained an appreciation for music and art, as well as a mastery of chess. His membership in the Falcon, a Polish nationalist group, led him to further develop his mind as well as his body, and by age twenty-one he had packed 260 pounds of muscle onto his five-foot, eight-inch physique.

Inspired by the growing success of George Hackenschmidt on the continent, he took an interest in becoming a wrestling star himself, first gaining the attention of local promoters by defeating an experienced wrestler in a traveling Polish circus. By his mid-twenties, he was making a name for himself in the industry, taking the ring name of Zbyszko, after a medieval knight of Polish legend. He achieved notoriety for a two-hour draw in 1906 against feared Russian competitor (and former Cossack) Ivan "Bigfoot" Poddubny, on his way to winning his first tournament in Paris.

Zbyszko came under the management of prototypical promoter C. B. Cochrane, who had also managed Hackenschmidt's career. While working with Cochrane, Zbyszko would be embroiled in controversy when one of his opponents, the supposedly Turkish Kara Suliman, was exposed as Bulgarian Ivan Offtharoff. It was revealed that Offtharoff, who had engaged in a series of matches with Zbyszko, was actually in the employ of Cochrane. Although not shocking by modern wrestling standards, the revelation meant that the two grapplers were actually in cahoots—in other words, performing rather than competing.

But Zbyszko was still the real deal, as his grueling 1910 battles with world champion Frank Gotch and Indian icon the Great Gama prove. Gama, in particular, would become something of a career rival for Zbyszko, and their epic draw made Zbyszko one of the only wrestlers ever to face the Great One without being pinned. It is believed that a staggering sixty thousand spectators were on hand some eighteen years later when the two behemoths met one last time in Patiala, India.

By the end of the 1910s, both Stanislaus and his younger brother Wladek had established themselves as major players on the U.S. grappling scene. With the business under the control of the infamous Gold Dust Trio of Ed "Strangler" Lewis, manager Billy Sandow, and booker Joe "Toots" Mondt, the onetime sport became a performance attraction, and Zbyszko was a major part of the development. Recruited by the trio, he was selected to win the World Heavyweight title from Strangler Lewis on May 6, 1921. But Zbyszko was already into his forties by that point, and the aging competitor proved to be lackluster at the box office. He dropped the title back to Lewis ten months later.

However, Zbyszko would experience one more reign as world champion, even if it wasn't in the script. After the Gold Dust Trio put the World title on former football player Wayne "Big" Munn—a popular star with little to no real wrestling ability—Zbyszko was hired by rival promoter Tony Stecher to betray the trio and double-cross Munn in the ring. On April 15, 1925, Zbyszko shot on the champion and claimed the crown, losing it shortly thereafter to Tony's brother Joe Stecher—which had been the plan all along.

Following his rematch with Gama in 1928, Zbyszko retired from the ring. In the ensuing decades, he and his brother became talent scouts and trainers, scouring the world for new wrestlers while maintaining a chicken farm in Missouri. It was in Argentina that Zbyszko discovered future legend Antonino Rocca in the 1940s. He also started the careers of future legends Johnny Valentine and Harley Race, breeding a toughness in them that they would carry for their entire careers.

The legacy of Zbyszko was still blazing strong in 1950, when he was chosen by film director Jules Dassin to play a major role in his noir masterpiece *Night and the City* (Dassin had remembered Zbyszko as a wrestler from his youth). As retired old-time grappler Gregorius the Great, Zbyszko turned in an eye-opening performance full of pathos and credibility. It was life imitating art, and a fitting cap to the Polish strongman's life in the public eye. He would live quietly on his farm in Missouri for another seventeen years before passing away on September 23, 1967, at the age of eighty-eight. His mantle would be taken up a few years later by a young rookie named Lawrence Whistler, who would take the name Larry Zbyszko. And while most modern fans may remember him first when they think of that name, for true students of the game there is still only one Zbyszko.

4

Slam Bang Western Style

How the Gold Dust Trio Invented Modern Pro Wrestling

An honest man can sell a fake diamond if he says it's a fake diamond.
—Jack Pfefer

By the dawn of the Roaring '20s, professional wrestling had experienced both its first major boom period, and its first major bust. The American public seemed to have grown a bit fatigued of the sport, such as it was. Competition for the attention of the masses was at an all-time high, with the explosion of radio, the growth of motion pictures, and the rise of boxing as a popular (and most importantly) legal sport.

A change was in order—and the source of that change would be an alliance of three unique individuals, each with his specific strengths. They would have a significant impact on the development and evolution of the wrestling business. They were known as the Gold Dust Trio, and although the true nature of their influence is as debatable as so much of wrestling's early lore, one thing is certain: professional wrestling changed dramatically in the 1920s, and these men reaped the benefits. Even after their alliance crumbled, they went on to achieve great things individually, and remained as formidable as they had been when they were together.

Champion, Manager, and Mastermind

As far as the public was concerned, the most important member of the trio—that is to say, the most visible—was a strapping young grappler named Robert Friedrich, who had learned his trade via the legendary correspondence course of Farmer Burns. Friedrich became known as Ed "Strangler" Lewis, the name under which he would become the most dominant pro wrestler of the decade. An athlete of considerable true wrestling ability, he would become a credible World Heavyweight Champion, winning the title for the first time at the end of 1920 from Joe Stecher.

Behind this new Strangler was one Billy Sandow, a former middleweight wrestler of the 1910s who had taken to managing talent after losing his health club business to fellow wrestler Fred Beell in a wager over a private match. Born Wilhelm Bauman (he took his ring name from nineteenth-century strongman Eugen Sandow), he was a born showman with a flair for the dramatic who took to barnstorming across the country with a stable of wrestlers, working local rubes for their hard-earned cash wherever they could. For Sandow, meeting up with a twenty-three-year-old Lewis in 1914 was just the break he was looking for.

The final piece of the puzzle was one of the most dangerous "hookers" in the business—a wrestler named Joseph Mondt, who had learned his trade directly from the great Burns. Mondt was touring the carnival circuit with the Farmer as what was then known as a "policeman": a keenly skilled grappler whose job it was to make sure all the other wrestlers stayed in line, and to step in whenever it seemed like a local boy might actually win one. But beyond just a rugged prodigy in the ring, Mondt (nicknamed "Toots" by Burns due to his young age and babyish looks) had a sharp head for business and a gift for innovation that would serve him throughout his long life.

"He had a rep for being pretty clever when it came to manipulations," *Wrestling Observer* editor Dave Meltzer says of Mondt. "He was a power broker from the 1920s to the 1960s. To last that long in this business you must be pretty clever, or know all the dirty tricks."

When the Lewis-Sandow team came calling for an enforcer to join their clique, Farmer Burns was only too happy to suggest Toots Mondt, and so was formed the group that would later be known as the Gold Dust Trio (a moniker that was coined in the seminal 1937 book *Fall Guys: The Barnums of Bounce*). Together, they would quickly exert a stranglehold on the wrestling business, changing it fundamentally in the process. With Lewis as the top star, Sandow as the manager, and Mondt as the enforcer/booker, the influence they enjoyed was like nothing the business had seen up to that time.

From Sport to Show

One of the issues that wrestling struggled with at the time was the undeniable fact that the matches could often be long, tedious affairs, lasting many hours, with very little movement between the competitors. Over the years, fans had grown tired of it, and their patience wore increasingly thin as their entertainment options expanded. Also, matches were often made in a haphazard fashion, with very little rhyme or reason, and almost no sense of continuity between events. The athletes involved did not have much in the way of color or charisma, and the result was a product whose blandness had become all too apparent. The Gold Dust Trio, and Toots Mondt in particular (or so many believe), was about to introduce dramatic change.

Among the many innovations attributed to Mondt during this period were:

- The introduction of time limits to keep matches shorter
- Allowing striking blows for the first time
- Creating ongoing "programs" in which two wrestlers would have a series of matches against one another over a perceived issue or grudge
- Touring with a set troupe of wrestlers who would travel to each town, performing as a packaged event
- Introducing colorful, if unrealistic, maneuvers like bodyslams and suplexes
- Presenting wrestlers as "good guys" and "bad guys" (known in the business as "babyfaces" and "heels") in order to give fans clear-cut people to root for and against
- Working out dramatic finishes to matches designed to entertain and to bring the crowds back for more

Mondt called it "Slam Bang Western Style" wrestling, and combined with Sandow's business acumen, the Gold Dust Trio was able to implement the new format with great success, using Ed Lewis as their public focal point. Matches would now be contested in a more histrionic fashion closer to a performance than an actual competition, with exaggerated holds applied in such a way as to elicit a broad reaction from an audience that didn't know how to respond to the earlier, more subtle style of shoot wrestling. By crafting ongoing programs between wrestlers that would sustain fan interest in their upcoming matches, Mondt had hit upon the element that would eventually morph into the elaborate storylines that would come to characterize pro wrestling.

For the first time, wrestlers began to take on roles in the ring. And although it started very simply (nothing like the cartoonish characters to come in later years), the use of babyfaces and heels would become an integral part of the overall product. In fact, as world champion, Lewis himself would play a subtle heel, traveling from town to town, inspiring fans to root for whatever opponent was trying to take his title away that night. By "packaging" wrestling as a traveling show, Sandow had given fans more reason than ever to come out, promising a stacked lineup of exciting matches (between seasoned colleagues who grew accustomed to working with each other night after night), instead of just one big match.

It is worth noting, however, that there has always been a shadow of doubt as to exactly how much of a role Toots Mondt and the Gold Dust

Trio played in the sport's transformation in the 1920s. Much of our modern understanding of the matter comes from the book *Fall Guys*, and it has often been speculated that the author, Marcus Griffin, may have been a PR writer in Mondt's employ, spinning history in the favor of his boss. It has even been postulated by some that "Marcus Griffin" may have even been a pseudonym for Mondt himself. Historian Steve Yohe is among those who rejects the Mondt hype and offers a different explanation as to why wrestling changed the way it did:

> In 1919, after the World Series was fixed, the government clamped down hard on pro sports. The worked sport of pro wrestling realized it had to stop relying on gambling money, and was maybe the first major sport to go without it. Breaking the law was no joke, and they knew a worked sport ripping off gamblers was trouble. It was then that the working of pro wrestling turned to entertaining fans. It no longer had to look completely real. By that time, bigger arenas had been built and you could make a good living off the gates alone.
>
> A lot of reporters have said that the sport stopped being "real" after 1921. This was the period when Strangler Lewis was champion. It didn't stop being real, it stopped *looking* real. The money then came from casual fans, looking for a good time, and not from the old wrestling fans that thought they were watching true wrestling.

The First Modern Wrestling Company

Whatever the reasons, the 1920s saw pro wrestling become outright performance, and although this was not directly acknowledged to the paying public, the change was noticed and business picked up with the Gold Dust Trio at the helm. Raiding talent from bookers and promoters far and wide, they consolidated the business under their control, attracting a stable with enough wrestlers to put on shows all over the country. Matches were made, finishes carefully planned in advance, programs carefully crafted, and talent booked all over from one central office. Lewis, Sandow, and Mondt had succeeded in creating pro wrestling's first national promotion. Predictably, however, the egos involved wouldn't allow it to last too long, and the business wouldn't see anything like it again for sixty years.

One of the most important ingredients in controlling the wrestling business was controlling the World Heavyweight Championship, and the trio did just that for years. For much of the time, Lewis himself—a consummate wrestler who could legitimately defeat any opponent who might get ideas about muscling the gold away from the conglomerate—held the crown. But they were also smart enough to know that fans would grow tired of him being perpetually at the top, and so he would occasionally drop the title to cooperating parties like Stanislaus Zbyszko, only to eventually win it back.

After a three-year promotional war with a rival organization run by Joe Stecher, his brother Tony, and East Coast impresario Jack Curley, during which both Lewis and Stecher claimed different versions of the world championship, the reign of the Gold Dust Trio finally came to an end. Toots walked away from the group in 1928 after a spat with Billy's brother Max, aligning himself with Philadelphia promoter Ray Fabiani before eventually muscling his way into the New York wrestling scene following the death of Jack Curley in 1937. Soon after Mondt's departure from the trio, Sandow and Lewis parted ways as well. Sandow would continue to manage wrestlers (including future world champion Everett Marshall), and Lewis still had a few more go-rounds as world champion in the 1930s—under new management, of course.

Showmanship over Sportsmanship

Despite the dissolution, the legacy of the Gold Dust Trio lived on. Colorful competitors began to take a larger role in the business, and serious wrestling skill was no longer a mandatory requirement. The trio's own Wayne Munn had been the first in 1925—a former football star elevated to world-title status thanks to his enormous crossover popularity. The sport would see more such crossovers. "Dynamite" Gus Sonnenberg, a Dartmouth football standout, snatched the world championship away from Strangler Lewis in 1929 and brought it under the control of Boston promoter Paul Bowser. The Beantown grappling kingpin would place the emphasis on marketability and box-office draw over ability, later taking Irish import Danno O'Mahoney from an unknown of untested wrestling skill to his newest superstar world champion by the mid-1930s. The drawback of such practices was that these manufactured attractions were vulnerable to potential double-crosses by the "legit" wrestlers who could still be found in relative abundance.

"There is a theory that the number of true shooters in wrestling always remained the same," says Steve Yohe. "But the need for performers [arose] to fill all the new arenas built after network radio made the sport popular with the general public starting around 1922, so the 'worker'-type wrestler was developed to fill the need."

With the most widely recognized version of the world championship in his camp, Bowser created an organization he called the American Wrestling Association (not to be confused with the later AWA of the 1960s–1980s). This move would be indicative of the trend in wrestling following the demise of the Gold Dust Trio: the world championship splintered into fragments, and rival territorial promotions were cropping up everywhere.

The New York State Athletic Commission established a world champion-ship, with Jack Curley and the clout of Madison Square Garden on its side. The National Boxing Association formed its own wrestling subdivision, the National Wrestling Association (not to be confused with the National Wrestling *Alliance* that would take shape in the 1940s), which recognized its own world champions, including a twenty-one-year-old St. Louis standout named Lou Thesz, who captured his first world title under the National Wrestling Association banner in 1937.

"Before, you always had the sense that, if nothing else, the illusion that maybe pro wrestling isn't real, but the world championship is real," explains Dave Meltzer. "All of the machinations with the world champion in [the 1930s], and the selling of the title to the highest bidder . . . that told you that the world championship was worked, too."

The Darling of the Depression

By far, the top star to emerge during this era of fragmented championship lineages and white-hot promotional rivalries was a handsome, chiseled Greek immigrant going by the name of Jim Londos. Groomed for great-ness by the Mondt-Fabiani combine, Londos burst on to the scene, first in Philadelphia and then in New York. With his matinee-idol looks and deep tan, he was wrestling's first sex symbol, and the start of a long-running tradi-tion of ethnic-based drawing cards in the Northeast.

With Mondt, Fabiani, and later New York kingpin Jack Curley behind him, Londos quickly became a sensation, packing houses throughout the Northeast on a consistent basis, to a degree that had never quite been seen before. The National Wrestling Association recognized him as world champion from 1930 to 1935, and he would continue to hold one version or another of the title well into the 1940s.

But a promotional rift separated him for years from his longtime rival of the era, Ed "Strangler" Lewis. Owing in part to bad blood from the breakup of the Gold Dust Trio (and perhaps the fact that Londos feared locking up with the formidably skilled Strangler), a match could not be worked out between the two opposing factions. Lewis had aligned himself with Boston promoter Paul Bowser, and the "Golden Greek" had Curley and Mondt in his corner. The waters became further muddied when Lewis and his com-bine invaded New York, gaining world-title recognition from the New York State Athletic Commission in 1932. Now both men had a claim to the crown.

The warring sides at last came to agreement in 1933, forming what became known in the business as "The Trust," an unspoken alliance among promoters that included Jack Curley, Ray Fabiani, Toots Mondt, "Carnation" Lou Daro (Mondt's newest ally out of Los Angeles), Paul Bowser, and both

Londos and Lewis. The dream match between the Strangler and the Golden Greek took place on September 20, 1934, at Chicago's Wrigley Field. It would be the most talked-about and highest-drawing match the business had seen since another mega match in that same town, the 1911 return bout between Frank Gotch and George Hackenschmidt. A record-shattering crowd of 35,265 fans paid $96,302 to witness Londos vanquishing his rival (and new business associate) Lewis to settle the feud. That new record would stand for nearly twenty years.

The Business Exposed

Despite the doldrums of the Great Depression, stars like Lewis, and especially Londos, were helping to keep the business afloat, but a major blow was coming in the form of a highly damaging reprisal from a vengeful rival promoter who was bitter over having been left out of the promotional "Trust." Eastern European immigrant Jack Pfefer was a colorful, eccentric visionary who saw pro wrestling, first and foremost, as an entertainment spectacle—the more ridiculously over-the-top his stable of characters, the better for business. And so he had no qualms about going to *New York Daily Mirror* sports writer Dan Parker—a longtime exposer of pro wrestling's "fakery"—and spilling the beans about the true nature of the business.

"People for the most part always knew wrestling was a work, but when Pfefer exposed the business, he did it in a cynical way that made the fans ashamed to be involved with it," says Yohe. "He told them that everyone in the sport was a creep, and that they were just 'marks' for watching."

The scorned Pfefer told Parker all about the predetermined nature of the bouts, and how the championship was decided in backroom meetings rather than in the ring. There had been exposés in the press before, but nothing like this. This was one of wrestling's own doing the talking. And worst of all, Pfefer's diatribe was damning of wrestling fans themselves. The damage would be immediate and far-reaching. An angry fan base turned its back on the business, which wouldn't fully recover for a decade. Even after the business recovered, the damage done to the mainstream's perception of professional wrestling would be permanent.

"The expose in the '30s did, in fact, kill the business for many years in a lot of [areas of] the country," says Meltzer. "That's why promoters were so scared of [breaking] kayfabe. There was a time when that did kill wrestling."

Wrestling Regroups

In the wake of the scandal, the wrestling business scrambled to survive. By the end of the '30s, Jack Curley was dead and Toots Mondt, ever the survivor, had formed a new partnership with New York's latest promotional powerhouse, Rudy Dusek, leader of the infamous troupe of wrestling brothers known as the Dusek Riot Squad. With Dusek as promoter and Mondt booking talent (as well as "angles," as pro wrestling storylines are called), the organization would control wrestling in the area for years. But it wouldn't be easy: the sour reputation the sport had earned caused influential boxing promoter Tex Rickard to have the grunt 'n' groan game banned from the hallowed halls of Madison Square Garden in 1940.

In the Midwest, a loose confederation of promoters began gradually to take shape. The trials of the Great Depression had been followed by the onset of World War II, and times were lean. It was a good time for promoters to stick together. St. Louis impresario Tom Packs was establishing a territory that would eventually become one of the sport's major hotbeds, and also had gained the attention of the National Wrestling Association; it was during this period that such Packs products as the aforementioned Thesz enjoyed reigns as World Heavyweight Champion, as well as tough shooter Ray Steele, Hungarian import Sandor Szabo, and Wild Bill Longson, the roughhousing inventor of the piledriver who would become the longest-reigning titleholder of the 1940s.

Nearby, in a territory spanning parts of Missouri, Nebraska, and Iowa, promoter P. L. "Pinkie" George and wrestler/promoter Orville Brown had formed the Midwest Wrestling Association, which recognized its own champion. The seeds planted during this era across the Midwest would soon yield great fruit; following the war years, an alliance between the MWA group and Packs's St. Louis outfit would produce a monopolistic organization that would help reinvigorate the business, as it simultaneously tried to control every aspect of it from coast to coast. Inter-promotional cooperation was about to reach an all-time high. Not since the halcyon days of the Gold Dust Trio itself would the business be so unified.

Major Stars of the Era

As pro wrestling changed from sport to show during the 1920s and '30s, these colorful individuals made the transition with ease.

- Bronko Nagurski
- Danno O'Mahoney
- Dick Shikat
- "Dynamite" Gus Sonnenberg
- Ed Don George
- Ed "Strangler" Lewis
- Everett Marshall
- The French Angel
- Gino Garibaldi
- Jim Browning
- Jim Londos
- "Jumpin'" Joe Savoldi
- Man Mountain Dean
- Ray Steele

- Sandor Szabo
- Steve "Crusher" Casey
- "Tiger Man" John Pesek

- Wayne "Big" Munn
- Wild Bill Longson
- Yvon Robert

The Scissors King

Although not as well remembered today as his predecessors Gotch and Hackenschmidt, or his contemporaries Lewis and Londos, Joe Stecher was one of the most popular wrestlers of his time, and for a short while, the top-drawing star in the sport. His story is one of great triumph, and, ultimately, great sadness.

He was born on April 4, 1893, to Bohemian immigrants, on a four-hundred-acre farm in Dodge, Nebraska. The youngest of eight children, Joe, along with his older brothers Lewis and Tony, were enrolled in the YMCA's wrestling course by their father at an early age. Seeing his brothers excel at the sport made the adolescent Joe want to do the same, and by sixteen he was already a local high-school standout, known for his lanky body and tremendous leg strength. After opening a lot of eyes by nearly defeating touring professional Dr. Benjamin F. Roller in 1909, it became clear that a pro career was in Joe's future.

Joe was clearly the best athlete of the Stecher clan, while Tony possessed the business acumen; so the two hit the professional ranks in 1912 as a wrestler-manager tandem. Joe rose through those ranks, making short work of all comers with a unique body-scissors hold he had developed, using his powerful legs to trap opponents and force their shoulders to the mat. The move earned him the lifelong nickname of "The Scissors King." He soon caught the attention of Farmer Burns and his protégé, World Heavyweight Champion Frank Gotch. When it came time for Gotch to walk away from the sport and the title, he gave his blessing to Stecher, who beat American champion Charlie Cutler in Omaha, Nebraska, on July 5, 1915, to become the next World Heavyweight titleholder. At age twenty-two, he was the youngest to do so.

Unfortunately, Stecher never quite escaped the shadow of Gotch, whom he hadn't beaten for the title, and a match could not be made prior to the former champ's untimely death in 1917. Instead, on April 9th of that year, Stecher would lose the title via forfeiture to Earl Caddock, refusing to finish their match. This match (and others like it) led to speculation that Stecher may have suffered from some form of mood disorder that caused periods of deep depression and, at times, made him prone to uncontrollable outbursts and unpredictable behavior, while at other times he would be completely passive and agreeable.

With the more level-headed Tony guiding his career, Joe remained in the public eye as a major player even after losing. He sparked a rivalry with new-comer Ed "Strangler" Lewis that would define the rest of his career, engaging in several marathon draws with the tough Wisconsinite before the decade was out. Then, on January 16, 1920, in one of the last shoot-style World Heavyweight title matches, he beat Earl Caddock, recently returned from serving in World War I, to become the first man to regain the championship. In between falls, Stecher's handlers once again noted his erratic behavior and reluctance to continue. Held at Madison Square Garden, this match is the oldest wrestling bout for which motion picture footage is still in existence.

Stecher would hold the gold for the majority of 1920 before dropping it to his nemesis Lewis in December. With Lewis and his Gold Dust Trio now in control of the business, the Stecher boys found themselves out in the cold. They sided with influential promoter Jack Curley in a bitter war with the trio. After treading water for a few years, Tony masterminded the plot that eventually put the title back around his brother's waist in 1925, thanks to an assist from veteran hooker Stanislaus Zbyszko. It took three years for Strangler Lewis and the Stechers to work out their differences, leading to a match on February 20, 1928, that saw Lewis unify both title claims with a win over Joe in St. Louis.

Now a former three-time champion and no longer the youngster he once was, Joe attempted to retire and return to his farm. But some bad investments forced him to return to the business the following year. So desperate was he, in fact, that he went to work for his former rivals Billy Sandow and Paul Bowser, who ordered him to do jobs for (translation: lose to) world champions like Lewis and newcomer Gus Sonnenberg, a footballer of limited wrestling ability, for whom a win over a star like Stecher would go a long way.

"He was right there when the business changed," says Mike Chapman, an expert on Stecher's life and career. "He saw what was happening to the sport he loved. He gave his life to it. Joe had to endure the trauma of seeing what he loved turn into a sham. He eventually had to lose lots of matches to people who weren't worthy to carry his jock strap."

After a few years of doing similar "jobs," Joe retired for good in 1934, at age forty-three. More bad investments left him destitute by the middle of the decade, and that, combined with his continued bizarre outbursts and irrational behavior, led his wife to divorce him and take custody of their children. Forced to take action, his older sibling Tony, who had once done all he could to protect Joe's professional life, stepped in and had his baby brother committed to a mental institution in St. Cloud, Minnesota. Tony went on to run the Minnesota wrestling territory for twenty-five years before selling to Verne Gagne, founder of the AWA. Joe Stecher never left the institution, remaining there until his death on March 29, 1974, at age eighty-one.

The Second Strangler

Babe Ruth. Jack Dempsey. Red Grange. Bill Tilden. These men, and several others, dominated what would come to be known as America's Golden Age of sports; a period in the 1920s when athletics first consumed the mainstream American consciousness. But one of the men who stood right alongside these luminaries during his own time, and yet whose star has since dimmed, is professional wrestling's own Babe Ruth: Ed "Strangler" Lewis.

He was born Robert Herman Julius Friedrich in Nekoosa, Wisconsin, on June 30, 1891. By the tender age of fourteen he had already taken to wrestling, participating in his first match on July 18, 1905. In tribute to Evan "Strangler" Lewis, legendary star of a previous generation and a fellow Wisconsin native, the youngster took on the bold moniker of Ed "Strangler" Lewis. To back up his new name, he developed a "stranglehold" finisher, which, unlike that of his predecessor, was actually a combination of a side headlock and a sleeper hold, intended to pin his opponent, not force them into submission.

In later years, Lewis would take to famously practicing his pet hold on a specially made spring-loaded dummy head, a publicity stunt that made him a media darling. This kind of business savvy made Lewis a standout in his time, especially since it was paired with a dangerous grappling ability that led him to be considered unbeatable in a legitimate contest. In fact, later shooters like Lou Thesz and Verne Gagne claimed emphatically that Lewis could only be defeated when he allowed himself to in order to further a storyline angle.

Confident in his abilities, Lewis had no problem "doing business" when the situation called for it, and perhaps this also contributed to his enormous success. Paired with manager Billy Sandow, Lewis quickly climbed the ladder in the period between World War I and the start of the 1920s by holding his own against former World Champion Joe Stecher in a series of brutal encounters. By the time he ascended to the position of the World Heavyweight Champion in the early 1920s, he had firmly built the entire wrestling business around himself. Only a skilled and dangerous wrestler as he could have done this

As the superstar of the Gold Dust Trio, Lewis enjoyed more than a decade of dominance, winning five World Heavyweight Championships between 1920 and 1932. During much of this period, he played the part of one of wrestling's first true "heels," taunting opponents and fans with his dreaded stranglehold, building interest in feuds, and drawing attention to forthcoming matches. His name became synonymous with pro wrestling, and he rubbed shoulders with all the pop culture icons of his day. He also made himself the husband of a grand total of four wives (the last of whom stayed with him for the remaining twenty-nine years of his life).

After the breakup of the Gold Dust Trio, Lewis remained an integral part of the mat game for years, but the paunchy, salt-and-pepper-haired grappler of the 1930s was not quite the same Strangler. In place of Stecher, he had a new rival, Jim Londos, with whom he vied for world-championship status. After Lewis defeated Jack Sherry in a number-one contender's match at the new Madison

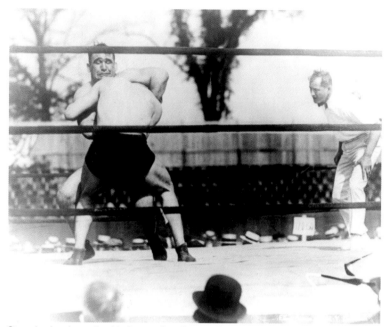

Strangler Lewis applies his famous headlock to Russian competitor Ivan Linow at an international tournament, c. 1920.   *Library of Congress*

Square Garden Bowl in Long Island City, New York, he gained recognition from the New York State Athletic Commission as World Heavyweight Champion. It was a maneuver he and his promotional backers had orchestrated against Londos, who had refused to defend his title against the Strangler. It would be Lewis's final title.

Lewis went into semi-retirement in the late 1930s, his eyesight ravaged by the effects of trachoma, a disease that afflicted wrestlers in those days due to unclean ring mats. Falling on some hard times in the 1940s, he was eventually recruited by the brand-new National Wrestling Alliance, a conglomerate of wrestling promoters, to be the sanctioning body's goodwill ambassador. In this role, he would also be brought on as the figurehead manager of the NWA's undisputed World Heavyweight Champion, Lou Thesz. Lewis would remain very close friends with Thesz for the remainder of his life.

Relying on the financial support of his wife as well as that of fans and acquaintances at the end of his life, a legally blind Ed "Strangler" Lewis died broke in New York on August 8, 1966, at the age of seventy-five. And although the struggling reputation of pro wrestling over the years caused his name to leave the company of the likes of Ruth, Dempsey, Grange, and Tilden, no one can take away the towering celebrity status once enjoyed by this titan of the mat.

The Golden Greek

During the depths of the Great Depression, one wrestler continued to inspire fans in urban centers on both the East and West coasts to fill arenas to capacity. On the New York scene, he was the first true wrestling superhero, an unstoppable drawing card for Madison Square Garden who set the pattern later followed by MSG headliners like Antonino Rocca, Bruno Sammartino, and Hulk Hogan. Jim Londos set the template for wrestling's reliance on ethnicity as a tool for selling tickets, a tradition that would live on for decades. Some call him the greatest live draw in the history of the business.

"Londos was the greatest wrestling star the sport had ever seen," opines historian Steve Yohe, an expert on the Golden Greek. "He was a draw from his first match in 1915 until he retired in 1958."

He was born Christos Theofilou on January 2, 1897, in Argos, Greece, the youngest of thirteen children. In 1910, a teenaged Theofilu ran away from home and immigrated to the United States, where he took on a series of manual jobs, including that of a plasterer on a construction site. A student of bodybuilding and weight lifting, he trained his body to near perfection, and although he stood only five-nine, his adult weight reached as high as 205 pounds. This helped him to find work as a nude art model and as a circus acrobat.

The circus world inevitably led him to cross paths with the world of professional wrestling, which captured his imagination instantly. He trained feverishly for the sport, and debuted in 1915 at age eighteen, using the unfortunate name of "The Wrestling Plasterer" Christopher Theophelus. Before long, he abandoned the plasterer gimmick and rechristened himself Jim Londos, in honor of the early twentieth-century journalist and novelist Jack London, of whom the well-read young man was a great admirer.

"He worked out every day, and kept a strict diet," says Yohe. "He studied every form and style of wrestling, including jiujitsu, which he came in contact with living near the Chinatown of San Francisco as a teenager. He seemed to have his whole life planned before he started, and no wrestler ever worked harder for what he got."

What he got was a position at the very top of every promoter's wish list. Facing all the top competitors of the 1920s, Londos's star rose even in defeat. Crowds took an instinctive liking to the tough, good-looking underdog with a body that looked like it had been cut out of marble. His immigrant status also endeared him not just to Greeks, but also the many Italians, Jews, Poles, and other ethnic groups that made up so much of the growing urban populations of the day.

His shot at greatness finally came on June 6, 1930, when he toppled fellow immigrant Dick Shikat for the New York State Athletic Commission's recognition

Flanked by ring announcer Joe Humphries (left) and promoter Jack Curley (right), Jim Londos exults in his World Heavyweight Championship win over Jim Browning, who is being tended to by referee George Bothner. Madison Square Garden Bowl, Long Island City, New York, June 25, 1934.   *Author's collection*

as World Heavyweight Champion. With the victory he also gained the recognition of the newly formed National Wrestling Association, a division of the National Boxing Association (now the WBA). However, a white-hot behind-the-scenes feud with another giant of the ring, Ed "Strangler" Lewis, would throw a monkey wrench into things.

Londos had the backing of New York and Pennsylvania area promoters Toots Mondt, Ray Fabiani, and Jack Curley, who found themselves on the other side of a war with Lewis and his backer, Boston promoter Paul Bowser. Lewis used his influence to have the NYS Athletic Commission strip Londos of the title in 1932 when he refused to face him. Nevertheless, Londos would continue to claim the National Wrestling Association title for another two years, before losing it to Danno O'Mahoney in Fenway Park. By that point, Londos had abandoned Curley and aligned himself with Bowser, in a move typical of the Byzantine wrestling intrigue of the 1930s.

"He was bigger than any promoter of his time," says Yohe. "Many times these promoters would resent him, but when they kicked him out of their city, they would always come crying to get him back."

His appeal extended far beyond just the Northeast, as could be seen in October 1934 when he journeyed to Los Angeles for promoter Lou Daro to defend his title before a crowd of twenty-five thousand (in a typical case of wrestling hyperbole, Daro claimed the number was closer to thirty-nine thousand) against the West Coast's number-one attraction, the massive Man Mountain Dean. Indeed, Londos held attendance records in most major cities where he wrestled, throughout the U.S. and Canada. Ever the smaller underdog, he innovated a match style that is still copied to this day, that of the hero who takes tremendous punishment over a long period of time, only to make a dramatic comeback in the end and vanquish his more intimidating opponent. He was one of the first to understand how to properly "sell" the suffering he endured at the hands of his enemies, so it would be apparent all the way to the cheap seats.

Londos claimed world-championship status well into the 1940s, before he finally wound down his historic career. With or without the title, he was a top-drawer attraction and a regular main-eventer. He was also wise enough to save his money, and therefore was able to retire in comfort to California, where he lived as a millionaire farmer to the end of his days. He passed away from a heart attack on August 19, 1975, at the age of seventy-eight.

5

Wrestling as You Liked It

The Golden Age of Television

A lot of people will pay to see someone shut your mouth. So keep on bragging, keep on sassing and always be outrageous.
—Gorgeous George, to Muhammad Ali

It was a match made in heaven. Starting in the late 1940s, professional wrestling crossed paths with a brand new medium that was about to take the nation by storm and transform the way we experience entertainment. A natural fit for television technology, wrestling not only benefited from the TV boom, it helped to shape and define it. Colorful characters and their in-ring antics were brought into viewers' living rooms for the first time, taking a business that had been on life support and turning it into a household word. As the product became more histrionic to fit the in-your-face format, the emphasis moved more than ever away from genuine grappling and toward flamboyant showmanship. Many athletes benefited from this transition, but none more so than a high-school dropout from Houston, Texas, who reinvented himself as wrestling's first TV superstar.

World War II was a tough and transformative time for America in general, as it was for the wrestling business in particular. The box office was lacking, as was the star power needed to draw fans out to the arenas. With so many of the game's talent serving their country in the armed forces, the ranks were significantly depleted, and as a result, desperate promoters began to rely more than ever on cartoonish performers who might not have been Olympics-worthy wrestlers, but could get the job done in terms of marketability and fan appeal. They started relying more on gimmickry, adding titillating women's matches to the card, as well as varied types of matches, from tag teams to mud wrestling and everything in between. Were it not for the birth of television, it might very well have been on the road to obscurity and oblivion.

Boob Tube Renaissance

But we don't have to speculate about that, because television *did* come along after the war, lighting up the homes of Americans with a cold, blue glow that translated to cold, green cash. In those early days of the late 1940s, the brand new television stations popping up across North America were looking for cheap, dependable programming to fill their daily timeslots, and professional wrestling provided just that. Los Angeles outfit KTLA became the first, kicking off a program in 1946 that was aired from the famed Olympic Auditorium. Other local programs would soon follow, but the granddaddy of them all would be *Wrestling from the Marigold*, a national broadcast that debuted in 1949 and ran on the DuMont Network for six years. Presented by Chicago promoter Fred Kohler, *Wrestling from the Marigold* helped take pro wrestling mainstream, and its stars became bona fide celebrities.

In those early years, TV and wrestling went hand in hand, with the sport drawing higher ratings than almost anything else on the tube. Although some early scripted programs like *I Love Lucy* and Milton Berle's *Texaco Star Theatre* already existed, there wasn't a lot of pre-produced entertainment to choose from, and so sporting events like wrestling and boxing provided a simple alternative—easy to shoot, with ready-made characters and compelling storylines. The result was an era often referred to today as the first Golden Age of pro wrestling.

Although storylines and characters had existed in wrestling before TV, the dynamic, visual medium helped bring things to a whole new level. With regular broadcasts being offered, it was easier for promoters and bookers to employ ongoing, episodic angles that would capture viewers' attention and entice them to come down to their local arena and pay money to see live matches. Wrestlers now had the opportunity to speak into a microphone and get their points across verbally, and if they didn't possess the skill to do so, a new type of performer, the wrestling manager, was created to do it for them. This new element of the show, known in the business as "cutting a promo," not only enabled wrestlers to propel storylines forward, it also allowed them to further establish and develop their onscreen personas.

"Television was the new thing, and wrestling came off really well on TV," says *Wrestling Observer* editor Dave Meltzer. "It had colorful characters . . . and was a very simple morality play. TV increased wrestling's exposure so much. The concept of hyping arena shows on TV was created. Before, they would use newspapers, but TV is far more effective for projecting your personality than stories in the newspapers."

And what personalities they were. Wrestling had been home to outlandish types from the beginning, but thanks to TV, the business produced a new cast of characters that was just as engaging and bombastic as any cast of a television program could be expected to be. There were flamboyant heroes like Ricki Starr, the ballet-dancing wrestler from Greenwich Village; the superhero-esque "Mr. America" Gene Stanlee; the high-flying Antonino Rocca, New York's hottest attraction since the days of Jim Londos. And more than ever, there were heinous villains who made it their life's work to draw the ire of the first generation of couch potatoes with their carefully honed routines: the arrogant "Nature Boy" Buddy Rogers, whose style became the template for scores of copycats; goose-stepping Nazis like Hans Schmidt, Karl Von Hess and Fritz Von Erich; the bellowing Canadian behemoth Killer Kowalski; the "Mormon Giant" Don Leo Jonathan.

"The environment was right," says Tim Hornbaker, accomplished historian and author. "Post World War II, people were looking for an outlet to vent their aggressions. The wrestling arena, where they could yell and scream at heels like German sympathizer Hans Schmidt, was the perfect place to have an entertaining time. People wanted to get out of their house and there wasn't cable TV, the Internet or other distractions around to keep them sitting on their butts. So they got up and went to their local arena to enjoy wrestling."

The Toast of the Coast

But no character—in wrestling or on TV, for that matter—equaled the stature of George Wagner, a journeyman wrestler who stumbled upon the gimmick of a lifetime and rode it to pop-culture immortality. When his no-nonsense grappling style didn't pay the bills, he rechristened himself Gorgeous George, adopting a persona that included elaborate robes, perfectly coiffed platinum blonde hair, entrance music ("Pomp and Circumstance," thirty-five years before Randy Savage co-opted it), even a valet to accompany him to the ring and spray the canvas with a perfumed atomizer. After a dozen years spent in relative obscurity, Gorgeous was suddenly the "Toast of the Coast."

To a business that had consisted largely of hard-nosed, straight-ahead grapplers with minimal color, the impact of a figure like Gorgeous George cannot be overstated. His elaborate, decidedly effeminate act was pure gold, as fans sat glued to their TV sets in the hopes that someone—*anyone*—could take the wind out of the sails of this shamelessly preening peacock of a wrestler. To the staid audiences of the 1950s, with their traditional concepts of masculinity, his very existence was an affront. It also didn't hurt that he could perform well in the ring, and seemed to be having quite a bit of fun with the whole thing. His fame transcended the business, and looking back, it's clear that Gorgeous George was one of the first television-manufactured

American celebrities. From a performance standpoint, he was professional wrestling's first genius.

From humble beginnings in Texas, Gorgeous was suddenly in demand from promoters all over the country. The same could be said to a lesser degree for any wrestlers who were getting television exposure, and Kohler's talent in particular was suddenly being requested by many of his rivals in other territories, making him for a few years the most influential and powerful promoter in the business. Although some of the old-timers mistrusted TV because they thought it would keep people from going out and buying tickets, the opposite turned out to be true. The omnipresent new medium gave promoters a way to sell their product in people's homes, just like so many other products. Pro wrestling had a higher profile than it had ever enjoyed.

"Pro wrestling was perfect for TV in so many ways because you really just needed a single camera, and you could follow the action," explains Greg Oliver, author of the *Pro Wrestling Hall of Fame* book series. "It was a lot more photogenic than even boxing, which was another early one, because you could see it from further away and follow the action. Over time, pro wrestling had to adapt to TV, and TV adapted to pro wrestling. There were opportunities for guys to get more colorful, and therefore the stories themselves had to get more dramatic."

An Alliance Forged

Just as TV was expanding the horizons of the business in a big way, a new confederacy of wrestling promotions was coming together, first in the Midwest, then spreading outward, unifying operations within the industry in a manner not seen since the days of the Gold Dust Trio in the 1920s. But unlike that organization, the National Wrestling Alliance, as it would be called, was not a single company. Rather, it was a collection of organizations, forming an agreement to work together to share talent, promote the business, and most importantly, not compete with one another.

The grouping came together officially in 1948, made up of such founding members as Ohio's Al Haft, Minnesota's Tony Stecher, Missouri's Sam Muchnick, and the original organizer and president, Iowa impresario P. L. "Pinkie" George. One of the most important aspects of the NWA was the emphasis on recognizing a single World Heavyweight Champion, to give unity to the business, and provide a major attraction to all members. For the majority of the NWA's early years, and during the entirety of wrestling's TV Golden Age, this role would be consummately filled by one Lou Thesz, the son of a Hungarian shoemaker from St. Louis who was a throwback to the old days of shooters like Strangler Lewis (his manager), Stanislaus

NWA World Heavyweight Champion Lou Thesz, featured on the cover of *Wrestling As You Like It*, the premier magazine of wrestling's TV Golden Age.   *Author's collection*

Zbyszko and Frank Gotch; a respected, legit wrestler who gave credence to the title and to the business as a whole. (For more on the NWA and Thesz, see Chapter 10.)

The birth of the NWA came along at just the right time, with TV giving the various Alliance promoters the perfect outlet to help popularize their new idea. Kohler, naturally, came on board, as did many other promoters nationwide who had their own local TV shows. Thesz defended his crown in territories across North America and even internationally, engaging in a series of title unification matches with other claimants like Gorgeous George and Baron Michele Leone, a long-haired faux nobleman who reigned supreme in California and who, in his 1952 match with Thesz, wound up drawing the first $100,000 gate in the history of the business.

The NWA and the popularity of wrestling in general crested during the first half of the 1950s, but between Eisenhower's first and second terms, the steam began to run out. As modern TV watchers are well aware, the medium gives rise to fads which come and go over time, and pro wrestling turned out to be one of those fads, having a finite shelf life before viewers moved on to something else. In 1955, the DuMont Network canceled *Wrestling from the Marigold*; there would not be another national network TV wrestling broadcast for thirty years. Meanwhile, what remained were the local broadcasts, creating local stars helping to strengthen and grow local territories and the promoters who ran them.

A Family Dynasty Begins

One of these new promoters on the scene was a Washington, D.C.–based entrepreneur named Vincent James McMahon, owner of a company called the Capitol Wrestling Corporation. Running out of D.C.'s Turner Arena (which McMahon bought from aging wrestler-turned-promoter Joe Turner) since 1953, by the middle of the decade McMahon got his product on local television. One of the savviest visionaries around when it came to the possibilities of TV, McMahon invested money in updating his arena and wiring it for proper TV lighting. The DuMont Network soon came calling, and the local Capitol Wrestling matches were being broadcast throughout much of the Northeast.

Thanks to the power of television, McMahon was able to gain enough influence and momentum to begin knocking on the door of the big boys, which in New York meant that old warhorse Toots Mondt, the former Gold Dust Trio cornerstone who now ran the Manhattan Booking Office; Rudy Dusek, leader of the Dusek Riot Squad and the top promoter in the region going back to the 1930s; and Charlie and Ned Johnston, whose family had run wrestling at Madison Square Garden for more than a generation.

At first, the old guard tried to fend off the upstart McMahon, but his stars were the ones TV viewers wanted to see. McMahon presented his first show at Madison Square Garden in 1956; by the end of the decade, he was the sole promoter of wrestling at the venue. The Johnstons were out, as was Dusek. Mondt, ever the survivor, chose to join forces with McMahon and his Capitol Wrestling Corporation. Toots had enjoyed great success at the Garden for years with Argentine acrobat Antonino Rocca as his top draw, and with the merger, Rocca became McMahon's top draw as well, second only in the nation to Gorgeous George himself.

The New York machinations of McMahon and Mondt in the late 1950s were typical of the scrambling that was going on in the wake of wrestling's disappearance from national television. Everyone wanted a piece of the pie, and regional television was now where it was. The business was becoming fragmented again, and a new territorial era was on its way, defined by sharp boundaries and regional fiefdoms. Wrestling was leaving the mainstream consciousness for a time, even if it was a healthier business overall than ever before.

Major Stars of the Era

The early days of television brought a host of outrageous characters into the living rooms of wrestling fans. Here are just a few:

- Antonino Rocca
- Baron Michele Leone
- Bobo Brazil
- "Classy" Freddie Blassie
- Crusher Lisowski
- Edouard Carpentier
- Gorgeous George
- Hans Schmidt
- Haystacks Calhoun
- Irish Danny McShain
- Killer Kowalski
- Lou Thesz
- Mildred Burke
- "Mr. America" Gene Stanlee
- "Nature Boy" Buddy Rogers
- Pat O'Connor
- Primo Carnera
- Ricki Starr
- Verne Gagne
- "Whipper" Billy Watson

The Human Orchid

In terms of celebrity status, no professional wrestler other than Hulk Hogan ever achieved the level of mainstream fame and notoriety enjoyed by Gorgeous George, the original gimmick wrestler and the man almost single-handedly responsible for transforming television into a viable American entertainment medium. At one point in his career, he was the highest paid athlete in the world, and he would later be cited by the likes of Muhammad Ali, Bob Dylan, and many others as a direct influence. Few performers can claim to have changed the business as dramatically as he did, turning it from a dying sport into a colorful, highly lucrative American spectacle.

He was born George Raymond Wagner on March 24, 1915, in Butte, Nebraska—humble beginnings for the future Toast of the Coast. His family later relocated to Houston, Texas, where he would eventually take to wrestling in school and at the local YMCA. He would turn this into a professional career when he started wrestling for Houston promoter Morris Siegel in 1938.

But Wagner didn't make much of a splash in those days, being a rather nondescript fellow who got lost in the mix of hard-nosed grapplers who populated the business at the time. It would take something a little extra for him to get noticed; something to help him stand out from the pack. Reading in a magazine about a wrestler named Lord Patrick Lansdowne who was using fancy robes and an elaborate ring entrance to get himself over with fans, Wagner decided to take that idea to the next level. He invented a gimmick for himself that was unlike anything the business had seen up to that point—that of a wrestler who was more image than athleticism, a character that would magnetically draw the attention of fans by his very presence.

He debuted his new image at a card in Eugene, Oregon, in 1941, inspiring the ring announcer to refer to him as "Gorgeous George." The name stuck, as did the image. Coming to the ring in outrageously ornate outfits provided by the prestigious boutique Frank and Joseph of Hollywood, and accompanied by a solemn valet spraying perfume, George was now making an entrance that would often take longer than his matches. His long hair was done up in platinum bobby pins, which he would refer to as "Georgie Pins" and toss out to the crowd. His elaborate histrionics included refusing to be touched by referees or opponents, playing the coward, and, of course, cheating at every possible turn. His effete dandy persona played on the homophobic tendencies of mainstream American culture in the 1940s and '50s. He knew fans would pay good money to see his pretty blonde hairstyle ruined and the smug arrogance beaten out of him, and they did.

With the advent of television in the late 1940s, Gorgeous George's popularity skyrocketed. He made his TV debut in a November 11, 1947, match, and almost instantly became a household name. His celebrity rivaled the likes of other early TV superstars, including Lucille Ball, Bob Hope, and Milton Berle, all of whom he knew personally. He

"The Human Orchid" blesses a Chicago crowd with his presence, in a photo taken by twenty-one-year-old photojournalist Stanley Kubrick in the summer of 1949.
Look *Magazine Photograph Collection (Library of Congress)*

appeared in films, was lampooned in Warner Bros. cartoons, and became the biggest drawing card the business had ever seen. Based out of Los Angeles, where he wrestled regularly for promoter Johnny Doyle, he made headlines everywhere he went, including New York, where in 1949 he appeared in the first wrestling event held at Madison Square Garden in a decade.

"You had only a few stations, and TV was the in thing," explains Dave Meltzer. "The TV ratings for wrestling in the late '40s and early '50s were huge. Everybody watched it, and the famous wrestlers were real famous. More famous than John Cena, by far. Gorgeous George was a legit TV celebrity that they made jokes about on late-night TV shows. Everybody in the country knew who he was."

In May 1950, George won World Heavyweight Champion recognition in Paul Bowser's Boston-based AWA after beating Native American competitor Don Eagle. He would later lose the title in a unification match with NWA World

Heavyweight Champion Lou Thesz, a legit grappler who always respected the consummate wrestling skill that hid under George's outrageous act.

As the '50s wound down, so did the career of Gorgeous George. Wrestling was no longer featured on national TV, and a few poor business investments led George to wrestle longer than he would have liked. In 1959, he suffered humiliation when a loss to Whipper Billy Watson at Toronto's Maple Leaf Gardens led to him having his gorgeous locks shorn in the middle of the ring. He was instructed to retire by doctors in 1962 after being diagnosed with liver disease resulting from years of hard drinking. The day after Christmas, 1963, George Wagner died of a heart attack at the age of forty-eight. It is rumored that he was so poor by that point that his fellow wrestlers had to raise money to buy him a headstone.

Gorgeous George turned wrestlers into showmen, and turned wrestling into television's most successful early programming, all while demonstrating a level of self-awareness that made him an icon of unprecedented proportions. He once remarked, "I don't think I'm gorgeous, but what's my opinion against millions of others?" Who are we to argue with that?

The Argentine Backbreaker

What Gorgeous George was to the West Coast, Antonino Rocca was to the East Coast, and only the Human Orchid himself was a greater box-office attraction during the 1950s. Rocca also played a major part in the early success of promoter Vincent J. McMahon, whose Capitol Wrestling would eventually morph into WWE. A dazzling acrobat of the ring, his thrilling aerial maneuvers helped him almost single-handedly invent a new style of wrestling.

He was born Antonio Biasetton on April 13, 1927, in Treviso, Italy, a small town near Venice. By the time the Fascists gained control of his homeland in the late 1930s, he and his family relocated—along with many other Italians—to the South American nation of Argentina. His early years are shrouded in mystery, as Rocca enjoyed stretching the truth when it came to his background; it's possible that he excelled in rugby and soccer, and would have had a career in either, were it not for a knee injury.

In 1947, the twenty-year-old was trained for the ring by the legendary Stanislaus Zbyszko, who was running the local wrestling promotion at the time. Biasetton changed his name to Rocca to play up his Italian heritage, and started employing previously unheard-of high-flying maneuvers, using the natural flexibility originally intended for the soccer field. He was discovered by retired American wrestler Nick Elitch, who convinced Rocca to bring him on as a manager and come to the United States to wrestle for Houston promoter Morris Siegel. After making a major splash in the Lone Star State, it was only a matter of time before New York came calling—in the form of Kola Kwariani, a gruff Eastern European shooter who scouted talent for Toots Mondt's Manhattan Booking Office.

Rocca debuted in the New York City area at Brooklyn's Ridgewood Grove in 1949, and never looked back. As they had in Texas, fans in New York responded wildly to the Argentine's dynamic style, characterized by a fast-paced excitement that was a dramatic departure from the mat-based clinching that grappling fans of the time had come to expect. And even though shooters including Lou Thesz liked to point out his lack of wrestling ability, it didn't matter in the end. Fans ate up his amazing dropkicks, victory rolls, flying head scissors and other dazzling maneuvers that changed the definition of what pro wrestling performance could be.

In a rare battle of the babyfaces, U.S. champion Verne Gagne attempts to take down Rocca with a flying-headscissors in Madison Square Garden, February 15, 1954.   *Author's collection*

Before long, Rocca was the top sensation of the Northeast, selling out Madison Square Garden and other major venues with a regularity not seen since Jim Londos was Jack Curley's headliner during the Depression (Rocca's Garden debut against Gene Stanlee drew the largest crowd MSG had seen for wrestling in nineteen years). Also like Londos, Rocca appealed to the massive immigrant fan bases of many urban centers, particularly those of Italian and Hispanic descent, both of which groups claimed him as their own. For the first time since the early 1930s, pro wrestling was a major attraction in the New York area, and Rocca was the reason.

Mondt was a major force in the business once again, and began booking his cash cow for other promoters all across the country. "Rocca has done more for legs than Betty Grable," Toots once said of his aerial marvel. One of these other promoters was Vincent J. McMahon, who started booking Rocca as one the top stars on his earliest shows in the Washington, D.C. area. When McMahon's stock began to rise in the mid 1950s thanks to TV, he convinced Rocca to leave Mondt (an old-timer who had always been wary of TV), and come work exclusively for him. This helped cement the D.C. impresario as the Northeast's wrestling czar, and soon Mondt took up the philosophy, "If you can't beat 'em, join 'em."

Under McMahon, Rocca entered a new phase of his career, forming a vastly popular tag team with Puerto Rican sensation Miguel Perez in the late 1950s. For years the duo held Capitol Wrestling's version of the World Tag Team Championship (forerunner to today's WWE Tag Team Championship), and between 1958 and 1960 headlined the Garden in a celebrated series of seven main events against the hated team of Dr. Jerry Graham & Eddie Graham. By the early '60s, he parted ways rather acrimoniously with McMahon after Bruno Sammartino was selected to be the company's next top star.

After trying to run opposition for years, financial need caused Rocca to eventually patch things up with the McMahon family. In the 1970s, he returned as a TV announcer, calling the action with a young Vincent K. McMahon, son of Vincent J. McMahon and future head of the company. In February 1977, he was honored by Staten Island promoter Tommy Dee during a special event called "Rocca Night." One month later, he was admitted to Roosevelt Hospital for a urinary tract infection, believed to be the result of alcohol abuse. After a two-week stay, during which he battled complications from the infection, Antonino Rocca died at age forty-nine. An innovator of the ring and the first major attraction for the company that would one day become WWE, Rocca will never be forgotten for his contributions to the history of the business.

The Original Nature Boy

When naming the most influential wrestling performers of all time, the name of Buddy Rogers needs to be at or near the very top of the list. Creating the template persona followed by so many who came after, he was a major innovator as well as a colossal box-office draw. He is a person of great historical importance, and as the first WWWF World Heavyweight Champion, he was a pivotal figure in the establishment of the most dominant pro wrestling company of the past half-century.

He was born Herman Rohde to German immigrants in Camden, New Jersey, on February 20, 1921. After becoming a police officer shortly after his eighteenth birthday, the young man also began simultaneously wrestling on a local basis. Initially calling himself Dutch Rogers (a nod to his *deutsche* ancestry), by the mid-1940s, while wrestling in Texas, he took to calling himself "Buddy Rogers," after a popular movie star of the day.

It was also around this time that Rogers began crafting a unique persona. Taking his cue from Gorgeous George, who was becoming the talk of the business due to his over-the-top flamboyance and in-ring arrogance, Rogers began donning sequined robes and took on a cocky, obnoxious demeanor. Tweaking what was working for George, he created something that was completely his own: a strutting, loud-mouthed, bleached blonde heel character that would directly inspire countless imitators over the years, including "Classy" Freddie Blassie, "Mr. Perfect" Curt Hennig, and, of course, the man who even adopted Rogers's own "Nature Boy" nickname, Ric Flair.

Rogers was the prototypical wrestling heel in the modern sense, bragging about himself on the mic and putting his opponents down at every chance he got. He represented the new type of performer that was coming into favor at the time, and has dominated ever since, with a combination of athleticism, interview ability, attitude, and a great overall "look." He interacted directly with the crowd, responding to what got them riled up and emphasizing it to further enhance his villainous image. A master of what would come to be known as "ring psychology," he redefined the manner in which wrestlers performed matches.

Rogers became such a box-office draw that promoters everywhere broke with tradition in pushing a wrestler based solely on his persona and marketability rather than his actual grappling ability. After spending a decade as United States Champion, he was rewarded with the ultimate prize on June 30, 1961, when he took the NWA World Heavyweight Championship from Pat O'Connor in Comiskey Park before the largest wrestling crowd in American history up to that point, in the same spot Gotch had battled Hackenschmidt fifty years prior. The move was a major vote of confidence from the NWA, which, until then, had selected shooters rather than performers as its champions.

By that point, Rogers's career was under the management of Northeast kingpins Toots Mondt and Vince McMahon, who were using the Nature Boy as the attraction of Capitol Wrestling, based in Madison Square Garden. Originally, Rogers had been in the stable of Ohio promoter Al Haft, who would lend him out to eccentric showman Jack Pfefer for occasional dates in the lucrative New York area during the '50s. Pfefer, a fan of the more theatrical side of the business, loved Rogers's act and helped make him a superstar. But when Pfefer got pushed out of the New York wrestling scene by Mondt and McMahon in 1960, the duo also pulled off the master stroke of signing Rogers to an exclusive deal. And so, when Rogers won in Comiskey that meant that the NWA World Championship was theirs to control.

NWA officials didn't appreciate the maneuver, and in January 1963 had Rogers lose the title back to their dependable former champion Lou Thesz, whom they had called out of retirement. Nonplussed, Mondt and McMahon ignored the loss and announced Buddy Rogers as the first World Heavyweight Champion of their own independent organization, the World Wide Wrestling Federation. On May 17, 1963, he lost the WWWF World Heavyweight title to Bruno Sammartino in forty-eight seconds in Madison Square Garden, ushering in an era of dominance and prosperity for the company.

The forty-two-year-old Rogers retired later that year, his health in question after suffering a heart attack not long before the Sammartino match. He would later come back in the early 1980s to work for the World Wrestling Federation, now run by Vince McMahon's son, as an announcer and manager for "Superfly" Jimmy Snuka. At the time of his death in 1992 at age seventy-one, he had been planning a big return match in Philadelphia. As always, Buddy Rogers was looking to the future.

6

Gentlemen's Agreement

The Glory Days of the Territorial System

In the old days, there were wrestling fiefdoms all over the country, each with its own little lord in charge. Each little lord respected the rights of his neighboring little lord. . . . I, of course, had no allegiance to those little lords.
—Vince McMahon, *Sports Illustrated*, March 25, 1991

It was a time after wrestling had faded from attention on national TV in the 1950s and before it again became a national force in the 1980s, when the game was divided into a complex map of neatly (and sometimes not-so-neatly) defined territories, complete with their own home town cast of characters, and local TV programs with their own unique, regional flavor. From Cowboy Lutrell and Eddie Graham in Florida, to the Shires and LeBells on the West Coast, to the Crocketts in the Carolinas and beyond, being a wrestling fan in those days was defined by where in North America you happened to live.

So What Are Wrestling Territories, Anyway?

There had been promotional territories going back to the 1920s and '30s, so they weren't necessarily anything new, per se. But most fans will point to the late 1950s through the early 1980s as professional wrestling's "Territorial Era." Most, if not all, of the major territories during that time period were members of the National Wrestling Alliance, or at least affiliated with it in some way. That meant that territorial boundaries would be respected, and with the exception of occasional "outlaw promotions" that would crop up from time to time, promoters agreed not to present shows in areas designated as another promoter's specific region. In the case of the NWA territories, talent was usually shared between promotions, and wrestlers enjoyed the ability to move freely from one territory to another. This kept them from getting stale by performing for any fan base for too long a time, and it also helped the promoters keep their product fresh as well by ensuring a steady flow of new performers.

Television helped establish the territorial order, as each region had its own TV program, which it used to help promote its own regional live events and further its own storyline angles. In addition to TV, each territory ran regular live events at certain venues that made up a specific regional circuit; often, a central booking office would supply talent to individual promoters who ran certain towns within the territory. Championships multiplied at an astounding rate, with each territory recognizing its own local titleholders. And although wrestlers moved regularly from area to area, each region came to spotlight its own local favorites—regulars who would go on to inspire the adoring loyalty, or enduring hatred, of local fans.

"Wrestling went down for a while when they lost national TV," explains Dave Meltzer of the *Wrestling Observer*. "The second rise of wresting, the territorial rise, came with the advent of UHF television, because now instead of having three or four TV stations, you had maybe 10 or 12, but they were all local. Wrestling thrived on UHF because you just needed a solid weekly audience to do well. In a lot markets, the pro wrestling show was the highest rated locally produced TV show, and in some markets, it was even higher than some networks. You could serve your local customer base, and the promoter was more in control, because instead of booking guys off a national TV show that were stars and paying a percentage to the big promoter who had the TV, now its *your* TV and you're in control, so you make your own stars."

Fans also came to expect a different type of product in different regions. Detroit came to be known for a chaotic, proto-hardcore style; Memphis was the home of Southern-style barroom brawling; wrestling in the WWWF's Northeast area was dominated by ethnic athletes; the AWA gave white bread fans of the Midwest a squeaky-clean, amateur-based style. Each area was its own contained wrestling universe; fans were fixated only on the sports' goings-on in their own territory, which was exactly how the promoters wanted it.

"Every place went up and down based on their stars—who was on top, who the villains were," says wrestling historian Greg Oliver. "Fans knew that every week to two weeks, there'd be a show in their area, and just like a season ticket subscriber to opera or football, getting this was part of their life, a regular thing."

"The Big Three"

The rise of the territories was typified by the establishment of three different organizations in the early 1960s that dared to defy the dominance of the NWA. In 1959, Los Angeles promoters Jules Strongbow and the married duo of Cal and Eileen Eaton formed what would come to be known as the World Wrestling Association, recognizing Edouard Carpentier as world champion after a controversial win over NWA title-holder Lou Thesz. The following year, 1950s superstar Verne Gagne, who had bought the Minnesota territory from Tony Stecher, established the American Wrestling Association, recognizing himself as the first AWA World Heavyweight Champion with the excuse that then-NWA titleholder Pat O'Connor refused to defend against him. And, in 1963, Capitol Wrestling kingpins Vince McMahon and Toots Mondt broke off from the NWA to create the World Wide Wrestling Federation, recognizing recently dethroned NWA titleholder Buddy Rogers as their first WWWF World Heavyweight Champion.

And so the Territorial Era was a time of multiple world champions. The WWA relinquished its claim, rejoining the NWA in 1968, but the AWA and the WWWF (which would

Prior to establishing the modern American Wrestling Association (AWA), Verne Gagne was one of the top stars of the 1950s.

Jack Pfefer Collection, University of Notre Dame

shorten its name to WWF in 1979) remained independent. Fans of the 1960s through the 1980s would grow used to the great triumvirate of NWA, AWA, and WWF World Championships that dominated the wrestling landscape.

Stars Without Boundaries

Most territories were able to supply enough work to their stable of talent to allow them to make a decent, regular living at their chosen profession, and sometimes a lot more than decent. Most wrestlers enjoyed moving from one territory to another during the Territorial Era, and several of them reached a level where their star power would transcend territorial boundaries, making them major drawing cards everywhere they went. The NWA World Champions like Dory Funk, Jr., Jack Brisco, and Harley Race were always in a position to be stars in every territory they toured. Long-running WWWF World Champion Bruno Sammartino became a big enough phenom on the Northeast that he was in demand to defend his title in California, Ontario, Florida, and many other places. There was the plumber's son from Austin, Texas, "The American Dream" Dusty Rhodes, whose irresistible charisma and captivating interview style made him a top-shelf national attraction with or without the NWA World Championship.

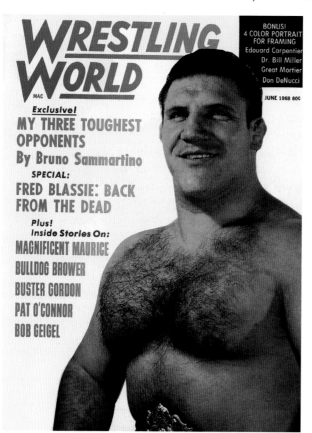

And then there was the massive Frenchman who became the single-hottest wrestling attraction of the 1970s and early 1980s, as well as a legitimate crossover celebrity. Andre the Giant became a legend quickly among fans, and promoters in every territory clamored to add him to their shows. Managed by Vincent J. McMahon, Andre spent years being booked out of the WWWF office to territories all over the nation, as well as the world, and was the most sought-after talent in the business since Gorgeous George.

Due to his main-event status in New York City, the center of the publishing world, Sammartino was probably featured on more magazine covers during the 1960s and '70s than any other wrestler. *Author's collection*

The Business Booms

Although the industry was fragmented during the days of the territories, for many of the regions, business had never been better. In the 1970s, wrestling mega-events, or "supercards," became more and more common. California's Mike LeBell presented the first major wrestling show broadcast over closed-circuit TV, headlined by Freddie Blassie taking on John Tolos in a white-hot grudge match. Now, thanks to closed circuit, crowds in remote theater locations in other parts of the country could see the event live. The WWWF presented a series of major events at Shea Stadium: a 1972 dream match between World Champion Pedro Morales and former champ Bruno Sammartino; a 1976 show that included a revenge match between Bruno and the man who broke his neck, Stan Hansen, as well as coverage of the boxer/wrestler match between Muhammad Ali and Antonio Inoki live from Japan; and a 1980 show headlined by the likes of Bruno Sammartino, Hulk Hogan, and Andre the Giant. In 1978, Eddie Graham presented a show in the Miami Orange Bowl he ostentatiously called *The Superbowl of Wrestling*. With a main event pitting NWA World Champion Harley Race against WWWF World Champion Superstar Billy Graham, it was hard to argue with that claim. During the early 1980s, Bill Watts's Mid-South Wrestling Association became known for a series of supercards at the Superdome in New Orleans.

Territorial boundaries eventually blurred thanks to the beginnings of cable TV, which provided the opportunity for programming to reach a national audience without being on network TV. In 1973, the fledgling HBO started featuring WWWF events from Madison Square Garden. Georgia Championship Wrestling became the first weekly wrestling show carried over cable TV when its local Atlanta channel, WTBS, rose to be a national cable powerhouse. In the early 1980s, Southwest Championship Wrestling out of San Antonio got a deal with the USA Network. Some regional promoters complained about the unfair advantage this gave to their colleagues, but there was no stopping the march of technological progress.

"All of a sudden you could see guys from outside your region, and it just meant a lot more," says Greg Oliver. "You could see the guy from Atlanta, and you wanted to see him in *your* territory. You had national stars in a way that you really didn't before."

But it was more than just technology that began to spell the end of the territorial system; it was also ingenuity—specifically, the ingenuity of Vincent Kennedy McMahon, the son of WWF founder Vincent James McMahon. On June 6, 1982, in a meeting at New York City's Warwick Hotel, the younger

McMahon made a deal with his father and business partners Robert "Gorilla Monsoon" Marella, Arnold Skaaland and Phil Zacko to purchase the Capitol Wrestling Corporation, putting the WWF brand under his new TitanSports corporate banner. With visions that reached far beyond the northeastern United States, and no loyalty whatsoever to the traditional way promoters did business, he would bring the entire territorial system crashing down before the decade was out.

Breaking Down the Major North American Territories

All-Star Wrestling

At one time broadcast across Canada, this territory originated in Vancouver, British Columbia, as Rod Fenton's "Big Time Wrestling," but later changed over when Sandor Kovacs and Gene Kiniski (then the NWA World Heavyweight Champion) took over. Former AWA promoter and wrestler Al Tomko became the top dog in the late 1970s, and even tried to take the company independent as the Universal Wrestling Alliance in the mid-1980s to combat the encroaching WWF. All-Star ceased operations in 1989.

Map by Kyle Kusch of the Basement Geographer (basementgeographer.com)

American Wrestling Association

The AWA was to the Midwest what the WWWF was to the Northeast: a major-league alternative to the NWA, with its own recognized world championship. Founded by Verne Gagne in 1960 after he bought out the old Minnesota territory from Tony Stecher, the AWA focused on scientific grappling, largely owing to Gagne's own amateur background. Although Gagne pushed himself as the AWA World Champion for much of the company's history, other top AWA stars included Nick Bockwinkel, Mad Dog Vachon, and The Crusher. The company was raided heavily by the WWF in the mid-1980s, but limped on until 1991.

Atlantic Grand Prix Wrestling

A fixture in the Maritimes region of Canada from the 1960s, Grand Prix ran regularly in New Brunswick, Nova Scotia, and Prince Edward Island. Its main titles included the European Championship, Maritimes Championship, North American Tag Team Championship, and a version of the U.S. Championship. Emile Dupree took over the company in 1977 and ran it until selling out to the WWF in 1986. In 2001, Dupree brought Grand Prix back to the Maritimes, and continues to promote there to this day.

Big-Time Wrestling (San Francisco)

> *I always thought San Francisco wrestling was the best promotion. It was like Madison Square Garden, with good workers.*
> —Steve Yohe

The 1920s mat star Joe Malcewicz had been the original boss of the San Francisco territory from way back, originating the sport's first World Tag Team Championship there with the Sharpe Brothers as his top titleholders. One of Malcewicz's other tag team attractions, Roy Shire, took over in the 1960s and made the territory an NWA member. Shire was responsible for making men like Ray Stevens, Pat Patterson and High Chief Peter Maivia into stars, and helped establish the Cow Palace as one of the top venues in the business (the Cow Palace battle royals are still the stuff of legend). Shire closed up shop in 1981.

Big-Time Wrestling (Detroit)

Nick Londos (no relation to Jim) ran Detroit in the 1920s and 1930s, and later Johnny Doyle and Jim Barnett had success there in the '50s. But it would be Ed Farhat, better known as The Sheik, who would become forever associated with Detroit wrestling. The Sheik's battles in the fabled Cobo Arena with archenemy Bobo Brazil are remembered to this day, and the territory is credited with helping to popularize the hardcore style of wrestling during the 1970s. The company closed in 1980, but its glory days can be witnessed in the classic mockumentary *I Like to Hurt People*.

Central States Wrestling

The birthplace of the National Wrestling Alliance, this territory was founded in the '40s by NWA forefathers Pinkie George and Orville Brown. Bob Geigel and his Heart of America Promotions took over in 1958, booking shows throughout Kansas, Missouri, Nebraska, and Iowa, and forming a close relationship with St. Louis promoter Sam Muchnick. Geigel would help propel both Pat O'Connor and Harley Race to the NWA World Heavyweight title, and even served as NWA chairman from 1978 to 1987. In 1986, he sold the Central States territory to Jim Crockett, who was expanding his company in an attempt to go national.

Championship Wrestling from Florida

Florida was the place where some of the most creative stuff came out.
—Greg Oliver

Enjoying a close working relationship with the WWWF, CWF was run by Eddie Graham, who had been a top tag team star for the WWWF in the 1950s. After taking over from original Florida promoter Cowboy Luttrell, Graham went on to produce one of the most consistently popular territories of the 1970s and 1980s. His TV programs featured Gordon Solie, "Dean of Wrestling Announcers," on the mic, as well as such stars as Kevin Sullivan, Barry Windham, Mike Rotunda, and his greatest attraction of all, "The American Dream" Dusty Rhodes. Graham committed suicide in 1985, and the company was sold to Jim Crockett two years later.

Continental Championship Wrestling

Covering portions of Tennessee and Alabama, this territory was, at different times, also known as Gulf Coast Championship Wrestling and Southeast Championship Wrestling. Little footage still exists, and the territory often ran in relative obscurity under the Welch/Fuller wrestling family, due to their belief that coverage in wrestling magazines or other outlets would break the illusion of kayfabe. The Continental name change in later years was done in a failed attempt to compete with the WWF. The promotions finally ceased operations in 1989.

Continental Wrestling Association

Better known to fans simply as "Memphis," this territory was established by Jerry Jarrett in opposition to fellow Tennessee promoter Nick Gulas, and went on to become one of the hottest companies of the '70s and '80s, known for its cards at the Mid-South Coliseum. With Lance Russell's distinctive voice calling the action and Jerry "The King" Lawler as the top star, Memphis helped define the Southern "rasslin" style, and received national headlines due to Lawler's on-air feud with comedian Andy Kaufman. The CWA later morphed into the United States Wrestling Association, which survived as the last of the full-time territories, soldiering on until 1997.

Georgia Championship Wrestling

GCW changed the business.

—Greg Oliver

Following a turf war between Ann Gunkel and Cowboy Bill Watts for control of the Georgia territory after the death of Ann's husband, Ray, ubiquitous wrestling mastermind James E. Barnett swooped in and took over. A slot on Ted Turner's Atlanta-based WTBS became fortuitous when TBS grew to be a national cable channel, pumping GCW into homes across America. By the 1980s, Barnett changed the company name to World Championship Wrestling. In 1984, the coveted timeslot was sold to Vince McMahon, who was eager for a national spotlight, and replaced the Georgia show with his own WWF programming. Dubbed "Black Saturday" by fans, the initial McMahon broadcast was met with an extremely negative backlash—a rare case of pushback against his company's expansion. His product rejected by the TBS audience, McMahon soon sold the timeslot to Jim Crockett, and it became the cornerstone of the company that would evolve into WCW.

Hollywood Wrestling

Wrestling had always been popular in the surreal world of L.A. and was a staple of early promoters like Lou Daro and Johnny Doyle. The LeBell family took center stage in 1959, when their L.A. territory formed the original World Wrestling Association, which had its own world championship until rejoining the NWA in 1968 and renaming itself Hollywood Wrestling. The Olympic Auditorium was the home turf for stars like "Classy" Freddie Blassie,

September 8, 1972: Ernie Ladd (left) battles Mil Mascaras at the Olympic
Auditorium, the main venue for the Los Angeles territory.

Photo by Pro Wrestling Illustrated

the Guerrero family and Mil Mascaras. The LeBells enjoyed national TV on
Spanish UHF channel Univision and promoted the first closed circuit supercard from the L.A. Coliseum in 1971, but would close down ten years later.

Houston Wrestling

Morris Siegel had been the first licensed wrestling promoter in the state of
Texas, and for years ran the region's most successful promotion before turning over the reigns to his one-time assistant, veteran grappler Paul Boesch.
Boesch was a beloved fixture of the Houston community for decades,
earning the friendship and support of fellow Texan and future president
George H. W. Bush. Boesch's territory earned a rep among wrestlers as one
of the best in which to work. Despite a tumultuous relationship with ally/
rival Fritz Von Erich in Dallas, Boesch continued to promote successfully
until selling his promotion to Vince McMahon in 1987.

Lutte Internationale

Also known as International Wrestling, this Montreal-based territory was
owned and operated for many years by early promoter Eddie Quinn,
who was later superseded in the 1960s by Jacques Rougeau, Sr., and Bob

Langevin. The 1970s saw a promotional war with a rival faction called Grand Prix Wrestling that was run by the Vachon brothers. It was during this time that Montreal gave fans the North American debut of Andre the Giant. A later Montreal faction run by Gino Brito formed a partnership with the WWF in 1985, but the Montreal territory gave way fully to the WWF in 1987.

Maple Leaf Wrestling

Founded by Jack Corcoran in 1930, the Toronto territory was, for decades, under the control of Frank Tunney, who presented regular cards in the historic Maple Leaf Gardens, the home of Toronto wrestling for more than half a century. For many years, Tunney's top star was Whipper Billy Watson, who enjoyed two reigns as NWA World Champion during his Ontario heyday. Tunney also had a working relationship with The Sheik's Big-Time Wrestling on the other side of the Great Lakes. After Frank Tunney died, the promotion went to his brother Jack Tunney, who sold it to Vince McMahon in 1986 and became the WWF's figurehead president.

Mid-Atlantic Championship Wrestling

Jim Crockett Promotions began life in 1935, and for many years was known as a territory devoted to tag teams. Jim Crockett, Jr., took over from his father in the early '70s, and, with booker George Scott, transformed the company into one of the hotbeds of the NWA. Based in Virginia and the Carolinas, it would become almost synonymous with the NWA, boasting World Champion Ric Flair as one of its top attractions. Crockett launched *Starrcade* and other yearly supercards, and went toe-to-toe with the WWF, taking over territories like Florida, Central States, and Mid-South. In 1988, Crockett sold the company to Ted Turner, who turned it into WCW. It existed until 2001, before finally being purchased by the WWF.

Mid-South Wrestling Association

Leroy McGuirk ran Tri-States Wrestling out of the Oklahoma-Arkansas-Lousiana-Mississippi region, becoming known for highlighting talented light-heavyweights like the great Danny Hodge. When his assistant Cowboy Bill Watts bought him out in 1979, he launched Mid-South, one of the most revered territories of the era. Known for its innovative episodic TV and rugged, reality-based storylines, Mid-South helped launch the careers of the Fabulous Freebirds, Ted Dibiase, Jake Roberts, and The Junkyard Dog, who became some of the most popular wrestlers in the country under Watts's watch.

National Wrestling Federation

After being banished from the Manhattan Booking Office following the merger between New York impresario Toots Mondt and up-and-comer Vincent J. McMahon, Pedro Martinez established a new territory for himself based in Buffalo, New York. The NWF promoted in Upstate New York, as well as portions of Pennsylvania and Ohio, and was a top competitor to McMahon's WWWF during the 1970s. The NWF had working relationships with both New Japan and Quebec's Lutte Internationale.

Pacific Northwest Wrestling

A founding member of the NWA, Don Owen remained a member longer than any other promoter, running his Oregon/Washington–based territory for nearly half a century. He was known for treating wrestlers fairly, and thus everyone wanted to work for him. For years, one of his top local attractions was Dutch Savage, who eventually bought into the company. Among the talent who made their names in PNW were Jimmy Snuka, Jesse Ventura, Billy Jack Haynes, and Roddy Piper. Carrying on as the WWF and WCW fought for national domination, the highly respected Owen finally closed down PNW in 1992.

Polynesian Pacific Wrestling

As early as the 1930s, Al Karasick controlled the much-sought-after Hawaii territory, a coveted destination for wrestlers looking for "working vacations." After Karasick's retirement, Ed Francis (father of future NFL player Russ Francis) and Lord James Blears took over the Honolulu booking office, maintaining strong ties to both the AWA and NWA. In 1979, they sold out to High Chief Peter Maivia (grandfather of The Rock) and his wife, Lia, who took over after the high chief died in 1982. Under the Maivias, PPW established a strong relationship with New Japan Pro Wrestling across the Pacific.

Southwest Championship Wrestling

Joe Blanchard enjoyed success in the 1970s and early '80s with this territory based in San Antonio, Texas. SCW benefited especially from a crucial TV deal with upstart cable channel USA Network, which televised its show nationally for a few years until an especially bloody match between Joe's son Tully and Bob Sweetan got the company booted in favor of Vince McMahon's WWF. SCW had working arrangements with the AWA, World Class and the World Wrestling Council in Puerto Rico, and even tried to establish its own world championship. In 1985, the company was sold to indie-league Texas All-Star Wrestling.

St. Louis Wrestling Club

St. Louis was the heart of wrestling in the central part of America. I think it will always be associated with wrestling.

—Harley Race

Thanks to the influence of Sam Muchnick, who took over the St. Louis office from Tom Packs, this small territory, based around a single city, was the soul of the NWA during the '50s, '60s, and '70s. During this period, Muchnick served as perennial chairman of the NWA, presenting a serious-minded product that stayed away from the cartoonish elements of the business for the sake of credibility. NWA World title matches at the Kiel Auditorium delivered the finest mat wrestling to be found anywhere, and Muchnick's weekly *Wrestling from the Chase* TV show ran for twenty-four years. Muchnick sold his company in 1982, and three years later it was absorbed into Jim Crockett's growing territory.

Stampede Wrestling

The vast western wiles of Canada were covered by tough Stu Hart, a renowned shooter trained by Toots Mondt. He established Stampede Wrestling in 1948, and for four decades it was a veritable star-making machine, churning out greats like Chris Benoit, Bad News Brown, Chris Jericho, Brian Pillman, Davey Boy Smith, Dynamite Kid, and, of course, Stu's celebrated wrestling sons, most notably Owen Hart and multi-time world champion Bret "Hit Man" Hart. Stu's basement "Dungeon" was known for being the toughest wrestling dojo in existence. Although Stu was bought out by the WWF in 1984, his sons continued promoting Stampede Wrestling for many years thereafter.

Western States

In Amarillo, the Funks made sure that everything they did on TV looked pretty solid, and as real as it could get.

—Dr. Tom Prichard

In the old days, wrestling in West Texas was the province of wrestler/promoter Karl "Doc" Sarpolis. But it was when the Funk family stepped in that the Amarillo territory truly came into its own. A wrestling hotbed during the 1960s and 1970s, the region was headlined by Dory Funk, Sr., and his two sons, Dory Funk, Jr., and Terry Funk, both of whom had go-rounds with the NWA World Championship in the 1970s. Declining attendance led the Funks to sell to Dick Murdoch and Blackjack Mulligan in 1980, and the promotion soon closed for good.

World Class Championship Wrestling

They had some visionary guys in World class that understood how society was changing, and they took advantage of that with many different things, including music videos and entrance music, that hadn't been done before.
—Greg Oliver

The name "World Class" will forever be associated with the fabled and infamous Von Erich family. Patriarch Fritz Von Erich, along with promoter Ed McLemore, founded the Dallas-based promotion in 1966 after breaking

away from the Houston group run by Paul Boesch. Fritz took total control after McLemore died three years later, and both he (and, later, his sons) would come to dominate the in-ring product for many years. During 1982–1984, World Class was arguably the hottest territory in the country, owing to the legendary Von Erich/Freebirds feud. World Class was eventually sold to Memphis promoter Jerry Jarrett in 1989.

The old Madison Square Garden, on 8th Avenue and 49th Street in Manhattan, was the WWWF's home arena during the 1960s. *Author's collection*

World Wide Wrestling Federation

The company that would ultimately swallow up all the rest originally began life as a regional territory based out of the Northeast, with Madison Square Garden as its mecca. Breaking away from the NWA in 1963, it created its own World Heavyweight title, which was, for years, held by such popular babyfaces as Bob Backlund, Pedro Morales, and, of course, "The Living Legend" Bruno Sammartino. Vincent J. McMahon, founder of the company, eventually sold out to his son Vincent K. McMahon in 1982, and from there the company (renamed the World Wrestling Federation in 1979) would expand from coast to coast, and beyond.

World Wrestling Association (Indianapolis)

Stealing its name from the popular earlier territory out of Los Angeles, the WWA was the brainchild of Dick "The Bruiser" Afflis and Wilbur Snyder, who took over the NWA's Indianapolis region from Jim Barnett and turned it into a sister promotion to the AWA. Many future legends would benefit from the talent-sharing agreement between the two territories, including The Crusher, Baron Von Raschke, and manager Bobby "The Brain" Heenan. The WWA lasted until 1989, when AWA talent raids by Vince McMahon proved too much to withstand.

World Wrestling Council

For over forty years, wrestling in Puerto Rico has been synonymous with one name: Carlos Colon. The New York–area wrestler returned to his native island in 1973 to form a company called Capitol Sports Promotions, with Dominican Republic promoter Victor Jovica. The two would dominate the Caribbean grappling scene for decades, giving fans intense, blood-soaked action, featuring the likes of Abdullah the Butcher and Bruiser Brody. The company changed its name to the World Wrestling Council in the 1990s, and continues to promote in Puerto Rico to this day.

Major Stars of the Era

The heyday of the territories saw the business populated by a wide array of performers both regional and national in appeal.

- Andre the Giant
- Bob Backlund
- Bruno Sammartino
- Danny Hodge
- Dick the Bruiser
- Dory Funk, Jr.
- Dusty Rhodes
- The Fabulous Moolah
- Gene Kiniski
- Gorilla Monsoon
- Harley Race
- Jack Brisco
- Jerry "The King" Lawler
- Mad Dog Vachon

- Mil Mascaras
- Nick Bockwinkel
- Pedro Morales

- The Sheik
- Superstar Billy Graham
- Terry Funk

The Living Legend

The holder of the WWWF World Championship for eleven of the first fourteen years of its existence, Bruno Sammartino was the number-one star of the 1960s and '70s for the company that would one day become WWE. On May 17, 1963, he kicked off the longest world championship reign in the history of the business when he beat Buddy Rogers by submission in Madison Square Garden. That would be the first of two reigns that spanned years. Possessing a connection with fans like no other, he rallied them passionately to his cause in one title defense after another.

He was born October 6, 1935, in Pizzoferrato, a small town in the Italian province of Abruzzi. As a child, he and his family went into hiding in a nearby mountain range when Italy fell under the control of fascist Benito Mussolini and his Nazi cohorts. When World War II finally ended, the family, having suffered fourteen months of near-starvation, was able to relocate to America, settling in Pittsburgh, Pennsylvania. Young Bruno was a scrawny, sickly teenager who often found himself picked on in his new school. This wouldn't go on for long.

Determined to build up his body, he began lifting weights at the local YMHA, and, by high-school graduation, was tipping the scales at 257 pounds. He made the decision to use his impressive size in a career as a professional wrestler, landing a tryout with longtime Pittsburgh promoter Rudy Miller, which led to a 1959 debut match that was won in nineteen seconds. Miller groomed Sammartino for an eventual introduction to Northeast wrestling czar Vince McMahon, who, after persuasion from his elder partner, Joe "Toots" Mondt, began preparing the Italian strongman to become his company's top star.

McMahon wanted to use Sammartino as an asset to help him establish his organization as an entity independent of the NWA, which he did in 1963 when he transitioned his brand new WWWF World Heavyweight title from first champion, Buddy Rogers, to Bruno, who, in a couple of short years, had become a fan favorite par excellence.

As champion, Bruno Sammartino was the idol of millions, a hero to the immigrants and descendants of immigrants who packed arenas throughout the Northeast, but especially at Madison Square Garden, where his monthly title defenses sold out on a regular basis. After a record-shattering seven-and-a-half years, an exhausted Bruno, longing for time to rest and be with his family, finally convinced McMahon to relieve him of his championship duties, and he dropped the gold to Ivan Koloff in a January 18, 1971, bout that left fans in such silent shock that it was said you could hear a pin drop in the arena. By 1973, McMahon was able to convince Sammartino to come back for another three-and-a-half years as champ, extending his legacy well into the 1970s.

"Bruno Sammartino represented something that transcended ethnicity," says veteran wrestling scribe Keith Elliot Greenberg. "At the time, living in New York City, my grandparents believed in Bruno . . . that he somehow represented them. There was something about him that hit an emotional nerve."

Sammartino lost his title for the final time to Superstar Billy Graham on April 30, 1977, and retired four years later, while still the company's most adored athlete. He spent some time as a WWF-TV announcer in the 1980s, but longstanding bad blood with the McMahon family (which intensified due to

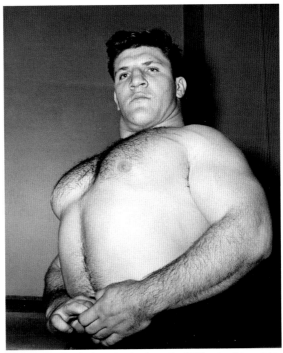

Sammartino broke into the business in 1959, using his weight-lifter's physique to impress promoters like Pittsburgh impresario Rudy Miller.   *Jack Pfefer Collection, University of Notre Dame*

Bruno's disillusionment with the company's steroid culture) led to a bitter grudge that lasted for a quarter-century. Sammartino finally relented, accepting induction into the WWE Hall of Fame in 2013.

For the countless fans who had been heartbroken during Bruno's long sabbatical, it was a deserving reward for the man who embodied the WWWF for two decades. Specifically for those of Italian descent, the name Bruno Sammartino occupies a spot in a rare pantheon of ethnic legends that includes the likes of Joe DiMaggio and Frank Sinatra. If any wrestler is deserving of the moniker of "Living Legend," it is he.

The Eighth Wonder of the World

Billed as the largest athlete in the world, Andre the Giant enjoyed a level of notoriety experienced by very few professional wrestlers. His actual height was a "mere" seven feet or so, compared to the seven feet five inches at which he was often billed—always given to hyperbole, wrestling promoters couldn't resist exaggerating even his enormousness, and would sometimes have him stand on a

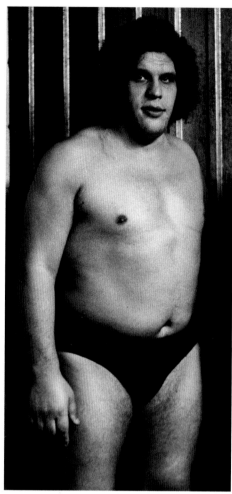

The top-drawing star of the 1970s, Andre was a main-event performer everywhere he appeared.

Brandon Seigler/Wikimedia

box during interviews to make him seem even taller. But regardless of his exact size, Andre was a giant in the business and in the hearts of fans worldwide.

Andre Rene Rousimoff was born on May 19, 1946, in a small French village, the son of Russian immigrant parents. Born with acromegaly, a disease that caused his body to grow at an alarming rate, he was already six feet three inches and two hundred pounds by age twelve. After spending some time working on a nearby farm as a teenager (and gleaning life lessons from playwright Samuel Beckett, his next-door neighbor), the gigantic teenager decided to use his unusual size to his advantage, and began wrestling at local shows in France and throughout Europe.

Now over four hundred pounds, Andre began turning heads within the business. Wrestler/manager Frank Valois brought him to North America for the first time in the early 1970s, where he went to work in Montreal for Paul Vachon under the name Jean Ferre (taken from that of a Paul Bunyan–like giant of French Canadian folklore). Promoters from other territories, hearing of this new French giant, began to ask for his services, and it would be Chicago-area wrestler/promoter Dick the Bruiser who rechristened him "Andre the Giant."

But it was under the managerial auspices of the WWWF's Vince McMahon, who made an exclusive promotional deal with Andre in 1973, that the Giant's legend would really take hold. McMahon was smart enough to promote Andre as a unique, almost mythical, attraction, having him work in a style that emphasized his large size, and playing up his height and weight—as well as an undefeated streak that may have been more ballyhoo than statistics bear out—to cultivate his intimidating reputation. Under the WWWF banner, Andre was booked to territories all over the world, and his arrival was much heralded wherever he went. Fans adored him, and promoters adored the money they knew he was guaranteed to bring in.

For a time, he was the most famous wrestler in the world, making appearances on *The Tonight Show Starring Johnny Carson*, and appearing on TV shows like *The Six-Million-Dollar Man* (playing a Sasquatch) and movies like *The Princess Bride*. Fans seemed to tap into his natural gentleness, which could turn into an awesome, unstoppable force when he was unleashed against whatever local bad guys they wanted to see get squashed. Away from the ring, he was larger-than-life as he was in it, earning the nickname "The Boss" from his peers, and becoming renowned in the business for his boisterous love of life, which included drinking on an epic scale.

Once the younger Vince McMahon took over the WWF and began to take it national, Andre began to work exclusively for the company, and played a pivotal role in its successful expansion. After a shocking heel turn, he took on an alarming villainous persona and challenged WWF World Heavyweight Champion Hulk Hogan at *WrestleMania III* in the Pontiac Silverdome before the largest crowd ever gathered to witness a professional wrestling event in North America (the WWF has famously given the attendance figure as 93,173, although many speculate the real figure is somewhere around eighty thousand). In a true "changing of the guard" moment, Andre the Giant was pinned by the Hulkster, losing his first WWF match in fifteen years and completely establishing Hogan as the industry's unrivaled top banana.

His lifelong affliction of acromegaly ultimately caught up with him, and the nearly wheelchair-bound Andre was forced to retire in 1991. While visiting France for his father's funeral on January 27, 1993, Andre Rousimoff died quietly in his sleep, at age forty-six. His name continues to resonate with fans due to the manner in which his legacy has been warmly carried on by present-day WWE, the company that owes him so much. In 1993, he became the first WWE Hall of Famer, and in 2014, a new annual battle royal was named in his honor, to be held every year at *WrestleMania*, the event he helped put on the map.

The American Dream

Ever since the advent of TV, pro wrestlers have required a lot more than pure athleticism to be successful and "get over" with fans. They needed to be uniquely charismatic, and, if possible, have a special way with words that could win the attention of fans, as well as convince them to turn over their hard-earned money, of course. In the annals of wrestling history, Dusty Rhodes is a watershed figure— a talent who was able to establish himself as a national attraction based on pure charisma and determination. It was of little consequence that he couldn't really wrestle technically, or that he appeared overweight and out of shape. For the first time, the *character* was everything.

He was born Virgil Riley Runnels, Jr., in Austin, Texas, on October 12, 1945—the "son of a plumber" as he would famously and passionately intone during countless TV promos. Growing up against a working-class background that would be represented by the persona he would cultivate for years, the young Runnels became a football standout during his college days at West Texas State, an institution known for the many future pro wrestling legends it boasted on its team.

Changing his name to the catchy "Dusty Rhodes," he enjoyed his first taste of wrestling success as a heel, one-half of a tag team known as The Texas Outlaws, rampaging through the AWA with fellow Lone Star native Dick Murdoch. But Dusty was a born babyface, and when fans in Florida embraced him after he turned on his former partner, the villainous "Korean Nightmare" Pak Song, he never looked back. He took to calling himself "The American Dream" (a response to Song's moniker), and became the biggest superstar ever produced by Eddie Graham's Sunshine State promotion.

Rhodes was one of a kind, a dynamic performer who spoke to his audiences like a zealous gospel preacher, relating to fans as one common man to another. His interviews were even more entertaining than his matches. Just as Elvis did for rock 'n' roll, Rhodes co-opted mannerisms and vocalizations identified with African-American culture, and it made him one of the most beloved fan favorites of his generation. His drawing power extended way beyond Florida, and his 1970s exploits in the WWWF, the Sheik's Detroit territory, Georgia Championship Wrestling, and other locales, are the stuff of legend.

Up to that point, the National Wrestling Alliance had been careful to place its World Heavyweight title on "credible" athletic competitors only, preferably those with solid amateur credentials. But the overwhelming popularity and ticket-selling charisma of Rhodes led the NWA brain trust to dramatically break from tradition. Between 1979 and 1986, Rhodes would win three NWA World Heavyweight Championships, defeating Harley Race for the first two, and Ric Flair for the last. The shift to the concept of wrestler-as-entertainer was complete.

More than just a talented performer, Rhodes also demonstrated a great creative mind for behind-the-scenes booking. He first spent time as one of the main bookers for Jim Crockett Promotions in the mid-1980s, crafting the storylines during the company's hottest period, and also infamously coming up with what would become known as the "Dusty finish"—a choreographed match conclusion in which a referee is knocked out and later controversially overturns the original, more popular decision. Innovative ideas like this have made Rhodes a creative groundbreaker, and he has since enjoyed booking stints in more recent years, first for TNA Wrestling, and currently for WWE, for whom he has been a member of the creative team since 2005.

Dusty wound down his in-ring career during the 1990s, enjoying final runs in both the WWF, where his "common man" gimmick was accentuated with ill-conceived polka-dot attire, and in WCW, the company for whom he had first made his creative bones during its previous incarnation as Jim Crockett Promotions. In recent years, he has enjoyed watching the careers of his wrestling sons, Dustin "Goldust" Runnels and Cody "Stardust" Rhodes in WWE. Most recently, he has been given creative control over WWE's NXT farm system, using his enormous talents to help groom the next generation of pro wrestling superstars.

7

Rock and Wrestling

The '80s Explosion

I'm speechless. It's just so exciting, I don't know what to say. It's the best thing I've ever seen in my whole life.
— Andy Warhol, backstage at Madison Square Garden
for the WWF's *War to Settle the Score*

In the days of Ronald Reagan and MTV, wrestling experienced a renaissance like never before. With Vince McMahon's World Wrestling Federation going national and rival Jim Crockett Promotions rallying the vestiges of the old territorial system, it was a truly great time to be a fan, even if many of the time-honored conventions were going out the window. This was the era of Hulkamania, of stylin' and profilin', and of pro wrestling's reinvention as pay-per-view home entertainment.

Since purchasing his father's wrestling company in 1982, Vince McMahon was intent on expanding the WWF into the first truly national professional wrestling promotion of the industry's modern era. To do this, he would use a combination of talent raiding, television wheeling and dealing and raw, brutal ambition. The gentlemen's agreement that characterized the Territorial Era (in which promoters respected regional boundaries) was something for which he had no respect. To realize his dream, he would obliterate every one of those boundaries.

The WWF Goes National

It started with a cable TV deal on USA Network in 1983 that would see the WWF product broadcast nationwide for the first time. But to truly spread out into rival territories, McMahon would need the local syndicated channels, which were then the backbone of the business. He began buying up timeslots in TV markets far from his Northeastern base, immediately angering promoters in those areas, with whom he was now in direct competition. Many tried complaining to Vince's father, their old comrade, but to no avail. The son was now in charge, and the old ways were done.

To amp up his product and make WWF wrestling the most popular brand around, he started luring top stars away from other companies, beefing up his own roster with a kind of "Justice League" of wrestling luminaries: The Junkyard Dog and Jake "The Snake" Roberts from Mid-South, Roddy Piper and Ricky Steamboat from Jim Crockett Promotions, Mike Rotundo and Barry Windham from Florida, The Hart Foundation and The British Bulldogs from Calgary's Stampede, Paul Orndorff from Georgia Championship Wrestling, and Randy Savage and manager Jimmy Hart from Memphis. Perhaps more than any other rival, McMahon raided the AWA, from whom he acquired the services of Adrian Adonis, Ken Patera, Jesse "The Body" Ventura, announcer Mean Gene Okerlund and manager Bobby "The Brain" Heenan, among others.

Randy "Macho Man" Savage was one of the premier stars of the WWF during Vince McMahon's national-expansion effort in the 1980s. *Rob DeCaterino/Wikimedia*

Hulkamania Runs Wild

No other AWA acquisition would serve McMahon's cause quite like the tan, towering, superhero-come-to-life known as Hulk Hogan. Jilted by AWA owner Verne Gagne, a pure wrestling enthusiast who refused to change with the times and grant him a shot at the top, Hogan agreed to become the foundation upon which McMahon's national expansion would be built. It started in Madison Square Garden on January 23, 1984, when he beat The Iron Sheik in five minutes to become WWF World Heavyweight Champion—a moment often viewed by modern fans as professional wrestling's BC/AD moment.

Hogan's popularity skyrocketed, as fans responded instantly to his charisma and larger-than-life aura. He had previously touched the mainstream consciousness with an appearance in the film *Rocky III*, but as WWF World Champion, Hulk Hogan became not only a legitimate mainstream 1980s celebrity, he also is, quite possibly, the most famous pro wrestler of all time. Leading a troupe of talent McMahon promoted as "WWF Superstars," Hogan was the ace in the hole with which McMahon would topple the territories.

In some regions like St. Louis and Los Angeles, the local promotion had already gone belly up, allowing McMahon to easily step in and take over. Some, like Stu Hart in Calgary, Paul Boesch in Houston, the Brisco brothers in Georgia, and Jack Tunney in Toronto, he bought outright. Those who wouldn't sell, like Verne Gagne, Bill Watts and Jim Crockett, he would engage directly in bitter promotional wars. Once his WWF programs began appearing in markets throughout North America, McMahon was able to start promoting live events in those areas as well, as local fans became interested in seeing the new show in town.

"Vince changed the business, not to hurt it, but to do what was best for him," says wrestling historian and biographer Scott Teal. "To be honest, by 1986, a lot of the territories were headed downhill, anyway. If Vince hadn't changed it, I think it would've been gone anyway."

McMahon clamored for mainstream attention, and Hulk Hogan was just part of the plan. He courted celebrities like pop-music breakout sensation Cyndi Lauper and action star Mr. T, and got his wrestlers appearances on late-night talk shows and *Saturday Night Live*. He negotiated a deal with NBC to bring professional wrestling back to network television with a program called *Saturday Night's Main Event*. In the process, he orchestrated something called "The Rock 'n' Wrestling Connection," a union of pro wrestling and popular culture that captured America's zeitgeist in a way pro wrestling hadn't since the 1950s. The WWF became a mainstream entertainment force.

What the World Is Watching

This was solidified on March 31, 1985, when the ultimate culmination of McMahon's plan took shape in the form of *WrestleMania*, a pro wrestling mega event broadcast from Madison Square Garden to the largest closed-circuit audience in U.S. history. Hogan teamed with Mr. T to take on top heels Piper and Orndorff that night, and guest appearances were made by Liberace, Billy Martin, Muhammad Ali, and others. It would become an annual event, one of many presented by the WWF using the brand new medium of pay-per-view television. Just as much an innovator of TV technology as his father, Vince McMahon helped popularize the pay-per-view concept, in which fans could watch a live event from home by paying a one-time fee. The business model would become the company's bread and butter for nearly thirty years.

"Hogan couldn't have done it without Vince, and Vince couldn't have done it without Hogan," says Dave Meltzer of the *Wrestling Observer*. "I don't think he could've done it without Mr. T and Cyndi Lauper [either]. He was on the verge of failing, but was able to get all that national TV. I really believe that the Verne Gagnes and the Jim Crocketts, had they have gone national, they couldn't have been as big as Vince, because they didn't have the creativity of Vince."

The mid-to-late '80s saw the WWF become the "cool" thing to watch—but the old school regional promoters weren't about to ride off quietly into the sunset. Bill Watts attempted to take his Mid-South territory national as well, renaming it the Universal Wrestling Federation. World Class Championship Wrestling left the NWA and tried to use the star power of the Von Erich family and an ESPN-TV deal to do the same. The AWA brought in former WWF stalwarts Sgt. Slaughter and Bob Backlund, and presented *SuperClash*, an imitation *WrestleMania* held at Chicago's Comiskey Park.

Crockett Strikes Back

But the WWF's main rival for dominance would be Jim Crockett Promotions. Based originally in the Carolinas and Virginia, the company had ceased being referred to as "Mid-Atlantic" in an attempt to counter the WWF's big-time feel. Taking advantage of the crumbling National Wrestling Alliance infrastructure, Crockett positioned his company as the new heart of the NWA, even going so far as to promote his product in such a way that fans referred to it simply as "the NWA," ignoring the fact that the NWA was actually an association of many organizations.

Crockett knew what McMahon was up to from the beginning. One month prior to Hulk Hogan winning the WWF World Championship, Crockett presented *Starrcade '83* from the Greensboro Coliseum. The event would become his company's signature annual show. When McMahon failed in his initial attempt to infiltrate the Georgia territory, Crockett was there to buy him out, taking over the coveted TBS timeslot. In addition to Georgia, Crockett began expanding into other regions, eventually taking over the Central States, Florida, and Mid-South/UWF territories, as well.

Just like McMahon had Hogan, Crockett had his own ace in the hole in the NWA World Heavyweight Champion, a bleached-blond Buddy Rogers disciple who was everything the Hulkster was not: a cocky, wheelin' and dealin', limousine ridin' and Lear-jet flyin' ladies man who strutted to the ring and whose untiring in-ring prowess earned him the nickname "The Sixty-Minute Man." Ric Flair epitomized the Crockett product, which emphasized wrestling athleticism over goofy caricatures. Whereas McMahon had opted to make the WWF into a child-friendly pop confection, Crockett Promotions was smash-mouth, old-school wrestling, with intense, violent storylines. In addition to Flair, Crockett gave them such rugged performers as The Midnight Express, Arn Anderson, Wahoo McDaniel, Nikita Koloff and Magnum T.A. It was the anti-WWF, and, as such, appealed to a segment of fans disenchanted with McMahon's attempts to sanitize their sport.

"The greatest wrestling I've ever seen was the NWA in the '80s," recalls Evan Ginzburg, co-producer of the 2008 motion picture *The Wrestler*, and a lifelong fan. "I would go see the NWA every month in Philly: Ric Flair and the Horsemen. The absolute greatest was The Midnight Express. They elevated tag team wrestling to an art form. Those shows were so loaded. It was the most amazing talent roster that I've ever seen. They promoted a very different product. It was about wrestling."

Working along with other companies like the AWA, the CWA in Memphis, World Class and Mid-South, Crockett helped form a loose confederation of territories known as "Pro Wrestling USA," banding together to try to combat the WWF phenomenon. But the grouping proved short-lived, as predictable infighting between the rival promoters brought the whole operation crashing down. McMahon had something they didn't: unity of vision. He didn't play well with others; and with his plan now bearing fruit, he didn't need to.

"Eventually you learn what makes people watch," says Dave Meltzer. "They want to see stars. It didn't matter how well the guys worked. That's the most overrated part of the wrestling business. Work had nothing to do with it, it was all who had the best TV, who had the stars, and who got there first."

By the latter part of the decade, the territorial system was in tatters. *WrestleMania III* in the Pontiac Silverdome had put the icing on the cake for McMahon. Before, he was bluffing his way to the top, borrowing money to do everything in his power to make the WWF seem like a national company. But with the success of his third installment of *WrestleMania*, broadcast before a record-breaking live crowd and featuring a generation-defining main event pitting Hulk Hogan against Andre the Giant, the WWF was bluffing no longer. It really *was* a national company, and well on its way to being a worldwide attraction. Almost all the territories had died or were on life support.

At the end of 1988, financially outpaced by McMahon and unable to keep up in the expansion game, Jim Crockett sold his company to cable TV mogul Ted Turner, whose TBS channel had been airing his programming for years. Turner took the name of the company's flagship TV show, World Championship Wrestling, and made it the name of the company brand. Jim

Crockett Promotions was now WCW. Crockett may have been out of the race, but the race was far from over.

Pulling the Curtain Back

In February 1989, Vince McMahon and his wife, Linda, appeared before the New Jersey State Senate and broke decades of industry secrecy by declaring that professional wrestling be defined as "an activity in which participants struggle hand-in-hand primarily for the purpose of providing entertainment to spectators rather than conducting a bona fide athletic contest." Their goal, as it would be in all other states, was to get pro wrestling out from under the jurisdiction of the State Athletic Commission, which would save them countless dollars in the form of TV rights taxation and licensing fees normally levied against professional sports entities. In doing do, they put the final nail in the coffin of kayfabe, the time-honored code of silence about wrestling's true nature, which had been steadily eroding since Jack Pfefer's tell-all newspaper interview a half-century earlier. McMahon had long presented his product as entertainment; in fact, he had already renamed his product entirely, phasing out references to "professional wrestling" and instead terming it "sports-entertainment." His move with the athletic commissions simply wrote it down explicitly in black and white.

"Vince did it for the good of the business, but he also did it to save money," says David Shoemaker, author of *Squared Circle: Life, Death and Professional Wrestling*, "which is a perfect analogy for the business in its entirety, because it's never *not* been a carny sideshow act. It's always been equal parts entertainment, and equal parts conning people out of cash."

Scandal and Stagnancy: The '90s Slump

Unfortunately, this wouldn't be the last time Vince McMahon would find himself taking part in public legal proceedings. After years at the top of the wrestling world, the early 1990s saw him and his company rocked with a series of debilitating scandals. Front and center was a steroid trial that threatened to send him off to prison and sink his entire company. Clearly, it took more than exercise and diet to produce athletes that looked the way McMahon's WWF Superstars did, and once former ring physician Dr. George Zahorian was brought up on charges of possession and distribution, what most already assumed became a matter of public knowledge: anabolic steroid abuse had become rampant in the pro wrestling business.

While McMahon battled it out in court, the WWF product also suffered. The early 1990s saw a downturn in the business as the euphoria of "Rock and Wrestling" wore off. Attempts to recapture Hulkamania with the likes of

Randy Savage and The Ultimate Warrior failed. Meanwhile, WCW began to provide growing competition with young performers like Sting, Lex Luger and Sid Vicious. In response to dwindling crowds and a desire to get back some of that "old school" feel, the WWF launched a new flagship program in January 1993. Broadcast live and initially from the intimate Manhattan Center (a wrestling hotbed going back to the infamous 1915 international tournament), *Monday Night Raw* represented a dramatic shift in the way the WWF presented wrestling.

Distancing itself from the very stars who had helped build up the company in the 1980s—many of whom, like Hogan and Savage, were swiftly jumping ship to WCW—the WWF introduced what it called a "New Generation" of top talent. This included longtime tag team regular Bret "Hit Man" Hart, who was elevated to main event, world-champion status; another former tag teamer, Shawn Michaels, whom many would consider the finest in-ring performer of his era; the Undertaker, an enigmatic hold-out from the Hogan days who ascended to legendary status; Tony Montana wannabe Razor Ramon, who had been plain old Scott Hall in the AWA; and the towering Diesel, known to his friends as Kevin Nash.

Extreme Competition

The WWF was the weakest it had been since its explosive expansion, and the rest of the business took notice. In the void left by the territories, a disjointed but surviving independent circuit of small-time local promotions cropped up. Chief among these would be a company called Eastern Championship Wrestling, run by former WCW manager Paul Heyman out of a south Philadelphia bingo hall, which would grow into so much more than an indy, shaking up the entire business by changing its name to *Extreme* Championship Wrestling and pioneering an in-your-face, anti-establishment style that would come to be known as "hardcore." It was the ultimate alternative to what mainstream wrestling had to offer at the time.

"ECW was the broad street bullies of wrestling," says Brian Heffron, better known to fans of extreme as The Blue Meanie. "We came along at the right time. People complain today that [WWE] wrestling is rated PG. Back in the early '90s, it was almost rated G! They called wrestling a circus before, but now they literally had a clown! You don't get any more circus than that! I'm a dedicated wrestling fan, and there's a period where even *I* stopped watching."

Meanwhile, WCW was certainly taking notice for the perfect time to strike, and did so. The company had been growing since Ted Turner's 1988 acquisition, and by the mid-1990s was snatching up WWF talent left and right, doing exactly to McMahon what McMahon had done to Crockett and so many others. In September 1995, WCW launched a live program called *Monday Nitro*, running it head-to-head against *Monday Night Raw*. A full-on war was brewing, for which the 1980s territorial war was a mere dress rehearsal.

Major Stars of the Era

For a generation of fans that first discovered wrestling in the glorious '80s and early '90s, there are certain performers who will always embody the soul of the business.

- Bret "Hit Man" Hart
- Big Van Vader
- Diesel
- The Honky Tonk Man
- Hulk Hogan
- The Junkyard Dog
- Lex Luger
- "Mr. Perfect" Curt Hennig
- Randy "Macho Man" Savage
- "Ravishing" Rick Rude

- Razor Ramon
- Ric Flair
- Ricky "The Dragon" Steamboat
- "Rowdy" Roddy Piper
- Sgt. Slaughter
- Shawn Michaels
- Sid Vicious
- Sting
- The Ultimate Warrior
- Undertaker

The Second Nature Boy

Smoke fills the arena. Strobe lights flash. Over the loudspeakers come the strains of *Also Sprach Zarathustra*. A silhouette appears out of the darkness, wearing a flowing, feathered and sequined robe, held open to reveal an impossibly huge gold belt. As he struts down the aisle to the ring, his peroxide blond locks blown out and resplendent, he purses his lips into an oval and lets out a loud "Wooooo!!!" He is "The Sixty-Minute Man," "The Dirtiest Player in the Game." He is "Nature Boy" Ric Flair.

He was born on February 25, 1949, to a young, disenfranchised mother in Memphis, Tennessee, who was conned out of her baby by the infamous Tennessee Children's Home Society. Adopted by an affluent couple (a doctor and an actress) who named him Richard Morgan Fliehr, he was raised in the town of Edina, Minnesota, eventually attending the University of Minnesota on a football scholarship. He was a member of the wrestling team as well, but it would be a totally different kind of wrestling that soon led him to drop out of school and start on his road to immortality.

After meeting aspiring wrestler and former Olympic weightlifter Ken Patera, Flair was invited to join the legendary training camp of AWA owner Verne Gagne. In a barn outside Minneapolis, Flair was trained by renowned shooter Billy

The Nature Boy before an Ontario title defense, wearing the classic NWA World Championship belt he carried for most of the first half of the 1980s.

Photo by Terry Dart

Robinson, and debuted in the AWA in December 1972 in a ten-minute draw with journeyman George "Scrap Iron" Gadaski. A chubby, auburn-haired greenhorn, he was nothing like the Slick Ric he would later become.

Not long after transitioning to Jim Crockett's Mid-Atlantic Championship Wrestling, the territory that would be his home for the majority of his salad days, he had his back broken in an October 1975 plane crash that ended the life of the pilot, and the careers of veteran wrestler Johnny Valentine and rookie Bob Bruggers. Doctors told the twenty-six-year-old that he'd never wrestle again, but he'd spend the next three decades proving them wrong.

Crockett groomed him to be his company's top star, and as he captured one U.S. championship after another, he honed the persona that would turn him into a wrestling legend. Taking his cue from 1950s and 1960s icon Buddy Rogers, he took to wearing flashy robes, and adopted arrogant mannerisms and a flowing mane of blond hair. He even took Rogers's figure-four leglock finisher and "Nature Boy" nickname after beating the original in a 1978 match. Also like Rogers, but even more so, he was gold on the mic. A brash, bold talker, he enjoyed singing his own praises and running down his opponents with disdainful ease. Fans couldn't get enough of it.

Eventually, Crockett would persuade the NWA brass that his boy was world-championship material. On September 17, 1981, he won his first NWA World Championship, beating Dusty Rhodes. Over the course of his illustrious career, his grand total of world championships, ranged from sixteen to twenty-five, depending upon who you ask. Most agree that it was more times than any other performer in the history of the business.

The reason was simple: Ric Flair was the embodiment of a professional wrestling champion, possessing all the tools promoters looked for in a top hand. He had the look, he had the mouth, he had the attitude, and he most certainly had the ability to work inside the ring. Appearing night after night, year round, in matches all over the world in defense of his title, he was known for his amazing stamina and able to put on a great match no matter the capability of his opponent. A master of ring psychology, he's considered by many to have been the greatest all-around performer the business has ever known. He was also the face of the NWA during its last years, and even survived (for a time) the transition of Jim Crockett Promotions into WCW.

The type of heel fans loved and hated in equal measure, his charisma was such that people couldn't help but cheer for him despite themselves. Although he spent portions of his career as a hero and a villain, he's best remembered for being the heel champion, the bad guy who is chased by earnest babyface challengers. This role was further accentuated thanks to his leadership of the infamous clique known as The Four Horsemen, pro wrestling's ultimate supergroup stable.

After a conflict with WCW's corporate bosses, he would go to work for Vince McMahon's WWF, adding that championship to his resume. He eventually returned to WCW and remained there until the company's end, despite a bitter real-life feud with executive producer Eric Bischoff. The conclusion of his full-time career took place when he made his triumphant return to WWE in 2001, enjoying a run that included several high-profile *WrestleMania* matches and membership in yet another powerful heel stable, Evolution.

Although some of his most recent years have seen him wander from TNA to Ring of Honor to the indy circuit, allegedly due to hard financial times, he currently enjoys WWE royalty status, and still pops up on *Monday Night Raw* here and there, just to walk that aisle one more time. As the man himself has been known to say on many an occasion, "Diamonds are forever, and so is Ric Flair."

The Immortal One

There are few performers who literally transcend the entire pro wrestling business. In fact, you could probably count them on one hand, and still have fingers left over. But one man who absolutely transcended the business, transforming it forever in the process, is Hulk Hogan, the catalyst who helped turn WWE into what it is today, and arguably the most famous professional wrestler who ever lived. Vince McMahon and others have called him the "Babe Ruth of Wrestling," and with good cause. In the past fifty years, there is certainly no other performer who matched his level of celebrity and notoriety. In the pantheon of icons, he is *the* icon.

He was born Terry Eugene Bollea on August 11, 1953, in Augusta, Georgia, the son of a dance teacher and a construction foreman. His family soon moved to the Tampa, Florida, area, where the young Bollea became a fan of Eddie Graham's Championship Wrestling from Florida promotion. Inspired by Florida headliner Superstar Billy Graham, he tried to match the Superstar's unique look, dying his

hair blond and developing huge muscles (using Graham's method of injecting anabolic steroids, as would later be revealed in legal testimony). He began to gain
attention in the crowd at local events, and Graham eventually got him a tryout.

Supporting himself with his side career as a rock bassist and recording studio
session musician, Bollea was trained by the unyielding Hiro Matsuda and debuted
in Florida in 1977. He quickly transitioned to the Alabama territory, where he
wrestled under the names Sterling Golden and Terry "The Hulk" Boulder. After
getting his first taste at main-event status in the Memphis-based CWA promotion, he was brought into the WWF by Vincent J. McMahon, who gave him the
name Hulk Hogan in order to promote him as an ethnically Irish competitor.

Hogan's star rose mightily in the early '80s, and during a stint in the
Midwestern AWA territory, he started a movement that would come to be
known as "Hulkamania," turning babyface for the first time and rallying fans to
his cause. An appearance alongside Sylvester Stallone in the 1982 hit *Rocky III* as
the wrestling champion Thunderlips only increased his mainstream appeal. The
Hulkster was a star in the making.

"Stallone's office called and I took the call," remembers former *Pro Wrestling
Illustrated* editor Bill Apter. "They said they were looking for a certain type. So I
sent photos of . . . Hulk Hogan, who was pretty new on the scene. They called
back and asked if I could get in touch with him. I don't know if they had anyone
else in mind, but Hogan was perfect for it."

When Vincent K. McMahon, new owner of the WWF, needed a superhuman champion around which to build the company he hoped to turn into a
national powerhouse, he came knocking on Hogan's door. The rest is history. As
the WWF's top superstar of the 1980s and early 1990s, Hulk Hogan embodied
a sea change in the pro wrestling business. Although chided by critics for his
lack of "credible" wrestling ability, none of that mattered. Fans wanted a real-life
action hero to get behind, and Hogan provided them with just that. Although
steroid-enhanced bodybuilder physiques had first been popularized in wrestling
by Graham some years before, Hogan solidified that look as the new standard.
Going forward, for better or worse, pro wrestlers would be expected to look like
superheroes.

A generation of youngsters grew up worshipping Hogan and following his
"Four Demandments": train, say your prayers, eat your vitamins, and believe in
yourself. His lack of technical prowess was compensated for with an ability to
connect with live audiences in an unprecedented way. A mere finger point to an
opponent, a hand cupped to his ear, or a simple pose would elicit titanic crowd
reactions, and his penchant for making exciting comebacks in the ring by "hulking
up" against his opponents was exhilarating. With Hogan on top, the WWF established *WrestleMania* as the industry's premier annual event, and soon the company's dominance reached worldwide levels.

"Whatcha gonna do?" The Hulkster marches to the ring in 1988, not long after losing his first WWF World Championship.   *John McKeon/Wikimedia*

As if that weren't enough to cement his legacy, in the mid-to-late 1990s, Hogan reinvented himself by switching to rival company WCW and changing allegiances in the most shocking heel turn in wrestling history. Growing out a stubbly beard and calling himself "Hollywood" Hogan, he became the leader of an invading faction called the New World Order (nWo). Just like that, Hogan was once again relevant, and the nWo storyline would help to reinvigorate the whole business during a down period.

The twenty-first century saw the Hulkster triumphantly return to WWE, and with the exception of a 2010–13 run in TNA Wrestling in an on-air general manager role, he has continued to appear on and off for Vince McMahon, the businessman who turned him into a household name in the first place. In spite of a steroid scandal that threatened to tarnish his legacy, he is fondly embraced by nostalgic fans and new fans alike, the living, breathing personification of modern professional wrestling.

The Heartbreak Kid

The 1990s was a period of transition in the industry, starting out with struggling business and creative doldrums, and ending on a very lucrative and refreshingly innovative note. Spanning that entire period was a wrestler who emerged from the tag team ranks to become the most purely talented in-ring performer of his generation, and some would argue, of all time. Shawn Michaels was the epitome of the contemporary pro wrestler, crafting a style that would be copied by countless American stars in later years, and would come to typify what fans currently

Michaels (right) tangles with Razor Ramon during the historic Intercontinental Championship Ladder Match in Madison Square Garden at *WrestleMania X*, on March 20, 1994.

Photo by Pro Wrestling Illustrated

expect to see once the bell rings. They called him "The Showstopper," a nickname he earned each and every night for the better part of two decades.

He was born Michael Shawn Hickenbottom on July 22, 1965, growing up in San Antonio, Texas, as the youngest of four children in a military family. A football standout in high school and college, he decided instead to pursue a career in professional wrestling, of which he had been a fan since the age of twelve. He left school after his freshman year at Southwest Texas State University, and went to work for Southwest Championship Wrestling (by then known as Texas All-Star Wrestling), the San Antonio-based company whose shows he had been attending since he was a kid.

Bouncing around the territories, the newly christened Shawn Michaels spent time in Mid-South and Central States, where he and Marty Jannetty formed a tag team known as The Midnight Rockers, which would eventually win the World Tag Team Championship in the AWA. Michaels and Jannetty continued with the team for the next six years, joining the WWF at the end of 1988 with the shortened name of The Rockers. The partnership would define the early portion of his career, but there was much more in store.

After infamously splitting with Jannetty by tossing him through a window on the set of Brutus Beefcake's "Barber Shop" interview segment, Michaels went full-on heel, and began to come into his own. The cocky new persona seemed tailor-made for the brash young athlete, who quickly established himself as an impressive singles talent on the WWF roster, earning several runs as Intercontinental Champion, and even challenging WWF World Heavyweight Champion Bret "Hit Man" Hart—the man with whom he'd remain locked in a years-long rivalry for dominance in the era both in the ring and behind the scenes.

More than just a flashy gimmick, as an in-ring performer, Michaels was nothing short of a revelation. A master of the art of "selling" for his opponent, he could make anyone look like a million bucks, and wasn't afraid of taking all manner of high-risk bumps, often bouncing around the ring like a rubber ball in his efforts to make every match a breathtaking nail-biter. A show-stealing ladder match with Razor Ramon at *WrestleMania X* in Madison Square Garden took him to another level, and helped establish the new style as the expected norm for big-money bouts. He was eventually rewarded in 1996 with his first reign as WWF World Heavyweight Champion, fittingly dethroning Bret Hart at *WrestleMania XII*.

As the WWF transitioned into the edgy Attitude Era of the late 1990s, Michaels's heel persona took on new dimensions as he became the leader of the innovative D-Generation X faction. But years of punishment to his body, including one particularly bad bump in a casket match with the Undertaker at the 1998 *Royal Rumble*, caused him to step away from the ring for four years after dropping his World Heavyweight title to newly minted main-eventer Stone Cold Steve Austin at *WrestleMania XIV*.

But things were far from over. Michaels defied the odds in 2002, returning to action in the recently renamed WWE for what would be another eight years before finally calling it quits after a retirement match with the Undertaker at *WrestleMania XXVI*. In that time, he provided a whole new generation of WWE fans with even more thrilling, show-stealing encounters with the likes of Triple H, Ric Flair, and Randy Orton.

Although often difficult to handle behind the scenes, any diva behavior on the part of the Heartbreak Kid was made up for by his unique ability to turn every match into a classic. It's that natural gift that made him the entertainer he was, and will ensure that he is never forgotten. A whole generation of young performers try every night to emulate what he did back then, but there is only one original.

8

Are You Ready?

How Wrestling Got "Attitude"

Wrestling is one of the last truly rebellious American things left.

—Billy Corgan

Following the highs of the 1980s, the wrestling business found itself going through a bit of the doldrums during the 1990s. A stagnant product, declining ratings and a dearth of dynamic new stars led some to think the best days were in the past. That is, until a bold and dramatic overhaul took place at the end of the decade that has come to be known as "The Attitude Era." It was a no-holds-barred time of raucous storylines, outrageous characters, and edgier programming than had ever before been seen, when Monday nights became must-see TV.

Thanks to the efforts of creative individuals both behind the scenes and in the ring, professional wrestling was transformed. For the first time, "meta" storylines began to be presented, deconstructing the traditions of the inner workings of the business and blurring the lines between fiction and reality. Angles gained as much TV attention as actual matches, becoming more sophisticated and shaking up a product that had been thought of as family entertainment for years. Propelled by an unprecedented national TV ratings war, changes were set in motion that continue to characterize the business to a certain extent today. This evolution of the business has its supporters and its detractors, but none can deny its importance.

E-C-W! E-C-W!

Although major North American groups WCW and the WWF were competing for dominance, the creative impetus would come initially from outside of the "Big Two." Run out of a bingo hall on the corner of Swanson and Ritner in seedy South Philadelphia, a local promotion called Eastern Championship Wrestling was poised to change the industry. Started by Todd Gordon from the ashes of Joel Goodhart's Tri-State Wrestling, the company's product morphed from your typical run-of-the-mill 1990s indy fare to a much more intense, reality-based, ultra-violent and ultra-sexualized product that ran counter to the ultra-kiddy movement that had taken over mainstream wrestling.

The changes were largely due to booker Eddie Gilbert and a subversive mastermind from Scarsdale, New York, who had gotten his break in the business when he was a kid, hanging out backstage at Madison Square Garden with "Classy" Freddy Blassie, Capt. Lou Albano, and The Grand Wizard, and later came to work in WCW and other companies as manager "Paul E. Dangerously." His real name was Paul Heyman, and his goal was to give fans something they weren't getting anywhere else; something *extreme*. Under his watch, the company changed its name to Extreme Championship Wrestling, and Gordon was pushed out, leaving Heyman in full control.

Thanks to ECW, American wrestling fans became familiarized with things like flaming tables, barbed-wire wrapped two-by-fours, titillating ringside valets whose behavior was decidedly R-rated, and in-ring promos that hinted at reality and contained language usually reserved for the locker room. Performers like the daredevil Sabu, wily Brooklyn native Taz, the beer-swilling Sandman and the "Innovator of Violence" Tommy Dreamer tore into each other with reckless abandon, and perhaps more importantly, their conflicts played out in storylines that didn't insult the fans' intelligence, referencing wrestlers' past personas and real-life grudges. And thanks to a growing UHF and cable presence in the Northeast and other areas, people were taking notice.

"People find it hard to believe, but Paul could come up with a whole angle in the blink of an eye," says Brian Heffron, ECW's Blue Meanie. "In the ECW locker room, his table was right in the middle. If you had an idea, you'd walk over a couple feet and talk to Paul. You'd see him sitting there with a tablet of paper, staring off into space, in deep thought. He was always open to suggestions. He could just come up with stuff. You'd see him walk in and he'd have something written on the back of a restaurant napkin. A little germ of an idea would grow into such a great angle."

A New World Order

The first to take notice would be Eric Bischoff, a former AWA announcer and front-office gofer who had risen to the position of executive vice president of Atlanta-based World Championship Wrestling. Bischoff was intent on making WCW competitive with the WWF, and had already recruited a bunch of former WWF luminaries, including Hulk Hogan, Randy Savage, and many others. The combination of ECW's edgy content and a unique angle being run in Japan, in which New Japan Pro Wrestling suffered a scripted "invasion" by rival organization the Universal Wrestling Federation,

Scott Hall (left) and Kevin Nash (right) shocked the wrestling world when they recruited Hulk Hogan to the New World Order in July 1996.   *Photo by* Pro Wrestling Illustrated

gave Bischoff an idea that would finally help him overtake Vince McMahon, if only for a time.

Starting in 1996 with the recruitment of former WWF stars Kevin "Diesel" Nash and Scott "Razor Ramon" Hall, Bischoff masterminded an invasion storyline in which WCW would appear to be infiltrated by a renegade group known as the New World Order. Originally composed of Hall, Nash, and a newly heel Hulk Hogan, the nWo eventually expanded to include much of the roster, and the overall storyline involved the group's attempt to take over WCW. Now commonplace in American pro wrestling, this was the first storyline that revolved around control of an entire company, transcending the typically personal grudges between wrestlers that usually drove storylines. The nWo invasion angle was orchestrated to come off as a "worked shoot," that is, an angle that played off fans' understandings of the reality behind what goes on as part of the show.

The nWo invasion would grow more complex as time went on, and the angle would stretch on for years. Bischoff beefed up his roster with talent from all over the business, including former ECW talents Dean Malenko, Eddie Guerrero, Chris Jericho, and Chris Benoit; performers from New Japan, Masa Chono and The Great Muta; and even prominent *lucha libre* stars from Mexico, Rey Mysterio and Psicosis. A one-man phenomenon known simply as Goldberg also captured fans' attention as he mowed down one opponent after another in a seemingly unstoppable march to the top. His defeat of Hulk Hogan for the WCW World Championship in the Georgia Dome would be one of WCW's most highly rated episodes of *Monday Nitro*.

Not Your Father's WWF

There would be a lot of those highly rated episodes, as *Monday Nitro* finally overtook the WWF's *Monday Night Raw* in the weekly TV ratings, and WCW pushed ahead of the WWF in overall prominence on the American wrestling scene. The conflict would come to be known as the Monday Night War, and saw both organizations locked in mortal combat, not only for control of the industry, but also for survival. Week after week during the late 1990s, and into the new century, both companies strove mightily to one-up each other, crafting more bizarre storylines and shocking turns of event designed to keep viewers from changing the channel to the competition.

Bischoff and WCW had caught Vince McMahon and the WWF off guard, during a time when the company's creativity was lacking and the vacuum left behind by departing stars had yet to be filled. But as the competition heated up and WCW began to win the war, it seemed that the powers that be inside the WWF's Titan Tower headquarters were motivated to shake things up in a big way. McMahon began listening to the advice of Vince Russo, the editor of his magazine division, who, along with his partner Ed Ferrara, urged McMahon to abandon the safe route he had been taking and get edgier. Inspired by what they saw in ECW, Russo and Ferrara helped lead the WWF in a direction that would soon be dubbed "Attitude."

"He was opening the curtain," says longtime WWE magazine writer Keith Elliot Greenberg, who worked with Russo during his days heading the publications department. "I'm not going to give him the entire credit for the Attitude Era, but he greatly contributed to it."

Adds Kevin Kelly, then a member of the announce team as well as a magazine staffer:

> It was born out of the pages of *Raw Magazine*. It wasn't so much that Vince McMahon or Vince Russo ripped off ECW. Vince called a meeting, and he invited Russo, who had helped out with TV writing, as well as Jim Cornette and Jim Ross, Pat Patterson and Bruce Prichard. The ratings in February 1997 were not good. He said, "I want some fresh ideas, I want to know what direction we should go." And Russo said, "I think we should have the same tack that we have when it comes to *Raw Magazine*. We need to be smart, we need to be edgy, we need to not be afraid to take chances and say things that are controversial." And that was really it.

Austin vs. McMahon

It started with a character called Stone Cold Steve Austin, a rough-and-tumble Texan whom McMahon had hired away from ECW and transformed into wrestling's ultimate anti-authority malcontent. Taking some cues from the persona he had developed under Heyman, Austin began to cut scathing promos in which he ridiculed other WWF performers in vulgar ways and even called out the WWF brass, in more blurring of the lines of reality. Starting out as a heel, Austin's personality became so popular with fans that he eventually found himself as a full-blown babyface.

"It was when [producer] David Sahadi at the TV studio changed the look and feel of *Raw* to make it '*Raw is War*,'" remembers Kevin Kelly. "That meant they were going to war against WCW, and that gave the show the new look it needed, to match the attitude that it would soon be bringing out."

Vince McMahon himself would become the company's ultimate embodiment of evil as a result of a real-life incident in the main event of the 1997 *Survivor Series* in Montreal, Quebec. WWF World Champion Bret "Hit Man" Hart had signed with WCW and, worried that he might defect while still holding his company's top title, McMahon secretly instructed referee Earl Hebner to ring the bell at a crucial moment in the match and award the championship to challenger Shawn Michaels, in conflict with the agreed-upon script that originally saw Hart winning by disqualification. Hart decked the chairman in the locker room after the match, and happily left for WCW. McMahon, meanwhile, came off in a profoundly negative light with fans, who were convinced that "Vince screwed Bret" and referred to the incident as "The Montreal Screwjob."

"We had our biggest ratings right after Bret left," says Kelly. "It provided a huge boost. I think there was a sense of betrayal on the part of the boys towards Vince, at least that next day. A lot of people felt Bret had gotten done dirty. Then Vince's side of the story came out, and everyone was able to make their own decisions. Once Vince went on TV with the camel hair jacket and the black eye, and was able to tell the story, [saying] 'Bret screwed Bret,' that was it."

Ever the opportunist, McMahon turned lemons into lemonade by playing up his new heel status, and positioned himself into a major on-air rivalry with the WWF's new top rebel, Steve Austin. It was yet another "meta" storyline, in which wrestler and boss engaged in a power struggle for control of the company, each rallying others to their side. Austin bucked his employer's decrees at every turn, growing more and more popular in the process.

A Roster of Renegades

The sleeping giant had awoken, and the newly christened WWF Attitude Era would soon turn things around for the once-beleaguered company.

Business boomed again in the late 1990s with the transition to a more adult-oriented product. Michaels, along with one-time "Connecticut blue blood" Hunter Hearst Helmsley, who morphed into the cocky bad boy "Triple H," banded together to form D-Generation X, a foul-mouthed faction for whom no sacred cow was off-limits. Mick Foley, an early proponent of the hard-core style who had performed in WCW and ECW as Cactus Jack and more recently in the WWF as Mankind, redefined what was considered acceptable for the WWF's in-ring product, infusing the kind of ultra-violence and weapon-oriented action that had previously been exclusive to the land of Extreme. There was the wrestling porn star Val Venis, as well as the brash tag team of The New Age Outlaws, made up of formerly struggling mid-carders Billy Gunn and Road Dogg. The Undertaker went from an Old West archetype to a more sinister, even satanic, figure. And then there were the women, whom the WWF would eventually brand as "Divas," a new breed of female performers like Sable, Sunny and Terri Runnels, who traded in the coyness of past beauties (like Miss Elizabeth) for overt sexuality.

While the Austin/McMahon storyline raged, Stone Cold would be rivaled as the top main-eventer in the WWF by one man—a third-generation performer who would eventually become wrestling's most successful crossover celebrity since Hulk Hogan. Debuting in 1996 as the amiable Rocky Maivia, he got himself some "Attitude" and reinvented himself as the arrogant yet irresistibly funny scoundrel known as The Rock. Just as with Austin, The Rock's act would become such a hit with the WWF fan base that he'd soon be one of the company's hottest attractions.

The two Vinces, McMahon and Russo, had successfully taken the WWF in a whole new direction, and by the end of the decade WCW was being left in the dust. The nWo invasion had grown stale over time, and increasing attempts to keep it fresh only made things worse thanks to a disjointed booking committee that seemed incapable of crafting storylines that actually made sense. Even the shocking and sudden departure of Vince Russo for WCW did little to hurt the WWF's momentum, as the former head writer of WWF programming seemed unable to recapture lightning in a bottle while working with Bischoff.

"WCW had the greatest talent any company ever had," marvels Dave Meltzer, who covered the war extensively at the time in his *Wrestling Observer* newsletter. "They were owned by this media conglomerate that was filled with money. They had everything going for them, and should've never lost. It was a combo of Vince and Steve Austin and The Rock and dX, but the key to Vince winning the war was the absolute, complete incompetence on the other side. Also, with Austin and Rock, he lucked into two of the most charismatic guys in the history of the business at the same time."

War Is Over

By the start of 2001, WCW had gone out of business, losing their TV deal when new head honchos at Time-Warner decided against continuing to air pro wrestling on their cable networks. McMahon swooped in and purchased all of WCW's assets for a mere $5 million, ironically outbidding Bischoff himself. Just like that, the Monday Night War was over. Weeks later, ECW went under as well after their own TV timeslot on cable network SpikeTV was taken over by the WWF. In what seemed like the blink of an eye, the professional wrestling landscape was suddenly and permanently altered.

To all intents and purposes, WWE became the only show in town as far as major league pro wrestling in North America was concerned. But even with the war over, many of the changes remained; storylines were more mature in tone, as well as much more complex, as it became commonplace for performers to spend just as much time talking on the mic as wrestling in the ring. Backstage vignettes became a standard part of the show. To combat the lack of competition, the WWF first tried an invasion storyline involving the WCW and ECW brands it had recently purchased, but when that fizzled, they instead opted for a more long-term solution in 2002, splitting the roster into two distinct in-house brands named for their two flagship TV shows, *Raw* and *SmackDown*. Designed to keep things fresh, the brand extension was maintained for nearly a decade before the roster was finally reunited.

Some New Alternatives

The brand extension was intended to create the illusion of competition, but a handful of companies would attempt to create some real-life competition to shake up the industry seemingly ruled by WWE (the company name changed from WWF following a long and protracted legal battle with the World Wildlife Fund that was finally lost in May 2002). Foremost among them would be a group called Total Nonstop Action, or TNA Wrestling, which was founded by longtime Memphis promoter Jerry Jarrett and his son Jeff, and included the likes of Vince Russo as booker.

TNA landed many former WWF and WCW performers such as Kurt Angle, The Dudley Boyz, Jeff Hardy, Scott Hall, Kevin Nash, Ric Flair, and Hulk Hogan, and also created new stars, including Abyss, A. J. Styles, and Christopher Daniels. For a time they were even affiliated with the venerable NWA, which had been limping along ever since cutting ties with WCW in 1993. Initially pioneering the concept of weekly, low-priced pay-per-view events, TNA eventually settled into a cable-TV deal that saw their program *Impact Wrestling* offer a viable weekly alternative to WWE.

Additionally, a company called Ring of Honor began operations in 2002, initially founded by Rob Feinstein, a wrestling video merchant looking to create his own product, along with booker Gabe Sapolsky, who had made his bones as a booking assistant to Paul Heyman during the dying days of ECW. Running contrary to the emphasis on entertainment and soap-opera angles in mainstream pro wrestling, ROH placed the emphasis squarely on athleticism and match quality with an old-school, no-nonsense approach, accented by a high-octane, very modern in-ring style. The company would help establish standout performers, including future WWE World Heavyweight Champions CM Punk and Daniel Bryan, and typified the new face of the American independent wrestling scene, which would later feature such companies as CHIKARA, Dragon Gate USA, and EVOLVE.

Emerging from the Attitude Era

Not to be outdone in the athleticism department, the WWE of the 2000s started putting the focus on pushing talented, hard-working performers of smaller size, as well as creating brand new stars for the future. Longtime fan darlings like Chris Benoit, Chris Jericho, Eddie Guerrero, and Rey Mysterio, often considered the antithesis of the "WWE look," were given opportunities as main-event performers.

Fostering a growing developmental system that included organizations like Ohio Valley Wrestling, Memphis Championship Wrestling, and the Heartland Wrestling Association, WWE started calling up some rookies and giving them the stage: "The Animal" Batista, who would join forces with Triple H and Ric Flair as part of a faction called Evolution; third-generation standout Randy Orton, whose natural talent would often be stymied by his backstage attitude; the massive NCAA Heavyweight Champion Brock Lesnar, a throwback to the shooters of old who eventually dominated the UFC as well; and a young man from West Newbury, Massachusetts, named John Cena, who would go on to become the face of WWE for well over a decade.

Eventually, the excesses of the Attitude Era were scaled back, due in part to changing audience tastes, as well as several unfortunate incidents and the media attention they attracted. Tragedy struck WWE in November 2005 when the very popular Eddie Guerrero was found dead in his hotel room just hours before an event of an apparent heart attack many attributed to the damage done by years of steroids and other drugs. Unthinkably, that tragedy was actually overshadowed by what happened in June 2007, when Guerrero's best friend, Chris Benoit, murdered his wife and child and then committed suicide at his home in Atlanta. And these were not the first deaths of recent WWE performers, as the company had lost Brian Pillman to a heart attack in 1997, as well as Owen Hart, who died at a pay-per-view event in May 1999 when a harness used to lower him into the ring snapped, dropping him seventy-eight feet.

WWE had already been reining things in for years due to their status as a publicly traded company, as well as pressure from advertisers, but the Guerrero and Benoit incidents clinched it. The company instituted a wellness program designed to curb the substance abuse rampant in the industry. And while some have cast doubts on its effectiveness, it has indeed resulted in a generally safer environment. Show content was noticeably toned down, resulting in what some skeptical fans have referred to as the "PG Era." Nevertheless, the influence of "Attitude" continues to be felt to this day, and probably always will be.

Major Stars of the Era

The business changed radically around the turn of the twenty-first century, and these men and women played major parts in affecting that change.

- The Big Show
- Booker T
- Chris Benoit
- Chris Jericho
- Chyna
- Diamond Dallas Page
- Eddie Guerrero
- Edge
- Goldberg
- Kane
- Kurt Angle
- Mick Foley
- Rey Mysterio
- Rob Van Dam
- The Rock
- Sabu
- Scott Steiner
- Stone Cold Steve Austin
- Triple H
- Trish Stratus

The Hardcore Legend

Few performers have helped transform the public's perception of what a professional wrestler should look like, or what he can and should do in the ring, the way that Mick Foley did. His moniker of "The Hardcore Legend" may have been a bit of sarcastic self-deprecation on his part, but it nevertheless became a very accurate description for his multitudes of supporters and imitators. Whether as Cactus Jack, Mankind, and, yes, even Dude Love, Foley never failed to entertain the fans by putting his body on the line like no other. More than just a fearless artist of the squared circle, he has transitioned from a wrestling career to that of a respected best-selling author and humorist, whose warm heart belies the lunacy he displayed between the ropes.

He was born in Bloomington, Indiana, on June 7, 1965, but soon relocated to the place with which he would become most associated in later years: Long Island, New York. And although he was both a lacrosse player and a wrestler in high school, it would be a very different kind of wrestling that would shape his destiny. The young Foley was a died-in-the-wool pro wrestling fan, particularly of the Bob Backlund–era WWF. He and his friends created their own fantasy wrestling storylines and personas, and the video exploits of his teenaged "Dude Love" character would later be a testament to his passion for the business from an early age. He famously hitchhiked to Madison Square Garden in November 1983 to witness his hero Jimmy "Superfly" Snuka leap from the top of a steel cage in his match with The Magnificent Muraco. It was then that he became sure of what he wanted to do with his life.

After training under longtime WWF journeyman Dominic Denucci, Foley debuted that same year, and spent several years as a jobber, an "enhancement talent" hired to make other stars look good, and most importantly, to lose. He would even fill this role in the WWF during the mid-1980s. It wasn't until he made his way to the Memphis territory that he first adopted the maniacal Cactus Jack gimmick, and things started to turn around. During the dying days of the territories, Cactus appeared in places like World Class and even had a brief stint in WCW during the late 1980s. All the while, he was honing his hardcore style, and after an ultra-violent indy match in Philadelphia with "Hot Stuff" Eddie Gilbert, he earned a second stint in WCW.

It was during that run that he really cemented his reputation, attracting a devoted cult following of fans who couldn't get enough of his unhinged persona, riveting interview style, and seemingly reckless behavior. There appeared to be nothing he wouldn't do to get a rise out of the crowd, and he was more than willing to endure great punishment, as can be evidenced by his brutal series of matches with Big Van Vader, one of which, contested in Germany, resulted in the loss of most of his right ear. With his overweight appearance and unkempt ring attire, he drew a stark contrast from the chiseled Adonises who populated most of the show, and fans couldn't care less. In a way, he represented all of them, and through sheer willpower and determination he made himself a star.

After a stint in ECW, where one would think he would be most at home, he finally made it to the company he had enjoyed as a kid, debuting in the WWF in 1996 under the persona of Mankind, an even more bizarre permutation of the Cactus Jack gimmick. During the deconstructionist Attitude Era, he would eventually perform under all three of his personas: Cactus, Mankind, and Dude Love (or "The Three Faces of Foley," as they came to be known). He would capture three WWF World Heavyweight titles and etch his name among the wrestling immortals thanks to an infamous Hell in a Cell match with the Undertaker at the 1998 *King of the Ring* in which he would plummet through the ceiling of the cell to the mat below. By the time of his 2000 retirement, he had already revealed himself to fans as Mick Foley, which only increased their adoration of him.

Foley would continue to appear for the WWF/WWE as a goodwill ambassador over the years, and even spent a bit of time in TNA as well, briefly returning to action to win their version of the world championship. He would also reveal himself to be a captivating writer, and starting with the 1999 autobiography *Have a Nice Day: A Tale of Blood and Sweatsocks*, would eventually pen four memoirs, two novels, and four children's books, many of which have appeared on the *New York Times* bestseller list. He remains an inspiration to fans young and old, with a brutal wrestling legacy matched only by his boyish sense of humor about it.

The Texas Rattlesnake

Stone Cold gives his trademark salute during his final run with WWE as an active wrestler in 2003. The "OMR" on his vest stands for "One More Round." *Mshake3/Wikimedia*

If ever there was a face of the Attitude Era, it was the face of Stone Cold Steve Austin, the one-man phenomenon who rallied fans to his anti-authoritarian cause, battled WWF Chairman Vince McMahon in one of the company's hottest angles of all time, and probably made more money for the company than any other single performer in its history. There was a time during the late 1990s and early 2000s when the "Austin 3:16" T-shirt became ubiquitous, when Austin's on-air struggles offered catharsis for the masses in a way that only professional wrestling can.

He was born Steven James Anderson in Victoria, Texas, but after his father abandoned the family he took on the last name of his stepfather, Ken Williams. Coincidentally, when he first expressed interest in becoming a professional wrestler in his twenties, there already was a Steve Williams in the business, and so it was suggested to him by booker Dutch Mantell (a.k.a. WWE manager Zeb Coulter) that he take the name

Steve Austin, after the popular bionic main character of the '70s action TV series, *The Six-Million Dollar Man*.

Austin first broke into the business in Texas during the dying days of World Class Championship Wrestling, where he was trained by "Gentleman" Chris Adams (whose wife, Jeannie, would, incidentally, wind up becoming Austin's own second wife). After a run in the Memphis-based USWA, he took on the nickname "Stunning," and soon got his big break in WCW in 1991. He became a member of Paul Heyman's Dangerous Alliance stable, and enjoyed lengthy reigns as WCW World Television Champion, as well as a groundbreaking turn as tag-team partner to Brian Pillman in the infamous Hollywood Blondes tandem. But although the Blondes gimmick was a hit, Austin didn't survive the mid-1990s influx of former WWF talent to WCW, and was notoriously fired by WCW boss Eric Bischoff for being "unmarketable."

Bischoff's poor judgment would eventually come back to haunt him. After honing a new foul-mouthed, shoot-from-the-hip persona in ECW (run by his former on-air manager Heyman), Austin was picked up by the WWF, dropping the "Stunning" moniker for "Stone Cold." He also adopted an exciting new finisher, the Stone Cold Stunner. Although not an immediate hit (he was originally presented as "The Ringmaster"), Austin's no-nonsense tough-guy persona grew on fans, and a titanic 1997 feud with Bret "Hit Man" Hart helped make him a main-event star. Not even a severe neck injury in a match against Bret's brother Owen at *SummerSlam '97* could halt his forward momentum, although it would later catch up with him.

Launching into an epic onscreen struggle against Vince McMahon, Stone Cold became more than a main-event star; he became an icon. Toppling Shawn Michaels for his first WWF World Championship at *WrestleMania XIV*, he embarked on a run the likes of which has probably never been equaled in company history. Thanks to an expertly crafted storyline from "Mr. McMahon" and head WWF creative writer Vince Russo, Austin was positioned as the ultimate rebel, unwilling to be made into a corporate pawn by the powers that be. Through him and his antics, frustrated fans got to work out their own pent-up frustrations, fantasizing about having the freedom to ridicule their own bosses and leave them lying in the middle of the ring. He galvanized the fan base as Hulk Hogan had done a generation earlier, and his merchandize sales, ever the measuring stick for modern-day wrestling success, surpassed even those of Hogan's heyday.

Eventually, that nagging neck injury, as well as serious wear and tear on both knees, forced the Texas Rattlesnake to cut his career short. He slowed things down in the early 2000s, and missed some time due to several periods in which he walked out of the company due to creative differences, often feeling that his character was no longer being handled as well as it had been in previous years.

Eventually, he had his final match against his classic Attitude Era rival, The Rock, at *WrestleMania XIX* in 2003.

Austin has continued to appear for WWE as a goodwill ambassador, ironically enough, and crowds never fail to erupt when that broken glass music cue hits. Currently, his podcast, *The Steve Austin Show*, is a major hit with fans who still enjoy listening to Stone Cold spout off in his classic style. The man has never been afraid to give the middle finger to social norms, both literally and figuratively, and his followers, far and wide, continue to live through him.

The People's Champion

He is the "Most Electrifying Man in Sports-Entertainment," The Brahma Bull. A natural performer who can light up a crowd just by raising an eyebrow, he could get the job done both on the mic and in the ring. Few athletes in pro wrestling history put it all together the way The Rock did, and that was the reason he became, alongside Steve Austin, one of the defining performers of the Attitude Era. A total package entertainer, he has understandably become a mainstream celebrity who continues to electrify audiences on movie screens as well as occasionally still in the ring.

He was born Dwayne Johnson on May 2, 1972, in Hayward, California, the son of 1970s and '80s wrestling superstar Rocky Johnson and his wife, Ata Maivia-Johnson, herself the daughter of the late Samoan wrestling legend "High Chief" Peter Maivia. The young Dwayne grew up in the business, as his grandparents also ran the local Hawaiian territory, Polynesian Pacific Wrestling. A college football standout who won a national championship with the University of Miami's Hurricanes in 1991, he went on to a brief career in the Canadian Football League; when he was cut in 1995, he opted instead to channel his athleticism into his family's business of choice.

Johnson was not only a third-generation performer, he was a member of the legendary extended family of Samoan superstars that includes the likes of The Wild Samoans Afa & Sika, Yokozuna, and many more, and these connections helped him get a WWF tryout. He was sent to the Memphis-based USWA, which was then engaged in a developmental agreement with the WWF. There, he competed as Flex Kavana and got his feet wet while the WWF waited to sign him to a long-term deal. The deal finally happened in late 1996, and Johnson made his WWF debut at the *Survivor Series* in Madison Square Garden, using the name Rocky Maivia as a tribute to his father and grandfather.

But Rocky's squeaky-clean babyface persona was a dud with fans of the burgeoning Attitude Era, and it wasn't until he took on a more arrogant, heelish demeanor and started referring to himself egotistically as The Rock that he finally got over. And, boy, did he get over. During 1997 and 1998, The Rock emerged as the ultimate performer fans loved to hate. They loved it so much, in fact, that it was inevitable for him to eventually become a good guy, despite the fact that his onscreen personality had changed very little.

His weekly in-ring interviews became the highlight of the show; with the help of WWF writers, as well as his own natural charisma, he became the single-most entertaining performer on the roster. He coined catch-phrase after catch-phrase, asking fans if they could "smell what The Rock was cookin'" or intoning, "Finally, The Rock has come back to [*insert city name here*]!" He typified the push under the Attitude Era toward extended promos that often overshadowed the in-ring action, and definitely raised the bar when it came to what performers would be expected to do from a verbal point of view.

A crossover Hollywood star, Dwayne "The Rock" Johnson makes an appearance at the 2009 Tribeca Film Festival.
David Shankbone/Wikimedia

Inevitably for a performer of such talent and good looks, Hollywood came calling, and starting in 2001, The Rock began appearing less and less in the ring and more and more on the movie set. His credits include starring turns in such films as *The Scorpion King* (2002), *Southland Tales* (2007), *Race to Witch Mountain* (2009), *G.I. Joe: Retaliation* (2013), and three entries in the *Fast and Furious* series. But despite disappearing from action for years at a time, The Rock remains a part of the WWE firmament to this day.

He confirmed that in 2012 when he returned to challenge John Cena, the star who had risen in his absence to become the new top dog in WWE. The Rock and Cena faced off in the main event of *WrestleMania* two years in a row, giving the Brahma Bull the chance to show the WWE Universe that he still had what it took to electrify them like he had done so many times in the past. For those who have thrilled to his exploits over the past two decades, there was never any doubt.

9

Theater of the Absurd

Wrestling as Performance

There's no drama like wrestling.

—Andy Kaufman

ome folks enjoy high-end cable shows like *Mad Men, Game of Thrones,* or *Breaking Bad.* For others, afternoon soap-opera fare is more their speed. Still others go in for Broadway shows, while grand opera might suit some tastes. And yet to millions of fans, there is one kind of staged entertainment that speaks to them like nothing else, a modern-day passion play that encapsulates elements of all of the genres mentioned above, but designed for a much broader (some might say lower) common-denominator audience. And yet, some of the world's foremost intellectuals have been ardent supporters, including classical conductor Arturo Toscanini, respected actor Sir Peter Ustinov, and eminent sports journalist Bob Costas. Professional wrestling has often been called the "king of sports," although, perhaps, it should more accurately be called the "king of drama."

It may have started out as a pure sport, but for the past ninety years, pro wrestling has been something closer to performance art, with each match a kind of mini one-act play, and the overarching storylines that link them together more of an ongoing saga. It is unquestionably theater for the masses, performed for many who probably would never even consider themselves fans of theater. Drawing on traditions that date back as far as Japanese kabuki and ancient Greek tragedy, pro wrestling taps into something deep within us, which probably accounts for why its popularity continues unabated, regardless of how openly scripted it is. A highly ritualized form of entertainment, it provides a satisfying catharsis for people of all ages, genders, races, and creeds. We know exactly what to expect, and that's exactly what we enjoy so much about it.

A Crucial Dichotomy

The drama of professional wrestling hinges primarily on the good vs. evil dynamic, or more appropriately to the context, the conflict between faces (short for babyfaces) and heels (short for shitheels), as the good guys and bad guys are called in the business. Wrestlers portray specifically heroic or villainous roles, which have grown increasingly complex over the years to the point that in recent decades they can legitimately be termed "characters." This gives the fans a very clear choice as far as who to root for, and who to root against, making them much more invested in the choreographed contest. Granted, there have always been fans, now more than ever, who choose to root for the heels and against the faces, and in our own postmodern world of moral gray areas, the lines between the two are not as clearly defined as they once were. Nevertheless, the central conflict remains the heart and soul of what pro wrestling is all about.

Often, the role of the heel is the harder of the two to perform, and the more valuable. After all, a face doesn't need to do much to get a crowd on his side, and charisma goes a long way. Typically, faces can sometimes be bland or even saccharine (sometimes referred to as a "white meat babyface"). But a heel needs to openly court the derision of the audience with histrionic mannerisms and vocalizations. Some variations can be the obnoxious and cowardly "chickenshit heel," as well as the brutal and intimidating "monster heel." By being hateable enough, the heel becomes the main reason people are drawn to a particular event; in other words, they're willing to pay to watch someone finally shut him up and give him his comeuppance. Getting people to dislike you that intensely—particularly if they know you're just playing a part—is an art form in itself, often referred to in the business as "getting heat."

"There were abrasive villains that were so great on the microphone, they became cult heroes," says Keith Elliot Greenberg, biographer of top heels Fred Blassie, Superstar Billy Graham, and Ric Flair. "It's a certain raw charisma, a bravado that borders on the comical, and an ability to talk people into the arena. And that's before any of them get into the ring."

By following the specific pattern of most matches, and in the bigger picture, most storylines, fans experience an emotional release. Suspense is built up, whether over minutes, or over weeks and months, until the outcome they have been hoping for is at last achieved. There are many ways to achieve this. For example, the traditional approach taken with the WWF/WWE World Championship has often been to have the title held by a very popular face that must overcome obstacle after obstacle in the form of diabolical threats. The traditional approach of NWA bookers in the 1970s and '80s was often to have their title held by a heel, who would be chased by an inspirational face, allowing fans to rejoice when he finally won—if only for a time. This is not to say that heels always lose, and faces always win. After all, that would make things far too predictable, even for something as ritualized as wrestling. Now and then, heels will triumph, but usually to serve some greater storyline purpose; for example, to build that heel up to an eventual loss to an even more beloved babyface.

"In the old days, wrestling was proletarian theater for the masses," says Evan Ginzburg, lifelong fan and co-producer of the 2008 motion picture *The Wrestler*. "Ultimately, good overcame evil. In the WWF, it was always about Bruno defending the belt, Backlund defending the belt, Pedro defending the belt, Hogan defending the belt. It was very simple, and it always worked. It's not Shakespeare—not to demean wrestling fans, because I've met some of the most interesting, eclectic people through wrestling."

What's the Angle?

In order to generate interest in the matches (promoters long ago realized there weren't enough fans who'd pay money to see clean, straightforward, honest-to-goodness wrestling), a carefully crafted storyline, or "angle" must be put together, usually by the booker or booking committee, which has today evolved into the more modern-sounding "creative team." These creative types bestow characters upon the performers, and place them into adversarial on-air relationships called "programs." Usually, a championship is a great concept around which to build an angle, and that's why they continue to be so important to the business. They instantly create the sense of something important being fought over, and are at the root of wrestling's nature as simulated sport. However, in the absence of titles, or to further enhance them, bookers script grudges generated by manufacturing personal animosity between the performers, such as when Andre the Giant famously went from face to heel in 1987 due to his perception of having been passed over for a shot at Hulk Hogan's WWF World Championship.

In recent years, the pure good vs. evil passion play that has driven wrestling for generations has become a bit more convoluted, as the business adapts to a more nuanced, and (some would say) more cynical pop-culture sensibility. Smiling and waving white meat babyface types, who in the past might have been portrayed in a positive light, are now often presented as annoying, self-righteous bads guys, such as Olympic gold medalist Kurt Angle. Meanwhile, nihilistic, sarcastic ruffians who might have once been clear-cut heels will today be cheered by fans and presented as the good guys, à la Stone Cold Steve Austin.

Speaking of Stone Cold, the famous program he had with WWF Chairman Vince McMahon in the late 1990s has now become something of a template for most main-event storylines going forward. Rather than wrestlers working out personal one-on-one grudges, it has become more about factions vying for corporate control, or evil authority figures battling it out with rebellious loners. Recently, Daniel Bryan became WWE's most popular face due to a storyline in which he struggled to overcome corporate overlords Triple H and his wife, Stephanie McMahon, on his quest for the WWE World Heavyweight Championship. The angle was based, in part, on the real-life belief of some inside the company that Bryan was not suitable championship material, but WWE was able to shift gears and use that backstage intrigue to fuel the scripted storyline once they decided to capitalize on the support Bryan enjoyed from fans.

"In some sense, it's unavoidable," explains David Shoemaker, author of *Squared Circle: Life, Death and Professional Wrestling*. "In the post-modern wrestling world, if we're going to be honest about the fact that these guys are in charge, they're almost forced to be villains. You need the real-life 'corporate COO vs. the rest of the company' aspect for it to have legitimacy in the fans' eyes. As much as people complain about Triple H and Vince being on screen, if you're not acknowledging that truth within the fabric of this falsehood, then you're just leaving out a huge component. That's where the most poignant soap-opera aspect comes from, and it's impossible to get away from it. As much as fans might complain, that's what they're interested in."

Stirring the Pot

Although the employee vs. boss trope is a relatively new development for pro wrestling, the use of social issues to further angles is certainly nothing new. Austin tapped into working-class angst during his feud with the evil Mr. McMahon, but so did old-school WWWF World Champion Bruno Sammartino, who channeled the rage of the crowd against challengers (and their managers) who frequently hurled ethnic slurs and other condescending putdowns his way.

Pro wrestling has never shied away from sensitive issues of race, ethnicity, gender or sexual orientation; rather, it has openly courted them. Some would even say it has downright exploited them. Preening, feminized performers like Gorgeous George, Exotic Adrian Street, Goldust, and Billy & Chuck have played upon audiences' sexual insecurities and homophobia, inviting them to wish for the tougher, manlier babyface to set things right. There has been no shortage of foreign menaces to challenge American

Alongside his manager, Abdullah Farouk (left), the savage Sheik whipped crowds into a frenzy with his Arabian madman gimmick.

Jack Pfefer Collection, University of Notre Dame

supremacy: "Russians," like Ivan Koloff and Nikolai Volkoff; "Japanese," like Mr. Moto and Kinji Shibuya; "Nazis," like Killer Karl Krupp and Fritz Von Erich; and "Arabs," like The Sheik and Muhammad Hassan (sometimes, these performers actually boasted the same ethnicity as their characters, but this was far from necessary). Female performers, typically, are there to titillate, to play on male sexual hang-ups, or for a subversive combination of both.

Physical Storytelling

While the angle sets the stage, what goes on between the ropes is still the meat and potatoes, and where performers are expected to provide viewers with an appropriate payoff. Talented participants and savvy observers will tell you that there is a psychology to a wrestling match, and that those who engage in them are cooperating with each other to tell a story to the audience. True ring artists can bring a crowd down, up, then down and up again, over and over, leading to a big, orgasmic finish. Most importantly, it all needs to make some kind of sense—within the greater fiction, of course. Fans are programmed to sympathize with the babyface as he takes a pounding, to jeer the heel for doing so, then to cheer on their hero when he makes his dramatic comeback. They express frustration when the villain cheats, usually unbeknownst to the intentionally oblivious referee.

"It's easy to watch, but it's hard to explain," says Dave Meltzer of what makes for a great match. "It's a matter of knowing what your end result is, and then listening to the crowd and improvising on the way how to best get there. That's why the experienced guys are so much better than the new guys, because they recognize the crowd more. You want to build them up for certain peaks, but not big peaks, and then at the end you want the biggest peak. You want to do something early to hook them. You want to get heat on the babyface, so there's a feeling of him coming back, and then at the end have the big shebang."

Matches are broken into "spots"—that is, specific moments of action, usually choreographed either loosely or down to the last detail, depending on the preferences of the performers and the necessities of blocking out segments of a television program. Long holds are often employed to let the performers rest and lull the crowd into a sense of calm before exploding into fast-paced "high spots" designed to get a strong reaction, or "pop the crowd." At all times, performers must play relatively broadly to the audience. This was even more the case when each move had to be registered in the cheap seats; the emergence of close-up TV camera shots has allowed for a little bit more subtlety, but not much.

"Even if they had one hold on, they had those fans' complete attention the whole time," explains historian Scott Teal. "Because they did it in such a way that the fans would be on the edge of their seats wanting to see if this guy would break out of that hold. If they could hold the fans attention in so-called 'rest holds,' who cares if it was a rest hold? They had the fans' attention."

This kind of histrionic performance is known as "selling"—in which wrestlers register pain, anger, or other emotions to make the match appear as convincing as possible. Often, the wrestler who appears to be losing is actually working much harder than the wrestler who appears to be on the offensive, since that "losing" wrestler must put in a great effort to "sell" his opponent's moves and make them look harmful, which usually involves "bumping" around the ring to put over an opponent who may only be making limited physical contact. The better the selling, the more fans buy into the match and willingly suspend their disbelief.

"I think fans want to share in the passion of a big match," offers wrestling historian Tim Hornbaker. "It is something that is palpable under the right circumstances. But the psychology begins in the promotion, then plays out in the ring. It can be remarkably special if worked the right way."

When watching highly talented participants, it is not that hard to understand why some refer to professional wrestling as an art form. For all its crudeness, simplicity, and predictability, in the hands of genuine ring artists and booking visionaries, a great wrestling match can be a thing of beauty, and a well-crafted angle can be just as compelling as the greatest "legitimate" drama. Fulfilling a purpose served by popular entertainment for millennia, professional wrestling provides structured ritual and thrilling spectacle in the form of carefully controlled chaos.

A Modern Mythology

Pro wrestling has fascinated and confounded cultural critics for decades, its broad psychology and theatricality providing excellent fodder for literary essays, anthropological expositions and dramatic critiques. In 1965, *Baltimore News American* columnist Steve Gavin invited Edward J. Golden, Jr., director of Baltimore's Center Stage Theater Company to attend a WWWF event at the Civic Center, and printed his reaction. Golden noted:

> It has the basic elements of children's theater—it is not appealing to anything sophisticated and it is keyed to an almost total naïveté. In some ways, it reminds me of a Jacobean tragedy. . . . Becket[t] has this too: man does nothing but contest and there is no intelligibility, just a series of images coming at you and some subliminal logic functioning. Wrestling has all the grace and simplicity of a folk ballad, but none of the significance. It is totally physical, a physical battle of strength beautifully keyed to illicit primitive titillations. In that way, you could call it unfocused theater, since it has no point other than arousing primitive emotions spuriously. . . . Wrestling's appeal is a world beyond reason, a purely instinctive world, and it succeeds beautifully. It's all done very well.

Celebrated *New York Times* theatre critic Brooks Atkinson once opined, "These mugs are terrible actors. They lack spontaneity. Once you have seen one meatball with blond hair step belligerently outside the ring and shake his fist at a jeering audience, you have seen them all. Their fake rage and savagery have become repetitious and tiresome . . . . They represent the lowest level of ham."

Atkinson's opinion notwithstanding, pro wrestling has provided scholars with much to write about over the years, and there is perhaps no scholarly work on the subject more respected and oft-quoted than the 1957 treatise, "The World of Wrestling," by French philosopher Roland Barthes, featured in his essay collection *Mythologies*. In many ways, Barthes cut right to the heart of what wrestling is from a thematic point of view, focusing on the struggle of good and evil, wrestling's preoccupation with justice, as well as the importance of the spectacle of suffering. Seeing through the tightly drawn curtain of kayfabe, Barthes recognized that the purpose of wrestling is not the actual sportsmanlike demonstration of athleticism, but the social concepts that are acted out by characters portraying overblown human stereotypes.

Typical of Barthes's keen insight into the psychology of wrestling is the following passage:

> We are therefore dealing with a real Human Comedy, where the most socially-inspired nuances of passion . . . always felicitously find the clearest sign which can receive them, express them and triumphantly carry them to the confines of the hall. It is obvious that at such a

pitch, it no longer matters whether the passion is genuine or not. What the public wants is the image of passion, not passion itself. There is no more a problem of truth in wrestling than in the theater. In both, what is expected is the intelligible representation of moral situations which are usually private. This emptying out of interiority to the benefit of its exterior signs, this exhaustion of the content by the form, is the very principle of triumphant classical art.

Those Fabulous Fans

What wrestling is about is the father and his children. It's about taking your children to something that's magical. When you're a kid, they're ten feet tall. And you're sharing this with your father, and it's something very, very special. It's Marvel Superheroes and DC Comics come to life.
                    —Evan Ginzburg, associate producer of *The Wrestler*

There are few connoisseurs of any particular genre of popular entertainment as dedicated and passionate as wrestling fanatics. Many of them will save their hard-earned cash and travel great distances to support their chosen "sport." They will debate its nuances with great zeal, and thoroughly give themselves over to the performance while in the moment. Indeed, the audience can be seen as part of the show, and that role has only increased

Although they've changed significantly over the years, wrestling fans remain more a part of the show than in virtually any other form of sport *or* entertainment.
Look *magazine Photograph Collection (Library of Congress)*

over the years. There is no more surefire ingredient to a successful wrestling event than a very loud, very "hot" crowd.

Over the decades, there have even been fans who made such an impact on the proceedings that they are remembered as characters themselves. The 1950s gave us Hatpin Mary, a bespectacled granny known for prodding the heels with her eponymous weapon of choice, as well as anything else she could get her hands on. WWF viewers of the 1980s and '90s were very familiar with Vladimir, the muscular superfan seen in the front row of so many events. The crowd at ECW Arena featured the infamous Hat Guy (also known as Hawaiian Shirt Guy), as well as his compatriot, Faith No More Guy. Most recently, WWE fans are well aware of Tie-Dye Guy and "Sign Guy" Rick Achberger, known to follow WWE to every stop on its road tour with witty placards worthy of his nickname.

Those placards are among the ways fans interact with the live action. Chanting, too, has become one of the most standard, ritualized aspects of the fan experience. Today's live (or live-to-tape) event-based TV programming, unlike the more canned, re-edited shows of decades past, encourages active fan participation, which is just what the contemporary breed of fan is looking for.

While traditionally, wrestling fans have been cynically referred to as "marks" for their gullibility and manipulability, over the past thirty years there has been a gradual "smartening up" of the fan base. First came insider newsletters (a.k.a. "dirtsheets") like the *Wrestling Observer*, started in the early 1980s by obsessively dedicated fan and journalist Dave Meltzer. The earliest publication to ignore kayfabe and cover the real behind-the-scenes dealings of the wrestling business, it has since become the industry's version of *Variety*. The 1990s brought fan access like never before in the form of the Internet, which obliterated any attempts at secrecy much as it did for most other forms of human endeavor.

The digital revolution changed the nature of wrestling's fan base forever. Now armed with all the information promoters wanted to keep away from them, including backstage gossip and insider terminology once sacredly hidden from the masses, a new hybrid fan was created: a mark who had been made "smart" to the business, often referred to as a "smart mark" or simply a "smark." Although they originally tried to fight the tide, these days wrestling companies actively court the smartened-up fan base. WWE is an entertainment industry leader in utilizing social media, and smaller companies like Ring of Honor and Dragon Gate USA depend on the smarter Internet fan as their bread and butter. But true to its nature as a carny business, pro wrestling has found a way to adapt by creating angles that play to the smarks' appetite for backstage reality, thus continuing to work the fans, albeit in a very postmodern way.

10

National Wrestling Alliance

Grappling's Venerated Monopoly

> *The Alliance was not intended only for the benefit of one man or a small group.*
> *It was intended to be a cooperative for the benefit of the whole membership. If I*
> *can't clean it up, I am going to the Justice Dept. Someone has to.*
> —P. L. "Pinkie" George

Prior to the rise of Vince McMahon's WWF in the 1980s, the NWA controlled and governed wrestling's big leagues with an iron fist. A promotional cooperative that stretched across state and even national boundaries, reigning supreme from the time of Truman to the time of Reagan, the NWA was not a single company, but an alliance of promoters, who agreed not to compete with one another and to recognize a single World Heavyweight title. For years, that title was the undisputed property of the legendary Lou Thesz, and the whole shebang was moderated by promoter Sam Muchnick from his offices in St. Louis, for decades the ultimate wrestling mecca. From its conception at the dawn of television, to its modern-day incarnation as a loose conglomerate of independent promotions, the rise and fall of the once-mighty NWA spans nearly seventy years of wrestling history.

Wartime Genesis

The 1940s was a time of fragmentation and marginalization for professional wrestling. Rocked by exposés and banned from Madison Square Garden, the business was re-centralized in the Midwest. At the time, several groups simultaneously vied for power and legitimacy. Among them was the St. Louis outfit run by Tom Packs, which had control of the World Heavyweight title as recognized by the National Wrestling Association, a collection of state athletic commissions organized as part of the National Boxing Association. Packs's top stars of the 1940s were the roughhousing "Wild" Bill Longson and Lou Thesz, who would buy the promotion from the bankrupt Packs in 1947. There was Kansas City–based wrestler/promoter Orville Brown, who had established himself as the World Heavyweight Champion of a group he called the Midwest Wrestling Association. And then there was P. L. "Pinkie" George, a promoter out of Des Moines, Iowa, who saw the potential for something a whole lot bigger.

To quell the territorial conflicts, Pinkie George called a meeting of promoters on July 18, 1948, at the Gold Room of the Hotel President in Waterloo, Iowa. Joining him were Orville Brown, Max Clayton of Omaha, matchmaker Wally Karbo (representing the interests of Tony Stecher's Minneapolis operation), and Sam Muchnick, a Ukrainian-born sportswriter and entrepreneur who had started out as an assistant to Tom Packs before forming his own opposition group in St. Louis. Chicago kingpin Fred Kohler, who had become one of the first promoters to benefit from the exposure of TV, was unable to attend, but consented via telegram to the decrees established that day.

And the decrees were quite bold. With George's leadership, the group established what they called the National Wrestling *Alliance*, taking its name from that of George's own Iowa-based company. This would not be one wrestling company, but rather a consortium of companies (which would eventually be incorporated by George). They would agree to establish clear lines dividing their respective wrestling territories; promoters would be prohibited from competing with one another directly; talent would be exchanged among the promoters; and the group would recognize one World Heavyweight Champion, and one World Junior Heavyweight Champion. Groups like this had been attempted in the past, but usually collapsed quickly due to infighting. This would not be the case with the NWA, which succeeded in providing relative unity to a disjointed business for many years.

The NWA grew dramatically in its early years, going national as it added more members like Morris Siegel in Houston; Don Owen in Portland, Oregon; Joe "Toots" Mondt in New York; Al Haft in Columbus, Ohio; Joe Malcewicz in San Francisco; Paul Bowser in Boston; Johnny Doyle in Los Angeles; Paul Jones in Atlanta; Frank Tunney in Toronto; and Salvador Lutteroth in Mexico City, among many others. For the first time, a well-organized, durable network of promotional territories now existed.

"The formation of the NWA . . . advanced the cause of the industry, allowing it to thrive at a very specific time, the late 1940s and early 1950s TV boom," says Tim Hornbaker, author of the definitive NWA history, *National Wrestling Alliance: The Untold Story of the Monopoly That Strangled Pro Wrestling*. "The Alliance streamlined the sport from its disorganized standing and created singular champions, defined territories and promoters worked together to spotlight wrestling's top stars. I think fans appreciated the newfound structure of pro wrestling and if it hadn't taken place, the sport would have never seen the growth and success that it did in the 1950s. . . . Promoters knew they had to work together to survive."

A Champion to Be Proud Of

Central to the success of the venture was cleaning up the title picture and setting up one World Heavyweight Champion to be recognized by all the territories. The first National Wrestling Alliance World Champion selected was Orville Brown, who was already the MWA World Champion. After coming to an agreement with Lou Thesz's St. Louis office, a title unification match was set up between Brown and Thesz, who was recognized as world champion by the National Wrestling Association. This was intended to unite the two titles and strengthen the Alliance's standing—but when Brown's career was tragically cut short in an auto accident, it was decided that Lou Thesz would be automatically recognized as the unified World Heavyweight Champion.

The fledgling National Wrestling Alliance couldn't have hoped for a better standard-bearer than Thesz, whose solid fundamentals and classic look harkened back to the days of shooter champions like Strangler Lewis and Frank Gotch. With Thesz as the face of the NWA, the network had credibility, and a champion that promoters could be proud to present in their territories. Thesz toured through all the regions governed by the NWA, not only defending his title, but unifying it with others as the Alliance made further deals with other promoters to join the fold.

"No one was better for the NWA as world champion than Lou Thesz," says Tim Hornbaker. "To the public, he was the face of pro wrestling and he was an admirable sportsman. Without Thesz, the NWA would never have succeeded in terms of respect and visibility."

On July 27, 1950, he bested AWA World Champion Gorgeous George in Boston, putting to rest that version of the title. On May 21, 1952, he toppled Baron Michele Leone in Hollywood's Gilmore Baseball Park, ending Leone's claim to the world title. That particular encounter, presented by L.A. promoters Cal Eaton and Johnny Doyle, drew 25,256 fans (with thousands turned away), and professional wrestling's first $100,000 gate. Thesz even helped take the NWA international when he traveled to Japan to face Japanese Wrestling Association champion Rikidozan on October 13, 1957, in a match that remains the single-highest-rated TV program in Japanese history. The NWA would retain ties with the JWA, and later with All-Japan Pro Wrestling. It was a classic example of the NWA's consolidation of power with Thesz as champ.

"Thesz looked and acted the champion, and wrestling gained respect having him as a representative," says noted wrestling historian Steve Yohe. "Wrestling went into a slump in 1955 and the government almost killed it in 1956. Without Thesz it did poorly, until Buddy Rogers became champion. The greatest compliment in wrestling history took place when the NWA asked Thesz to return and win the title back from Rogers in 1963."

The Feds Come Calling

The mid-1950s brought the NWA its first wave of major tribulations, and challenges to its absolute power; the remainder of the decade would get rocky. A number of individuals who felt slighted by the promotional conglomerate, including California promoter Nick Lutze, who felt targeted by NWA members in his home state; former World Champion Stanislaus Zbyszko, displeased at what he felt the NWA was doing to his beloved sport; and former Women's Champion Mildred Burke, who took issue with her ex-husband, the NWA's supplier of female wrestlers, began to complain to the federal government about what they saw as monopolistic practices. Federal investigators looked into whether the Alliance was blackballing noncompliant performers and preventing non-NWA promoters from earning a living. The blackball issue was compounded by the plight of one Harold "Sonny" Myers, a popular NWA-booked wrestler who found himself out in the cold when he refused to kick back royalties to the NWA for events he was promoting independently.

The NWA was shepherded through these difficult times by Sam Muchnick, the St. Louis impresario who had helped found the group and who, for the better part of twenty-five years, served as its president. Muchnick's connections to the "legit" sports community and his background as a sportswriter inspired him to make pro wrestling as respectable as possible under his watch. He affirmed St. Louis as the "home town" of the NWA, effectively shifting the power away from founder Pinkie George (in response, George would resign from the NWA in 1959). He also did his best to corral and placate the many warring factions which constantly threatened to tear the NWA apart, both from without and from within. Booking control of the NWA World Champion Lou Thesz certainly didn't hurt, either.

"Sam Muchnick was the number-one reason the NWA was successful," states Hornbaker. "He was the perfect leader for the Alliance and maintained the organization's structure in spite of fellow members basically doing everything possible to undermine him. He held them all together, and really kept the NWA going through thick and thin. It was unbelievable the way he preserved the Alliance during the government's investigation in the 1950s."

From his desk at the offices of the St. Louis Wrestling Club, Sam Muchnick presided over the National Wrestling Alliance during most of the 1950s, '60s, and '70s.
Jack Pfefer Collection, University of Notre Dame

Using connections in the U.S. justice system, as well as his own skills as a diplomat, Muchnick helped the NWA survive a federal anti-trust suit, as well as Myers's allegations of blacklisting. As part of the deal, the NWA agreed to loosen up its tyrannical practices, allowing wrestlers to perform for non-affiliated companies and relinquishing their self-declared rights to territorial exclusivity. The Alliance would continue to dominate the business, but some wiggle room had been made for outside forces to gain momentum.

A Shared Playing Field

In June 1957, a plan was devised to have Thesz drop his NWA World Championship to French-Canadian Edouard Carpentier, only to have some promoters dispute the title change, leading to a series of lucrative title unification matches around the horn. But the plan went awry when things got a little too "real": Promoters who had been lying in wait to double-cross the NWA decided to use the "disputed" title loss as an excuse to sever ties with the NWA and recognize Carpentier as their own champion. What had started as a scripted storyline turned into reality, as Thesz's long-running status as undisputed champion was shaken. The pattern continued in

1960 when Verne Gagne bought out Minneapolis promoter Tony Stecher and decided to secede from the NWA, forming the American Wrestling Association and crowning himself as its champion. Gagne further cemented his claim by defeating renegade champ Carpentier shortly thereafter.

Another group making waves was Capitol Wrestling, a Northeastern combine headed by promoter Vincent James McMahon and matchmaker Toots Mondt. With Madison Square Garden as its home base, the Capitol group had a lot of power in the NWA, and a new inter-promotional deal made with Fred Kohler's Chicago territory only strengthened them further. Kohler had lost momentum since losing his national TV deal, but became a player in the NWA once again, thanks to his connection to New York. Through Kohler, McMahon and company also gained control of long-running NWA United States Champion "Nature Boy" Buddy Rogers, originally a Kohler creation.

The rising power of McMahon was evident when he was able to push Rogers all the way to the NWA World Championship. The match occurred on Kohler's home turf, in Chicago's historic Comiskey Park before a record-shattering 38,622 fans who witnessed the Nature Boy take the crown from New Zealander Pat O'Connor. In an unprecedented move, the match was even broadcast live on television. It would be the single-most-watched pro wrestling match in U.S. history up to that time, and the attendance record would stand for a quarter of a century.

But NWA promoters were soon rankled at McMahon's growing power, made worse by his hesitancy to share Rogers with the rest of the territories. The decision was made to bring Thesz out of retirement to take the prize back from the Nature Boy in January 1963, a maneuver that led Capitol Sports to secede from the NWA and form the World Wide Wrestling Federation, recognizing Rogers as its first world champion.

The NWA's once-uncontested North American dominance was now contested, and would remain so. During the 1960s and '70s, the Alliance would have to share the playing field with the AWA and the WWWF, which continued to promote their own talent and recognize their own world champions. Nevertheless, the NWA remained the major power in the business, with control over the majority of the landscape; despite their secessions, the AWA and WWWF continued to work with the Alliance, and even attended the annual conventions and aided in the decision making, perhaps a nod to the NWA's superiority as a network that outranked any one organization.

The Times, They Are a-Changin'

Post-Thesz, the NWA carefully protected its World Heavyweight title, bestowing it to tough, rugged, credible athletes like Alberta, Canada's Gene

The classic World Heavyweight Championship belt used by the NWA from 1973 through 1985, at which time it was replaced by the "Big Gold Belt."

Simon from United Kingdom / Wikimedia

Kiniski; second-generation standout from Amarillo, Texas, Dory Funk Jr.; and the movie-star-handsome NCAA National Wrestling Champion from Oklahoma State, Jack Brisco. Wrestling territories had become more distinct than ever, each with their own local TV programming and roster of stars—but the arrival of the NWA World Heavyweight Champion was still a major event, and local performers stood to get instant legitimacy (known as "the rub") just by going toe-to-toe with the titleholder, whether they won the belt or not.

Muchnick finally stepped down as NWA president in 1975. It was a time of flux, as the wrestling industry became more sensationalized and more localized than ever. The NWA World Championship, rather than being the undisputed symbol of excellence in the business, became more of a prop to help build regional talent. A new booking strategy took hold with the ascension of Harley Race, a working-class tough guy heel who would go on to hold the NWA World Heavyweight title a record-setting eight times. Now, the approach would be to have the heel champion tour the territories, being chased by the local babyfaces as the crowd prayed for the villainous titleholder to finally lose. And this occurred often, as Race dropped his gold to the likes of Brisco, Dory's brother Terry Funk, Georgia's rookie sensation Tommy "Wildfire" Rich, even Japan's Giant Baba. Another change in the NWA philosophy occurred with Race's loss of the NWA World title to Florida's Dusty Rhodes, a rotund, flamboyant performer whose claim to fame was not the classic appearance and real wrestling skill of past NWA champions, but rather his color, charisma, and popularity. It was a sign of the times, as the NWA gave up its past pretense toward "legitimizing" pro wrestling.

Crockett Takes Control

By the beginning of the 1980s, the NWA's power base had shifted to the Mid-Atlantic territory operated by Jim Crockett, Jr.'s Crockett Promotions. Just as McMahon and Kohler had done with the original Nature Boy, Crockett had his own Nature Boy, Ric Flair, whom he elevated to NWA World Champion status for the first time, in 1981. Under Crockett's watch, Flair would come to dominate the title during the 1980s, its final years as a major championship. Seeing changes afoot as Vincent K. McMahon, son of Capitol/WWF founder Vincent James McMahon, began targeting the NWA's territorial system in a move to take his company national, Crockett started consolidating his own power.

With the NWA's long-running status as a conglomerate of wrestling promotions in danger, Crockett began to monopolize the NWA "brand," often referring to his product simply as "NWA Wrestling." To newer fans, he even gave the impression that the NWA only referred to his own organization. And more and more, this was becoming true, as Crockett began swallowing up other regional groups. By the mid-1980s, the NWA World title was hardly even being defended outside of Crockett's territory, as Flair began to work exclusively for Crockett. By the end of the 1980s, the NWA's territorial system had been destroyed by the WWF, and Crockett had morphed into Ted Turner's World Championship Wrestling.

WCW continued doing business with the NWA for a few years, but after a title dispute with Ric Flair that occurred when Flair jumped ship to the WWF with his NWA World title belt in 1991, causing the NWA to strip him of champion status, the once-glorious NWA World Championship was regarded as a secondary title by WCW, which now had its own independent world championship. In 1993, WCW permanently severed ties with the NWA, leaving the group weaker than ever, and without a national platform.

Surviving Post-WCW

Under the leadership of promoters like Howard Brody and Dennis Coralluzzo, the NWA tried to regroup, forming a partnership with ECW, then becoming the most popular indy league in America. But ECW honcho Paul Heyman wanted no part of the group, and masterminded a humiliating double-cross in which ECW star Shane Douglas, having won the NWA World title in a tournament, threw the belt to the ground and relinquished it, verbally denigrating the neutered NWA in the process. Reeling, the NWA was forced to limp on as a group of regional independent promoters without national television. Former UFC Champion and legit tough guy Dan Severn, a throwback to the NWA World Champions of old, saved them some face as titleholder for a few years, but it was clear the glory days were over.

The NWA enjoyed just one more moment in the sun in 2002 when it cut a co-promotional deal with newly formed company TNA Wrestling, which saw the NWA World Heavyweight title (and World Tag Team title) return to national television. However, TNA soon grew tired of being associated with the devalued NWA name, and canceled its membership in the organization in 2005. (TNA retained use of the NWA World title until 2007.)

Today, the NWA is once again a loose organization made up of local independent groups, including Georgia-based NWA Wildside, David Marquez's Championship Wrestling from Hollywood, and others. Legal wrangling over the rights to the NWA name have threatened to sink the network once and for all, and recent rumors of turning the NWA into a franchising organization have only added to the controversy. With WWE now ruling the roost in the wrestling business, there no longer seems to be a place on the national stage for the once-great and powerful NWA. Nevertheless, for wrestling historians and history-minded fans, those three letters will always inspire awe and reverence. They will always mean something special.

THE BEST IN THE BUSINESS
A Look at Some of the Great NWA World Champions

Lou Thesz

Born Lajos Tiza on April 24, 1916, Aloysius Martin "Lou" Thesz was the champion's champion. Debuting in the 1930s in the St. Louis territory he would always call home, Thesz would eventually win a record-setting six World Heavyweight Championships over the course of his career, three of those under the auspices of the National Wrestling Alliance.

Trained by renowned "hooker" George Tragos, Thesz possessed the genuine ability that had once been essential to professional wrestling in the days of earlier champions like Ed "Strangler" Lewis, who would go on to become his mentor and best friend. This quality was highly respected by the old-school NWA promoters, and Thesz was talented enough as an athlete and as an astute businessman who allowed no one to take advantage of him. He called the shots wherever he went, and made the NWA title into the undisputed heavyweight wrestling championship of the world. His initial NWA reign, from 1948 to 1956, comprises the NWA's most powerful era, and remains one of the longest World title reigns in the history of the business.

"Lou not only had great wrestling coaches, he had phenomenal business coaches: Ed 'Strangler' Lewis and Ray Steele," explains Thesz's widow, Catherine

Thesz, during his final reign as NWA World Champion, in the mid-1960s.
Jack Pfefer Collection, University of Notre Dame

"Charlie" Thesz. "They taught him his value, and he was champion so long because he was a credible champion that all the promoters agreed on. So they would get mad at him because he wanted what was fair. They would get rid of him, but then they'd come back, hat in hand."

Thesz tired of the wear and tear of being champion, and finally convinced promoters to let him lose the title to Whipper Billy Watson in 1956. Those promoters kept coaxing him back, however, and he'd recapture the gold in 1957 and in 1963, losing it for the final time in 1966 to Gene Kiniski. Of course, for a wrestler of the caliber of Lou Thesz, who could defeat just about anyone anytime he wanted to, losing had to be on *his* terms.

As the business moved further and further away from wrestling fundamentals and more toward performance, Thesz became disillusioned with it. Nevertheless, he remained in top physical condition, and even came back for one last match, at the advanced age of seventy-four, against Japanese protégé Masahiro Chono in 1990. He helped to found the George Tragos/Lou Thesz Professional Wrestling Hall of Fame in 1999, and just three years later, on April 28, 2002, Lou Thesz passed away at the age of eighty-six.

"It always amazed me that while he was saddened and sometimes disgusted by the way things were going, he respected the boys' right to have their own era," says Charlie. "A lot of the older guys resented it, and railed against it. But I think Lou felt like he'd had his moment, and he'd done what he thought should be done, and it wasn't his position to tell these guys how they should run their business. Lou had done it all, and he did it all his way. But he realized that his time had passed."

Pat O'Connor

Born Patrick John O'Connor on August 22, 1924, in Raetihi, New Zealand, this amateur standout represented his country as a wrestler in the 1948 Pan American

Games, and captured New Zealand's amateur heavyweight title in 1949 and 1950; he also competed in the 1950 British Empire Games.

As a professional, he rose through the ranks, working for such NWA promoters as Mid-Atlantic's Jim Crockett and St. Louis's Sam Muchnick. It was Muchnick, in fact, who helped propel him to the NWA World Championship, with a January 9, 1959, win over Dick Hutton. Chicago promoter Fred Kohler balked at the move, claiming that he had not been consulted, and, for a time, prevented O'Connor from working in his city. Nevertheless, when it came time for O'Connor to lose the title two years later to Buddy Rogers, it was Kohler who hosted the match at Comiskey Park.

O'Connor was part of a group of promoters who purchased the St. Louis territory from his retiring mentor Muchnick in 1982. He passed away on August 16, 1990, at age sixty-five, after a battle with cancer. In his honor, the NWA presented the Pat O'Connor Memorial Cup International Tag Team Tournament at WCW's *Starrcade '90* event that December.

Gene Kiniski

Dubbed "Canada's Greatest Athlete" a generation before Iron Mike Sharpe co-opted that title, Kiniski was one in a long line of performers (including Gus Sonnenberg and Bronko Nagurski) who made the transition from football to wrestling. Born Eugene Nicholas Kiniski on November 23, 1928, outside Edmonton, Alberta, to Polish immigrants, he was a stellar high school athlete on both the gridiron and the wrestling mat. He was playing for the University of Arizona when he was recruited to the professional ranks by Arizona promoter Rod Fenton in 1952.

Trained by Dory Funk, Sr., the massive Kiniski became an instant contender for the NWA World Championship, perennially challenging such titleholders as Lou Thesz, Whipper Billy Watson, Dick Hutton, Pat O'Connor, and Buddy Rogers. In 1961, during a stint in the Midwest, he captured the AWA World Championship from Verne Gagne (this would eventually make him the only wrestler to hold both the AWA and NWA titles).

In St. Louis's fabled Kiel Auditorium, he achieved the pinnacle of his career, ending Thesz's final reign as NWA World Champion on January 7, 1966. He would hold the title for over three years, only the second NWA World Champion after Rogers to work as a heel. Finally, an exhausted Kiniski dropped the gold to Dory Funk, Jr., in Tampa on February 11, 1969.

In November 1983, he refereed the famous steel cage NWA World title match between Harley Race and Ric Flair at the original *Starrcade*. He retired for good in 1992, and died of brain cancer at his home in Blaine, Washington, on April 14, 2010. He was eighty-one.

Dory Funk, Jr.

Funk as a rookie, fresh out of West Texas State, c. 1963.
Jack Pfefer Collection, University of Notre Dame

Born Dorrance Earnest Funk, Jr., on February 3, 1941, in Hammond, Indiana, this second-generation performer was destined for the business. His father, Dory Funk, Sr., had been a major star in the Texas area, running the Amarillo territory since the younger Dory was just a teenager. After a successful college football career at West Texas State University, he debuted for his father's promotion in January 1963.

By the end of 1960s, Dory Funk, Jr., was high on the NWA's radar, and was finally selected to be the one to dethrone long-running World Champion Gene Kiniski on February 11, 1969, in Tampa, using his dreaded spinning toe-hold. Funk's reign would last four and a half years, making it the second-longest NWA title reign behind Thesz, and only the sixth-longest World Heavyweight title reign of any kind in the history of the business. A cleancut, soft-spoken, no-nonsense babyface, Funk as champion was a throwback to the respectable days of Thesz and O'Connor, and he did the NWA proud until finally losing to Harley Race in Kansas City on May 24, 1973.

Funk later enjoyed a run with his younger brother Terry in the mid-1980s heyday of the WWF, and in the 1990s he operated the Funking Dojo training camp for the WWF, producing such performers as Kurt Angle and The Hardy Boyz. Dory Funk, Jr.'s school, the Funking Conservatory, continues to train aspiring wrestlers, and also produces the Florida-based independent promotion known as !BANG!

Harley Race

A tough street fighter from Quitman, Missouri, Harley Leland Race was born April 11, 1943. After being kicked out of high school for scuffling with a teacher, Race chose a career in pro wrestling, receiving training from early twentieth-century legends Stanislaus and Wladek Zbyszko, who owned a nearby ranch.

After surviving a devastating car accident at age twenty that killed his pregnant wife and nearly severed his leg, Race returned to the ring in 1964. He made a name for himself as tag team partner of Larry Hennig in the AWA, and was a dependable wrestler in many NWA territories. In May 1973, Race was selected to take the NWA World Championship from long-reigning champ Dory Funk, Jr., in Kansas City; rumors abounded that Funk refused to drop the belt to the popular Jack Brisco and had been faking injury. Race was brought in to act as a transitional champion, losing the prize to Brisco in Houston two months later.

But that reign would be no fluke. Race would dominate the title in the late 1970s, finally regaining it from Dory's brother Terry in Toronto on February 6, 1977, and holding it for much of the next four years. Doing business whenever asked, he would occasionally lose his title, only to win it back until he amassed a record eight NWA World Championships. One of the hardest-working champions in the ring, he defended his title almost every night in marathon-length matches. He ultimately passed the

Race dominated the NWA World Championship in the late 1970s.   *Photo by Terry Dart*

torch to Ric Flair in a bloody steel cage match at *Starrcade '83* in Greensboro, North Carolina.

Jack Brisco

He was born Freddie Joe Brisco in Seminole, Oklahoma, on September 21, 1941, and was raised in the nearby town of Blackwell, along with his five siblings (including his brother Jerry, who would also become a successful wrestler). He attended Oklahoma State, where he became the first Native American to win the NCAA National Wrestling Championship in 1965. Later that year, he transitioned to the professional ranks.

A pure wrestler of great skill, Brisco is believed to have been second only to Thesz in shooting ability among NWA World Champions, and was unquestionably the most accomplished amateur wrestler to capture the prize. That designation came on July 20, 1973, when he defeated Harley Race in Houston on the same night that a brand new version of the belt was presented by NWA President Sam Muchnick. He had originally been scheduled to take the gold from Dory Funk, Jr., with whom he had been competing for years in one of the most fondly remembered "pure wrestling" rivalries.

Brisco dropped the title briefly to Giant Baba in December 1974 as part of an agreement with Baba's All-Japan promotion, and, after taking it back, would continue to hold it for another year until finally losing it to Dory's younger brother Terry on December 10, 1975.

Jack Brisco wrestled another nine years before appearing in his last match, teaming with his brother Jerry in a WWF World Tag Team title bout in Madison Square Garden. He operated the famous Brisco Brothers Body Shop in Florida for thirty years, and died on February 1, 2010, at age sixty-eight, due to complications from open-heart surgery.

For other prominent NWA World Champions, see Chapter 5 (Buddy Rogers), Chapter 6 (Dusty Rhodes), Chapter 7 (Ric Flair), and Chapter 19 (Terry Funk).

What the World Is Watching

WWE, Wrestling's Most Powerful Empire

It is not enough to succeed. Others must fail.

—Gore Vidal

From a regional promotion based in the northeastern United States, it grew to become the ultimate entity in the wrestling business, spreading out on a global scale and taking a product that was once based on arena ticket sales and making it a merchandising and media powerhouse. Formerly known as the WWF but now known as WWE, it is the most powerful force in the industry—so much so that it has even sought to rename the industry itself, rebranding professional wrestling as "sports-entertainment." Whatever you call it, the industry is currently defined by one extremely powerful and influential organization, and has been since the century began. What Coca-Cola is to soft drinks, what Disney is to animation, what McDonalds is to fast food, WWE is to pro wrestling.

The McMahon Dynasty

The story of WWE is the story of a family. It was Vincent James McMahon who founded it in the 1950s; Vincent Kennedy McMahon, who reinvented it as "sports-entertainment" in the 1980s; and now, the new generation of Stephanie McMahon Levesque and her husband, Paul "Triple H" Levesque, is poised to take the entertainment juggernaut well into the twenty-first century. All told, the McMahon family encompasses four generations (thus far) of wrestling impresarios, an involvement in the wrestling business that dates back over eighty years, and an involvement in the promotions business that dates back close to a century.

First Generation

It all starts with Roderick James "Jess" McMahon, who was born in New York City on May 26, 1882, the youngest of four children, to Roderick and Elizabeth McMahon, recently emigrated from Galway, Ireland. Along with his older brother Eddie, Jess McMahon decided to take his degree from Manhattan College and go into the promotions business in the early 1900s, taking over managerial duties at venues throughout Manhattan. Boxing was, first and foremost, what he promoted, but he was also a pioneer in black baseball, founding such early Negro League teams as the New York Lincoln Giants. Disappointed in what he perceived as the corrupt business his children had entered, Roderick the elder disowned his two sons, leaving everything to his daughters, Lauretta and Catharine.

This unfortunate turn of events didn't deter Jess McMahon. He went on to become the matchmaker for top New York boxing promoter Tex Rickard, and was involved in the promotion of the 1915 battle between heavyweight champ Jack Johnson and "Great White Hope" Jess Willard in Havana, Cuba. Rickard and McMahon also opened up the newly constructed reincarnation of Madison Square Garden to boxing in 1925 with a light heavyweight clash between Jack Delaney and "Astoria Assassin" Paul Berlenbach.

Although Rickard himself disapproved of pro wrestling, Jess had no such qualms, and in 1932 started presenting cards at the Municipal Stadium on Long Island. For twenty years, he was a trusted associate of such New York wrestling kingpins as Jack Curley, Rudy Dusek, and Toots Mondt, booking their talent regularly for his shows. On November 22, 1954, while in Wilkes-Barre, Pennsylvania, to oversee an event, he died in his sleep at the age of seventy-two.

Second Generation

Jess may have made a good living dabbling in wrestling promotions, but his son would take it to another level. Vincent James McMahon was born to Jess and his wife, Rose, on July 6, 1915, in Harlem, New York, although the family relocated to the Far Rockaway section of Queens when he was a boy. The child grew up around the great sports stars and promotion figures of the 1920s, as his dad regularly took him backstage with him at the Garden, a place that would remain special to him throughout his life. By 1935, Jess had set his twenty-year-old son up with his own office in Hempstead, Long Island, where he promoted boxing, wrestling and music concerts.

Following World War II, Vincent J. McMahon relocated to Washington, D.C., where he hoped to set up his own wrestling fiefdom far away from those like Mondt and Dusek, who controlled the game in New York. He

Vince McMahon "Senior," seen here literally wielding the pencil. This photo was prominently featured in the opening montage of WWE programming in recent years.   *Photo by* Pro Wrestling Illustrated

purchased Turner's Arena from the widow of local promoter Joe Turner, renamed it Capitol Arena, and began presenting regular events there under the banner of Capitol Wrestling, with the first being held on January 7, 1953. Understanding the importance of television from the start, he was able to convince DC DuMont Network affiliate WTTG to begin airing Capitol Wrestling in 1956, and it eventually infiltrated New York. When Mondt had his promoter's license temporarily suspended, Vince seized the opening to present his first show at Madison Square Garden; before long, he and Mondt had partnered to control much of wrestling in the Northeast, with additional TV shows airing from Bridgeport, Connecticut, and the Sunnyside Gardens in Queens.

The Capitol Wrestling Corporation became so powerful that, in 1963, Vince J. McMahon was able to declare independence from the NWA and establish his product under the name of the World Wide Wrestling Federation. Spreading into Boston after the death of longtime beantown impresario Paul Bowser, Vince's WWWF next expanded through all of New England. With Bruno Sammartino as his top attraction, he turned the WWWF into arguably the most successful wrestling territory in the United States throughout much of the 1960s, '70s, and early '80s. On May 27, 1984, he died at the age of sixty-eight, following a four-month battle with pancreatic cancer.

Third Generation

Just as Vincent James McMahon had exceeded his father's accomplishments in the business, so would his own son exceed his. While stationed with the Coast Guard in North Carolina during World War II, Vincent J. McMahon had met and married a waitress named Vicky Askew, who bore a son, Vincent Kennedy McMahon (often erroneously called "Vince Jr."), born on August 24, 1945. Unfortunately, the marriage did not last long, and the younger

Vince was raised by his mother and an abusive stepfather, Leo Lupton. He wouldn't be reacquainted with his birth father until the age of nine, and began regularly spending time with him and his new wife, Juanita, in his teenage years, getting his first taste of the business by following his dad around, just as his dad had once done. (In 1961, sixteen-year-old Vince was present for the famous Comiskey Park match between Pat O'Connor and Buddy Rogers, an event that left a strong impression on him.)

By the 1960s, he had changed his name from Vince Lupton to Vince McMahon, and was living with his father full-time. Attempting a career as a traveling salesman after getting a business degree from East Carolina University, in 1969 he was finally given a ring announcer position by his father on the WWWF program *All-Star Wrestling*. Although "Vince Sr." was reluctant to have his son work in the business, "Vince Jr."

Vince McMahon "Junior," here seen during one of WWE's annual tours of U.S. Army bases for the *Tribute to the Troops* show.

Airman 1st Class Nicholas Pilch, U.S. Air Force

took to it right away, replacing regular WWWF play-by-play announcer Ray Morgan in 1971 and starting out with his own small satellite promotion in Maine. He helped his father broaden TV syndication rights, and pushed for the brand name to be shortened to WWF. He purchased the Cape Cod Coliseum in 1979 and began promoting concerts and other events there under the banner of his own company, TitanSports.

In 1982, Vincent K. McMahon purchased the Capitol Wrestling Corporation from his father and his father's business partners Phil Zacko, Arnold Skaaland, and Robert "Gorilla Monsoon" Marella (to whom the elder McMahon had sold Toots Mondt's piece of the company after Toots retired in 1969). He then promptly set to work transforming the regional WWF into a national organization. With crossover sensation Hulk Hogan leading the way, he made the WWF into a household name and eclipsed nearly all other pro wrestling groups over the course of the 1980s. He pioneered pro wrestling on pay-per-view television, and made *WrestleMania* into the industry's number-one yearly event. By the end of the 1990s, he even went so far as to do something his father would never have dreamt of doing: playing a part in WWF storylines as the evil "Mr. McMahon" character during a time when the company reached greater heights than ever during its so-called "Attitude Era."

"There was consistent leadership at the top," says announcer Kevin Kelly of his experience working for Vince in the late '90s/early '00s. "There was one point of contact. All decisions end with Vince. . . . Not every decision he made was good or right, but at least the company had its center. So even though Vince would change his mind often, there would be a consistent person that everybody looked to for guidance. We just had to figure out which way he was pointing that day."

Vince McMahon took his company public in 1999, making himself a billionaire in the process, and before long he had also put his only remaining rivals, WCW and ECW, totally out of business. Although forced to change the company name yet again to WWE as a result of legal threats from the World Wildlife Fund, he continued to build his organization into a worldwide phenomenon. He also branched out into other business ventures, including motion picture production, a recording label, and, most recently, a streaming WWE Network that may just redefine the business yet again. Although his on-air role has diminished, he remains the guiding force of WWE.

"He was a guy who had a lot of drive, and he was real smart and saw things other people didn't see," says journalist Dave Meltzer of the *Wrestling Observer*. "Sometimes he was wrong. But he had a vision of what he wanted wrestling to be. I think he wanted to be a lot more than just a wrestling promoter, and I think in that sense he didn't fully achieve his dream."

Fourth Generation

While attending church in his native North Carolina at age sixteen, Vince met the woman he would marry five years later, in 1966: Linda Edwards. The young couple struggled in the early years before Vince found steady work

The latest generation of the McMahon family to step into a leadership role with WWE, Stephanie is the heir apparent to that wrestling dynasty.

Mshake3/Wikimedia

in his father's company, but then were finally able to settle down and have children: a son, Shane, born January 15, 1970, and a daughter, Stephanie, born September 24, 1976.

Shane and Stephanie would go on to help their father in different ways. Shane paid his dues from an early age by working in the company warehouse, on the ring crew, and even as a referee, before taking on an administrative role at his father's side after graduating Boston University. He would take over the company's newly created digital media department in 1998, and, eventually, was put in charge of print media as well. He was also taking an on-air role as the daredevil performer affectionately called "Shane-O Mac," known for putting his body on the line in hair-raising matches. He later took on an exclusively behind-the-scenes role, spearheading broader international TV distribution rights before departing the company in 2010 to start his own company called YOU On Demand, China's largest supplier of pay-per-view movies.

Starting as a receptionist after her own Boston University graduation in 1998, Stephanie would eventually head WWE's creative department in 2002, charting the direction of all on-air characters and storylines. Originally linked to wrestler Paul "Triple H" Levesque as part of a 2000 storyline, the two became romantically involved in real life, and eventually married in 2003. Today, she serves as chief brand officer of WWE. She and Triple H, who is now an executive vice president, currently supervise not only on-air creative, but also talent development, live event booking, marketing, and much more. Their backstage role was recently amplified by an on-air one in which they portrayed The Authority, a power-mad couple that ruled over WWE with a tyrannical vengeance.

Seats of Power

From the establishment of Capitol Wrestling in 1953 to modern-day WWE, the company has been headquartered in various locations, including:

- Franklin Park Hotel: A historic art deco tower in downtown Washington, D.C., at 1332 I Street N.W., the seventh floor of which housed the original Capitol Wrestling Corporation offices in the 1950s and '60s.
- Holland Hotel: At 351 West 42nd in the heart of Manhattan (and a stone's throw from Madison Square Garden), the WWWF had its main office here from 1971 until "Vince Sr." sold the company to his son in 1982.
- Greenwich, Connecticut: After running TitanSports out of the Cape Cod Coliseum in South Yarmouth, Massachusetts, Vince and Linda McMahon relocated to 81 Holly Hill Lane in their new home town.
- Stamford, Connecticut: Following the success of *WrestleMania* in 1985, the WWF main offices were moved to the heart of one of the state's biggest cities, at 1055 Summer Street.
- Titan Tower: In April 1991, the company settled into the $10 million, four-story complex it calls home to this very day, a gleaming cube of steel and glass at 1241 East Main Street in Stamford, overlooking I-95. There is also a state-of-the-art TV studio around the corner, at 120 Hamilton Avenue. The company currently maintains branch offices in Miami, London, and Singapore. WWE's music division is headquartered in New York City, and WWE Studios, its film division, resides in Los Angeles.

Promotional Partners

Back in the territorial days, when the (W)WWF ruled the Northeastern United States, there was a whole cast of localized promoters who worked under the McMahons, running local shows in their designated sub-regions using talent supplied by the main office. It was a smaller version of what the NWA had been doing nationwide, and this network of promoters helped the WWF to establish its independence from that group and be self-sustaining. Vince himself ran Madison Square Garden, but here are a few of the others and their respective turf:

- Arnold Skaaland: White Plains, New York
- Willie Gilzenberg: Northern New Jersey (also the WWWF's figurehead president)
- Phil Zacko: The most powerful of McMahon's lieutenants, with control over eastern Pennsylvania, D.C., Maryland, and parts of New Jersey. He

also ran the WWWF's weekly TV tapings in Hamburg and Allentown, Pennsylvania.

- Tommy Dee: Brooklyn and Staten Island, New York
- Tony Santos, Abe Ford, Angelo Savoldi: Massachusetts
- Ray Fabiani: Philadelphia, Pennsylvania
- Rudy Miller: Western Pennsylvania

Ten Pounds of Gold

The WWE World Heavyweight Championship has been in existence, in one form or another, since April 1963, when the WWWF was first formed and recognized former NWA titlist Buddy Rogers as its inaugural titleholder. In the intervening half-century, it has grown to become the most coveted prize in the business and has been held by a veritable who's who of wrestling greats, from Bruno Sammartino to Daniel Bryan. Over that time, it has gone through several transformations:

- Buddy Rogers belt: The original WWWF World title belt was actually the Nature Boy's United States Championship, thus its central medallion was in the shape of the USA.
- Classic Bruno belt: Held by Sammartino during his historic seven-and-a-half-year title reign of the 1960s.
- Mulkavitch "Chicken" belts: Wrestling championships in the 1970s were dominated by the iconic design of Nikita Mulkovich, known for the broad eagle jokingly referred to by fans as a "chicken." The WWWF used at least two versions held by such champs as Pedro Morales, Superstar Billy Graham, and Bob Backlund.
- Big Green belt: When Graham destroyed Backlund's belt in an infamous 1982 angle, this one was introduced, featuring a large round plate on green leather.
- The Hogan belts: The Hulkster held not one, not two, but three different versions during his historic four-year reign. These were the first designed by longtime WWF belt-maker Reggie Parks.
- Winged Eagle belt: Probably the most well-known version of the title, introduced in 1988 for the *WrestleMania IV* championship tournament, and kept around for a decade.
- Big Eagle belt: Much larger than the winged eagle belt, this one was bestowed to Stone Cold Steve Austin after his *WrestleMania XIV* victory in 1998.
- Smoking Skull belt: Wanting something a little more personalized, Stone Cold commissioned a strap with his own signature iconography.

- Undisputed belt: Designed by WWE graphic artist Keith Ciaramello, this version was created for the unification of the WWE and WCW World Heavyweight Championships in 2001. It remained in use even after WWE reactivated the WCW title a year later as a separate title known simply as the "World Heavyweight Championship."
- Spinner belt: To match John Cena's hip-hop persona, this blinged-out strap, complete with spinning center medallion, was introduced in 2005.
- Big Logo belt: After The Rock captured the gold at the *2013 Royal Rumble*, WWE unveiled its boldest design yet, featuring a gigantic WWE logo and side plates that reflect the character of whichever performer currently holds it.

The Face of the Company

Being WWE World Heavyweight Champion is an important responsibility for a performer, and makes him, in many ways, the physical embodiment of WWE. Much thought is put into who gets to wear the coveted crown, as doing so is an overnight ticket to pro wrestling immortality. Here is a rundown of some of the more notable luminaries to hold that distinction over the years:

John Cena sports the spinner belt that was made specifically for him in 2005.   *U.S. Dept. of Defense*

Pedro Morales

The Puerto Rican sensation galvanized New York–area fans with almost as much fervor as his Italian predecessor, Bruno Sammartino, holding the belt for nearly three years after winning it from Ivan Koloff in Madison Square Garden in February 1971. He was known for his fiery temper, and later made a comeback in the early 1980s, becoming the longest-reigning Intercontinental Champion of all time.

Superstar Billy Graham

"The man of the hour, the man with the power, too sweet to be sour," Graham was a performer ahead of his time, possessing dynamic mic skills and a "cool heel" persona that led fans to cheer for him in spite of themselves. His massive, steroid-enhanced physique was also a sign of things to come, and when he toppled Sammartino for the gold in 1977, he looked like nothing fans had seen up to that point.

Bob Backlund

In the entire history of professional wrestling, only Bruno Sammartino, Lou Thesz, and Verne Gagne have enjoyed a World Championship reign longer than that of the All-American Boy, who reigned atop the WWF from 1978 through 1983. An accomplished collegiate grappler, he was one of the finest ring technicians ever to hold the title, and the closest thing WWE ever had to the classic NWA World Champions of yore.

Randy "Macho Man" Savage

Hitting the ring to the strains of "Pomp and Circumstance," the Macho Man was a ball of irresistible energy, rivaling Hulk Hogan for dominance during the WWF's 1980s Golden Age. With the lovely Miss Elizabeth by his side, he won the title in a *WrestleMania IV* tournament and held it for a full year, winning it again three years later. His intense interview style is often imitated, but never duplicated.

Bret "Hit Man" Hart

Just as Hogan and Savage rivaled each other in the '80s, so, too, did Shawn Michaels and the Hit Man in the '90s. Unlike the high-flying Michaels, Hart was a hard-nosed, rugged mat wrestler, trained in the bowels of his father's infamous "Dungeon" in Calgary, Alberta, Canada. Dubbed "The Excellence of Execution," Hart was a master of ring work, and captured the championship five times between 1992 and 1997.

Triple H

With thirteen total World Championships to his credit, there seems to be no stopping "The Cerebral Assassin." It doesn't hurt to be married to the boss's daughter, but that doesn't take away from the palpable desire and

The Hit Man greets fans on his way to defending the WWF World Championship.
Mandy Coombes/Wikimedia

passion that Triple H brings to every in-ring effort. With Stone Cold Steve Austin, The Rock, and Mick Foley, he played an integral part in the forging of the WWF's "Attitude Era." Although he is now an executive officer in WWE, he continues to play an on-air role and can still get the job done between the ropes.

CM Punk

Not many people can get away with calling themselves "The Best in the World," but the Straight-Edge Superstar made it hard to deny during his epic run as WWE Champion from 2011 to '13. In a time when titles switch so frequently, Punk was deemed compelling and talented enough to run with the gold for fourteen months—the longest reign of the past quarter-century. Although he shocked fans by abruptly quitting the business at the start of 2014, insiders feel it is only a matter of time before the pride of Chicago returns.

For more notable WWE World Heavyweight Champions, see Chapter 6 (Bruno Sammartino), Chapter 7 (Hulk Hogan and Shawn Michaels), Chapter 8 (Stone Cold Steve Austin and The Rock), Chapter 15 (Undertaker), and Chapter 26 (John Cena and Randy Orton).

The Crown Jewel of Pay-Per-View

Vince McMahon took a major gamble in 1985, when he funneled all his available funds into a venture that was intended to be the official clarion call for his aggressive national expansion. Signaling a new era in professional wrestling in the process, it was held in the WWF's traditional "home field" of Madison Square Garden and featured mainstream celebrities rubbing elbows with McMahon's performers. Had it been a failure, it most assuredly would have sunk the WWF for good, but instead, its success opened the doors for the growth of the company into the mammoth multimedia giant it is today. Dubbed *WrestleMania* by longtime McMahon employee and legendary ring announcer Howard Finkel, it has gone on to become known as "The Showcase of Immortals"—an annual mega-event that is pro wrestling's answer to the Super Bowl, and so much more. Today, appearing in the main event at *WrestleMania* has arguably become the most coveted achievement in sports-entertainment, surpassing any championship belt.

- *WrestleMania*; March 31, 1985; Madison Square Garden; New York, New York; Hulk Hogan & Mr. T vs. "Rowdy" Roddy Piper & Paul Orndorff
- *WrestleMania 2*; April 7, 1986; Nassau Coliseum, Rosemont Horizon, L.A. Sports Arena; Uniondale, New York, Rosemont, Illinois, Los Angeles, California; Hulk Hogan vs. King Kong Bundy
- *WrestleMania III*; March 29, 1987; Pontiac Silverdome; Pontiac, Michigan; Hulk Hogan vs. Andre the Giant

The 80,676 fans who packed MetLife Stadium for *WrestleMania 29* set an all-time gate record for pro wrestling: $12.3 million.   *Schen Photography/Wikimedia*

- *WrestleMania IV*; March 27, 1988; Trump Plaza; Atlantic City, New Jersey; Hulk Hogan vs. Andre the Giant, Randy Savage vs. Ted Dibiase
- *WrestleMania V*; April 2, 1989; Trump Plaza; Atlantic City, New Jersey; Randy Savage vs. Hulk Hogan
- *WrestleMania VI*; April 1, 1990; SkyDome; Toronto, Ontario; Hulk Hogan vs. Ultimate Warrior
- *WrestleMania VII*; March 24, 1991; L.A. Sports Arena; Los Angeles, California; Sgt. Slaughter vs. Hulk Hogan
- *WrestleMania VIII*; April 5, 1992; Hoosierdome; Indianapolis, Indiana; Hulk Hogan vs. Sid Justice, Ric Flair vs. Randy Savage
- *WrestleMania IX*; April 4, 1993; Caesars Palace; Las Vegas, Nevada; Hulk Hogan & Brutus Beefcake vs. Money, Inc., Bret "Hit Man" Hart vs. Yokozuna
- *WrestleMania X*; March 20, 1994; Madison Square Garden; New York, New York; Yokozuna vs. Lex Luger, Yokozuna vs. Bret "Hit Man" Hart
- *WrestleMania XI*; April 2, 1995; Hartford Civic Center; Hartford, Connecticut; Lawrence Taylor vs. Bam Bam Bigelow, Shawn Michaels vs. Diesel
- *WrestleMania XII*; March 31, 1996; Arrowhead Pond; Anaheim, California; Bret "Hit Man" Hart vs. Shawn Michaels
- *WrestleMania 13*; March 23, 1997; Rosemont Horizon; Rosemont, Illinois; Sycho Sid vs. Undertaker
- *WrestleMania XIV*; March 29, 1998; FleetCenter; Boston, Massachusetts; Shawn Michaels vs. Stone Cold Steve Austin
- *WrestleMania XV*; March 28, 1999; First Union Center; Philadelphia, Pennsylvania; The Rock vs. Stone Cold Steve Austin
- *WrestleMania 2000*; April 2, 2000; Arrowhead Pond; Anaheim, California; Triple H vs. The Rock vs. Big Show vs. Mick Foley
- *WrestleMania X-Seven*; April 1, 2001; Reliant Astrodome; Houston, Texas; The Rock vs. Stone Cold Steve Austin
- *WrestleMania X8*; March 17, 2002; SkyDome; Toronto, Ontario; Hulk Hogan vs. The Rock, Chris Jericho vs. Triple H
- *WrestleMania XIX*; March 20, 2003; Safeco Field; Seattle, Washington; The Rock vs. Stone Cold Steve Austin, Triple H vs. Booker T, Kurt Angle vs. Brock Lesnar
- *WrestleMania XX*; March 14, 2004; Madison Square Garden; New York, New York; Triple H vs. Shawn Michaels vs. Chris Benoit, Eddie Guerrero vs. Kurt Angle
- *WrestleMania 21*; April 3, 2005; Staples Center; Los Angeles, California; Triple H vs. Batista, John "Bradshaw" Layfield vs. John Cena
- *WrestleMania 22*; April 2, 2006; Allstate Arena; Rosemont, Illinois; John Cena vs. Triple H, Kurt Angle vs. Rey Mysterio vs. Randy Orton

- *WrestleMania 23*; April 1, 2007; Ford Field; Detroit, Michigan; Bobby Lashley vs. Umaga, John Cena vs. Shawn Michaels, Batista vs. Undertaker
- *WrestleMania XXIV*; March 30, 2008; Citrus Bowl; Orlando, Florida; Big Show vs. Floyd Mayweather, Jr., Randy Orton vs. Triple H vs. John Cena, Edge vs. Undertaker
- *WrestleMania 25th Anniversary*; April 5, 2009; Reliant Stadium; Houston, Texas; Triple H vs. Randy Orton, Edge vs. John Cena vs. Big Show
- *WrestleMania XXVI*; March 28, 2010; University of Phoenix Stadium; Glendale, Arizona; Batista vs. John Cena, Chris Jericho vs. Edge
- *WrestleMania XXVII*; April 3, 2011; Georgia Dome; Atlanta, Georgia; Edge vs. Alberto Del Rio, The Miz vs. John Cena
- *WrestleMania XXVIII*; April 1, 2012; Sun Life Stadium; Miami, Florida; The Rock vs. John Cena, CM Punk vs. Chris Jericho, Daniel Bryan vs. Sheamus
- *WrestleMania 29*; April 7, 2013; MetLife Stadium; East Rutherford, New Jersey; The Rock vs. John Cena, Alberto Del Rio vs. Jack Swagger
- *WrestleMania XXX*; April 6, 2014; Superdome; New Orleans, Louisiana; Randy Orton vs. Daniel Bryan vs. Batista
- *WrestleMania 31*; March 29, 2015; Levi's Stadium; Santa Clara, California

The Most Powerful Person in WWE You've Never Heard Of

Behind the scenes in the world's largest pro wrestling organization, there is arguably no one, with the exception of Vince McMahon himself, with as much influence as Kevin Dunn, executive vice president of television production. Since the late 1980s, when the WWF brought all of its TV production in-house for the first time, Dunn has been the man in control, directing all programming and helping to shape the company's entire vision. Although he keeps a notoriously low profile to the public, so integral a part has Dunn played in the growth of WWE's TV product that he has, for years, been Vince McMahon's most trusted associate, and is believed to have the chairman's ear like no one else.

The relationship between the Dunns and McMahons actually goes back a generation, as it was Kevin's father, Dennis Dunn, who supervised TV production for Vince's father back in the 1970s and early '80s. A legendary tale is told of how the elder Dunn once saved weeks' worth of TV film footage from a car fire, cementing the bond between the two families with his valiant act. As a result, the younger Dunn was first hired by Vince McMahon in 1984 and played a role in the early days of the WWF's national expansion before completely taking over the director/producer reins at the end of the '80s.

Crucial to the developmental of WWE's impressive production values and the overall look and feel of the television product, Dunn shapes what we see each and every week. Known as a hard taskmaster who expects excellence from his staff, he is infamous for barking orders to production crewmembers over their headsets. He is considered pivotal to the transformation of pro wrestling into sports-entertainment, and his controversial philosophies about the business have made him unpopular with some old school purists—most vocally, longtime manager and creative consultant Jim Cornette—who believe that Dunn views traditional notions about wrestling with disdain.

12

Lucha Libre

A Proud Mexican Tradition

In a society like Mexico there is the need for cultural heroes, the idea of someone who is going to avenge the wrongs of the world.
—Dr. David William Foster, Arizona State University

South of the border, there is a very different brand of professional wrestling, which, in recent years, has encroached more and more on the mainstream American consciousness. With its origins in the early twentieth century, the Mexican style of wrestling called *lucha libre* is known for its exotic masked performers, wild tag-team encounters, and innovative high-flying maneuvers. The international *lucha* phenomenon really began with the Lutteroth family, who founded Mexico's (and the world's) oldest wrestling company. Major luminaries of *lucha libre* such as El Santo, Blue Demon, Mil Mascaras, Perro Aguayo, Rey Mysterio, and Mistico have become cultural icons in their native country, and the mystique of the mask in *lucha* culture has taken on almost sacred proportions.

Much more surreal and stylized than its American counterpart—some would even say more cartoonish—*lucha libre* presents professional wrestlers as comic-book superheroes come to life. In recent decades, *lucha* iconography has even taken on something of the mythic, with the mask itself becoming a visual cue for Mexican culture in general. Nearly as popular in Mexico as pro sports like soccer and baseball, *lucha libre* is a breed apart from American pro wrestling. Nevertheless, its fast-paced, high-energy and high-risk style has infiltrated U.S. rings in recent years, as *luchadores* have traveled north, and as American grapplers have also adapted some of their signature maneuvers.

The Godfather of *Lucha Libre*

There is evidence that pro wrestling in Mexico goes back nearly as far as it does in the U.S., all the way back to the late-nineteenth century. In the early twentieth century, Italian entrepreneurs Giovanni Reselevich and Antonio

Fournier achieved some success promoting a style of combat sport they first referred to as "*lucha libre*," translated as "freestyle wrestling." But it wouldn't really be until the 1930s that *lucha libre* first took hold of the national consciousness, thanks to an enterprising government official who took a liking to what he witnessed in the rings of El Paso, Texas, and decided to bring the unique form of entertainment back to his native land.

Raised in the Jalisco region of Mexico, Salvador Lutteroth Gonzalez had been serving the government ever since battling the forces of Pancho Villa during the Mexican Revolution as a teenager. While working for the Tax Department, he was relocated to the border town of Cuidad, Juarez, in 1929. While there he began attending wrestling matches presented by promoter John McIntosh in nearby El Paso. Watching the finest stars of the era colliding during the early '30s, Lutteroth became enamored of the exciting style of wrestling performance that was emerging at the time, and, by 1933, he had invested his money in creating an organization called *Empresa Mexicana de Lucha Libre* (Mexican Wrestling Enterprise). This entity still exists today as *Consejo Mundiale de Lucha Libre* (World Wrestling Council—not to be confused with the Puerto Rican league of the same name), and has been passed down through three generations of the Lutteroth family. It single-handedly launched the *lucha libre* phenomenon in Mexico, and remains today the single-oldest professional wrestling company in the world.

Investing even more money won in a national lottery, Lutteroth was able to build his company into a national force during the mid-1930s. In the beginning, the EMLL style was not much different than American wrestling, but things changed quickly. When an American performer debuted for him wearing a black leather mask, Lutteroth presented him as Maravilla Enmascarada (The Masked Marvel). The mask became such a popular accessory with fans that more and more *luchadores* (as Mexican wrestlers were called) began adopting it. Although not all *luchadores* wear masks, to this day the mask is the single-most defining element of *lucha libre*, and has helped *luchadores* create colorful, unforgettable characters.

The Mask

One of these was a particular masked character that Lutteroth developed into the most beloved *luchador* of all time, as well as the face of *lucha libre* itself: El Santo (The Saint). Debuting in the early 1940s, El Santo became a celebrity who transcended the business; a cult hero whose silver-masked visage adorned the pages of comic books, and whose exploits were chronicled in a series of action films during the 1950s, '60s and '70s. He was joined by other *lucha* legends like Blue Demon, the Villanos, and a *luchador* who actually started out as a movie character before crossing over into "real life"; he was billed as Mil Mascaras (The Man of a Thousand Masks).

Along the way, the mask would become something more than just a method of obscuring one's face. Drawing on cultural memory dating back to Aztec and Mayan imagery, the masks became symbols, as *luchadores* could use them to represent gods, animals, mythical creatures or any other larger-than-life being. Even more than in America, the secret code of kayfabe was strictly observed, as masked *luchadores* appeared in public wearing their masks, guarding their secret identities in the manner of superheroes. The

The *lucha libre* mask is an integral part of Mexican pop culture.

Christine Zenino/Wikimedia

mystique of the mask gave *lucha libre* something completely unique from anything seen in the U.S. *Luchadores* tied up their entire identities with their masks, and fans thus learned to disregard any distinction between the person and the performer.

To unmask was considered devastating, and could legitimately damage a performer's career; for this reason, the most grave stipulation match of all became the "mask vs. mask" encounter, in which the losing competitor would be forced to reveal himself to the world. For those *luchadores* without masks, wagering their hair was a suitable alternative. This particular stipulation even gained some traction in the U.S., with American performers like Gorgeous George, Adrian Adonis, and CM Punk falling victim to the clippers over the years.

Essential *Lucha* Elements

Ironically, although the code of kayfabe was taken very seriously, the actual product itself was far more flamboyant than anything seen in the business up to that point. Realism was not a high priority when it came to what actually went on in the ring; promoters and fans were much more interested in sensationalistic action. Along with the proliferation of masks, capes and other outlandish accoutrements came the development of a much more aerial-based style that emphasized acrobatic maneuvers over mat wrestling, and saw an array of unique moves added to the lexicon of pro wrestling, including the *plancha, senton, hurricanrana,* and many more. During the 1950s, '60s, and '70s, this stood in sharp contrast to the decidedly slower, brawling American style, and even caused some American stars (most notably the great NWA World Champion Lou Thesz) to look down on the *lucha* style as a bastardized form of wrestling that resembled choreographed tumbling more than anything else.

"In that era, all the American [wrestlers] always looked down on Mexico because their wrestling looked so fake," says Dave Meltzer of the *Wrestling Observer.* "You couldn't watch thirty seconds of *lucha libre* and believe you were watching a contest, even though the fans were every bit as fervent, and even more so."

Along with the new style, *lucha libre* developed its own set of rules that set it apart as well. To add even more action, six-man tag team encounters, or *trios,* became the standard *lucha* matches, with partners flying in and out of the ring with far more frequency than in American tag team matches. The outside area around the ring saw nearly as much action as the inside. Midget wrestling became an integral part of the product in the form of the *mini-estrellas,* many of whom were miniaturized versions of established characters. Similar to heels and faces, *luchadores* became divided into *rudos* and *tecnicos*, respectively.

Another type of character common to *lucha libre* is that of the *exotico*, a male wrestler who takes on decidedly feminine attributes, wears female attire, and projects a stereotypically homosexual attitude that directly flouts the macho sensibilities so intrinsic to Latin American culture. Although the feminized, pseudo-gay wrestler is also a traditional heel character in American wrestling as well, in *lucha libre* the *exoticos* take on much deeper implications, flying in the face of Latin masculinity as they do. Also distinctive is the manner in which legitimately gay performers have adopted the *exotico* character as part of their actual lifestyle; although the trope has existed since the 1940s, *exotico luchadores* have been openly proclaiming their real-life sexual preference since the '80s. And in a sign of more progressive times, they have also come to be portrayed much more often as *tecnicos* rather than *rudos*.

The Business Expands

EMLL/CMLL reigned supreme and uncontested over the *lucha libre* business for decades. Maintaining friendly relations with American promoters, the Lutteroths were among the founding members of the National Wrestling Alliance in 1948, and by the 1950s, when Salvador "Chavo" Lutteroth, Jr., had taken over, the NWA had granted their company control over the World Light Heavyweight, World Middleweight and World Welterweight Championships, reflecting *lucha libre*'s boxing-like emphasis on a wide array of different weight classes. This also placed the emphasis on the lighter weight performers better equipped for the aerial techniques fans came to expect.

The Arena Mexico in Mexico City became the "cathedral of *lucha libre*," and the main stage on which *luchadores* became legends. Among these many legends were the dreaded Medico Asesino, the innovative Rito Romero, and the hardworking Gory Guerrero, who would go on to found a dominant wrestling family composed of his sons Hector, Mando, Chavo, and the most famous of all, youngest son Eddie. Eventually, other *lucha libre* organizations would pop up, most notably the Universal Wrestling Assocation of the late '70s and early '80s, and a company founded by former head EMLL booker Antonio Pena that would eventually surpass EMLL itself: *Asistencia Asesoria Administracion* (AAA), founded in 1992.

"Of all the places I've gone to see wrestling, the best was Mexico, because of the fans," says Dave Meltzer. "Just being in the Arena Mexico, it was so much fun to watch wrestling, because the fan base was so passionate."

American Invasion

Despite what some American naysayers thought of it, the *lucha libre* style began to infiltrate the United States, and over the past fifty years that influence has grown to the point where many fans don't even realize its origins. First to popularize the high-flying approach in America was Mil Mascaras, who became a national star and appeared regularly everywhere, from L.A.'s Olympic Auditorium to New York's Madison Square Garden. Ironically, Mascaras was considered one of the more ground-based *luchadores* in his homeland; but nevertheless, American fans had never seen anything like him, and began to develop a taste for his acrobatic brand of performance.

This influence only grew stronger over time. By the mid-1990s, Pena was promoting AAA superstars like Rey Mysterio, Jr., La Parka, Juventud Guerrera, Psicosis, and Konnan to American audiences in areas with strong Hispanic populations like New York City and Miami, Florida. AAA co-promoted a 1994 pay-per-view with WCW called *When Worlds Collide*, and even enjoyed a brief partnership with Vince McMahon's WWF, the ultimate sign of American mainstream arrival. At the same time, visionary indy promoter Paul Heyman began incorporating many of the AAA standouts into his Philadelphia-based ECW, using their exotic flavor to add even more value to his groundbreaking, innovative product. Before long, U.S. powerhouse WCW had taken notice, and recruited the *lucha* stars as a key weapon in its arsenal during the ongoing Monday night ratings war with the WWF.

"Their moves were ahead of us," Meltzer says. "If you look at what guys do in the ring now, so much of the ring style has been developed by guys who grew up in the '90s and the 2000s and traded *lucha* tapes. As opposed to before, if you incorporated styles from another country into our wrestling, it was like you were doing it wrong."

In time, *lucha libre* would gain mainstream American attention as a pop-culture curiosity. It has inspired Saturday-morning cartoons, and even a 2006 cinematic comedy called *Nacho Libre*, starring Jack Black as a Catholic priest who becomes a *luchador* to help support his church (inspired by the real-life Sergio Gutierrez Benitez, who performed for more than twenty years as the masked Fray Tormenta). Today, the *lucha* mask is instantly recognizable as an element of vintage kitsch.

Eventually, *luchadores* would even become part of the fabric of WWE, and Mexican legends like Rey Mysterio and the late Eddie Guerrero would go on to become full-blown American main-event stars, apart from their *lucha* origins. This phenomenon has been most recently carried on by a young man named Luis Urive, who first achieved great fame in CMLL as the masked Mistico, and was able to translate that success in 2011 to a career in WWE as Sin Cara. Ironically, Urive parted ways with WWE in 2013 due to a combination of injuries and creative differences, and the company opted to bestow the Sin Cara identity on an entirely different performer—thus reinforcing that when it comes to *lucha libre*, the persona is most definitely of greater importance than the person.

Lucha Luminaries

Whether masked or unmasked, these larger-than-life personalities helped turn Mexico into a unique professional wrestling hotbed.

- Blue Demon
- Cibernetico
- Cien Caras
- Gory Guerrero
- Gran Hamada
- El Hijo del Santo
- Juventud Guerrera
- Konnan
- El Medico Asesino
- Mil Mascaras
- Mistico
- La Parka
- Perro Aguayo
- Psicosis
- Rey Mysterio, Jr.
- Rito Romero
- El Santo
- El Sicodelico
- Super Crazy
- Ultimo Dragon

The Saint

In the annals of *lucha libre*, there is one figure that stands head and shoulders above the rest—when it comes to El Santo, also known as El Enmascarado del Plata (The Silver-Masked One), the words "legend" and "icon" hardly suffice. A god of wrestling who became a folk hero in his native Mexico, El Santo was a symbol, an archetype who stood for heroism, courage in the face of oppression, and the indomitable human spirit. He galvanized a nation, became one of its most beloved sports figures, and, with the promotion of the Lutteroth family behind him, helped turn *lucha libre* into a full-blown national craze. Aside from his ring career, his larger-than-life exploits were chronicled in comic books, as well as a series of adventure films that are a subgenre all their own.

During his lifetime, he protected his real identity zealously, but even the great Santo had to start somewhere. He was born Rodolfo Guzman Huerta on September 23, 1917, in the town of Tulancingo in the Mexican state of Hidalgo, the fifth of seven children. After moving to Mexico City as a small child in the 1920s, Rodolfo took an interest in such sports as baseball, American football, and wrestling, training in both the *jiujitsu* and classical Greco-Roman styles. Although records are spotty, it is believed that he debuted as a professional wrestler at the age of sixteen on June 28, 1934, at Arena Peralvillo Cozumel. Then maskless, he wrestled simply as Rudy Guzman, on some of the earliest cards presented by EMLL founder Salvador Lutteroth.

But the mask phenomenon was already taking over *lucha libre*, and Guzman soon jumped on board. At first, he was known under such names as El Hombre Rojo, El Demonio Negro, and El Murcielago II ("The Bat II"—until the original Bat complained to the athletic commission about it). Then, when his manager put together a whole team of *luchadores* dressed all in silver, Guzman got in on the action, taking the name of El Santo. Donning his trademark silver mask, cape, trunks and boots for the first time, he stepped through the ropes at Arena Mexico on June 26, 1942, and the rest is history. El Santo (or just Santo for short) was an instant sensation, made even more so by the explosion of *lucha libre* into Mexican living rooms via television a few years later.

El Santo was the unquestioned leader of a pantheon of *lucha* heroes that arose over the course of the 1950s, '60s, and even into the '70s. He was rivaled by the great Blue Demon, who began as an enemy but turned from a *rudo* to a *tecnico* after a series of epic encounters in 1952 and 1953. Later, Santo and Blue Demon enjoyed a long-running partnership, almost like a *lucha libre* Batman and Robin. Santo also enjoyed an ongoing tag team partnership with Guerrero patriarch Gory Guerrero as La Pareja Atomica. Over the years, he grew to be the physical embodiment of *lucha libre*, and was worshipped by the Mexican working class to a degree that in America would be comparable to John Wayne.

In 1952, at the height of his popularity, comic book artist Jose G. Cruz kicked off a series based on Santo—a logical progression given the fact that most viewed him as a superhero already. The popular book ran for thirty-five years, even after Santo's death, and made him one of the most popular characters in the history of Mexican fiction. Just six years after the book launched, yet another multimedia chapter in his career began when he was invited by wrestler/actor Fernando Oses to appear in his first motion picture, 1958's *El Cerebro del Mal* (*The Evil Brain*), shot in Cuba mere weeks before Castro's takeover. The film would be the beginning of a nearly twenty-year run as an action movie star, as Santo battled aliens, werewolves, vampires, gangsters, and more in fifty-four films that raised his mythic status to greater heights. Today, the films are considered cult classics, and many remember Santo more for them than for his wrestling career.

In the late summer of 1982, Santo gave a farewell tour, culminating in one final match in September at Arena Mexico, teaming with Gory Guerrero, Huracan Ramirez, and El Solitario to take on Perro Aguayo, El Signo, Negro Navarro, and El Texano, just weeks after his sixty-fifth birthday. As part of that tour, he introduced his son Jorge, appearing under a similar silver mask as El Hijo del Santo (The Son of Santo). A little over a year later, in January 1984, he appeared on the Mexican talk show *Contrapunto* and shocked his fans by unexpectedly unmasking for a brief moment, revealing his face to the public for the first time ever. One week later, on the evening of February 5, 1984, Rudolfo Guzman Huerta, the great Mascarado de Plata, died of a heart attack during a live stage show at the age of sixty-six.

El Santo was buried in his classic silver mask, per his request, and his funeral was one of the most highly attended in Mexican history. Today, his legend is carried on by his son El Hijo del Santo, and most recently a grandson, El Nieto del Santo. His name has been immortalized in rock songs, inspired cartoon characters and ensured that the *luchador* mystique will hold sway over the imaginations of fans the world over for many years to come.

The Man of a Thousand Masks

If El Santo is the god of lucha libre, then Mil Mascaras is the archangel, bringing the style to the attention of American fans, as well as those around the world. Created to be a movie character, he was a real-life superhero if ever there was one, emerging from the motion picture screen to do battle in the pseudo-real world of professional wrestling. His high-flying abilities helped to link the *lucha libre* tradition with the aerial maneuvers he perfected, and he was one of the first performers American and Japanese fans had ever seen come off the top rope. Although his ego is almost as legendary as his influence, there is no denying the importance of the great Mil Mascaras.

He was born Aaron Rodriguez on July 15, 1942, in San Luis Potosi, Mexico, and took a strong interest in martial arts from an early age. By age twenty-two, he was getting his feet wet in the wild and woolly world of *lucha libre*, but it would take an unprecedented outside force to turn him into a national superstar. This force came in the form of Luis Enrique Vergara, the godfather of Mexican B-movies. Among Vergara's schlocky masterpieces were the burgeoning series of *lucha libre* action movies, and when he temporarily lost the services of his two top stars, El Santo and Blue Demon, Vergara decided he would create from scratch a new exciting masked *luchador* character. And the rookie Rodriguez would be the man behind the mask.

The character of Mil Mascaras first appeared in the 1966 film of the same name. It would be the first of an eventual twenty films that Rodriguez would make as Mascaras, often joining Santo, Blue Demon, and others. The youngest of the three major stars, he also had the longest movie career. The first *luchador* created specifically for the silver screen, his character was given a complete superhero-origin story, complete with special powers and a mission to protect the world from villains everywhere. His early films made the character so popular that it seemed only logical to carry it over into the actual ring, and Mil Mascaras embarked on a career of crossover proportions.

In 1968, he had his first American match, appearing at the Olympic Auditorium in Los Angeles for promoter Mike LeBell. He appeared in New York's Madison

Square Garden for Vincent J. McMahon, his prestige and fame so great that the New York State Athletic Commission exempted him from the sixty-year ban on masked wrestlers, making him the first to appear in a New York ring since the Masked Marvel debacle of 1915. He was a regular challenger to WWWF World Heavyweight Champion Superstar Billy Graham, and even held the World Championship of Eddie Einhorn's International Wrestling Association, a promotion that briefly arose to challenge the WWWF's New York dominance in the mid-1970s. In 1971, he made his first appearance in Japan, wowing staid Japanese audiences with his kinetic energy and engaging in a years-long feud with masked American wrestler The Destroyer.

Unlike other *luchadores* before him, Mil Mascaras was welcomed by international fans as a top babyface, his exciting arsenal of aerial maneuvers unlike anything they had seen. In time, fans would come to equate *lucha libre* with high-risk daredevil techniques, and, later, American wrestlers began to introduce the same moves into their repertoires, gradually moving pro

True to his name, Mil Mascaras appeared in a wide array of masks (and costumes).

Photo by Pro Wrestling Illustrated

wrestling off the mat and into the air. His colleagues, meanwhile, came to resent what they perceived as Mascaras's desire to "put himself over" at their expense. Over the years, performers ranging from Mick Foley to Chris Jericho to Superstar Billy Graham have cited his refusal to properly "sell" for his opponents, which, in turn, makes them look bad in the ring. On a 2012 WWE broadcast, announcer John "Bradshaw" Layfield went so far as to call him "the most egomaniacal, selfish human being that ever lived."

After nearly forty years of being the most popular international *luchador*, Mil Mascaras finally settled into semi-retirement in the early 2000s, although he has been known to occasionally enter the ring to this day, despite being in his seventies. He continues to make movies, his most recent being *Mil Mascaras vs. The Aztec Mummy* (2007) and *Academy of Doom* (2008), the first *lucha libre* movies to be filmed in English. He is the founder of a growing wrestling family that includes his brothers Dos Caras and El Sicodelico, as well as his nephews El Sicodelico, Jr., and former WWE World Heavyweight Champion Alberto Del Rio. To this day, his face has never been revealed in public.

The Strangest of All Movie Subgenres

Aficionados of B-movies all have personal favorites, whether it be Japanese *kaiju* flicks like *Godzilla, King of the Monsters!* (1954), horror gems from Britain's Hammer Studios, or blood-drenched Italian zombie films. But there is a special fan base that gravitates toward a very specific category of cheesefest, produced in Mexico predominantly during the 1950s, '60s, and '70s: *luchador* movies. An extension of the *lucha libre* tradition, *luchador* movies grew out of the public's perception of *luchadors* as real-life superheroes and supervillains, and gave film-going audiences a body of work that is truly in a class by itself.

Usually falling into the genres of science fiction and/or horror, *luchador* movies presented the stars of *lucha libre*—men like El Santo, Blue Demon, and Mil Mascaras—as macho, crime-fighting swashbucklers, whose wrestling careers are just a front to disguise their true nature as the defenders of Earth against evildoers of all stripes. Sexy female co-stars were almost inevitable, as were mad scientists, international spies, and all manner of supernatural baddies. It all started in 1952 with *Huracan Ramirez*, but it wasn't until the most famous *luchadores* became the centerpieces of the action that the subgenre really took off with grindhouse moviegoers.

Luis Enrique Vergara may very well have been the most prolific maker of *luchador* movies, and it was he who launched the cinematic careers of Santo, Blue Demon, and Mil Mascaras, whose character he created specifically for the screen. Merging superheroes and wrestling, the *luchador* movie phenomenon was a match made in heaven, and the films even gained an American audience thanks to the distributor K. Gordon Murray, who brought them to the U.S. in dubbed form (often changing the names of stars, such as Santo becoming "Samson"). Occasionally, even American actors (including horror veteran John Carradine) would appear alongside the masked protagonists.

Luchador movies peaked in the 1960s, but began to run out of steam by the mid-1970s, as audiences grew tired of the somewhat formulaic plots and lackluster production values. Matters were not helped when a new regime within the Mexican government, responsible for funding the film industry, pulled the plug on the production of *luchador* flicks, which they deemed unworthy of support. Nevertheless, they are today considered camp classics, adored by post-ironic hipsters and other boosters of obscure pop-culture ephemera. They are also a perfect example of the overarching influence of *lucha libre* on the popular consciousness. The stars of *lucha libre* straddled the realms of reality and fiction like no other pro wrestlers did, and their cinematic exploits helped them transcend the business even further.

Luchador Cinema: The Essentials

- *Santo contra el Cerebro del Mal* (*Santo vs. The Evil Brain*, 1958): Santo's very first starring vehicle.
- *Santo contra las Mujeres Vampiro* (*Santo vs. the Vampire Women*, 1962): This one received immortality in the United States when it was featured in an episode of *Mystery Science Theater 3000*.
- *El Santo en el Museo de Cera* (*Santo in the Wax Museum*, 1963): The Silver-Masked One investigates a series of kidnappings by a scientist intent on developing a monster army in this, the most critically acclaimed of *luchador* films.
- *Las Luchadoras contra la Momia* (*The Wrestling Women vs. the Aztec Mummy*, 1964): Part of a series of movies featuring a troupe of female *luchadores* known as *Las Luchadoras*.
- *Los Campeones Justicieros* (*The Champions of Justice*, 1970): A veritable who's who of *luchadores*, including Santo, Blue Demon, Mil Mascaras, Rayo de Jalisco, El Medico Asesino, and others do battle with a mad scientist and his army of superhuman midgets.
- *Santo y Blue Demon contra Dracula y el Hombre Lobo* (*Santo and Blue Demon vs. Dracula and the Wolf Man*, 1973): The title pretty much says it all.
- *El Castillo de las Momias de Guanajato* (*The Castle of the Mummies of Guanajuato*, 1977): The most financially successful of all *luchador* movies, it features Superzan, Blue Angel, and Tinieblas taking on the titular mummies, as well as zombies, Satanists, and more.
- *Misterio en las Bermudas* (*Mystery in Bermuda*, 1979): The end of the heyday of the *luchador* subgenre, and the final film for Blue Demon.

13

Puroresu

Japan's Wrestling Religion

Japan's very interesting. Some people think they copy things . . . I think they reinvent things . . . In some cases, they understand it better than the original inventor.

—Bill Gates

Outside of North America, there have been several enclaves throughout the world where professional wrestling has thrived. In the United Kingdom, Billy Riley's revered Snake Pit gym in Wigan has produced such serious grapplers as Karl Gotch and Billy Robinson, and British audiences have enjoyed the exploits of local heroes like Robby Brookside and Big Daddy Crabtree. In Germany, Otto Wanz's Catch Wrestling Association ruled the roost. South Africa and Australia have also been wrestling hotbeds over the years. But when it comes to pro wrestling beyond America's shores, there is one place which immediately comes to mind, where the success of the business has at times risen far beyond what it has even enjoyed in our own country: Japan.

In the Land of the Rising Sun, professional wrestling has enjoyed a level of culture and popularity that is truly unique. Treated much more like an actual sport than anywhere else, Japanese wrestling, or *puroresu*, is a throwback to the days when shooters ruled the game and personal honor was more important than storylines. Although it developed much later than it did in the United States, the national attention it enjoyed during its heyday is unequalled in America by anything short of the notoriety of Gotch, Hogan, and Gorgeous George. The Japanese are passionate about their wrestling, and there are those on our own side of the world who prefer their hard-hitting, serious approach over the more theatrical form it takes here.

Purofesshonaru Resuringu

Going back to the early years of professional wrestling's development in the United States, there had been occasional Japanese athletes who made the journey across the Pacific to prove their mettle against American competition. Sumo champion Sorakichi Matsuda toured the States in the 1880s, taking on the likes of William Muldoon, Evan "Strangler" Lewis, Farmer Burns, and other top competitors of the day. He even tried to bring the American version of the sport over to his native Japan, but without success. That would have to wait another half-century.

It would take a world war to bring Japan into close enough contact with professional wrestling for the sport to finally take hold. In the late 1940s, following the defeat of the Axis powers, American occupying forces began to import pro wrestling from the States as a form of entertainment for both the troops and the locals alike. A nation already rich in combat sport tradition, Japan began to embrace the foreign attraction, and the colorful good-guy/bad-guy dynamic held a certain appeal for a culture steeped in kabuki theatre and heroic epic poetry. Phoneticizing the sport's name in their own language, they called it *purofesshonaru resuringu*, a term which, in later years, would be abbreviated to simply *puroresu*. Eventually, a very specific face/heel relationship, that of Japan and the U.S. itself, provided the tinder needed to set *puroresu* aflame.

A Postwar Hero

When a former Korean sumo named Mitsuhiro Momota, performing under his sumo name of Rikidozan, made the transition to *puroresu* in the early 1950s, he helped usher in the sport's first Golden Age in Japan. Hiding his true Korean identity, he became a champion of the Japanese people, specializing in taking on evil American heels, usually much larger than he, and dispatching them in highly exciting matchups. Downtrodden after their wartime loss, it was just the kind of catharsis the Japanese needed, and they rallied to Rikidozan like no professional sports star in that nation's history. With television technology taking off in Japan just a few years after it had in the United States, it was a perfect storm that allowed for Rikidozan's ascension to national celebrity, and just as it had in the U.S., television was soon bringing wrestling into the homes of Japanese everywhere.

Riding the wave of his immense success, Rikidozan founded the Japanese Wrestling Association, the country's first native wrestling organization, in 1953. His matches against the likes of NWA World Champion Lou Thesz, massive masked villain The Destroyer, and the ultimate obnoxious blonde American, Fred Blassie, received TV ratings that today would be inconceivable, not just for pro wrestling, but for any broadcast of any kind. When Rikidozan wrestled in big matches, nearly everyone in the nation of Japan who owned a television was watching.

The Inoki/Baba Era

After Rikidozan's tragic murder in 1963, it fell to his two greatest pupils, Antonio Inoki and Shohei "Giant" Baba, to carry his mantle and keep the flame of *puroresu* burning. Rikidozan had been grooming them to be his successors, and after his passing, they dominated the JWA in the 1960s, very often as tag team partners. However, in the following decade, both men would strike out on their own, creating a business rivalry that has defined *puroresu* to this day. In 1971, after a failed attempt to take over the JWA, Inoki left the company to form his own group, New Japan Pro Wrestling. A few short months later, the JWA folded, and Baba created a second organization, All-Japan Pro Wrestling. Once in-ring allies, Inoki and Baba were now direct competitors. The two inheritors of the legacy of Rikidozan would dominate the *puroresu* landscape as promoters for the next thirty years.

Baba (an unusually large man who suffered from the same disorder that afflicted Andre the Giant) was an incredibly huge draw, and initially built All-Japan around himself as the top star. He was deeply influenced by the American style of professional wrestling that came to be known in Japan as "King's Road," inspired by the mat-based, scientific wrestlers like Harley Race and Dory Funk, Jr., who had come to Japan to defend the NWA World Heavyweight title. Under his watch, athletes such as Jumbo Tsuruta, Kintaro Oki, and Riki Choshu became popular by adapting the NWA style to American rings.

Inoki, meanwhile, focused on what would come to be known as the "strong style"—a more shoot-based performance style that made realism a top priority. Fascinated by various fighting styles, Inoki worked hard to protect his product. Although it was, of course, just as pre-arranged as all other kinds of pro wrestling, he instructed his wrestlers to "work stiff," which usually included hard-hitting blows that were not pulled, and submission holds that were really cinched in. Inoki's New Japan enjoyed an ongoing promotional relationship with the (W)WWF in America, and it was Vincent J. McMahon who helped to promote Inoki's most famous match and the ultimate ode to his desire to blend wrestling with other fighting styles: A mixed wrestler/boxer encounter that pitted him against none other than undisputed World Heavyweight Boxing Champion Muhammad Ali on June 26, 1976, in Tokyo's Budokan Arena.

As they competed for dominance throughout the 1970s and '80s, both All-Japan and New Japan stressed athleticism above all else. As wrestling became more cartoonish and storyline-based in the States, Inoki and Baba chose to keep their product relatively gimmick-free. Most angles, whenever they were used, were very basic, and usually focused on simple matters like heroic, never-say-die heroes using their "fighting spirit" to overcome great odds. It was important for matches to have clean, decisive finishes, without any of the screwy shenanigans designed to keep fans coming back for rematches in America. The attitudes of Japanese fans supported this approach; they treated their wrestling like a sport, and so the promoters gave them what they wanted. Some colorful characters did appear from time to time, like the high-flying Tiger Mask and Jushin "Thunder" Liger (inspired by *lucha libre* and a cartoon superhero, respectively), but, for the most part, Japanese wrestlers were relatively no-frills.

The Strong Style

The emphasis on athleticism was only further enhanced by the influence of Karl Gotch, a skilled shooter trained in the Wigan school of England, who, in the 1970s, traveled to Japan and taught many of the top stars the fine art of shootfighting. (Japanese fans would later honor him with the impressive nickname "The God of Wrestling.") More and more, *puroresu* put the emphasis on realism, and Japanese rings became known as a very tough place, where wrestlers had to be prepared to put their bodies on the line like nowhere else.

It was starting to appear that the original nineteenth century catch-as-catch-can origins of pro wrestling were making a comeback in Japan. This indeed came to pass in the 1980s as the trend led to the emergence of shoot-wrestling organizations like the Universal Wrestling Association, which presented a hybrid of legitimate fighting and worked wrestling. Later, in the 1990s, came Pancrase and Pride Fighting Championships, which presented legitimate, competitive professional wrestling. These Japanese groups would help give rise to the phenomenon of mixed martial arts, arguably the most popular combat sport today.

Meanwhile, the 1980s and '90s became a second Golden Age for *puroresu*, thanks to the continued business rivalry between Inoki and Baba. All-Japan's Triple Crown and New Japan's International Wrestling Grand Prix (IWGP) Heavyweight title became two of the most prestigious championships in the world. Wrestling in Japan received as much, if not more, mainstream attention than the WWF was getting in the U.S. during its own boom period. Cards at the Tokyo Egg Dome, the Budokan, and other fabled locations were among the biggest the industry had ever seen. Fans continued to believe in their "sport" with a passion that was quite different from that of American fans, who were being conditioned to look at wrestling as entertainment.

"The work is a lot more serious," explains Dave Meltzer, a passionate supporter of *puroresu* over the years. "In the '70s and '80s, there was more of a feel of realism. They protected the kayfabe. I don't know if more people thought it was real, but they did think Inoki was real. And not even that all his matches were real, but that some of them were real. There was that sense of, 'It may not be real, but these guys are really the toughest guys in the world.' There are moments in every match that are real, and we watch for those moments."

"Big in Japan"

Nevertheless, Japanese promoters continued to enjoy solid working relations with their American counterparts, and there was no greater evidence of this than the two-day event that occurred the weekend of April 28, 1995, in Pyongyang, North Korea. After long negotiations with the totalitarian government of that nation, Inoki was able to work out a deal in which he would co-promote the show along with American company WCW, as part of North Korea's World Peace Festival. A total of 340,000 packed May Day Stadium over the course of the two days, making it the most highly attended event in pro wrestling history (although it should be noted that the mandatory attendance enforced by Kim Jong-Il's oppressive regime likely had something to do with that). In the main event, Inoki himself faced WCW's "Nature Boy" Ric Flair.

As it had been from the very beginning, the popularity of pro wrestling in Japan had a lot to do with the involvement of foreign performers. Particularly, Japanese fans seemed to have a fascination with very large, raucous Western wrestlers, preferably with big muscles and blonde hair—some have speculated this may be due to how physically alien this look is compared to typical Japanese athletes. Among the many *gai jins* who have achieved particular fame in Japan are:

- Hulk Hogan
- Stan Hansen
- Bruiser Brody
- Abdullah the Butcher
- Andre the Giant

- Dory and Terry Funk
- Tiger Jeet Singh
- "Dr. Death" Steve Williams
- The Road Warriors

Some, like Hansen and Williams, enjoyed a level of notoriety and success that far exceeded what they achieved even in the United States, and so they wound up spending a great deal of time working in Japan. Usually, but not always, they worked as heels against the Japanese heroic babyfaces, in a complete reversal from the manner in which Asian wrestlers at the time would usually work heel in the United States.

Joshi Puroresu

The popularity of wrestling in Japan was even strong enough to support a women's division, and to a much greater degree than was ever viable in the United States. A tour led by World Women's Champion Mildred Burke in the 1950s was such a sensation that it led to the formation of the World Women's Wrestling Association in Japan, and during the 1970s–'90s, All-Japan Women's was one of the most successful promotions in the country, spotlighting the formidable talents of female athletes like Bull Nakano, Aja Kong, Akira Hokuto, and many others. In particular, the late '80s saw the rise of The Crush Gals, a tag team made up of Lioness Asuka and Chigusa Nagayo that achieved more mainstream attention than perhaps any other female performers in the history of professional wrestling.

As with their male counterparts, the difference in the presentation of women's wrestling in Japan as opposed to America is that the emphasis was on athleticism and putting on impressive matches. The women were not sexualized as their American counterparts usually have been, nor was titillation the underlying intent as it is in the U.S. Most women's wrestling organizations in Japan have existed independently of the male organizations, presenting women's wrestling as a product all its own, and there are many who have felt that the quality of that product was consistently superior to any male-based organization anywhere in the world.

Garbage Wrestling

But *puroresu* isn't just about honorable competitors performing clean, scientific matches before respectful, appreciative crowds. There is also an ultra-violent underbelly to *puroresu*, a counterpart to America's hardcore wrestling tradition known as "garbage wrestling." In fact, the development of garbage wrestling in Japan actually predates the proliferation of the hardcore style that exploded in America in the mid-1990s, due in large part to ECW. As early as 1989, Japanese groups like Frontier Martial Arts Wrestling and, later, Big Japan Pro Wrestling were popping up, offering extreme violence and borderline sadism as their stock in trade.

This legitimately dangerous product was championed by Atushi Onita, the mastermind behind FMW. Onita helped popularized the "deathmatch" concept, featuring matches that included such props as explosives, thumbtacks, and fluorescent light tubes. Often, the ring might be set on fire, or have barbed wire in place of ropes. This legitimately dangerous form of pro wrestling later spread to America, due to such Western performers as Mick "Cactus Jack" Foley, who first encountered it while overseas. Although this subgenre has its fans, it has largely been kept out of the U.S. mainstream due to its often brutal and bloody action.

Twenty-First Century Decline

Following the salad days of the 1990s, *puroresu* experienced increased fragmentation with the dawn of the new century, just as it had after Rikidozan's death decades earlier. After the death of Giant Baba in 1999, prominent All-Japan wrestler/promoter Mitsuhara Misawa departed to form his own company, Pro Wrestling Noah, leaving Baba's widow in charge of All-Japan. The following year, top New Japan attraction Shinya Hashimoto was fired, leading him to form his own group, Zero1. Both have gone on to become viable alternatives to the "Big Two" of All-Japan and New Japan, and other organizations like Michinoku Pro, HUSTLE, and Dragon Gate have enjoyed some success in their shadow over the years.

In recent years, *puroresu* has experienced a downturn in popularity; a marginalization similar to what American pro wrestling went through in the 1960s and '70s after the loss of national television. Today, New Japan (which Inoki sold in 2005) is the only *puroresu* televised on a major national network (Asahi TV), while Nippon TV, the longtime broadcaster for All-Japan (and Rikidozan's JWA before that), dropped All-Japan from its schedule in 2000 to make way for rival Pro Wrestling Noah, which held the spot until 2009. Today, All-Japan is aired on a small UHF network, and whatever wrestling there is on TV in Japan is relegated to obscure, late-night timeslots.

"What killed it was when they put the wrestlers in the MMA fights," says Dave Meltzer. "When they didn't do well in the MMA fights, that idea of watching wrestling to see the toughest guys—that went by the wayside when you saw how different an MMA fight looked from a professional wrestling match. That hurt wrestling bad there. It's started to rebuild, and now what exists is entertainment."

The glory days of Rikidozan, Antonio Inoki, and Giant Baba may have passed, but *pururesu* still has many boosters, both in its native land and around the world—fans that prefer their pro wrestling to be serious, athletic, and sports-like in its presentation. Perhaps, as with American wrestling, what is happening in Japan is merely a transitional phase, leading eventually to a glorious rebirth of the "fighting spirit" which made *puroresu* such a phenomenon for so long.

Puroresu Pioneers

Japan has produced some of the most popular legends the business has ever seen. Here are just a select few of them.

- Akira Maeda
- Atsushi Onita
- Genichiro Tenryu
- The Great Sasuke

- Hiroshi Hase
- Jumbo Tsuruta
- Jushin "Thunder" Liger
- Keiji Muto (The Great Muta)
- Kensuke Sasaki
- Kenta Kobashi
- Kintaro Oki
- Masahiro Chono
- Mitsuhara Misawa
- Nobuhiko Takada
- Riki Choshu
- Shinya Hashimoto
- Tatsumi Fujinami
- Tiger Mask
- Toshiaka Kawada
- Yoshihiro Tajiri

The Father of *Puroresu*

In the years after World War II, the Japanese needed a hero; someone to make them feel whole again after their demoralizing defeat at the hands of the United States and its Allies. Although diplomatic relations between the two nations were healing, many in Japan felt a sense of powerlessness, of going from a world power to a beaten nation. For those who felt that sense of loss, vindication came in the form of Rikidozan, a superstar of epic proportions, whose valiant exploits in the squared circle on the behalf of the people of Japan made him an object of worship. Most ironic of all was the fact that he wasn't even Japanese, and had to hide his Korean heritage during a career that was cut tragically short by murder. Nevertheless, in his dozen years in the spotlight, Rikidozan single-handedly established *puroresu* as the most passionate wrestling tradition in the world.

He was born Kim Sin-rak on November 14, 1924, in South Hamgyong, Korea (in present-day North Korea), but in his youth was adopted by a Japanese family living in Nagasaki Prefecture. Wishing to avoid the rampant anti-Korean prejudice in his new country, he was more than happy to take on his new family's name, calling himself Mitsuhiro Momota. That family would later disown him due to his involvement in pro wrestling, but before that he would achieve acclaim as a teenager competing in a very different form of wrestling more native to his part of the world, sumo. Debuting at age fifteen, Momota was given the sumo name of Rikidozan, which would stick with him for the rest of his life.

Rikidozan Mitsuhiro achieved some noteworthy success as a sumo, getting as far as runner-up to the top *yokozuna* champion position during his decade in the sport, before his Korean heritage eventually forced him out. Sumo, with its proud nationalistic tradition, wanted no part of him any longer, and so, in October 1951, he made the transition to the less-prestigious new form of American professional wrestling that was taking hold in Japan.

Promoters and bookers seized on the impressively built young man, having him win in matches against imposing and belligerent American villains. Up to then, the majority of wrestlers performing in Japan had been American, but now, with Rikidozan, a new dynamic developed. Playing off national insecurities and bitterness, the Americans were portrayed as evil and treacherous, and Rikidozan was

Rikidozan reigned as Japanese/International Champion from 1954 until his death in 1963.   *Public domain*

the inspirational vanquisher, toppling them one by one. The formula was an instant hit, and before long Rikidozan had achieved so much fame (and money) that he was able to create Japan's first native pro wrestling organization, the Japanese Wrestling Association.

Rikidozan's star rose to such a degree that he even started traveling to America to wrestle, even though while there he was presented in the same villainous light as most other performers of Asian extraction. But his massive international fame was really secured when he faced NWA World Heavyweight Champion Lou Thesz in October 6, 1957, in a sixty-minute draw that was broadcast in closed circuit on giant TV screens throughout Japan and scored a mind-boggling 87.0 rating, meaning that nearly nine out of every ten people in Japan with a television set were watching that match. Television was even newer in Japan at that time than it was in the United States, and Rikidozan galvanized the nation as the first superstar of the medium in a way that simply would be impossible to accomplish in the ensuing multimedia landscape.

"Rikidozan was the first cultural hero created by TV in that country," says Dave Meltzer. "He was much bigger than Gorgeous George in the sense that he was like a Martin Luther King. Gorgeous George was an entertainer, but Rikidozan was . . . the big-time public hero of the country. They had lost the war, there was very bad self esteem, and the idea of Rikidozan beating up the big Americans was great theater, and gave them the impetus to rebuild that country."

Other epic matches followed, including an August 27, 1958, rematch with Thesz, as well as an April 23, 1962, match against WWA World Champion Fred Blassie. The latter match was notorious for the way Blassie antagonized the relatively naïve and timid Japanese fan base by pretending to file his teeth into points in an attempt to draw their hero's blood. Blassie would become known in Japan as "The Vampire," and legend has it that the bloodletting in his matches caused some TV viewers to die of heart attacks in their homes. Whether true or not, the hype was indicative of the vast attention paid to Rikidozan's every move, culminating in his May 24, 1963, sixty-minute draw with The Destroyer that drew a staggering 67.0 rating (an even larger viewership than the Thesz match, due to Japan's much greater TV audience by that time).

By the early 1960s, Rikidozan's great wealth had enabled him to open a series of hotels, nightclubs, and other properties. It was in one of these nightclubs, on December 8, 1963, that he was stabbed by a member of the *yakuza* wielding a urine-soaked knife. The attack is believed to have been an organized crime revenge hit in retaliation for a match Rikidozan had with former judo champion Masahiko Kimura, in which he had legitimately roughed up Kimura. He neglected to take the wound seriously, and a week later, Mitsuhiro "Rikidozan" Momota died of peritonitis at the age of thirty-nine.

The Giant of the East

The Japanese have always been awed by wrestlers who are physically large and imposing. Usually, they get them in the form of the foreign *gai jin*; but in the case of Giant Baba, it was one of their own: a towering mountain of a man who lived up to his nickname, and who showed that not only did he have what it took to be a powerful drawing card, he also had the business acumen to build on the legacy of Rikidozan and create one of Japan's two major *puroresu* organizations. Being one of the most beloved Japanese professional wrestlers of the 1960s and '70s would have been enough to cement his historic status; add the fact that he founded All-Japan Pro Wrestling and it's easy to see why Baba is so revered.

He was born Shohei Baba on January 23, 1938, in the town of Sanjo, in the Japanese province of Niigata. Acromegaly would exaggerate his size and features in a similar way they did France's Andre the Giant, and by maturity he had grown to be nearly seven feet tall and well over 250 pounds, making him an anomaly among the diminutive Japanese. At first, the young Baba chose professional baseball as the field of endeavor with which to make best use of his size, and he was signed as a pitcher by the Yomiuri Giants at the age of seventeen.

Although he spent five years pitching, most of it was in the minor leagues. Baba's destiny lay in a different athletic pursuit, and he left the Giants to sign up for Rikidozan's training camp in April 1960, at age twenty-two. The great champion was looking for young lions to groom to take his place as Japan's next wrestling superstars, and he would find just that in Baba and his other newest trainee, a Japanese/Brazilian transplant named Kanji Inoki. Baba and Inoki debuted together on September 30, 1960, at the Daitu Ku Gymnasium in Tokyo, and both immediately began making waves on the *puroresu* scene.

Baba's size even made him a natural attraction for American audiences, and the Giant would gain some of his earliest experience working for Vincent J. McMahon's Capitol Wrestling in the early 1960s. While there, he battled such top stars of the era as Edouard Carpentier, Johnny Valentine, and Antonino Rocca, and even challenged Bruno Sammartino for the WWWF World Heavyweight title at Madison Square Garden. Just two months prior, Rikidozan had been murdered, leaving a major vacancy back home—a vacancy that would be filled by his two greatest pupils. The Baba/Inoki team would become the stuff of legend from the mid-1960s to the early '70s, frequently winning the NWA International Tag Team Championship.

But the collapse of Rikidozan's JWA in 1972 led both Baba and Inoki to found their own companies, and in the case of the giant that company would be All-Japan Pro Wrestling. Enjoying a strong relationship with the American NWA, All-Japan prided itself on presenting high-quality matches above all else. Baba based the style on that of NWA World Championship matches of the era, and made the most of the healthy talent exchange program that came with NWA membership.

Another perk of membership was the fact that Baba snagged the distinction of becoming the first Japanese to win the NWA World Heavyweight Championship. He did so on three occasions, defeating Jack Brisco in 1974, Harley Race in 1979, and Race again in 1980. In all three instances, the title changes were booked as a favor to All-Japan to help bolster the company's legitimacy and Baba's legendary status. All three reigns lasted a mere handful of days, but nevertheless added to Giant Baba's formidable mystique.

Baba's wrestling days began to wind down in the early 1980s and he started to focus completely on continuing to grow All-Japan. The company became a favorite of insiders and wrestling aficionados around the world, and drew even greater crowds during the late '80s and early '90s than at any point in its history, including a series of sellouts at Budokan Hall that regularly scored $1 million gates and attendances in excess of fifty thousand.

By the late 1990s, cancer forced Baba to step away from the ring for good, and he spent much of his time in bed fighting the disease. On January 22, 1999, he witnessed two of his homegrown discoveries, Mitsuhara Misawa and Toshiaka Kawada, tear the house down in Osaka in a hard-fought match for the All-Japan Triple Crown. Nine days later, he died at the age of sixty-one. Today, his legacy lives on as All-Japan remains one of Japan's primary wrestling organizations.

The Burning Fighting Spirit

For four decades he was the most powerful wrestling promoter in Japan, and the face of Japanese wrestling to the rest of the world. A student of all fighting disciplines, he helped to pioneer what would later come to be known as mixed martial arts, one of the first instances of which was a famous (and infamous) 1976 match he had with the greatest sports icon of all time. Transcending the business, Inoki has served as a politician in his native country, a role he recently returned to after a nearly twenty-year absence.

He was born Kanji Inoki on February 20, 1943, to a wealthy political family in Yokohama, the tenth of eleven children. His father, Sajiro, died when he was a boy, and, after falling on hard times, the family relocated to Brazil. It was there that the teenaged Inoki first met Rikidozan, the *puroresu* legend who happened to be on a world tour. In 1960, Inoki returned to Japan with the man who would become his mentor, and began to train to become a professional wrestler. Along with Rikidozan's other disciple, Shohei Baba, he debuted in September, taking the first name of Antonino in honor of his hero Antonino Rocca, whom he had seen perform while he was a boy in South America.

Inoki is one of the most decorated stars in the history of *puroresu*—or all of pro wrestling, for that matter.
Photo by Pro Wrestling Illustrated

Following Rikidozan's death in 1963, Inoki labored for a bit in the shadow of the more popular Baba. Starting in 1966, he formed a tag team with Baba that achieved great acclaim and headlined the Japanese Wrestling Association for years. Inoki's power in the organization grew, but when it was discovered in 1971 that he was planning a coup to take over the company, he was promptly fired.

Undaunted, Inoki leveraged his fame to form his own company, New Japan Pro Wrestling. Scoring a television deal on top Japanese network Asahi TV (which the company still enjoys to this day), Inoki began distinguishing his group via the establishment of what he called "strong style," incorporating real fighting techniques into his worked wrestling product. He became fascinated with different combat disciplines, studying *karate*, *judo*, *jiujitsu*, and more. In 1975, he was taken under the wing of the great Karl Gotch, who taught him the ancient art of catch wrestling, the legitimate grappling style from which professional wrestling had originally developed a century prior.

On a mission to prove the superiority of his chosen sport, Inoki started inviting fighters of all disciplines to compete in New Japan. It is unclear to what degree these matches were actual contests or pre-arranged wrestling "works"; they were perhaps a little of both. Nevertheless, they helped popularize the notion of mixing different fighting disciplines, which would eventually lead to the development of mixed martial arts as a sport in the 1980s.

The height of Inoki's inter-discipline craze came when he challenged Heavyweight Boxing Champion Muhammad Ali to a wrestler vs. boxer match in 1976, offering the champ $6 million to come to Tokyo's Budokan Hall and face him. The match was hyped throughout Japan and the United States, with many wrestling promoters getting in on the act, including Vince McMahon of the WWWF and Verne Gagne of the AWA. It was televised via closed circuit to a worldwide audience of over one billion. But the result was one of the most embarrassing debacles in the history of both sports.

Legend and fact mix when it comes to sorting out exactly what went down the night of June 26th, when the two finally met. Some suspect the match was supposed to have a scripted outcome, but both Inoki and Ali feared the other would try to go into business for himself and pull a double cross. Ali's camp reportedly imposed a series of rules on Inoki that would have seriously limited Inoki's offense. The match itself was a disaster, with both men afraid to mix it up, and Inoki spending the whole time on his back kicking Ali's legs, the champion unable to land a single punch. It is believed that Ali's boxing career may have even been shortened by the serious wounds he received to his legs that night. Nevertheless, the two men emerged from the incident as lifelong friends.

Inoki continued to champion shootfighting, eventually presenting MMA matches as part of his New Japan shows. He maintained a working relationship with the (W)WWF, even enjoying a short reign as WWF World Heavyweight Champion when he beat Bob Backlund during a tour of Japan (the reign remains unacknowledged in the U.S. to this day.)

In 1990, he followed in his father's footsteps, using his sports fame to launch a political career. Inoki served for five years as a representative in the Japanese House of Councilors, and is known for brokering a deal with Saddam Hussein that allowed for the release of Japanese prisoners in exchange for a wrestling event presented in Iraq. Unfortunately, Inoki was forced to step down in 1995 amid accusations of bribery, but would eventually return to the House of Councilors in 2013.

Although he remains active as a promoter, Inoki sold his interest in New Japan to the video game company Yuke's in 2009. Today, his political career is his focus, and he has made negotiations with North Korea his primary cause, using his deep connection to the North Korean–born Rikidozan as a diplomatic tool. And so, the legacy of the Father of *Puroresu* lives on through his greatest protégé.

14

Sex and Violence

The Queens of the Ring

I didn't ever want to see girl wrestling because women need to be in the kitchen, not in the ring. But if there ever was a woman who was born to be a wrestler, you're it!

—Ed "Strangler" Lewis to Mae Young

C ontrary to popular assumptions, women's professional wrestling has been around nearly as long as men's professional wrestling. It's just operated in the shadow of its male counterpart, often as a sideshow oddity designed for the titillation of a decidedly masculine fan base. Although there have been many female performers of great skill and exciting ability over the years, their craft has, unfortunately, been relegated to marginal status, particularly in the United States, and there is no question that it remains so to this day. However, when presented properly, women's wrestling can be just as thrilling as men's wrestling, and sometimes even more so, with fiery performances and fast-paced action.

In recent years perhaps more than at any other time, women do play an important role in the overall pro wrestling entertainment package. But that position is defined not so much by athleticism as by sex appeal. There can be no denying the sordid status women's wrestling has been stuck with, as part of a business that remains dominated by men and, even more importantly, by a male sensibility. Nevertheless, the business has boasted some truly impressive females who have struggled against the odds for generations, often carving out remarkable legacies in the process. Whether known as "lady wrestlers" or as "Divas," their efforts are well worth remembering.

Burlesque Beginnings

As far back as the prim and proper Victorian Era of the late nineteenth century, women wrestlers could be found appearing in carnivals and circuses—much like the men, only treated as much more of a freakish attraction, challenging as they were to the conservative mores of the day. Women might wrestle each other, or even challenge men out of the crowd. Eventually, women's wrestling migrated from the carnival sideshows to the burlesque houses and the back rooms of taverns, playing even more directly to the lascivious undertones of the proceedings involved, as throngs of rowdy men in various stages of inebriation cheered on the unseemly action. This era gave rise to a handful of very early standout female competitors, including Josie Wahlford, who defended her self-proclaimed women's championship against both male and female challengers; and Laura Bennett, who claimed the prize for most of the first decade of the twentieth century.

But it wasn't until the rise of the woman who bested Bennett for the title in 1910 that women's wrestling finally made it out of the back rooms and into the arenas, where Frank Gotch had already propelled men's wrestling. Cora Livingston (her name has often been misspelled as "Livingstone") was a powerful and talented grappler from Buffalo, New York, who would dominate women's wrestling for nearly two decades and be the first to be recognized as Women's Champion of the World. Her 1913 marriage to Boston promoter Paul Bowser no doubt helped her career as well, but Livingston nevertheless remains female wrestling's first true breakout star.

In the wake of Livingston's fame, many more female wrestling stars began to crop up in the 1920s and 1930s, as promoters became more open to the concept. Pro wrestling took more of the form of a colorful spectacle than it had taken before, and the still-unusual sight of women's wrestling lent itself to that spectacle. Performers came to prominence such as Oregon's Clara Mortensen, who was trained by her wrestler father from a very young age and debuted as a sibling act with her brother while still a child. Mortensen would be the next to lay major claim to the title of World Women's Champion starting in 1932.

The Girls Go Mainstream

Women's professional wrestling didn't start to become big business until the late 1930s, when a partnership arose between two individuals who would corner the market for the next fifteen years. One was a failed middleweight wrestler from Missouri named Billy Wolfe, who had taken to training and managing female wrestlers as a way to make a living. The other was an athletically gifted woman from Kansas named Mildred Bliss, whom Wolfe quickly realized was just the find he was looking for. Impressed by her muscular physique, Wolfe agreed to train her, changed her name to Mildred Burke, and groomed her to become the most dominant female performer the business has ever seen.

After defeating Mortensen in 1937, Burke laid claim to the World Women's Championship, and with Wolfe as her husband/manager, she became the top attraction of an entire troupe of women wrestlers. Before long, Wolfe had become the industry's ultimate broker for female talent: if a promoter wanted to add a woman's match to his card, Wolfe would be the guy he called. For the first time, women's matches began to appear regularly as part of events everywhere in the country. Throughout the 1940s Wolfe consolidated his control, and by the time the National Wrestling Alliance was formed in 1948, he had enough clout to become a crucial associate, providing women performers to cards held throughout the NWA's many affiliated territories.

It was a great deal, and helped to elevate women's wrestling as a top attraction, but it didn't last long. For years, stories of Wolfe's shady maneuvering spread throughout the business. There were allegations that he mistreated his female talent and was a flagrant womanizer who abused his position as the kingpin of women's wrestling. Some even went so far as to call him a pimp. When Burke finally got fed up with her husband's philandering, she filed for divorce in 1952, and the resulting dispute threatened to destroy everything the couple had built.

An Ugly Split

The NWA attempted to reconcile the two for the sake of the business, but when it became apparent that the bitterness ran too deep, the group responded by distancing itself from the ugly situation, and women's wrestling in general. Burke bought out Wolfe's half of their organization and formed her own independent group, which eventually morphed into the World Women's Wrestling Association. Wolfe had been prohibited from competing as part of the agreement, but true to form, he found ways around the prohibition, and embarked on a mission to ruin Burke and her world-championship claims.

Using his influence within the NWA, he first drove Burke's outfit into bankruptcy and attempted to regain control of her career and contract. He helped establish his daughter-in-law June Byers as the new NWA World Women's Champion in 1953, and when Burke continued to maintain her claim to the title, he pressured her into a two-out-of-three-falls match with Byers that devolved into something that hadn't occurred in pro wrestling in decades: a shoot fight. On August 25, 1954, in Atlanta, Georgia, the two women entered the ring with a legitimate beef to settle, and there was nothing scripted about it. This was Burke's chance to set the record straight, but when she allowed herself to be pinned for the first fall, expecting to come back strong in the second, she discovered that Wolfe's political stroke had struck again: the second fall was mysteriously called off, and Byers wound up continuing to claim the title as a result of the first fall.

Burke's career never recovered. Byers, meanwhile, would announce her retirement in 1956 and was stripped of her title by the NWA. Wishing to avoid the ongoing controversy and drama of the Wolfe-Byers-Burke debacle, they put their focus on a young newcomer who had the backing of influential veteran showman Jack Pfefer and was thankfully drama-free (for the moment): a thirty-three-year-old former valet from South Carolina named Lillian Ellison, whom Pfefer had taken to billing as "The Fabulous Moolah."

Absolutely Fabulous

One part Southern belle and two parts spitfire, Moolah was given recognition as the new World Women's Champion after winning a thirteen-woman battle royal on September 18, 1956. Wolfe and Byers tried to spoil the proceedings once again when Byers almost immediately came out of her retirement, but the NWA put its backing behind Moolah and so the Fabulous One defeated Byers in their highly anticipated match to make her claim undisputed. Although in actuality she would lose that title on several occasions over the years (to Betty Boucher in 1966, Yukiko Tomoe in 1968, and Sue Green in 1975), Moolah would later choose to ignore those brief losses, and insisted that she had been women's champion for a consecutive twenty-eight years.

Moolah gained the ability to rewrite women's wrestling history at will because she had installed herself as the ultimate controlling power in the business, a role that was cemented after Billy Wolfe's death in 1964. Establishing a company she called Girl Wrestling Enterprises, Moolah was now the one providing female talent to promoters throughout the NWA, and anywhere else they were required. She now literally owned the championship (she even put her picture on the belt), and all her challengers were among the stable of wrestlers she had trained herself at her wrestling school in Columbia, South Carolina.

She even came into direct competition with Mildred Burke, who was still running her WWWA as an outlaw organization, offering an alternative to Moolah's troupe. But with the backing of the NWA, Moolah's grip on the business was unbreakable. After parting ways with Pfefer, she became closely associated with some of the most powerful promoters in the nation: Paul Bowser and Tony Santos in Boston, and Vincent J. McMahon of the WWWF in New York. With McMahon in her corner, Moolah was even able to lift the ban on women's wrestling at the most famous arena in the world, when she defended her title against Vicki Williams in Madison Square Garden on July 1, 1972. Her pull within the industry was formidable by this point—arguably as strong as Wolfe's had been, if not stronger.

Girls Just Wanna Have Fun

Moolah was considered so integral to women's wrestling, in fact, that when Vincent K. McMahon was in the middle of launching his national expansion of the WWF and wanted women represented as part of his product, he got the Fabulous One to agree to appear strictly for his company, cutting the NWA out of the picture and making Moolah the first-ever WWF World Women's Champion. She had already been working with the McMahons for years, so the deal was a natural fit. As part of the agreement, Moolah was to pass the torch to McMahon's hand-picked successor, Moolah's star pupil Wendi Richter, whom the promoter envisioned as the female version of Hulk Hogan.

But although Richter was initially a success at the height of the "Rock 'n' Wrestling" revolution in the mid-1980s, paired up with pop-music sensation Cyndi Lauper as her manager, it didn't stick. Depending on whose story you believe, Richter's own instability coupled with shady backstage maneuverings from Moolah (who was reportedly unwilling to relinquish the spotlight just yet) caused Richter's star to fizzle prematurely. Women's wrestling in the WWF faded into the background despite another attempt to make a major star out of another Moolah student, Sensational Sherri Martel. By the end of the decade, Moolah had officially retired and the Women's Championship was put out of commission.

Several years later, the WWF attempted to take women's wrestling somewhat seriously when the championship was once again activated in 1993 and put around the waist of Alundra Blayze, a former AWA World Women's Champion who had come to prominence as Madusa Miceli. Formerly under contract to the most high-profile women's wrestling organization in the world, All-Japan Women's Pro Wrestling, she also helped the WWF to recruit some formidable opposition in the form of the fearsome Bull Nakano, the brutal Aja Kong, and others. Nevertheless, despite Vince McMahon's efforts, the American wrestling fan base wanted sexuality from its female combatants, and the new incarnation of the women's division just wasn't delivering in that department.

Dawn of the Diva

If sexuality was what the fans wanted, it would be delivered in spades during the Attitude Era, which changed the creative course of WWE at the end of the twentieth century. In the past, women's wrestling in America had always had an undercurrent of taboo eroticism, but never anything as overt as what happened when Vince McMahon and head booker Vince Russo decided to fully embrace a more adult product, with the ladies front and center. Of course, as with much of what the Vinces were attempting at the time, the origins were in Paul Heyman's ECW, where raunch was the name of the game and women like Beulah McGillicutty, Francine, and others had fully crossed over into R-rated territory. Not only were they flaunting their bodies in ways women in wrestling never had before, they were also mixing it up in the ring, taking bumps that previously would have been unthinkable.

When this sensibility was transplanted to the WWF, it led to the phenomenon that has defined women's wrestling ever since: "Divas." Rena "Sable" Mero, then-wife and valet to wrestler Marc Mero, was the first to be referred to as such, and it soon became a branding device for the WWF/WWE's entire women's division. By doing this, the company succeeded, for good or ill, in making women's wrestling as mainstream as it had been in the days of Mildred Burke.

Joanie "Chyna" Laurer (here with then-fiancé, Triple H) was one of the WWF's most popular stars—male or female—from 1999 to 2001.   *Mandy Coombes/Wikimedia*

Past ring queens like Sue Green, Penny Banner, and Leilani Kai, with their conservative leotards and flesh-tone pantyhose, now seemed downright demure in comparison to Divas like Debra McMichael, Miss Kitty, and Terri Runnels, who performed in ever-racier outfits and made it very clear that their number-one commodity was not their athletic ability but their physical sensuality. But the new approach fit right in with the edgy, anything-goes tone of the day, and the Divas became part of the package, branded in the same way the male wrestlers had been termed "Superstars" for years. Soon, rival WCW was even trying to replicate the Divas phenomenon with its own Nitro Girls dancing troupe.

A happy medium of sorts was reached, however, as the Attitude Era moved on and

McMahon began to catch some heat for the sleazier aspects of his television productions. Soon, women began appearing on the scene that were not only sexy but could also perform impressively in the ring. Female bodybuilder Joanie "Chyna" Laurer, who had started as a silent bodyguard for Triple H and Shawn Michaels's D-Generation X faction, broke out as a top-level performer in her own right, enjoying tremendous popularity for a short time in the early 2000s.

"She was absolutely top tier," says Dave Meltzer of the *Wrestling Observer* newsletter. "In her case, [it was] the way she looked, and the fact that she was beating up guys, which never would've been allowed in any other era. That made her a very intriguing figure. . . . We never had anyone like that in pro wrestling: a woman who was as big as the guys, and who was beating up the guys. Moolah and Mae Young never did that. Mildred Burke did it in carnivals, but that's different. Still, it got old really quick."

Chyna was followed by women like Ivory, Jacqueline, and Victoria, who combined sex appeal with the ability to actually put on a decent match.

The Trish and Lita Era

Chief among the performers of this particular era, which would come to be known as a modern-day Golden Age of women's wrestling, was a former Canadian fitness model named Patricia Stratigias, better known as Trish Stratus, and the high-flying punk rocker Amy Dumas, who emerged on the WWF scene in 2000 as Lita. Starting out as just another bleached-blonde valet, Stratus wanted to accomplish much more, and through hard work and training, she developed into one of the most impressive in-ring workers the company ever produced. Lita, meanwhile, gained instant notoriety with a wrestling style that was previously considered the sole domain of the men, incorporating aerial *lucha* tactics like moonsaults, suicide dives, tornado DDTs, and more.

The early to mid-2000s produced some of the finest women's matches WWE fans had ever seen, thanks to Stratus, Lita, and their contemporaries, who helped the division gain newfound respect. TNA Wrestling, the latest in the long line of WWE rival promotions, was also inspired to try and capture lightning in a bottle with their own division, terming their female performers "Knockouts" instead of Divas. But the temptation to abandon match quality and return to mere eye candy was always there, and began to gain ground again when Stratus, Lita, Victoria, and others began to fade from the WWE scene by the end of the decade. (Victoria migrated to TNA, where she became known as Tara.)

This is a struggle that continues to this day. Critics of present-day women's wrestling in America charge that many performers are nothing more

Known as the "Glamazon," former amateur wrestling champion Beth Phoenix was one the most dominant females of the early 21st century, holding the WWE Women's/Divas' Championship on four occasions, between 2007 and 2012, for a total of a year and a half.
Mshake3/ Wikimedia

than models hired to look pretty and are trained to do a passable amount of wrestling. Recent years have given us talented athletes like WWE's "Glamazon" Beth Phoenix, Natalya Neidhardt (niece of Bret "Hit Man" Hart), and TNA's Gail Kim, who can be depended on to provide great action; but also the likes of former swimsuit model Kelly Kelly and the Bella Twins, whose purpose on the show is clearly to pander to the male viewership. In 2010, WWE's Women's Championship was phased out in favor of the newly created Diva's Championship, ending a title lineage that dated back over a half century to the heyday of The Fabulous Moolah.

The move was made to help strengthen WWE's Divas brand, but it's also easy to understand why some also interpret it as a clear indicator of how WWE specifically, and the sports-entertainment industry in general, views women's wrestling: as a pretty confection intended to provide a titillating diversion and nothing more. Nevertheless, there remains hope for aficionados of "serious" women's wrestling in a new crop of performers being groomed in WWE's NXT developmental league, as a phenomenal match between Natalya and Charlotte (daughter of Ric Flair) at *NXT Takeover* in May 2014 demonstrated. Trained to work in the style of their male counterparts, these young women may one day help their division to generate the same interest and respect.

"It's changing now," Meltzer says. "When I watch the women wrestlers, they really want to be wrestlers. It's gone from pure T&A and really crappy wrestling, to very pretty girls who are trying to be wrestlers."

Leading Ladies

Over the course of more than a century, these accomplished women have helped establish that professional wrestling has enough room for both genders.

- A. J. Lee
- Beth Phoenix
- Clara Mortensen
- Cora Livingston
- Donna Christanello
- The Fabulous Moolah
- Gladys "Kill 'Em" Gillem
- Jacqueline
- Judy Grable
- June Byers
- Lita
- Madusa (a.k.a. Alundra Blayze)
- Mae Young
- Mildred Burke
- Penny Banner
- "Sensational" Sherri Martel
- Sue Green
- Trish Stratus
- Victoria
- Wendi Richter

The Kansas Cyclone

Mildred Burke was not just a women's wrestling superstar. Mildred Burke was a wrestling superstar, period. More than any other performer in the history of women's wrestling in North America, Mildred Burke was on a level comparable to nearly any man in the business during her time. For over a decade and a half, she was the embodiment of women's wrestling; her matches were very often main events, which was nearly unheard of for any female before or after her reign at the top. Guided to glory by the man she called both husband and manager, she would eventually suffer deep betrayal at his hands, both personal and professional, and lose the position she had worked so hard to achieve. But despite all the turmoil, she remains the ultimate "Queen of the Ring."

She was born Mildred Bliss on August 5, 1915, in Coffeyville, Kansas. As a teenager, she was working as a waitress on the Zuni Indian Reservation in Gallup, New Mexico, when she met her first husband, who whisked her away to Kansas City when she was just eighteen. A wrestling fan, he would introduce her to the business by taking her to the matches on a regular basis. The marriage may not have lasted, but her fascination with the squared circle did.

Intent on becoming a wrestler, she began training her body and developing her musculature to a degree that was quite rare for the 1930s. She eventually caught the attention of Billy Wolfe, the trainer and manager who saw in her the precious meal ticket he had been praying for. Together, they would form a unit that eventually took the wrestling business by storm—a unit made even stronger when the two eventually married. Changing her name to Mildred Burke, he booked her on carnival tours, where she regularly defeated male challengers.

Burke demonstrates a leglock on then-husband and women's wrestling czar, Billy Wolfe, c. 1940.   *Author's collection*

Finally, in January 1937, she got the big break she was looking for, defeating top 1930s female star Clara Mortensen to become recognized as World Women's Champion.

With women's wrestling as marginalized as it is today, it's hard to imagine a female star at the level of popularity Burke enjoyed from the late 1930s to the early 1950s. Promoters everywhere clamored for her services, and were willing to pay Wolfe handsomely for them. Rather than an oddity at the bottom of the card, she had great drawing power; her 1939 title defense against Lupe Acosta in Monterey, Mexico, and 1941 title defense against Elvira Snodgrass in Louisville, Kentucky, drew fourteen thousand and eighteen thousand fans, respectively, an unprecedented accomplishment in women's wrestling. Along the way, Wolfe leveraged her stardom to become the czar of women's wrestling in North America, and both he and Burke became very, very rich.

But by the 1950s, Wolfe's repeated indiscretions with other women in his stable, as well as his emotional abuse of Burke, became too much to bear for the female star, no matter how much money they were making. Her stepson George, Wolfe's son from a previous marriage, exacerbated the issue, acting as a harassing watchdog proxy for Wolfe while Mildred was on the road without him. Their acrimonious divorce was inevitable, and rocked the industry. Wolfe tried to destroy his ex-wife, taking advantage of the chauvinism of the NWA's good old boys' network, to send her into exile. Following the June Byers debacle in 1954, Burke established the World Women's Wrestling Association and continued to claim the World Women's Championship, even if the NWA no longer recognized her as such.

At first running opposition to Wolfe himself, she later found herself on the losing end of a promotional battle with the woman who had supplanted her as the face of women's wrestling and Wolfe's successor as female talent booker to the NWA: The Fabulous Moolah. Feeling threatened on all sides, she traveled with an escort for the remainder of her career. After the demise of the WWWA, she settled in Encino, California, where she ran a women's wrestling school in the 1970s and '80s. On February 18, 1989, Mildred Burke died of a stroke at age seventy-three. Although her legacy was tarnished by her enemies, contemporary historians have finally come to appreciate her tremendous contributions.

The Girl from Tookiedoo

To modern-day wrestling fans, The Fabulous Moolah is the unrivaled patroness saint of women's wrestling, a tough old broad who became WWE royalty thanks to a fifty-year relationship with the McMahon family. She dominated the female end of the business longer than any other individual, jealously clutching the World Women's Championship she herself owned for nearly thirty years. During that time, her training school produced a veritable who's who of female wrestling luminaries—a legion of women who populated the division from the 1960s through the 1990s. Many of these same women would, in later years, make allegations against Moolah and her practices, revealing a scandalous underbelly to the women's wrestling business.

She was born Mary Lillian Ellison on July 22, 1923, in Tookiedoo, South Carolina, the youngest of five children. After she lost her mother when she was only ten years old, her father began taking her to the local wrestling matches to cheer her up. She would eventually witness World Women's Champion Mildred Burke come to town to defend her title, and the experience convinced her that her destiny lay along a similar path. After an ill-advised and short-lived marriage during her adolescence (one that produced a daughter whom Lillian would leave to be raised by friends), she embarked on a wrestling career of her own.

To wrestle as a woman in those days meant doing business with Billy Wolfe, and that's how Ellison got started, tackling Wolfe's daughter-in-law June Byers in her first match on May 26, 1949. Growing tired of Wolfe's sexual advances and his practice of pressuring female talent to sleep with promoters for preferential booking, she soon defected to the camp of Jack Pfefer, who specialized in promoting women, giants, midgets, and other wrestling oddities. It was Pfefer who first gave Ellision the name "Moolah," when she explained to him that financial gain was the main reason she got into the business.

Working for a time as Slave Girl Moolah, a valet to male wrestlers like Elephant Boy and U.S. Champion Buddy Rogers, she eventually returned to full-time ring action as The Fabulous Moolah, and was chosen in 1956 to be the new NWA World Women's Champion. Backed by some of the most powerful promoters in the country, she used her growing influence to eventually take over Billy Wolfe's role as booker of all major-league female wrestling talent in North America. While no longer as high profile as it was in the Mildred Burke

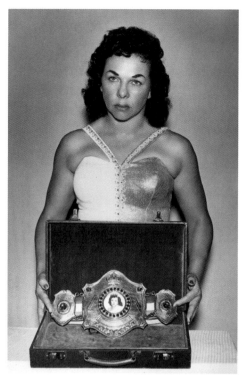

Moolah shows off the Women's Championship belt she proudly wore (and owned) for twenty-eight years.
Jack Pfefer Collection, University of Notre Dame

days, and once again relegated to glorified catfights on the undercard, women's wrestling still provided Moolah with a healthy living.

Her years as the controlling force behind the women's wrestling industry yielded many top performers, including Wendi Richter, Donna Christanello, Sherri Martel, Debbie Combs, Judy Martin, Velvet McIntyre, and others; still, Moolah has often been accused of Machiavellian practices, such as using her position to hold the title as long as she did, refusing to pass the torch to any of her students. This was typified in the manner in which she allegedly sabotaged Richter's rising career, eventually taking the title back from her in 1985 without her prior consent during a controversial match at Madison Square Garden in which Moolah donned a mask as the very weakly disguised "Spider Lady." Even worse than the political allegations were the claims that Moolah physically abused and bullied trainees in her school, and even pressured them to do the very same thing she had accused Wolfe of pressuring her to do early in her career.

Years after finally stepping out of the spotlight at the end of the 1980s, The Fabulous Moolah enjoyed a resurgence in popularity during the WWF of the late 1990s and early 2000s, when she and her best friend, fellow ring veteran Mae Young, began a beloved stint as recurring characters on *Raw* and *SmackDown!* Both well into their seventies by that point, Moolah and Mae didn't shy away from getting physical when the job called for it, and Moolah even enjoyed one last brief reign as women's champion at the age of seventy-six, defeating Lisa "Ivory" Moretti in 1999. During this period, Moolah and Mae were also featured prominently in the 2004 documentary film *Lipstick and Dynamite*, covering the halcyon days of women's wrestling in the 1940s, 1950s, and 1960s.

"The Fabulous Moolah" Lillian Ellison died on November 2, 2007, at age eighty-four, after suffering a heart attack as a result of shoulder-replacement surgery. Beloved by fans, she nevertheless has left behind a problematic legacy. As the face of women's wrestling for thirty years, she vigorously protected that position by any means necessary. Perhaps, in a field so thoroughly dominated by men, that's what she felt a woman had to do in order to survive. And in the end, she did far more than just survive: she endured.

Gorgeous Ladies of Wrestling

Ask a casual fan about pro wrestling in the '80s, and almost as likely as they are to mention Hulk Hogan, Ric Flair, the WWF or *WrestleMania*, they will very likely bring up a particular brand of women's wrestling that captured the attention of Gen-Xers at just the right moment in time: GLOW, the first televised all-female wrestling promotion in America. It aired from 1986 through 1990 in various syndicated markets across America, usually on Saturday mornings and usually in tandem with the WWF's own weekend programming. The Gorgeous Ladies of Wrestling is a camp classic that never tried to be anything more than a goofy, cheesy, thoroughly tongue-in-cheek take on the females of the ring.

The brainchild of hack Hollywood producer/director Matt Cimber, the last husband of '50s bombshell Jayne Mansfield, GLOW grew out of an original concept that was created by pseudo-sports promoter David McClane and Jackie Stallone, mother of longtime wrestling fan Sylvester Stallone and owner of Barbarella's, a women-only gym back in the '80s. When Cimber developed the GLOW concept, he enlisted McClane and Stallone to remain with the promotion as on-air personalities, which they did throughout the duration. Conceived as an episodic comedy series with distinct seasons, the program was filmed in Las Vegas at the Riviera Hotel initially, and then at a nearby warehouse.

With no pretense of realism whatsoever, GLOW embraced wrestling's silly side, and in a strange way was ahead of its time in its use of scripted backstage vignettes and its willingness to break the fourth wall. Nevertheless, the actresses and models hired to make up the GLOW roster were expected to learn how to wrestle, and were trained to do so by Mando Guerrero of the famous Guerrero wrestling family. The result was a bizarre and unforgettable cast of characters that included Babe, the Farmer's Daughter; the tag team of Hollywood & Vine; the disturbing Dementia; sexy Soviet Col. Ninotchka; the massive Matilda the Hun; and the exotic Spanish Red.

GLOW ran for four seasons, which just so happened to coincide with the height of Hulkamania and one of the industry's major boom periods. As a result, it is often linked in the minds of fans of a certain age with the wrestling they grew up with, despite its short run. With its opening rap video inspired by the Chicago Bears' "Super Bowl Shuffle," it was the perfect Saturday-morning companion to the WWF's cartoonish *Superstars of Wrestling.* One of its alumna, Tina Ferrari, even later made her way to the WWF as Ivory, an eventual three-time World Women's Champion—proving that the GLOW girls may have been the real deal, after all.

Exploited: Apartment Wrestling, Mud Matches, and More

Sexuality and women's wrestling have always, by definition, gone hand-in-hand. Yet there is also a much seedier and more explicit subgenre within women's wrestling that has sought to directly court this sexuality, dispensing with athletics to flirt with the realm of soft-core pornography.

Longtime readers of pro wrestling magazines recall a particularly unusual phenomenon known as "apartment wrestling." Beginning in the late 1960s in big cities like Manhattan, word spread of private apartments (more likely hotel rooms) where scantily clad/nude women would tussle with each other for the entertainment of an invitation-only group of (presumably male) onlookers. Capitalizing on the new development as a way to drive sales, wrestling magazines started dispatching photographers to the "matches," then running the photos with tawdry, fabricated tales that presumed to give some of the "backstory" of the proceedings. Soon, the matches were staged solely for the purposes of these photo spreads, and they became a common part of wrestling magazines of the 1970s, especially the London Publishing family of periodicals that included the likes of *The Wrestler, Inside Wrestling,* and *Sports Review Wrestling.*

It was a very permissive time for wrestling magazines, which already featured blood-soaked pictorials of the most violent matches imaginable; images of nearly naked women cat-fighting seemed a natural fit. The strange apartment-wrestling craze lasted until the beginning of the 1980s, when it was driven underground by the more family-friendly direction the wrestling magazine business, and the wrestling business in general, was taking. In recent years, it has experienced a mild resurgence thanks, predictably, to the Internet.

Apartment wrestling had a relatively short shelf life, but much more enduring has been the tradition of women wrestling in various wet, sloppy, and slimy substances. Mud is definitely the most popular medium, but women have wrestled in oil, Jell-O, chocolate syrup, and pretty much anything else promoters could think of.

Ironically, mud wrestling began not with women but with men. It all started in Seattle in 1937, when former World Champion Gus Sonnenberg and Indian grappler Prince Bhu Pinder were set to have a Hindu-style match in dirt, but too much water was added, accidentally resulting in mud. That last detail may have been an apocryphal one added later by grandiose promoter Paul Boesch, but whatever the reason, mud wrestling was one of the many gimmicks created to stir fan interest during the depths of the Depression. Soon after, women's wrestling impresario Billy Wolfe convinced his famous wife, Mildred Burke, to give it a try, and the rest is history.

Over the years, women have writhed around on the mat not only in mud, but also in ice cream, tomato sauce, and more. In the WWF during the height of the Attitude Era, the mud match made a brief comeback. Millions of *Monday Night Raw* viewers saw women wrestling in mud, in gravy (on Thanksgiving, of course), and in swimming pools, not to mention in "evening gown matches," in which the purpose of the encounter was to disrobe your opponent down to her underwear.

Today, women's mud wrestling and hot oil wrestling can be found as a regular attraction at strip clubs, bars, and bachelor parties, harkening back to the days when women wrestled each other for the leering male masses at burlesque halls and taverns. So much for progress!

15

From Parts Unknown

Wrestling's Most Bizarre and Unforgettable Gimmicks

When the going gets weird, the weird turn pro.

—Hunter S. Thompson

I n 1959, Stephen Sondheim wrote the immortal line for the Broadway musical *Gypsy*, "You gotta get a gimmick, if you wanna get ahead!"— and nowhere is this maxim more true than in the world of professional wrestling. Stemming as it does from the carnival circuit, wrestling has gimmickry in its DNA, and that has been, to a certain extent, true from the very beginning. Performers utilize gimmicks to add color to their performances and enhance their personalities—sometimes the gimmick can be an extension of their real-life identities (they may even use their actual names), or it may be a complete and radical departure into the fictional and fantastical.

It was during the 1930s that the surreal and the weird began to thoroughly infiltrate the professional wrestling product. Wrestlers of all shapes and sizes, with the most outlandish gimmicks imaginable appeared more and more, really taking hold, thanks to the advent of television. In more recent years, gimmicks have become so sophisticated and fully developed that they can be accurately referred to as "characters." In this chapter, we'll take a close look at the indispensable role of gimmicks, and some of the most colorful characters ever to set foot in a ring.

The Terrible Turk

A case can be made that the very first true wrestling gimmick was employed by one Yusuf Ismail, a mysterious figure billed by his manager William Brady and promoter Joseph Doublier as "The Terrible Turk." The first of several wrestlers to use that name, the original Turk was most likely a citizen of the

Ottoman Empire, or present-day Bulgaria, but some have even speculated he may have been a swarthy French dockworker capitalizing on his exotic looks.

The Turk first arrived in the U.S. in 1894, and created a major media stir with his claims of invincibility. Such a furor surrounded him that many of his matches, such as his bouts against Greco-Roman champion Ernst Roeber at Madison Square Garden and the Metropolitan Opera House, had to be stopped due to rioting. When he bested Evan "Strangler" Lewis for the American Heavyweight Championship in Chicago in 1898, he reportedly demanded the five-thousand-dollar prize money in gold, which he stored in a giant money belt he kept around his waist.

On his way back to Europe on July 4, 1898, The Terrible Turk drowned when the ship he was traveling on, the S.S. *La Bourgogne*, sunk to the bottom of the Atlantic. Legend has it that the mighty Turk was spotted shoving women and children aside to reach the lifeboats, but that he accidentally fell overboard and was dragged under the water by the weight of his ponderous money belt. Whether these details are true or just apocryphal flourishes, The Terrible Turk remains one of pro wrestling's most fascinating early characters.

The First Gimmick World Champion

Wildly disparate stories circulate about the origins of one Arteen "Harry" Akizian, with some claiming that he escaped the horrors of slavery and genocide in the Ottoman Empire of the 1910s, while others believe he may have just been an opportunistic ethnic Armenian from Pasadena, California. Wherever he was from, Akizian achieved immortality as the professional wrestler known as Ali Baba, one of the earliest examples of the bald-headed, handlebar-mustached Arabic heel gimmick later employed by the likes of The Iron Sheik.

Akizian had already been wrestling for years when, in 1936, he stumbled upon the Ali Baba character, which became a particular success in Detroit, thanks to its large population of Middle Eastern immigrants. He enjoyed so much immediate success with the gimmick, in fact, that promoters decided to put the World Heavyweight Championship on him, and so he defeated Dick Shikat on April 24, 1936, in the Motor City's famed Olympia Stadium to gain recognition from the National Wrestling Association. He held the title for seven months before losing to Everett Marshall in Columbus, Ohio.

Colorful gimmicks like Ali Baba's had been around for a long time, but what made this different was that it was the first time the World Heavyweight Championship, the pinnacle of the business and the trophy that helped maintain the illusion that pro wrestling was a competitive sport, was bestowed on a wrestler who was clearly portraying a character. Previously, world champions had been no-nonsense, meat-and-potatoes grapplers, whose straightforward presentation kept them at a distance from much of the theatrics that went on in the business. With Ali Baba's World Championship reign, theatrics took center stage for the very first time.

Ugly Angels

Wrestling fans of the 1940s and 1950s were witness to one of the spectacle's strangest fads, that of the ironically named "Angels": monstrous-looking individuals, usually suffering from some form of physical deformity such as acromegaly, who were promoted as frightening, often unstoppable heels. The Angels all had a similar look, with a bald head, as well as an overgrown cranium and facial features. They were a favorite attraction of itinerant showman Jack Pfefer, a promoter who specialized in the freak-show aspect of the wrestling business.

The first of the Angels was Maurice Tillet, a Russian-born Frenchman who entered the business in the late 1930s and rose to fame under the auspices of Boston promoter Paul Bowser as The French Angel. The story goes that Tillet, whose acromegaly did not set in until adolescence, was nicknamed "Angel" as a young boy due to his cherubic good looks at the time. Genteel and intellectual in real life, Tillet had been forced to abandon his ambitions of becoming a lawyer due to his deformity. (Rumor has it that his iconic visage was the inspiration for the animated film character Shrek.)

Tillet's success as The French Angel led to a myriad of Angels of various stripes, including The Swedish Angel (Phil Olaffson), The Super Swedish Angel (Tor Johnson), The Russian Angel (Tony Angelo), The Black Angel (Gil Guerrero), and even The Lady Angel (Jean Noble).

Who Were Those Masked Men?

Apart from the tradition of masked Mexican *luchadores* (see Chapter 12), pro wrestling in the United States has long been populated with performers who plied their trade under a hood. Ever since The Masked Marvel stole the show at the 1915 international tournament in New York City, there have been wrestlers who have seen the benefit of using a mask, whether to create an aura of mystery, to generate instant heel heat, or simply to protect one's identity away from the ring. Sometimes, a mask might even be used to repackage a performer under a different identity, so fans wouldn't realize they were watching someone they had already seen.

Prominent masked wrestlers have included:

- The Destroyer: Former Syracuse University wrestler and football player Dick Beyer, who first donned the mask in Los Angeles at the suggestion of "Classy" Freddie Blassie in 1962. The Destroyer became a legend both in the U.S. and Japan, and even held the AWA World Heavyweight title under the alternate name of Dr. X.

- Mr. Wrestling II: Longtime journeyman Johnny Walker, who finally achieved notoriety when he took to wearing a mask as the successor to the original Mr. Wrestling, Tim Woods. Wrestling II was one of the most popular performers in Georgia and Florida during the 1970s and 1980s, and was a favorite of Jimmy Carter and his mother, Lillian. He was invited to Carter's January 1977 inauguration, but declined when the Secret Service informed him he would have to unmask.

- The Spoiler: Canadian grappler Don Jardine, who is best remembered as the trainer of Mark Calaway, the man who would become the Undertaker. The top rope clothesline, one of The Spoiler's signature moves, was adopted by 'Taker as a tribute to his mentor.

- The Assassins: A storied tag team of the 1960s through the 1980s, known for their trademark gold-and-black masks. Founded by Jody Hamilton and Tom Renesto, Hamilton kept the gimmick going after Renesto retired by adding additional partners, such as Randy Colley and Hercules Hernandez

- Kane: Glenn Jacobs, who tried several unsuccessful gimmicks in the WWF, including that of deranged dentist Dr. Isaac Yankem, before settling in 1997 on the persona of the Undertaker's long-lost half-brother, on a mission of vengeful destruction. Kane's character has morphed drastically over the years, and he has even appeared in the ring without the mask. As of this writing, he is the company's longest tenured full-time performer.

- The Hurricane: Gregory Helms, an avid comic-book fan who used that background to create a masked superhero character that wound up being one of the highlights of early 2000s WWE.

- Abyss: A cross between Kane and Cactus Jack, daredevil performer Chris Parks has been with TNA Wrestling since the company's inception in 2002, and was the first masked wrestler to win the NWA World Heavyweight Championship.

Little People

It may not be politically correct, but midget wrestling has enjoyed a long appeal, for years existing right alongside women's wrestling as one of the most commonly found subgenres on the pro wrestling circuit. Owing to the industry's origins in carnivals and burlesque, there has long been a place for the unusual spectacle that midget wrestling provides, and many of its performers, including the likes of Little Beaver, Lord Littlebrook, Sky Low Low, and Fuzzy Cupid have gone on to become revered in the business.

The 1950s through the 1970s are generally considered the heyday of midget wrestling, thanks in large part to television. In fact, during this period it was not unusual to find TV programs that consisted entirely of midget wrestling. Nevertheless, most of the time the little people could be found performing on the same cards as their average-sized counterparts, and for a time the NWA even promoted a Midget World Championship, notably held by Low Low and Japanese competitor Little Tokyo on several occasions. The 1970s even saw the proliferation of female midget wrestling, featuring women such as Princess Little Dove, Darling Dagmar, and Fabulous Moolah protégée Diamond Lil'.

Although much of midget wrestling was and is just as athletic and competitive as other forms of pro wrestling, more often than not it has been played for laughs, and it is this aspect that has perhaps led to the downturn of the subgenre in recent decades, as audiences have grown less comfortable with it. Typical midget matches usually contained tried-and-true comedy spots that played up the diminutive nature of the performers, including running through the referee's legs, or being thrown around like children by the ref.

After the '80s, midget wrestling suffered a sharp decline, especially in the United States, where, typically, the performers were relegated to sidekick roles, such as Dink the Clown, the miniature version of Doink the Clown used by the WWF of the mid-1990s. Despite WWE's shortlived attempt to create a "juniors division" in the mid-2000s, little performers continue to this day as comic relief, an odd throwback to the sport's sideshow days. Most recently, WWE performers known as El Torito and Hornswoggle have continued the tradition on a mainstream level.

There are nevertheless some contradictions to this contemporary trend. Midget wrestling continues to thrive in the world of *lucha libre*, in which the performers are known as "minis" and are often packaged as miniature version of established, average-sized *luchadores*, including the likes of Mascarita Sagrada. The Micro Wrestling Federation, an independent company that was founded in 2000, continues to tour North America year-round. Also, the Half Pint Brawlers organization presents an ultra-violent hardcore brand of midget wrestling that is considered politically incorrect, even by midget wrestling standards.

Big People

Professional wrestling's voracious appetite for oddities has meant that it has always welcomed performers of unusually large size and girth. Put plainly, being extremely tall and/or fat has long been a very bankable commodity, usually superseding any lack of actual athletic ability. The greatest example of all, of course, would be Andre the Giant, whose already-massive dimensions were exaggerated to even greater proportions by hyperbolic promoters. But the ring has been home to many other assorted giants and behemoths over the years:

- Haystacks Calhoun: The 601-pound country boy from Morgan's Corner, Arkansas, who once killed his dog when he rolled over it in bed.
- Man Mountain Dean: The top-drawing monster of the West Coast in the 1930s, who was prominently featured in the film *Mighty Joe Young* (1949).
- The McGuire Twins: Listed in the *Guiness Book of World Records*, these scale-tipping brothers rode to the ring on tiny motorcycles.
- Martin "Blimp" Levy: One of the earliest wrestling giants, the 625-pound Blimp lived up to his name, and was known for basically falling on his opponents.
- Primo Carnera: The six foot nine inch, 265-pound mountain of muscle was the largest heavyweight boxing champ of all time, and later enjoyed a fifteen-year wrestling career.
- Great Khali: WWE's Punjabi titan, he stands over seven feet tall and weighs 350 pounds. Mobility is not his strong suit, nor does it need to be.
- The Big Show: Paul Wight was originally billed as Andre the Giant's son in WCW (he's actually even bigger than Andre was), and has been chokeslamming opponents into oblivion in WWE since 1999.
- Yokozuna: Rodney Anoa'i's weight went from 500 pounds to more than 750 pounds during his time in the WWF, and he enjoyed a lengthy run as WWF World Champion in 1993–94.
- Happy Humphrey: The heaviest pro wrestler of all time, Humphrey weighed in at over 800 pounds, and later approached 900 pounds. He's remembered for a match with Haystacks Calhoun, in which the two competitors were unable to touch hands while standing face-to-face.
- Earthquake: Former sumo John Tenta is best remembered as the Canadian powerhouse who put Hulk Hogan out of action by sitting on him in 1990.
- Giant Gonzalez: Failed basketball player Jorge Gonzalez was billed at eight feet tall (his actual height was a not-too-shabby seven feet seven inches). The tallest pro wrestler of all time, he was also known as El Gigante in WCW.

A Bear of an Opponent

Along with midget wrestling, the territorial days of the 1950s–1970s also boasted another unusual oddity: wrestling bears. Due to increased awareness of animal cruelty, as well as stricter safety precautions, the concept of bear wrestling has gone the way of the dodo, but it was once an exotic attraction at many smaller, local events, particularly throughout the southern United States. Often, the bear would work with a specific wrestler who might also be its owner and trainer, and the duo would perfect a choreographed match and take the act on the road. Sometimes, the bear might be trained to work with a different wrestler, most likely a heel who would play the coward and inevitably lose to the beast. Still other times, the promotion might challenge someone from the crowd to step up and face the bear in an actual competitive match, putting up money if said volunteer could triumph. Most, if not all, wrestling bears were declawed and detoothed.

The most famous of them all was an American black bear named Terrible Ted, who was the property of David McKigney, known in the ring as Gene Dubois. McKigney crossed paths with Ted, then a carnival bear, in the early '50s, and worked out a successful routine with the creature that remained a crowd-pleaser for nearly twenty years. The two performed their act everywhere, from Maple Leaf Wrestling in Toronto, to Georgia Championship Wrestling, to San Francisco's Big Time Wrestling, to the WWWF where they appeared in October 1971 at the Pittsburgh Civic Arena. Ted even boasted "victories" over such wrestlers as Angelo Savoldi, Baron Von Raschke, and a young Superstar Billy Graham. On several occasions, Ted met the challenges of fans from the crowd, and was even pinned on at least one of these occasions, leading to a lawsuit when McKigney and the promoter refused to pay the prize money. McKigney eventually added a second bear, Smokey, to the act, but retired them both for good in 1974.

It was Smokey who, in 1978, would maul McKigney's girlfriend to death when he accidentally left the animal's cage door open. This led to both bears being seized by the authorities. It is unknown what finally became of Smokey or Terrible Ted. As for McKigney, he was killed ten years later, when, on his way to a wrestling event in Newfoundland, he swerved his van to avoid hitting a moose and accidentally drove into a lake. McKigney's traveling partner, Keith "Adrian Adonis" Franke also died in the crash.

Man on the Moon

In the annals of pro wrestling history, there may have been no other angle as bizarre, as surreal, and as fascinating as what happened in Memphis, Tennessee, in the early 1980s. Longtime fans still speak in hushed tones about the headline-making feud that erupted between eccentric comedian and television star Andy Kaufman and Jerry Lawler, the King of Memphis Wrestling. At the time, there were many who truly believed that it was all real, which only added to its mystique; but even though later accounts would reveal that it was, of course, one of Kaufman's elaborate performance-art ruses, that takes nothing away from its brilliance.

A lifelong wrestling fan who worshipped at the altar of "Nature Boy" Buddy Rogers, Kaufman identified with the histrionic side of the business, and longed to get in the ring and play a villainous heel. In 1981, he began staging matches against women as part of his nightclub act, dubbing himself the "World Intergender Wrestling Champion." In an attempt to parlay the act into his dream career, he approached WWF promoter Vincent J. McMahon

After months of buildup, Kaufman and Lawler met in the ring at the Mid-South Coliseum for the first time on April 5, 1982.   *Photo by* Pro Wrestling Illustrated

in Madison Square Garden, but was rebuffed by the conservative elder McMahon. A friendship with prominent pro wrestling journalist Bill Apter helped Kaufman find someone with whom he could do business.

"He knew who I was from the magazines, and he asked me if we could go and talk after the matches," remembers Apter. "So here's Andy Kaufman from *Taxi* riding on the E train to the Van Wyck station, and walking to my apartment. . . . After about two hours of talking about wrestling, I said 'McMahon isn't going to let you do this. I have a friend in Memphis. Let's call him.' So I called Jerry Lawler and he said, 'You've got Andy Kaufman, the guy from *Taxi*, in your roach-infested apartment?' I said, 'Yeah, hang on,' and I put him on the phone. So that put the key in the ignition; a few days later Andy flew down there, and the rest is history."

Kaufman began appearing in the Memphis TV studios, challenging women to matches as he had been doing in clubs. He also shot a series of demeaning videos in which he lambasted the "rednecks" of Tennessee for their supposed lack of education and poor hygiene, and played up his sophisticated Hollywood origins. He was playing the obnoxious wrestling heel to the hilt, and soon drew the ire of Jerry "The King" Lawler himself, which had been the plan all along. Lawler and Kaufman finally met in the ring at the Mid-South Coliseum in April 1982, with Kaufman winning by disqualification when the King dropped him on his head with an illegal piledriver. Although legitimately injured, Kaufman exaggerated matters, going around for months in a neck brace and threatening to sue.

The feud drew national attention to pro wrestling for the first time since the 1950s. Mainstream audiences, particularly Kaufman's fans and co-workers, didn't know what to make of it. Here was the star of the NBC sitcom *Taxi*, mixing it up in a wrestling ring and braying on camera like an arrogant jerk. His shenanigans got him banned for life from *Saturday Night Live*, and the line between fantasy and reality was blurred even further when Kaufman and Lawler got into an obscenity-laced argument on *Late Night with David Letterman* that included Lawler slapping Kaufman, and the comedian tossing hot coffee at the wrestler.

Kaufman ignored the critics and continued working in Memphis for months, taking on Jimmy Hart as a manager and even touring the entire territorial circuit—not just TV tapings. He was paid regularly by Memphis promoter Jerry Jarrett, but never cashed a single check. He was finally living his dream, which was a reward in itself. He remained a fixture of Memphis TV, tangling with Lawler and other babyfaces, until he was diagnosed with cancer in December 1983. He passed away the following year, taking the secrets of the true nature of the incidents to his grave.

"He loved it," says Apter. "He wanted to be Buddy Rogers and Fred Blassie. He would've quit everything in show business had he been able to stay in pro wrestling and make a living with it."

The Kaufman/Lawler feud kept fans guessing for years, and even though the reality behind the planned storyline was officially revealed in later years, such as in the 1999 Milos Forman film *Man on the Moon*, and Lawler's 2002 autobiography *It's Good to Be the King . . . Sometimes*, it remains one of the most talked-about angles ever. If pro wrestling truly is performance art, then Andy Kaufman may have been the greatest pro wrestler of all time.

The Dead Man

It would be very difficult to decide, in a business based on gimmicks, what was the greatest or most successful one of them all. But if longevity is the measuring stick, then a case can be made that the Undertaker was—and is—the greatest gimmick of all time. Since 1990, he has been a mainstay of WWE, lasting as a main-event level talent longer than the likes of Bruno

Undertaker and Paul Bearer were inseparable during most of the 1990s, as is evident from this official publicity shot.

Sammartino, Andre the Giant, and Hulk Hogan. The concept behind his character—that of an undead, supernatural entity—may have been tweaked over the years, but it has had the kind of staying power with fans that bookers can only dream of when crafting a performer's persona. Every other ridiculous gimmick has come and gone over the past quarter-century, but the Undertaker remains a constant.

Believe it or not, the Undertaker wasn't always a zombie. He was born Mark William Calaway in Houston, Texas, on March 24, 1965, the fifth son of parents of Irish and Native American descent. He used his height early on as a basketball player in high school and college, attending Texas Wesleyan University. While in college, at age nineteen, he gave pro wrestling a try, appearing for the Von Erichs in the Dallas-based World Class Championship Wrestling.

At that time he called himself Texas Red, which would be the first in a line of short-lived gimmicks. He wrestled on the independent circuit as The Commando, and appeared in Memphis as The Master of Pain, even challenging Jerry Lawler for the USWA Heavyweight title. By 1989, he found his way to the national stage in WCW as "Mean" Mark Callous, appearing as part of The Skyscrapers tag team with "Dangerous" Danny Spivey and challenging Lex Luger for the United States Championship at *The Great American Bash '90*. But the stint was not a success, and he was let go later that year.

As luck would have it, a role alongside Hulk Hogan in the movie *Suburban Commando* brought Calaway to the attention of Vince McMahon, who promptly hired him and repackaged him as an Old West mortician character, debuting him at the 1990 *Survivor Series* in November. Clad in a wide-brimmed hat, long black duster, leather gloves and spats, the nearly seven-foot-tall Calaway was an instant sensation. The Undertaker had arrived—an unstoppable force from the netherworld that seemed to feel no pain and could bounce back from any form of punishment, seemingly unscathed. Was he dead or alive? Intrigued fans enjoyed playing into the awesome aura of the character.

Before long, Undertaker was joined by creepy manager Paul Bearer, and the duo became one of the WWF's most popular acts, whether performing as heels or babyfaces. He dethroned Hulk Hogan for the WWF World Championship in 1991, the first of an eventual seven world titles. But the character was such a success that he didn't need any championships—he seemed to operate outside the realm of other performers, a special attraction that was well protected by management, who were careful not to overexpose the white-hot gimmick.

Undertaker also began amassing a now-legendary undefeated streak at *WrestleMania*, appearing year after year at the industry's top event and always coming out the victor. It started at *WrestleMania VII* with a win over "Superfly" Jimmy Snuka, and continued for decades. "The Streak," as it came to be known, included victories over the likes of Jake "The Snake" Roberts, King Kong Bundy, Diesel, Sycho Sid, Triple H, Mark Henry, Randy Orton, Shawn Michaels, CM Punk, and many more, until finally reaching 21–0 in 2013. By that time, the forty-eight-year-old Undertaker had become a part-time WWE performer, mainly putting on the tights to defend his *WrestleMania* streak each year and nothing more. At long last, the streak came to an end at *WrestleMania XXX* in 2014 when, to the genuine shock of fans, 'Taker went down in defeat to Brock Lesnar.

Always finding a way to remain fresh, the Undertaker has managed to be a relevant member of the WWE roster longer than anyone else currently working for the company. Some of this success is due to his limited appearances in recent years, as well as the willingness of the WWE creative team to adapt his persona with the times. During the late-1990s Attitude Era, he took on more of a satanic air as the leader of the Ministry of Darkness. Through part of the 2000s, he was reinvented as the "American Bad-Ass," using a biker gimmick that was closer to his real-life identity. In recent years, he has returned to his undead roots to appeal to original fans' sense of nostalgia.

Semi-retired, the Undertaker remains one of the most popular figures in all of pro wrestling, and WWE's greatest active legend. Of all the outrageous gimmicks that have come and gone, his has lasted the test of time, possessing a certain something that has transcended the business. The Undertaker is so much more than a mere gimmick—he is, as Vince McMahon stated, a "Phenom."

The Weird, the Wacky, and the WTF

It's no secret that there have been some truly ridiculous, outrageous, and downright cringe-worthy gimmicks over the years. Many of them crossed into "so bad they're good" territory, and are fondly remembered by longtime fans despite their utter awfulness. The following is a list of twenty of the worst (best?):

Abe "Knuckleball" Schwartz

Following the Major League Baseball strike of 1994, the American people were pretty disillusioned with their baseball heroes, and the WWF decided to capitalize on this ill will by taking longtime company trouper "Brooklyn Brawler" Steve Lombardi and reinventing him as an evil ballplayer. Coming to the ring dressed in a full cap and uniform, with his face painted to look like a baseball for some reason, Schwartz only confused fans. Most confusing of all was how Lombardi went from Italian to Jewish.

Amish Roadkill

As the mastermind behind ECW, Paul Heyman was responsible for coming up with some brilliant gimmicks during the 1990s. But the creation of a mentally deranged Amish wrestler may not have been one of his shining moments. Nevertheless, the rotund, bearded Roadkill enjoyed a lengthy stay in the Land of Extreme during its final years, even sharing the ECW World Tag Team title with Danny Doring. Usually mute, Roadkill was known to menacingly intone the word "chickens" for no apparent reason.

Arachnaman

Taunting the Marvel Comics legal department with reckless abandon in 1991, WCW took second-generation star Brad Armstrong, slapped him in a yellow and blue web-covered costume and mask and called him Arachnaman. He even celebrated in the ring by shooting silly string from his wrists. In the end, WCW's wrongheaded gamble turned sour when

Marvel did indeed threaten a lawsuit, and Arachnaman quietly crawled off into the sunset.

Battman

No, that spelling is not a typo. With the *Batman* television show suddenly taking the nation by storm in 1966, perennial jobber Tony Marino had a bright idea: he had a cheesy knockoff of Adam West's already-cheesy costume from the TV show made up, and started parading around as Battman, even including a Robin-like sidekick in the act. Apparently, he somehow got away with the whole thing without suffering the wrath of DC Comics due to that extra letter *t*. The Battman turned Marino's career around for a short while in the late 1960s, when he was a big hit performing in the WWWF's Pittsburgh territory.

The Ding Dongs

From the mind of Jim Herd, the infamous former Pizza Hut executive who was given the reigns of WCW by Ted Turner, came this concept of a masked tag team, made up of two scrawny former jobbers who performed while wearing masks and leotards adorned with bells. The Ding Dongs weren't even the worst idea Herd came up with; wrestling fans are still grateful that WCW never had the nerve to introduce The Hunchbacks, a team of wrestlers who couldn't be pinned due to the enormous humps on their backs.

Doink the Clown

Doink almost doesn't belong on this list as, in the hands of veteran technician Matt Borne, the character actually worked on a weird level—at least in the beginning, when he was a sinister clown who performed sadistic pranks. Later, after Borne departed the WWF, the gimmick was bestowed on a variety of ignominious individuals, and inevitably became a kid-friendly babyface, complete with tiny sidekick Dink the Clown. Despite Borne's passing in 2013, the independent circuit continues to be plagued with random Doinks to this day.

Duke "The Dumpster" Droese

In the mid-1990s WWF, it seemed that every wrestler had to have another occupation of some kind. There were wrestling hockey players, wrestling accountants, wrestling plumbers . . . and a wrestling garbage man. Carrying a trashcan (what else?) to the ring with him, Duke the Dumpster proudly proclaimed that he was going to "take out the trash." He even took part in a feud with none other than Hunter Hearst Helmsley, the future Triple H. WWF fans endured Droese for two whole years before he was sent to the junk heap.

Eugene

Not even the mentally challenged are off-limits when it comes to bad gimmicks, which was proven when WWE gave us Eugene, the dimwitted "nephew" of Eric Bischoff. Portrayed by former developmental wrestler Nick Dinsmore as a wrestling savant who could mimic the moves of his favorite competitors, Eugene was pro wrestling's answer to *Rain Man*—minus the sensitivity and artfulness.

Glacier

Eric Bischoff is rightly praised for introducing the nWo to WCW in the late 1990s, but before we get too excited, let's remember that he also was responsible for Glacier, a character blatantly ripped off from the popular video game *Mortal Kombat*. Teased endlessly month after month, Glacier's debut on *Monday Nitro*, complete with outdated laser light show and fake snow, was a colossal dud. The company tried to match him up with other *Mortal Kombat*-inspired grapplers, including the masked Mortis, but soon dropped the whole fiasco.

The Gobbledy Gooker

The patron saint of bad gimmicks, The Gobbledy Gooker was second-generation grappler Hector Guerrero dressed in a turkey costume, and first emerged from a giant egg at the WWF's 1990 *Survivor Series*. After weeks of buildup, fans were dying to know what was in the egg, and when Mean Gene Okerlund revealed the Gooker to the live crowd at the Hartford Civic Center, you could almost feel their collective disappointment and disgust. Matters were not helped when Mean Gene proceeded to dance with the creature to the tune of "Turkey in the Straw."

Mantaur

When independent wrestler Mike Halac was offered the opportunity to work for the WWF in 1995, he jumped at it—even if it meant wearing a giant bull's head and furry singlet, and bellowing like a moose. Mantaur charged his opponents, stomped his feet as if they were hooves, and pretty much did whatever else was required of him. Despite his best efforts, however, Mantaur was very quickly put out to pasture.

Max Moon

It seems perfectly logical that, at some point, there would be a wrestler from outer space, and in 1993 the WWF gave him to us in the form of Max Moon. Originally designed for *lucha libre* superstar Konnan, the gimmick was hastily slapped on tag team also-ran Paul Diamond when Konnan balked at the idea and walked. Taking one look at Moon's cartoonish spaceman getup and confetti wrist-guns, it's not hard to comprehend Konnan's decision.

The Mummy

Not to be confused with the Yeti of mid-'90s WCW infamy, who only looked like a giant mummy, Benji Ramirez played an actual Egyptian mummy during the 1960s. Complete with mask and wrappings, the Mummy was a particularly big hit in the South, and even managed somehow to land a match in 1966 against former six-time World Heavyweight Champion Lou Thesz.

Naked Mideon

When the gritty Attitude Era hit the WWF in the late 1990s, it became clear that Dennis Knight could no longer be allowed to play the happy-go-lucky hillbilly Phineas Godwinn. First, the WWF creative team turned him into Mideon, a member of the Undertaker's diabolical Ministry of Darkness. When that fizzled out, desperation set in and he became Naked Mideon, which was basically Mideon as a streaker. Running through arenas wearing only a fanny pack, Naked Mideon understandably spelled the end of Dennis Knight's career.

Oz

Following Ted Turner's purchase of WCW in 1988, someone in Turner's organization had the bright idea to start using some of the company's other intellectual property as fodder for new wrestling characters. Since Turner Broadcasting owned MGM Studios at the time, what better idea than to rip off MGM's most beloved movie, *The Wizard of Oz*? The result was future World Heavyweight Champion Kevin Nash wearing a long green robe, an old man mask and wig, and a giant crown, being led to the ring by another guy who called himself Merlin the Magician.

Papa Shango

Charles Wright assumed many personas in the WWF of the 1990s, the first being a Caribbean voodoo master. With the inexplicable ability to make black slime pour from his opponent's bodies, Shango tangled with heavy hitters like Hulk Hogan, the Undertaker, and the Ultimate Warrior, whom he once caused to vomit in the ring on *WWF Superstars*. Wright would later be given a UFC gimmick as Kama the Ultimate Fighting Machine, and eventually achieved his greatest success as The Godfather, the wrestling pimp.

Phantasio

Yes, there really was a wrestling mime. Phantasio enjoyed initial success in Jerry Lawler's USWA as The Spellbinder, and it was Lawler who recommended him for Vince McMahon's WWF in the mid-'90s. Performing lame magic tricks in the ring that culminated in his making his opponent's underwear suddenly appear outside their clothing, Phantasio couldn't pull off the trick of having anyone give a damn about him. The character was phased out after one TV appearance.

The Shark

Poor John Tenta. After a successful run in the WWF as Earthquake, he was brought into WCW in 1994 and eventually transformed into The Shark. Wearing fake fins and a painted giant mouth with pointed teeth, he was known to scream "Shark attack!" before pummeling his opponents. Of course, when the gimmick tanked, he also became famous for cutting a promo on WCW TV in which he proclaimed, "I'm not a *fish*! I'm a *man*!"

The Shockmaster

The most notorious/hilarious moment in pro wrestling history occurred on August 18, 1993, when wrestler Fred Ottman, dressed in blue jeans, a furry vest, and a *Star Wars* storm-trooper helmet covered in glitter, accidentally fell through a sheetrock wall on live TV as part of WCW's *Clash of Champions XXIV*. The Shockmaster was supposed to be Sting and Davey Boy Smith's great equalizer in their battle with Sid Vicious and Harlem Heat, but instead turned into a punch line that is still eliciting laughs over two decades later.

The Zombie

ECW fans are still trying to forget WWE's ill-advised attempt to resurrect the defunct organization in the late 2000s, and this is one of the reasons. When it was learned that the new ECW would be airing its weekly program on the SyFy Channel, the WWE creative team felt they needed to add some elements of the supernatural to the show to please the network's usual fan base. And so, viewers tuning into *ECW on SyFy* for the first time were treated to the sight of a wrestler, made up as a zombie, staggering to the ring. After a predictably strong fan backlash, the undead grappler was never seen again.

Tag Team Turmoil

Wrestling's Dynamic Duos

It takes two flints to make a fire.

—Louisa May Alcott

O f all the permutations and variations on a theme that fans have witnessed over the years, the one that has survived the longest is tag-team wrestling. Originally an exotic oddity added to spice up a card, it has become so accepted and so commonplace that it is now just a regular part of the show. For nearly seventy years, tag-team matches have been lighting up crowds with the unique brand of drama and excitement that naturally occurs when you take a one-on-one encounter and up the stakes by turning it into a two-on-two affair. Tag-team wrestling has enjoyed varying degrees of popularity in different eras and in different companies; it has launched the careers of future Hall of Famers and given us some truly one-of-a-kind pairings.

Looking back now, it seems like an obvious enough idea to develop. Since the beginning of professional wrestling in the nineteenth century—or even, if one wishes to go back further, to the dawn of wrestling as a sport during mankind's antiquity—matches had always been contested as a single opponent against another. But as the sport moved more toward the realm of entertainment, an anything-goes attitude began to infiltrate the business, and promoters became open to trying whatever interesting gimmick would be likely to pack in the crowds. If fans got excited to see two of their favorite stars go at it, the thinking went, surely the excitement would double with four.

"Tag-team wrestling as a general concept makes sense," says Greg Oliver, who literally co-wrote the book on the subject, *The Pro Wrestling Hall of Fame: The Tag Teams* (2005). "Nobody goes through life by themselves. It always helps to have somebody there to help you out . . . . The idea is you're working with someone else to make a difference and succeed. So tag-team wrestling works on that level, and from an aesthetic standpoint, it adds to the number of people, so it's that much more excitement. The action can really get amped up; there are so many possibilities there."

A New Concept

Urban legend tells of the first tag-team match being held in San Francisco in 1901, but the more likely origin story points to Houston, where on October 2, 1936, promoter Morris Siegel and booker Karl "Doc" Sarpolis matched local favorites Whiskers Savage and Milo Steinborn against Indian imports Tiger Daula and Fazul Mohammed. That particular two-on-two presentation was not truly a tag match as we would conceive of one, as there was no tagging involved—rather, all four combatants took to the ring simultaneously, in what would eventually be termed a "Texas tornado match." Nevertheless, it is generally agreed upon as the first time more than two wrestlers performed in a ring at the same time.

An initial tag-team craze hit in the late 1930s, and it would be during the 1940s that the general "rules" of tag-team wrestling were solidified. Initially, they were referred to as "Australian tag team matches," with the story being that the concept had originated down under. However, there is nothing to support this origin, and it is likely a typical flourish devised by promoters to make the new idea seem even more exotic. According to these rules, only one member of each team would be allowed to compete in the ring at any given time; his teammate would stand outside the ropes, in a designated corner of the ring. Members would be able to switch once a tag had been made between them, at which point the inactive wrestler stepped through the ropes to take his partner's place. The wrestler who had tagged out then had until the referee's count of five to step outside the ropes and leave the fray (these five seconds, of course, allowed for all types of heel double-teaming shenanigans to take place). And so it went, until a fall occurred, just as it would in a singles match.

The division went from a bizarre attraction to an established part of the action in 1950, when the National Wrestling Alliance created its first World Tag Team Championship, under the promotional auspices of Joe Malcewicz's San Francisco territory. During the first decade of its existence, that prestigious championship would be dominated by the duo that deserves recognition as the first "star" tag team: Ben & Mike Sharpe. The Sharpe Brothers would hold the NWA World Tag Team title a staggering eighteen times between 1950 and 1959, and during that time even took the belts to Japan, where they became part of Japanese wrestling history, thanks to their landmark feud with Rikidozan & Rusher Kimura. Thus, they helped establish tag-team wrestling on two different continents.

"The Sharpes don't get enough credit for what they meant to pro wrestling," says Greg Oliver. "Joe Malcewicz had the idea that pro wrestling could be about more than just the singles, and tag teams really took off there. We almost all have brothers and sisters, so the family aspect of tag teams was really important, and why some guys became 'family' even if they weren't. That's something everyone could identify with."

The First Golden Age

With television encouraging ever more outrageous on-air characters, tag-team wrestling experienced its first Golden Age during the mid-1950s through the early '60s. It was then that teams generally began to be presented as a packaged unit, rather than just a loose partnership between two singles wrestlers. This was the rise of the "tag-team specialist," as duos like the Graham Brothers and the Fabulous Kangaroos took shape—teams with a specific look and theme to them. Before long, the NWA would be sanctioning several different versions of the World Tag Team title in different territories, and the AWA and (W)WWF would get in on the act, as well.

"In the post-war era, [the growth] of the tag teams had to do with the fact that there'd sometimes be only six wrestlers going to a town, or eight," explains Oliver. "Not a very big card, so the guys would work singles, and then they'd work in a tag-team match at the end, so those guys would work three matches and fill up a whole show in a small town. That's where tag-team wrestling started, and it grew from there."

This era would also see the beginning of the tried-and-true tradition of tag-team wrestling psychology. The thinking was that you wanted the crowd to be kept in suspense waiting for the babyface tag team to rally and give the heels their comeuppance. This was no different than in a singles match, except that the suspense was magnified, thanks to some clever manipulation of the tag team "rules." The heels would generally distract the referee, sometimes with the help of a manager, which would allow them to perform all manner of illegal double-teams and outside interference. Generally, one member of the babyface team would be made to suffer an inordinate amount of punishment while being cut off from his partner, just out of reach. The crowd's anticipation/frustration would build, until finally the downtrodden face would manage to make the "hot tag" to his exuberant teammate, and the place would come unglued as said teammate tore into the terrified heel tandem. Formulaic, perhaps; but it worked.

The Second Golden Age

Tag-team wrestling flourished during the Territorial Era, experiencing what is generally considered to be its second and greatest Golden Age of all during the 1980s. That decade was populated with more legendary teams, in more areas of the country, than one can shake a tag rope at. Down in Dallas, World Class Championship Wrestling showcased the groundbreaking feud between The Fabulous Freebirds and the Von Erichs. Bill Watts's Mid-South Wrestling and Jim Crockett's World Championship Wrestling spotlighted the innovative rivalry between The Midnight Express and The Rock 'n' Roll Express. The AWA featured The Midnight Rockers (later just The Rockers in the WWF), The East-West Connection (Adrian Adonis & Jesse "The Body" Ventura) and The High Flyers (Jim Brunzell & Greg Gagne). During the WWF's national expansion, that company boasted such tandems as The British Bulldogs and The Hart Foundation, fresh from Calgary's Stampede Wrestling; The Killers Bees (Brunzell, now teamed with B. Brian Blair); and Demolition, a frightening duo wearing facepaint and clad in spiked leather.

That latter team was a rare example of Vince McMahon aping an act he was unable to procure himself, as most fans today realize that Demolition was a pale imitation of a team that helped redefine tag-team wrestling and that became the most dominant pairing of all time: The Road Warriors. Hawk & Animal ran roughshod in the AWA, Jim Crockett Promotions and wherever else they went, and eventually even muscled their way into the WWF in 1990, taking the place of pretenders like Demolition and The Powers of Pain. Along with their many contemporaries, The Road Warriors were at the forefront of developing an even more high-impact, hard-hitting, and fast-moving form of tag-team wrestling than had ever been seen, with lightning-quick tags and innovative double-team maneuvers.

"Being in a tag team, you have to get along with your partner outside the ring and inside the ring," points out Dr. Tom Prichard, who achieved some of his greatest career success in tandems such as The Heavenly Bodies and The Bodydonnas. "You really do have to gel. People can tell the difference between great teams like the Freebirds and the Bulldogs, which had chemistry, and teams where they're just putting two guys together. Without that chemistry and that magic, its not gonna happen."

The Third Golden Age

Many feel that tag-team wrestling never again achieved the heights it did during the 1980s, when the tag team match(es) could typically be counted on to steal the show. Nevertheless, there was one last Golden Age, of sorts, that occurred during the late 1990s and early 2000s, particularly in the WWF/E, where a whole new crop of teams emerged to captivate fans' attention at the height of the Attitude Era. It started in 1997 with the rise of The New Age Outlaws, two former lower mid-carders, Road Dogg and Billy Gunn, who finally found their niche after going over the venerable Road Warriors in a true changing-of-the-guard moment.

The Outlaws were followed by the likes of The Hardy Boyz, Edge & Christian, and former ECW World Tag Team Champions The Dudley Boyz, all of whom upped the stakes of tag-team wrestling even further with all manner of death-defying, high-flying, heavily prop-laden matches. Add teams like the APA (veteran Ron "Faarooq" Simmons joined by longtime WWF mid-carder Bradshaw) and Too Cool (the hip-hop–inspired pairing of Brian "Grandmaster Sexay" Christopher and Scotty 2 Hotty that was briefly one of the WWF's most popular acts), and you have the last time that there was a truly coherent, heavily populated tag-team division.

Over the past decade, tag-team wrestling has had a tough time of it. Although there have been some bright spots, it is generally considered to be on the decline in comparison to the glory days of the '80s and '90s. Some in decision-making positions consider the subgenre to be passé, a gimmicky holdout from an earlier era. Many wrestlers fear getting pigeonholed as tag-team performers, and, thus, are hesitant to be placed in them. Also, the popularity of Triple Threat and Fatal Fourway matchups, which feature three and four singles competitors in the ring at the same time, has reduced the novelty tag-team wrestling once provided.

Still, that doesn't mean that there haven't been some hard-working tandems continuing to keep the tag-team torch burning bright in recent years. In WWE, The Usos have carried on the tradition of successful Samoan duos, and Cody "Stardust" Rhodes & Dustin "Goldust" Rhodes have kept the brotherly tag-team trope alive and well. In the grand tradition of The Fabulous Freebirds, The Shield was the most dominant three-man teaming in recent memory. In TNA Wrestling, The Dudley Boyz reinvented themselves as Team 3D, and Beer Money Inc. (James Storm & Bobby Roode) dominated the tag-team division for years. The independent circuit boasts The Briscoe Brothers (not to be confused with Jack & Jerry of old), who lay claim to being Ring of Honor's longest-reigning tag-team champions. The efforts of teams like these—and, most importantly, the promoters and bookers who believe in them—can help ensure that tag-team wrestling continues to thrive well into the twenty-first century.

Terrific Tandems

A look back at twenty-five of the most important tag teams to ever join forces:

Arn Anderson & Tully Blanchard

Also known as The Brain Busters during their short run in the WWF, Anderson & Blanchard achieved their greatest notoriety as members of the

Anderson & Blanchard left Jim Crockett Promotions and The Four Horsemen to join the WWF as The Brain Busters in the fall of 1988.

John McKeon/ Wikimedia

elite Four Horsemen in Jim Crockett Promotions. They were the first to win both the NWA and WWF World Tag Team titles, and brought an old-school, rough-and-ready approach to the flashy landscape of '80s tag-team wrestling. They each achieved greatness individually and with other partners, but Arn and Tully will always be best remembered as Horsemen.

The British Bulldogs

The British Bulldogs really set the stage for what pro wrestling has become, for good and for bad.

—Greg Oliver

Davey Boy Smith & The Dynamite Kid were among the acquisitions Vince McMahon made from Calgary's Stampede Wrestling during his national expansion of the WWF, and of the whole crop of exciting duos he imported during that time, they might have been the most talented. Combining the raw power of Smith with the crisp and brutal technical skills of the Kid, the British Bulldogs brought with them a style that WWF fans had never seen, and it took them all the way to the WWF World Tag Team title in 1986 at *WrestleMania 2*.

The Crusher & The Bruiser

Stomping their way to the ring to the strains of "The Beer Barrel Polka," Reggie "The Crusher" Lisowski and Dick "The Bruiser" Afflis were the ultimate blue-collar roughnecks, and they were adored by a fan base that was made up of largely the same. The Midwestern-based AWA was their home, and it was there that they spent more time as World Tag Team Champions than any other duo in wrestling history, capturing five titles for a total of nearly four years at the top between 1963 and 1976. Their record for most AWA World Championships would never be broken.

Demolition

Although they may have started out in 1987 as Vince McMahon's answer to The Road Warriors, Ax & Smash most certainly carved out an impressive place in wrestling history. With three WWF World Tag Team titles to their credit, they spent a total of nearly two years as champions, longer than any tandem in company history. Combining the talents of former "Masked Superstar" Bill Eadie (Ax) and former "Soviet" brawler Krusher Kruschev (Smash), they were one of the most "over" tag teams of the WWF's 1980s Golden Age.

The Dudley Boyz/Team 3D

The most decorated tag team in pro wrestling history, The Dudley Boyz have gone through some dramatic transformations over the years, but at the end of the day they're recognized as twenty-three–time World Tag Team Champions. Originally known as Buh-Buh Ray & D-Von Dudley in ECW in the late '90s, they made a major detour through WWE in the early 2000s, and later became Team 3D in TNA Wrestling during the late 2000s. Pioneers of the hardcore tag-team style, they are the only duo to win the WWE, NWA, WCW, ECW, TNA, and IWGP Tag Team titles.

The Eliminators

If Demolition was Vince McMahon's answer to The Road Warriors, then John Kronus & Perry Saturn comprised Paul Heyman's answer. Although they first formed in the Memphis-based USWA, where they won their first Tag Team Championship, it was in ECW during the mid-1990s that The Eliminators made a name for themselves, capturing three ECW Tag Team Championships and tangling with other classic ECW tandems like

The Gangstas, Cactus Jack & Mikey Whipwreck, and, of course, The Dudley Boyz.

The Fabulous Freebirds

Starting out in 1979 in Georgia Championship Wrestling as the pairing of Michael "P. S." Hayes and Terry "Bam Bam" Gordy, The Fabulous Freebirds added Buddy "Jack" Roberts to the team when they hit Mid-South Wrestling, where they also experienced their first taste of major success. By the time they got to World Class Championship Wrestling in Dallas in 1982, they were poised to become something very special. Utilizing Lynyrd Skynyrd's "Freebird" as their entrance theme, they were the first wrestlers since Gorgeous George to use music, and also innovated the industry's obsession with rock 'n' roll. Their ongoing war with the Von Erich family is the stuff of legend.

The Fabulous Kangaroos

The Kangaroos were the number-one team of all time. They set the standard.
—Greg Oliver

Since it used to be called "Australian tag team rules" back in the 1950s, it only made sense that one of the most prominent duos would come from Australia. The original Kangaroos, Al Costello & Roy Heffernan, were the first tag team to be packaged with a single theme, and set the template that would be followed by almost every tag team that followed. Managed by Wild Red Berry, they were the hottest tag team during the very early days of Capitol Wrestling (which would go on to become WWE), winning the United States Tag Team title three times. With their trademark boomerangs and outback gear, they were an act ahead of their time.

The Fabulous Ones

The innovative duo of Steve Keirn and Stan Lane, the brainchild of Jerry Lawler and Jerry Jarrett, created a mold that would be used many more times. And while they achieved success in a wide array of territories from Southwest Championship Wrestling and Florida to the AWA and Mid-Atlantic, it was in Memphis that The Fabulous Ones truly built their legacy, drawing tremendous crowds on a regular basis. The classic pretty-boy babyface tag team and their ongoing feud with the savage Sheepherders are fondly remembered to this day.

The Graham Brothers

Also known as The Golden Grahams, the team of Eddie Graham & Dr. Jerry Graham was one of many fictional "brother" tandems that have dominated wrestling over the years. Known for their white-hot feud with the team of Antonino Rocca & Miguel Perez, they sold out Madison Square Garden many times during the late 1950s. Under the management of the villainous Bobby Davis, they were among the most despised heels of their era.

The Hardy Boyz

Matt & Jeff Hardy emerged just at the height of the WWF's Attitude Era, and an eye-popping, take-no-prisoners aerial style was just what the weekly viewership of *Raw* and *SmackDown!* were looking for at the time. Distinguishing themselves in a ladder match against Edge & Christian at *No Mercy '99*, the unorthodox fraternal duo became an immediate sensation, and their tag-team career would forever be linked to that of their Canadian rivals.

The Hart Foundation

Many of the greatest tag teams of all time have been formed from two very different types of wrestlers; such was the case with Bret "Hit Man" Hart & Jim "The Anvil" Neidhardt, one of the most celebrated tag teams in WWE history. The slick technician Hart and the stocky bruiser Neidhardt complemented each other effortlessly, and their wars with The British Bulldogs over the WWF World Tag Team title during the 1980s produced some of the finest matches of the decade.

The Infernos

A gimmick that transcended individual members, this masked heel tandem was composed of several hooded grapplers during its heyday from the mid-1960s through the mid-1970s, including Frankie Cain & Rocky Smith (the originals), as well as replacement members such as Curtis Smith, Ron Gibson, Stan Pulaski, Stan Vachon, Doug Gilbert, Mike McManus, and Kurt Von Brauner. Infamous for their loaded boots and masks, as well as their flagrant illegal partner switching, they were mainstays throughout Florida, the Carolinas, Georgia, Tennessee, Texas, and California, and the various combinations held the NWA World Tag Team title on seven different occasions.

The Midnight Express

They had that intangible 'it' factor. They just went out there, and felt it, and did it.

—Dr. Tom Prichard

In 1983, Bill Watts proved once again why he had one of the keenest minds in wrestling when he teamed "Beautiful" Bobby Eaton and "Loverboy" Dennis Condrey under the management of Jim Cornette as The Midnight Express. The duo eventually went on to Jim Crockett Promotions, where they won the NWA World Tag Team title. When Condrey left the team and was replaced with "Sweet" Stan Lane, the success continued, as the new duo won the title as well. Known for their slick, highly coordinated in-ring style, The Midnight Express was one of the most exciting teams to watch, and were in demand by promoters all over the country.

The Minnesota Wrecking Crew

Arguably the dominant tag team of the 1970s, Gene & Ole Anderson were fixtures in both Jim Barnett's Georgia Championship Wrestling and Jim Crockett's Mid-Atlantic Championship Wrestling, winning a total of eight NWA World Tag Team Championships in both territories combined. Their rough-and-tumble, hard-hitting, methodical style was emblematic of the era, and made them one of the most feared duos anywhere in the business. The Wrecking Crew legacy was later enhanced with the addition of another "cousin," Arn Anderson.

The New Age Outlaws

As singles, not so much, but put Billy Gunn and Road Dogg together, and there was that magic and chemistry.

—Dr. Tom Prichard

"Oh you didn't know? Yo' ass better call somebody!" So went Road Dogg's trademark pre-match promo as he and partner Billy Gunn made their way to the ring during the WWF's no-holds-barred Attitude Era. As members of the D-Generation X faction, The New Age Outlaws were at the forefront of the edgy direction the company was going in at that time—a direction that saw them achieve greater success than they ever had apart. With no shortage of catchphrases and hand gestures, they were the epitome of the late-1990s WWF, and won five World Tag Team titles during that period.

Nick Bockwinkel & Ray "The Crippler" Stevens

They showed that tag team wrestling could be way more than just two guys paired together.

—Greg Oliver

Prior to becoming a dominant AWA World Heavyweight Champion, devious heel Nick Bockwinkel first made his mark as the tag-team partner of San Francisco legend Ray Stevens. Under the management of Bobby "The Brain" Heenan, they were the most hated AWA grapplers of the early 1970s, taking the World Tag Team title on three separate occasions for a total of more than three years as titleholders. The razor-tongued technician Bockwinkel and the alarmingly agile enforcer Stevens were the template for many teams that followed.

The Road Warriors

We came from the street, we always said we came from the street, and we never insulted the fans or talked above them. We were the guys that said what we were gonna do, and then we did it.

—Road Warrior Animal

Hawk & Animal won *PWI*'s Tag Team of the Year Award on four occasions, between 1983 and 1988, their most dominant period.

Photo by Pro Wrestling Illustrated

An apocalyptic vision from the future, Hawk & Animal seemed to have walked right out of the film from which they took their name. The business had never seen anything like them when they burst on the scene in the early 1980s—massive brawlers dressed in spiked shoulder pads, with demonic war paint and shaved heads. They were promoted as an unstoppable force (often drawing criticism from their peers for not selling their opponents' offense), and went on to become the only team to win the World Tag Team title in the NWA, the AWA, and the WWF, where they were alternately known as The Legion of Doom. They were arguably the most popular tag team in history.

The Rock 'n' Roll Express

First joining forces in Memphis in 1983, they were teamed by Jerry "The King" Lawler, who is known for his love of rock music and his desire to incorporate it in pro wrestling. Eventually making their way through Bill Watt's Mid-South Wrestling and Jim Crockett's World Championship Wrestling, The Rock 'n' Roll Express would win four NWA World Tag Team Championships, feuding nearly everywhere they went with their archrivals, The Midnight Express. There has perhaps been no other tag team that has been together as long as Ricky Morton & Robert Gibson, and the duo still makes appearances on the independent circuit.

The Sharpe Brothers

Unlike many so-called "brother" tag teams, this Canadian duo was made up of actual siblings. Ben & Mike Sharpe were the first major tag-team stars, dominating tag-team wrestling in the San Francisco territory of the 1950s, where it was first popularized by promoter Joe Malcewicz. Not only were they among the earliest World Tag Team Champions, they also became two of the earliest American performers to cross over into Japanese wrestling.

The Shield

Formed much more recently than the other groups on the list, this anarchistic team turned a lot of heads when they burst on to the WWE scene at the 2012 *Survivor Series*, and continued to dominate WWE TV thereafter. Initially featuring unhinged mastermind Dean Ambrose, intense powerhouse Roman Reigns, and high-flying daredevil Seth Rollins, the group even held the WWE Tag Team Championship when Reigns & Rollins captured the prize from Kane & Daniel Bryan. The trio imploded in 2014 when

Rollins shockingly turned on his partners, allowing all three members to go on to singles success.

The Steiner Brothers

Another legitimate brother duo, Rick & Scott Steiner were standout amateur wrestlers from the University of Michigan who formed one of the most gifted tag teams of the 1990s. Equally dominant in WCW and the WWF, they would capture a total of nine World Tag Team titles between the two promotions, and are responsible for some of the most thrilling matches of the decade. The Steiners were also a major sensation in Japan, where their combination of power moves and technical wrestling was extremely popular.

The Vachon Brothers

Although they achieved great success apart as both wrestlers and promoters, Paul "Butcher" Vachon and Maurice "Mad Dog" Vachon were also a phenomenon as a unit, and are best remembered for their nearly two-year reign as AWA World Tag Team Champions from 1969 to 1971. They also captured the Georgia version of the NWA World Tag Team Championship; Mid-Atlantic's Southern Tag Team Championship; the Texas Tag Team title in World Class; and the International Tag Team title in Stampede. Perhaps no other tag team achieved so much in so many different places during the '60s and '70s.

The Valiant Brothers

Unlike some teams like the Steiners and the Vachons, the Valiants weren't actual brothers, but in the end, that didn't matter. After former baby-face "Handsome" Jimmy Valiant turned on Chief Jay Strongbow and introduced his worked brother "Luscious" Johnny Valiant, a new WWWF tag-team dynasty was born. Feuding with top-level faces like Strongbow and world champion Bruno Sammartino, The Valiants dominated the WWWF World Tag Team title like no team had before, and took the bleached-blonde tag-team trope innovated by The Graham Brothers to a whole new level.

The Wild Samoans

Afa & Sika were the classic "wild-man" tag team, and what they lacked in political correctness they made up for in staying power. A top tag-team act everywhere they went, including Mid-South, Stampede, Mid-Atlantic, Memphis, Georgia, Vancouver, Detroit, and other locales, they accumulated more than twenty titles over the course of their tenure, most notably three WWF World Tag Team Championships under the management of Capt. Lou Albano. They are also the godfathers of a far-reaching family of Samoan wrestlers that includes The Rock and Roman Reigns.

More Top Teams

- Antonino Rocca & Miguel Perez
- Badd Company
- The Fantastics
- Harlem Heat
- The Hollywood Blondes ('70s, '80s, and '90s versions)
- The Kentuckians
- Larry "The Axe" Hennig & "Handsome" Harley Race
- The Mongols
- Pat Patterson & Ray "The Crippler" Stevens
- Prof. Toru Tanaka & Mr. Fuji
- Ricky Steamboat & Jay Youngblood
- Rip Hawk & Swede Hanson

Strength in Numbers

Aside from actual tag teams, which are typically composed of two or, at most, three rotating performers, pro wrestlers have also banded together over the years in larger groups, commonly known as stables or factions. These factions can create a sense of gang warfare within wrestling storylines, in which crews of allied wrestlers either do war with each other or target individual enemies. Factions can open up the possibility of many different angles; very rarely do they all compete together in the same match, but they can participate in several feuds at the same time, and in the process sometimes dominate a promotion. Heels apparently do better with a little backup, and so, usually, factions have been villainous in nature. Here are some of the best . . .

The Corporate Ministry

This big mishmash of a group actually came together as the combination of two different groups in the Attitude Era of WWF: Shane McMahon's evil Corporation, and the Undertaker's sinister Ministry of Darkness. The ultimate amalgamation of late '90s heels, they conspired to make life hell for Stone Cold Steve Austin and The Rock, and eventually revealed that the "Higher Power" pulling their strings was none other than WWF chairman, Vince McMahon.

D-Generation X

A rare babyface faction, the anti-authoritarian dX was one of the most popular forces in the WWF during the Attitude Era of the late 1990s and early 2000s. Originally headed up by WWF World Champion Shawn Michaels, it also featured Triple H and Chyna. After Michaels's retirement, X-Pac and The New Age Outlaws were recruited. In later years, Michaels and Triple H would get the band back together, but they never quite recaptured that original magic.

The Dangerous Alliance

Before he became the mastermind behind ECW, Paul Heyman was manager Paul E. Dangerously, and during his early '90s stint in WCW, he managed an impressive collection of heels that sought to replace the missing Four Horsemen as the company's dominant villains. Featuring U.S. champion Rick Rude, TV champion "Stunning" Steve Austin, World Tag Team champions Arn Anderson & Larry Zbyszko, and the lovely Madusa, the Dangerous Alliance did a lot more than just fill the Horsemen void.

The Dusek Riot Squad

"Never a dull match with a Dusek!" So went the slogan for what was perhaps the first stable in the history of professional wrestling. The Bohemian Dusek (real name: Hason) brothers set the business on its ear in the 1930s with their unprecedented roughhouse tactics and pack mentality. Rudy, the eldest, was a world championship contender and later became the czar of New York wrestling. Younger brothers Emil & Ernie were a common tag-team combo, and youngest brother Joe brought up the rear. Pioneering heels, they incited a riot at the Boston Garden in 1935 when Rudy violently interfered in Ernie's match with world champion Danno O'Mahoney, something unheard-of at the time.

"The Dusek Brothers were incredibly important," Greg Oliver states. "They introduced the idea that you couldn't mess with these guys because they'd watch out for each other."

Evolution

One of the factions most heavily influenced by The Four Horsemen was this group that dominated WWE during much of the first decade of the 2000s—it even featured Ric Flair as a founding member. Representing the past, present, and future of the business, Evolution also included world champion Triple H, as well as newcomers Randy Orton and Batista. The group would later reunite briefly in 2014, this time without Flair.

This particular lineup of The Four Horsemen, comprising (clockwise, from left): Arn Anderson, Barry Windham, Ric Flair, Tully Blanchard, and manager J. J. Dillon, was arguably the most successful of the group's incarnations.

Photo by Pro Wrestling Illustrated

The Four Horsemen

Without question, this impressively named group represents the gold standard of wrestling factions. Revolving around "Nature Boy" Ric Flair and his enforcer Arn Anderson, the original 1986 lineup also included Tully Blanchard and Ole Anderson, with J. J. Dillon as the manager. Later incarnations would feature Barry Windham, Sting, Lex Luger, Sid Vicious, and others. They dominated most of the championships in the NWA/WCW during their late '80s and early '90s runs, and seemed to live a glitz-and-glamour lifestyle that transcended the gimmick. To this day, their trademark four-finger salute remains "the symbol of excellence."

The Heenan Family

Stables were usually led by a manager, and in this case that manager was the great Bobby "The Brain" Heenan. The Heenan Family started in the AWA in the 1970s, and included the likes of Ray Stevens, The Blackjacks, Cowboy Bobby Duncum and AWA world champion Nick Bockwinkel. In the 1980s, Heenan brought the family to the WWF, where it featured Big John Studd, King Kong Bundy, "Mr. Wonderful" Paul Orndorff, "Ravishing" Rick Rude, and Mr. Perfect.

The Legion of Doom

The name would later become interchangeable with that of The Road Warriors, but it was originally used in the early 1980s as the title of a formidable stable in Georgia Championship Wrestling, of which Hawk & Animal were only a part. Under the leadership of "Precious" Paul Ellering, it also included the likes of Jake "The Snake" Roberts, King Kong Bundy, The Iron Sheik, The Original Sheik, The Spoiler, Arn Anderson, and Matt Borne.

The New World Order

Simply put, the nWo changed the pro wrestling business forever. Founded in WCW by former WWF stars Kevin Nash and Scott Hall (The Outsiders), as well as freshly heel-turned "Hollywood" Hulk Hogan, they were the first faction presented as trying to take over the entire company. They later recruited countless members, including Buff Bagwell, Konnan, and many more, eventually growing so bloated that they split into two rival groups, nWo Hollywood and nWo Wolfpac. And then, of course, there were the completely unrelated Latino World Order (lWo) and Blue World Order (bWo). (For more on the nWo, see Chapter 8.)

Raven's Nest/Flock

Originally formed in ECW by Scott "Raven" Levy in 1997, Raven's Nest, as it was first called, was a shady gang of reprobates presented almost like a cult of drug fiends, although drugs were never directly mentioned. After a long reign as ECW World Champion, Raven eventually jumped to WCW and took the concept with him, this time calling it Raven's Flock. Only one member, Stevie Richards, joined Raven in both of its incarnations.

17

Big Mouths and Bad Suits

The Vital Role of the Wrestling Manager

Some of those abusive, obstreperous, pernicious rumor-mongers who have sought to smear, besmirch, and destroy my reputation will never be able to take away my spirit of optimism because I will always be a ray of sunshine, a creator of gladness, and master of myself.

—Wild Red Berry

They scream at the top of their lungs, crying foul for every perceived injustice, while simultaneously refusing to take responsibility for the ones they themselves have perpetrated. They invite the hatred of the masses with open disdain. There is no illegal tactic or devious short-cut that is beneath their moral standards. They extol their own virtues and the virtues of the men they represent with a shameful lack of humility, and take pride in that which brings displeasure to as many as possible. They are a unique breed of characters resulting from the convergence of low theater and mass media. They are professional wrestling managers.

The idea of the modern wrestling manager is a product of the industry's transition to televised entertainment in the 1950s. In the earlier days, there had certainly been managers: Frank Gotch had Farmer Burns, Ed "Strangler" Lewis had Billy Sandow, Joe Stecher had his brother Tony. But these men were actual managers, handling the careers and training of their charges in a time before wrestling promoters became the ultimate power brokers in the game. This is not the type of manager we're discussing here. Rather, our focus is on the wrestling manager as fictional character—the caricaturized version created for television, which was loosely based on their real-life predecessors.

The Manager as Pitchman

In a way, the first modern wrestling manager may have been Ed Lewis himself, who was selected by the National Wrestling Alliance in the late

1940s to be a goodwill ambassador and the figurehead cornerman for its World Heavyweight Champion, Lou Thesz. Although Thesz and Lewis enjoyed a close friendship, with Lou considering Ed a mentor, the role of the retired Strangler was not that of the managers of yore, but really to be a promotional asset to help hype Thesz in the press and give a good outward impression to the public.

As television magnified wrestling's already-outrageous characters, there grew a need for more and more flash and color, and a new type of performer was created. Introduced as "managers," they were actually characters designed to do the talking for wrestlers who may not either have the skills or the comfort level to do it for themselves. With the cameras now rolling and wrestling being pumped into living rooms nationwide, the ability to speak convincingly and emotionally in order to advance storylines and promote ticket sales became a crucial part of a wrestler's skill set, right along with what he was able to do in the ring. And if he couldn't get the job done, a manager was assigned to do it for him.

By definition, nearly all wrestling managers were—and are—heels. There are several reasons for this. First and foremost, one of the most important functions of the manager is to draw heat from the crowd by inciting them directly, as well as distracting the referee and giving his men illegal assistance. Since babyfaces usually play by the rules and behave more honorably, a babyface manager doesn't have nearly as much of a reason to be there. Also, when it comes to talking, there has always been much more emphasis put on the heel, since he is usually the one who moves the storyline forward and needs to be as much of a character as possible. A babyface with weak mic skills is often forgivable; but for a heel, an acid tongue is more of a stock in trade. Essentially, a manager's main role becomes that of mouthpiece. In this way, he is the focal point of fan derision, so that a heel will automatically attract major heat just by being associated with him. Thus, the more brash, obnoxious, and arrogant a manager is, the better.

Rise and Fall of a Rogue's Gallery

Some of the earliest who rose to fill this increasingly important role were the likes of cocky Elvis wannabe Bobby Davis and the original walking thesaurus, Wild Red Berry. In some ways, these two created templates that have been copied ever since. A few of their successors in the 1970s certainly took more than a few pointers from Davis and Berry, including three devious souls who would form what is considered an "unholy trinity" of managers in the WWWF: Capt. Lou Albano, "Classy" Freddy Blassie, and The Grand Wizard. Meanwhile, in the AWA, a truly groundbreaking manager who went by the name of Bobby "The Brain" Heenan was doing something that was

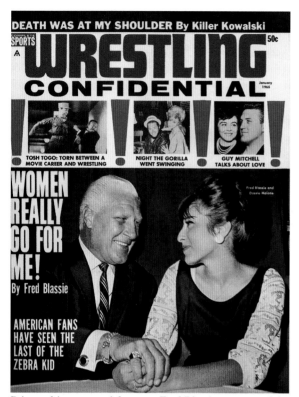

DEATH WAS AT MY SHOULDER By Killer Kowalski

COMPLETE SPORTS

A **WRESTLING** 50c

CONFIDENTIAL

January 1965

TOSH TOGO: TORN BETWEEN A MOVIE CAREER AND WRESTLING

NIGHT THE GORILLA WENT SWINGING

GUY MITCHELL TALKS ABOUT LOVE

WOMEN REALLY GO FOR ME! By Fred Blassie

Fred Blassie and Dessie Malone

AMERICAN FANS HAVE SEEN THE LAST OF THE ZEBRA KID

Prior to his managerial career, Fred Blassie was one of the top main-event performers in the world, and one of wrestling's bona fide celebrities, c. 1964.   *Author's collection*

fast becoming another prerequisite of the position: taking bumps. After all, if crowds would pay to see a heel wrestler get the stuffing beaten out of him, surely they would also pay to see his manager get the same treatment.

The territories produced a plethora of managers to plague fans in every part of North America. World Class Championship Wrestling in Dallas boasted "Playboy" Gary Hart and Gen. Skandor Akbar. Mid-South and Mid-Atlantic featured tennis racket–wielding Jim Cornette. Memphis was the stomping ground for the "Mouth of the South" Jimmy Hart. In the talent raids that occurred during the WWF's national expansion, Hart went to work for Vince McMahon, as did Bobby Heenan, where they joined the likes of retired longtime WWF heels Mr. Fuji, "Luscious" Johnny Valiant, and others.

The 1990s saw a steady decline in the role of the manager, and by the end of the decade they gradually vanished from the scene. For one thing, during the edgy late '90s and early 2000s period, promo skills for wrestlers were at a greater premium than ever before. Every athlete was expected to be able to speak for himself, and be entertaining on the mic, if he expected to get a serious push. Managers soon began to be seen as archaic, a corny relic of a more burlesque past. Another major factor in the de-emphasis of managers was the ever-increasing sex factor in professional wrestling. Whereas female "valets" had been around for decades, by the Attitude Era they became hyper-eroticized, and the thinking became: why use a goofy middle-aged guy in a sequined blazer when you could have a gorgeous half-naked blonde instead? And so, old school managing became something of a lost art.

"Over the last couple of years, I was the only male manager that was there," the late Paul Bearer, longtime Undertaker cornerman, told me in a 2002 interview. "I kind of had the feeling that when my run was over, they probably wouldn't be using anymore male managers. . . . The writers that we have, especially the young writers, they don't have a clue how to write for a male manager. I know that was one of the problems with me: they didn't know how to write for me. They didn't know what I did."

Carrying the Torch of Villainy

One whose presence in recent years has flown in the face of this trend has been former ECW honcho Paul Heyman, who, after the demise of his organization, returned to his original role as a professional on-air loudmouth. A manager in the classic mold, he has deftly represented WWE performers like Brock Lesnar, CM Punk, and Cesaro. Recently, he was joined by the former "Dirty" Dutch Mantell, whose managerial roots stretch back to 1980s Memphis. Now renamed Zeb Colter (in an apparent dig at conservative political pundit Ann Coulter), he and Heyman represent a minor resurgence in the importance of the wrestling manager.

For as long as professional wrestling remains the over-the-top theater of the absurd, someone will be needed to generate the all-important heat that keeps fans tuning in and buying tickets. Many wrestlers have been up to that task themselves, but, for a long time, managers were there to help them along; in essence, being the glue that held the angles together. Although neither as vital nor as plentiful as they once were, their entertaining contributions to wrestling (if not to fashion) are enormous.

Princes of Polyester

Here are twenty of the finest managerial mouthpieces of all time.

Arnold Skaaland

One of the very few babyface managers, longtime Capitol/WWWF stalwart Skaaland donned the suit after winding down his in-ring career in the 1960s. The squat, spit-curled "Golden Boy" was a fixture in the corner of Word Heavyweight Champions Bruno Sammartino and Bob Backlund, and although he never had much to do, his mere presence, like that of an old-school boxing manager, lent an aura of credibility to the proceedings. Ironically, his most famous act would occur on December 26, 1983, when

Fans were shocked when the heelish Heenan took on none other than the once-beloved Andre the Giant as his newest charge in 1987.

John McKeon/ Wikimedia

he threw in the towel on behalf of Backlund, conceding the WWF World title to The Iron Sheik.

Bobby "The Brain" Heenan

The man born Raymond Louis Heenan may have been the greatest all-around manager in pro wrestling history. Not only was he a master of ad-lib comedy with a polished presence, he was one of the first managers to take bumps, and was more than up to the task of bouncing around the ring like a champ when the situation called for it. Unfortunately, this would also cut his career short, as accumulated neck injuries forced him to step back into an announcer position. Nevertheless, for a guy this legitimately funny, that wasn't necessarily a bad thing.

Bobby Davis

One of the earliest modern wrestling managers, Davis was an arrogant pretty boy who rose to fame as the representative of U.S. champion Buddy Rogers in the 1950s. Although the Nature Boy didn't need a manager to do his talking, he and Davis made one of the most hated pairs in the business. Davis also managed such performers as The Graham Brothers and "Cowboy" Bob Orton, Sr., grandfather of Randy Orton.

Capt. Lou Albano

"Often imitated but never duplicated," Captain Lou was an eccentric, stogie-chewing blabbermouth who was, perhaps, the most directly influenced by Wild Red Berry in his penchant for verbal grandiosity. Specializing in tag teams, he managed an astounding sixteen different (W)WWF World Tag Team Champions between 1971 and 1994, and was in Ivan Koloff's corner when he unseated Bruno Sammartino for the World Heavyweight title. Despite a high-profile babyface run during the height of the Hulkamania era, Albano did his best work as a bad guy.

"Classy" Freddie Blassie

Of all the former wrestlers to settle into a managerial role, Blassie had been the biggest star. The one-time West Coast headliner was brought in by Vincent J. McMahon as part of a new crop of managers in the 1970s, replacing the ailing Wild Red Berry. "The Hollywood Fashion Plate" used his natural charisma and gruff stage presence to get over such heel acts as Waldo Von Erich, a rookie Hulk Hogan, and The Iron Sheik, whom he led to the WWF World Championship in 1983.

Dr. Ken Ramey

Starting out as an innovative referee in the 1950s and '60s, Ramey came up with the groundbreaking idea to turn himself heel and become the manager for the masked Interns tag team, initially in Florida, but later taking the highly successful act on the road to places like Nick Gulas's Tennessee territory, Leroy McGuirk's Tri-State Wrestling, and Mike LeBell's

Vince McMahon , Promoter   MONDAY, JUNE 16th

WORLD CHAMPIONSHIP
madison square garden **WRESTLING**

Sanctioned and Supervised by N.Y. State Athletic Commission   Chairman Edwin B. Dooley
With Approval of World Wide Wrestling Federation   Willie Gilzenberg, President

WALDO VON ERICH receives final instructions from MGR. FRED BLASSIE

The Box Office at Madison Square Garden is open daily, from 10 to 6

Blassie led many a nefarious villain to number-one contender status during the 1970s, including Waldo Von Erich, who challenged Bruno Sammartino for the WWWF World title more times than anyone else. *Author's collection*

Hollywood Wrestling. A master of psychology, he pioneered unique and subtle ways to distract the ref and draw crowd heat.

Eddie "The Brain" Creatchman

Pro wrestling's other "brain" manager was a retired Montreal-born grappler who perfected a stereotypically Jewish character that was so incendiary, he was known to start riots in the Montreal Forum. This quality actually endeared him to Ed "The Sheik" Farhat, who took him on as his manager, and the two had an ongoing relationship that lasted through much of the '70s. Creatchman alternated Sheik managerial duties with Ernie "Abdullah Farouk" Roth, and a classic confrontation between the two can be seen in the 1985 mockumentary *I Like to Hurt People*.

Gary Hart

Perhaps the greatest manager never to work for Vince McMahon, "Playboy" Gary Hart was gold on the mic, with an accomplished interview style that was way ahead of its time. One of the key architects behind the glory days of World Class as a booker in the mid-1980s, he also worked extensively in the Georgia and Mid-Atlantic promotions. Unlike most other modern managers, Hart reportedly worked as a real business and travel manager for the wrestlers with whom he was paired on TV.

Gen. Skandor Akbar

Texas-born Jimmy Wehba was given his name (Arabic for "Alexander the Great") by World Class promoter Fritz Von Erich to further emphasize his Middle Eastern ancestry, and he kept it when he transitioned from wrestling to managing in the late 1970s. The cigar-chomping, keffieh-wearing Akbar was known as the leader of a stable he called Devastation Inc., which made the rounds in both World Class and Mid-South throughout the 1980s. Among its multitudinous members were Abdullah the Butcher, Wild Bill Irwin, Dick Murdoch, The Missing Link, Kendo Nagasaki, Manny Fernandez, and The One Man Gang.

George "Crybaby" Cannon

Known for his tearful temper tantrums, the mammoth George Cannon was a retired wrestler who found new life as a manager in Canada, mainly representing The Fabulous Kangaroos in the late 1960s and early '70s. He often wore an army helmet when leading his protégés to action in the ring.

Later working as a booker and promoter, he helped promote Canadian events for the WWF in the 1980s until being forced to retire due to phlebitis.

The Grand Wizard

Along with Albano and Blassie, Ernie Roth completed a diabolical triumvirate of managers who made life hell for all (W)WWF babyfaces of the 1970s and early '80s. Known for his garish turbans, wraparound shades, and ridiculous sports jackets, he was the epitome of the obnoxious wrestling manager. In addition to his time in the Northeast, he had a successful run as manager of The Sheik, using the name Abdullah Farouk. Sadly, he died mere months before Vince McMahon's national WWF expansion. In the ultimate tribute to his talents, when it was announced that he had passed away, the live crowd cheered.

J. J. Dillon

What would any list of great managers be without the man behind the industry's most famous clique, The Four Horsemen? The weasely Dillon led the Horsemen during their original incarnation in the Jim Crockett Promotions/WCW of the mid- to late 1980s, and was known for blatantly interfering on their behalf time and again. In addition to his storied time with the Horsemen, Dillon also managed such talents as The Mongolian Stomper, Moondog Mayne, and Ox Baker throughout the NWA territories.

Jim Cornette

The Louisville Lip will never be forgotten by the countless fans who witnessed his talents as a top-flight manager in Memphis, Mid-South, Jim Crockett Promotions, WCW, and the WWF. Best known as the cornerman for The Midnight Express, his razor-sharp tongue and tennis racket were his greatest weapons, and his keen head for the business even helped earn him backstage creative positions in several of the companies for whom he worked.

Jimmy Hart

A former member of the 1960s one-hit-wonder vocal group The Gentries ("Keep on Dancin'"), the fast-talking "Mouth of the South" later made a perfect a wrestling manager, with his scrawny physique, airbrushed sports jackets, and the trademark megaphone he used to cheer on his charges and berate their opponents. Starting out in the Memphis-based CWA, he later made a big splash in the WWF as the spokesperson for the likes of Greg "The Hammer" Valentine, "Adorable" Adrian Adonis, The Hart Foundation, and, of course, The Honky Tonk Man.

Mr. Fuji

Although he was sometimes criticized for lacking in effective interview skills—one of the successful manager's most important attributes—the Devious One had enough accumulated caché as a loathsome heel from his days as an active wrestler to carry that over once he traded in his tights for a tuxedo and derby. Selected to fill the villainous void left when Capt. Lou Albano turned face in the mid-1980s, he was known for his gleeful sadism and fondness for throwing salt.

Paul Bearer/Percival Pringle III

William Moody will forever be remembered for standing alongside the Undertaker, holding his golden urn and moaning, "Oooohhh yessss!!" Brought into the WWF in 1991, he became a crucial part of 'Taker's act, and the two spent the better part of a decade together. As Bearer, he also introduced 'Taker's monstrous "half-brother," Kane, in 1997. Prior to his career-defining time in the WWF, Moody worked as Percy Pringle throughout the Southeastern United States. (Little-known fact: he was actually a mortician in real life.)

Paul Heyman/Paul E. Dangerously

The most visible and successful wrestling manager of the current century, Heyman made his bones as a photographer and writer for wrestling magazines in the '80s, working his way backstage at Madison Square Garden and learning the tricks of the trade from Fred Blassie, Lou Albano, and The Grand Wizard. In his "Psycho Yuppy" persona, the cell-phone–wielding Dangerously debuted in the dying days of Championship Wrestling from Florida, working his way through Memphis, the AWA, and WCW. In recent years, he has become a highlight of WWE programming, giving credibility to the talents he manages via his impeccable mic work.

Saul Weingeroff

Another villainous manager who played upon his audience's anti-Semitic tendencies, "Gentleman" Saul Weingeroff was more than willing to take advantage of his Hebraic ancestry during the 1960s and '70s throughout

Heyman, seen here with long-time protégé Brock Lesnar, is not only one of the best-talking managers of all time, but one of the best-talking talents, period.

Schen Photography/Wikimedia

Southern states like Tennessee and Texas. Making things even worse, he was best known for managing The Von Brauners, a tag team that used a Nazi gimmick. The ostentatious Weingeroff entered himself in the 1964 presidential election, and was also the first manager to employ fireballs as weapons.

Slick

It isn't everyone who is able to earn the title of "Doctor of Style," but if any manager deserved the moniker it would be Kenneth "Slick" Johnson, who stepped into the WWF in 1986 to take the place of the retiring "Classy" Freddie Blassie. Dancing his way to the ring alongside charges such as The Big Boss Man, Akeem the African Dream, and Power & Glory, he even had his own music video and entrance theme, appropriately titled "Jive Soul Bro."

Wild Red Berry

One of the most influential managers of all time, Berry was a leading light heavyweight grappler of the 1930s and '40s, known even then for his pompous way with words. Keeping a notebook of sayings and phrases gleaned from all manner of sources, including *Bartlett's Quotation*s, Berry took pride in his verbose and borderline nonsensical promos, in which he baffled announcers with one tortuous maxim after another. Manager of the likes of

The Fabulous Kangaroos and Gorilla Monsoon, he famously wore a jacket with the words "I Am Right" printed on the back.

Those Vivacious Valets

Promoters had long seen the obvious benefit to having beautiful women at ringside, dating as far back as the 1950s when a pre-fabulous Slave Girl Moolah accompanied Elephant Boy and "Nature Boy" Buddy Rogers to their matches. Gorgeous George was also known to have his wives escort him to the ring. But the practice did not take off in earnest until the 1980s, when it seemed every promotion was looking to add a little sex appeal to their product with some female talent. Unlike women wrestlers, valets were used mainly outside the ring, acting as eye candy, and more often than not enhancing the heel personas of the wrestlers with whom they worked.

Unlike managers, valets are not presented as leaders or decision makers, but as the companions—or, in worst-case scenarios, the possessions—of their assigned male performers. Occasionally, there have been some women who walked the line between the two roles: Sensational Sherri and Tammy "Sunny" Sytch, both of whom acted as ringside decorations and were positioned in some form of managerial capacity. But, for the most part, they were there to look good and, if they were with the bad guys, to mouth off and occasionally get disciplined by the good guys. Sexist, without question; but then, pro wrestling has always been a sexist business.

The role of valets was further emphasized in the 1990s and into the 2000s thanks to the Divas phenomenon, until they had all but eclipsed the male wrestling manager character. Over the years, there have been several valets who have become particular favorites of the (predominantly male) fans; here are just a few of these lovely ladies of the ring . . .

- Baby Doll: Known as "The Perfect 10," Nickla "Baby Doll" Roberts was the bad girl of the valet pack. Decked out in punk attire, she debuted in World Class with Gino Hernandez, and later appeared for Jim Crockett as a valet for Tully Blanchard of The Four Horsemen.
- Beulah McGillicutty: Of all the alluring females introduced in the sex-charged ECW during the mid-1990s, Trisa Hayes may have been the most memorable. Brought in as part of an intense storyline between Raven and Tommy Dreamer, she would even go on to mix it up in the ring in some of the promotion's most violent matches.
- Francine: Along with Beulah, Francine Fournier was one of the sexiest ECW valets, first appearing as the onscreen girlfriend of Stevie Richards before going on to memorable stints as the dominatrix manager of

The Pitbulls, and as "Head" Cheerleader for "The Franchise," Shane Douglas.

- Lana: Recent WWE programming has been highlighted by the appearances of the "Ravishing Russian," a.k.a. actress and dancer C. J. Perry, who was introduced as the microskirt-wearing representative of "The Bulgarian Brute," Rusev. Their relationship closely mimicked that of Russian boxer Ivan Drago and his wife, Ludmilla, in the 1985 movie *Rocky IV*.

- Miss Elizabeth: Arguably the most famous of them all, Elizabeth Hulette benefited from national WWF exposure as the maltreated valet for her real-life husband, "Macho Man" Randy Savage. For years, the lovely and demure Miss Elizabeth was the first lady of the WWF, eventually "marrying" Savage in a live ceremony in Madison Square Garden at *SummerSlam '91*.

- Missy Hyatt: This blonde bombshell started out as another in the explosion of valets that occurred in World Class in the mid-1980s. She later migrated to the UWF before settling into her most high-profile role in WCW alongside her husband, Eddie Gilbert, and The Steiner Brothers. She would later work with The Sandman in ECW.

- Precious: The real-life wife of "Gorgeous" Jimmy Garvin, Patti "Precious" Williams was the second valet he used in World Class Championship Wrestling, pushing out his cousin Sunshine in a memorable storyline. The duo was an NWA fixture of the '80s, later finding their way to Jim Crockett Promotions.

- Sable: Rena Mero set the WWF on fire when she first appeared at the side of then-husband Marc Mero in 1996. Never had a wrestling valet been so obviously sexualized on screen; she became a favorite of head creative writer Vince Russo, who positioned her as one of the company's top TV ratings draws. Her time in WWF would help to kick start today's Diva movement.

- Stacy Keibler: Before becoming a crossover TV star and girlfriend to George Clooney, the leggy Keibler made her name in pro wrestling— first as the bookish "Miss Hancock" in WCW, and later as one of WWE's premier Divas during the height of the division in the early 2000s.

- Sunshine: The very first of the wave of valets who hit in the 1980s, Valerie "Sunshine" French was brought into World Class in 1983 to accompany her real-life cousin Jimmy Garvin. In many ways, their on-air relationship inspired the more high-profile dynamic between Randy Savage and Miss Elizabeth in the WWF.

- Torrie Wilson: The former fitness model and future A-Rod girlfriend was one of WWE's two main Diva acquisitions (along with Stacy Keibler) when the company took over WCW in 2001. She was a top female talent throughout the first decade of the 2000s, gaining mainstream attention as one of the most beautiful women in show business.

- Woman: Longtime fan and occasional apartment wrestling model Nancy Toffoloni was recruited by future husband Kevin Sullivan, and first appeared with him in Championship Wrestling from Florida, as part of Sullivan's satanist faction. She would achieve greater notoriety through her association with The Four Horseman, and later reinvented herself in ECW alongside The Sandman. She divorced Sullivan and married Chris Benoit in a bizarre real-life extension of a wrestling angle. In 2007, she was brutally murdered by Benoit in the couple's Atlanta home. (See Chapter 21 for more information.)

18

A Head for the Business

Fifteen Visionaries Who Changed the Course of Wrestling History

When I look at my boys, I see stars.

—James E. Barnett

A s in most forms of show business and sports, when it comes to professional wrestling, the lion's share of the glory tends to go to those who are the most visible; namely, the talent. As fans, we celebrate the achievements of our favorite wrestlers. We hail those exceptionally gifted and accomplished performers as legends, and rightly so. Yet, with the exception of those who are especially attuned to the backstage goings-on of the business, we very rarely devote the same kind of attention to those individuals whose behind-the-scenes efforts have truly shaped the industry we love, and who allowed those performers to become the legends they are. We're referring, of course, to the promoters who run the show, and the bookers who create the feuds and storylines. In this chapter, we shine the much deserved spotlight on these men, the promoters and bookers, who made essential contributions to the growth and development of professional wrestling, whose greatest achievements occurred out of sight of the cheering masses.

Cowboy Bill Watts

During his time as owner and operator of Mid-South Wrestling from the late 1970s through the mid-1980s, Bill Watts championed the concept of professional wrestling as episodic television, building on storylines from one week to the next in a manner that always kept fans tuning in. He also stressed in-ring athleticism, resulting in a highly regarded product that featured both exciting matches and compelling angles. The booking style that he

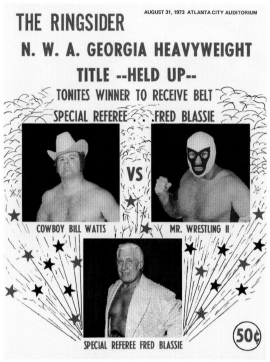

THE RINGSIDER

AUGUST 31, 1973 ATLANTA CITY AUDITORIUM

N. W. A. GEORGIA HEAVYWEIGHT

TITLE --HELD UP--

TONITES WINNER TO RECEIVE BELT

SPECIAL REFEREE... FRED BLASSIE

COWBOY BILL WATTS

VS

MR. WRESTLING II

SPECIAL REFEREE FRED BLASSIE

50¢

Like many successful wrestling promoters, Bill Watts was first a successful wrestler, enjoying superstar status throughout the 1960s.   *Author's collection*

pioneered along with his matchmaker Grizzly Smith (father of Jake "The Snake" Roberts) would have a profound affect on later WWF/E programs *Raw* and *SmackDown!*, which took the weekly, episodic approach to a whole new level, on an international scale.

Watts also became known for his colorblind attitude toward booking, regularly using African-American performers such as Ernie Ladd and Butch Reed, and making Sylvester Ritter, a.k.a. The Junkyard Dog, into one of the biggest stars in the business when he built his entire promotion around him in the early 1980s. Watts would later be hired as executive vice president of WCW, and, despite a controversy surrounding race-related comments that eventually led to his dismissal, Watts applied his colorblind attitude in the Turner-owned company as well, turning Ron Simmons into the first African-American titleholder in the history of the NWA/WCW World Heavyweight Championship.

Dusty Rhodes

No less than Ric Flair has stated that Rhodes had the greatest wrestling mind he ever encountered, and judging by what he accomplished in Flair's home territory, it's not hard to understand why. Dusty Rhodes was the head booker for Jim Crockett Promotions during the mid- to late 1980s, which is largely considered the company's most exciting and creative period. During his tenure, he masterminded the rise of The Four Horsemen, including their legendary feuds with the likes of Lex Luger, Sting (both of whom he helped make national stars), and, of course, himself. He was responsible for many of the company's pay-per-view and gimmick match concepts from that period, including *The Great American Bash*, *Halloween Havoc*, *Clash of the Champions*, and *War Games: The Match Beyond*.

An innovator of high spots, he came up with what would later be known as the "Dusty finish," a specific match conclusion in which a referee is incapacitated at the very moment when the face is triumphant, leading to the decision being reversed and the heel getting an ill-deserved win. Designed to draw heat for follow-up business, it became Rhodes's trademark as a booker, and although it later became infamous due to its overuse, it was effective when used sparingly.

Eric Bischoff

Whether you love him or hate him, not even Bischoff's detractors can take away from the fact that he was the man who led WCW to its most financially lucrative period; he also came closer than anyone in unseating Vince McMahon as the industry's leader. Taking over from the old-school Cowboy Bill Watts, Bischoff spearheaded dramatic changes in the organization, taking it from a regional enterprise with a Southern stigma to a legitimate contender for national power.

It was Bischoff who aggressively signed up major talents like Hulk Hogan, Randy Savage, Roddy Piper, and others, and expanded WCW's horizons to make room for exciting *luchadores*, cruiserweights, Japanese imports, and a slew of ECW defectors. And most dramatically of all, he devised the nWo invasion angle, arguably the most influential storyline in wrestling history, and the one that ushered in the contemporary era of the business. He also made himself into the first "evil boss" heel character, a now-standard trope in WWE, TNA, and elsewhere.

Fred Kohler

For nearly a decade, during the late 1940s through the mid-1950s, Fred Kohler was the most powerful promoter in all of professional wrestling, thanks to the national exposure he received from *Wrestling from the Marigold*, the seminal TV program that was broadcast across America on the DuMont Network. For the first time, all of the country was watching the product of a single wrestling promotion, right in their living rooms. As a result, the talent being featured on that program was in high demand from every other promoter. Naturally, Kohler was able to use this leverage to his advantage; he was also a key member in the early years of the fledgling National Wrestling Alliance.

Kohler leased out his top grapplers to every territory that could afford them. Meanwhile, his own business went through the roof—contrary to fears that TV would kill live attendance, the exact opposite occurred. Even after he lost his national TV deal, Kohler's reputation kept him going for years. An early partnership he had formed with Vincent James McMahon in New York helped sow the seeds for the eventual growth of another national power, WWE.

George Scott

Arguably the least known of this chapter's visionaries, Scott was enormously important to both the development of what is now WWE, as well as the company that would eventually become WCW. His initial impact was felt when he became head booker for Jim Crockett Promotions in the mid-1970s, and immediately set about changing the entire philosophy of the Mid-Atlantic–based organization. Moving the territory away from its traditional tag-team focus, he brought in such veteran talents as Johnny Valentine and Wahoo McDaniel, and helped groom future legends like Roddy Piper, Ric Flair, and Ricky Steamboat. Even after leaving Crockett in 1981, the changes Scott put in place would forever alter the course of the company.

At the request of Vincent J. McMahon, Scott jumped to the WWF in 1983 to help McMahon's son in his quest to take his company national. Scott became the head booker during the WWF's initial explosion during this period, overseeing the rise of Hulk Hogan as WWE World Champion, the establishment of *WrestleMania*, and the WWF's entrance into national network television with *Saturday Night's Main Event* on NBC. His influence during this crucial growth period in the company's history was essential to its success.

Jack Curley

The first major modern professional wrestling promoter, Curley started out in the boxing business at the turn of the twentieth century, but gravitated toward wrestling when the sweet science was outlawed in New York State for a number of years. After being catapulted to notoriety thanks to his involvement in the titanic 1911 rematch between Frank Gotch and George Hackenschmidt, Curley set about creating a wrestling empire that saw him become the first man to really control the business in New York City, the area that would long be its most profitable.

Curley envisioned pro wrestling as a regular running attraction, and turned it from a disorganized presentation built around specific matches made at the whim of the wrestlers and their management, into an organized, recurring series of events, driven by savvy promotion and the all-important use of media (which, in those days, consisted mainly of newspapers). Before Curley, the wrestling business was largely controlled by the athletes themselves, along with their personal managers. Due to Curley's influence, the promoter became the driving force behind the industry, for good or ill.

Jack Pfefer

Before Vince McMahon was even a twinkle in his father's eye, enterprising Eastern European immigrant Jack Pfefer was the first to view pro wrestling, first and foremost, as entertainment. Promoting in numerous areas throughout his nearly fifty-year career, he was a controversial figure in his time, but today is considered one of the most influential figures of modern wrestling, due to his propensity for spectacle and his disregard for the sanctity of kayfabe.

Pfefer's infamous exposure of that secret code in his 1937 interview with *The Daily Mirror* (see Chapter 4) was typical of his philosophy, and he repeatedly threatened to reveal the true nature of the business to the public if fellow promoters ever tried to deal dishonestly with him. It didn't matter to him; he was a stolid champion of the show-biz aspect of the industry, which was revolutionary at the time. Specializing in oddities, freaks, and other unique attractions, he roamed the nation for decades, an itinerant

The diminutive Pfefer was an outlaw promoter throughout most of his prolific career, and was often ridiculed for his appearance and heavy Eastern-European accent by his many professional rivals.

Jack Pfefer Collection, University of Notre Dame

entrepreneur with a circus-like product, whose way of thinking would eventually grow to dominate the entire business.

Jim Barnett

One of those odd, mercurial, ever-present figures that abound within the wrestling business, the flamboyant and eccentric James E. Barnett had a profound influence throughout the mat game from the 1950s all the way to the 2000s. He was a trusted advisor to some of the most powerful men in the industry, including Vince McMahon, Jim Crockett, and Fred Kohler, and played a crucial part behind the scenes throughout the second half of the twentieth century.

Barnett got his start working for the groundbreaking 1950s magazine *Wrestling As You Like It*, which soon helped him become a close associate of Kohler, the man who brought wrestling to national TV for the first time. In the 1960s, he introduced wrestling to Australia, kicking off a Golden Age for the business in that country. He owned pieces of many different promotions over the years, including Detroit and Indianapolis, which he eventually sold to The Sheik and Dick the Bruiser, respectively. After swooping in to take over Georgia Championship Wrestling in the early '70s, he oversaw the company's entrance to national cable TV on Ted Turner's WTBS. In later years, he would help McMahon take the WWF national, using his established connections in the TV industry, and oversaw the sale of Jim Crockett Promotions to his old ally Turner, resulting in the creation of WCW. A trusted advisor to Vince in his final years, one of his last pieces of influence came when he suggested that John Cena be pushed as WWE's next top star.

Pat Patterson

Those who know Patterson only as Vince McMahon's on-air "stooge" of Attitude Era WWF television, or even as the first Intercontinental Champion, don't know the true importance of the man. A trusted lieutenant to McMahon and one of his closest associates from the 1980s to the present day, Patterson has long been hailed as one of the business's true creative geniuses. Once closely involved in WWF booking, he was known for his innate ability to block matches, particularly finishes, which became his greatest asset. A veteran of the old-time San Francisco Cow Palace Battle Royals of the 1970s, he developed the concept of WWE's *Royal Rumble*, which was only one of his many innovations.

Patterson also worked for years as the company's main road agent, helping to train and advise one of the most talent-filled rosters in wrestling history. Although currently in semi-retirement and no longer involved in the day-to-day of WWE creative, Pat Patterson's contributions to the growth of the company from a creative standpoint during the 1980s and '90s in particular cannot be overstated.

Paul Heyman

The pride of Scarsdale, New York, Heyman was and is one of pro wrestling's truly innovative thinkers, a man whose outside-the-box ideas have had a profound effect on the development of the genre over the past two decades. A savvy and creative entrepreneur with a keen understanding for what wrestling fans want, he took Eastern Championship Wrestling and transformed it into Extreme Championship Wrestling, dictating the terms of the industry's edgiest era (not to mention its most financially lucrative) to date.

Although ECW itself had a limited shelf life, the "hardcore" sensibilities he popularized there would later be adopted by WCW and even more successfully by the WWF/E. Heyman's services would eventually be called upon by WWE, and he even spent time as head writer for *SmackDown!*, the company's weekly Friday night program. As with many great minds, Heyman has not always played well with others, and so his role with WWE would later be relegated to that of on-air talent only. Nevertheless, he has been instrumental in elevating the careers of several WWE performers, most notably CM Punk.

Pinkie George

An Iowa-based promoter of the 1940s and '50s, P. L. "Pinkie" George's central contribution to wrestling history was having the vision required to organize the formation of the National Wrestling Alliance. In 1948, the enterprising George saw the benefit of having all the nation's promoters join forces under one co-operational umbrella, to avoid harmful competition and share talent. Later, monopolistic practices set in, and, eventually, the NWA would be taken to task by the federal government.

George served as president of the NWA for its first two years, during which time he incorporated the group, helping to ensure its survival for many years to come. He was pushed out of his role in 1950 in favor of St. Louis promoter Sam Muchnick, and would be alienated from the organization in later years. Nevertheless, he will always be remembered as the man who helped to unite the business during one of its tumultuous eras, and created its most respected governing body in the process.

Sam Muchnick

For three decades, Muchnick was the face of the National Wrestling Alliance, serving as its president for much of the 1950s, 1960s, and 1970s. He oversaw the organization through most of its glory years, and worked hard to keep it together in the face of such controversies as the infamous federal anti-trust lawsuit. Many believe that without Muchnick's leadership ability, the NWA might not have survived its first decade of existence.

Promoting pro wrestling as a serious, sports-like product out of his home base in St. Louis, Muchnick was well liked both by those within the business, as well as sports industry figures with whom he had close working relationships. His diplomatic demeanor and forward-thinking approach helped the NWA grow to become what it had originally set out to be: the major-league organization of professional wrestling, governing the industry from coast to coast, as well as having far-reaching international influence.

Toots Mondt

Sources differ as to how much credit Mondt truly deserves for many of the innovations credited to him over the years, but it cannot be disputed that he was one of the industry's top promoters for an impressive forty-year span, stretching from the Roaring '20s era of Ed "Stranger" Lewis to the Swinging '60s era of Bruno Sammartino. A compulsive gambler and consummate con man, he was feared by fellow promoters and generally mistrusted by the performers who worked for him. But as with many such unscrupulous and Machiavellian individuals, his success is undeniable.

A key figure in the Gold Dust Trio promotional conglomerate of the '20s, it's believed that he helped to invent the modern concept of professional wrestling, including heels and faces, ongoing angles, traveling troupes of wrestlers, and the modern performance style (for more on this, see Chapter 4). He was a powerful force on the East and West coasts at various points throughout the 1930s, '40s and '50s, at one point controlling the legendary Manhattan Booking Office. Later, he joined forces with Vincent James McMahon to found the World Wide Wrestling Federation, using his influence over Madison Square Garden to help make the company one of America's most important promotions.

Vince McMahon

Without question the most polarizing figure in the history of the business, Vincent Kennedy McMahon is also the most powerful figure in the history of the business. It's been stated many times before, but he took an industry built largely around live events and outdated television deals, run locally by old-fashioned and outmoded power barons, and turned it into a modern multi-media and merchandizing powerhouse, thus making WWE the first truly worldwide wrestling organization.

McMahon has so thoroughly transformed the pro wrestling business, in fact, that he has even given it a whole new name, preferring to use the term "sports-entertainment"—a label that perhaps better fits the company's bold ambitions to be so much more than just your father's rasslin' promotion. He's made his fair share of enemies, but that will happen when you've run every one of your competitors out of business and control the entire fate of an industry. He may abhor the title of "wrestling promoter," but he can take solace in knowing that he is the most successful of them all.

Vince Russo

Highly unpopular with many pro wrestling purists and those Internet "smart marks" for whom second-guessing has become an art form, "the other Vince" deserves credit nonetheless for kick starting the most successful period in WWE history, and for helping to shift the creative course of the business. His legacy may have been tarnished by some less-than-successful stints in places like WCW and TNA Wrestling, but it can be argued that the Attitude Era never would have happened without him.

A gruff New Yorker with an iconoclastic philosophy, Russo rose through the ranks as the editor of *WWF Magazine*, eventually developing the edgy *Raw Magazine* and transferring its take-no-prisoners sensibilities to TV when he was appointed head WWF creative writer. Instrumental in the creation of the villainous Mr. McMahon character, the legendary Austin/McMahon War, D-Generation X and many more popular angles and characters, he also adopted a controversial booking style known as "hot-shotting," presenting sensational incidents such as title changes and heel/face turns at a much faster and less conservative pace than tradition dictated. Designed to increase TV ratings, this approach helped the WWF win the Monday-night ratings war with WCW, and is largely in use to this day.

19

This Is Extreme

ECW and the Rise of Hardcore Wrestling

We [didn't] have the budget to compete with WWE and WCW on lighting and pyro. Why go there? Hide it! Accentuate the positives: best interviews, most action, wildest brawls, best wrestling, highest-flying cruiserweights, all these different things that we could do better than everybody else. . . . Why be second best at anything? Why not say, "Screw the lights, screw the pyro, here it is, down and dirty."

—Paul Heyman

Professional wrestling is a violent, potentially dangerous form of entertainment; there can be no doubt about it. And yet, for those fans with a particularly bloodthirsty bent, there is a subgenre to the business, one which takes the usual violence to another place entirely—a place of intense action that goes beyond what might strictly be termed "wrestling," and can include the implementation of foreign objects, a general relaxation of the "rules" that results in a more wild and wooly product, and perhaps most strikingly, lots and lots of blood. More than any other aspect, the phenomenon known as "hardcore" has taken the industry further than ever from its roots as a genuine, competitive sport, turning it into a hyper-violent, chaotic spectacle.

The term "hardcore wrestling" has its origins in the organization that would popularize it in the United States in the 1990s to a degree that had never been seen before, turning it into a genuine category unto itself, Extreme Championship Wrestling. And yet, for decades before ECW first set up shop, the hardcore phenomenon had been gradually taking shape and becoming an integral part of the fabric of pro wrestling. In recent years, it has fallen out of favor, as many things do after being fully embraced by the mainstream. But for those looking for just a bit more than traditional holds and between-the-ropes action, hardcore wrestling still provides a thrilling, and sometimes shocking, alternative.

The Birth of Hardcore

When searching for the origins of hardcore wrestling, one can travel as far back as the 1930s, a time when professional wrestling had been transformed into a histrionic caricature of its former self. It was also a time when promoters were first learning to employ whatever tricks possible to boost business during a period when Depression-struck patrons were strapped for cash and protective of their entertainment dollar. Upping the stakes seemed like a logical thing to do, and it is during this period that we find the birth of the "no-holds-barred" match, an encounter in which rules are purportedly thrown out the window to allow two competitors to settle their differences once and for all. On June 25, 1937, in Atlanta, Georgia, Jack Bloomfield and Petro Rossi did battle within the confines of a cage made out of chicken wire. This extreme stipulation, devised to provide the ultimate culmination (or "blow-off") to an ongoing feud, would soon evolve into pro wrestling's most famous gimmick encounter, the steel-cage match (with the first known use of an actual steel cage being a 1942 match between John Katan and Ignacio Martinez in Hamilton, Ontario).

By the 1950s, certain performers began to emerge who specialized in a brawling style of wrestling that resembled barroom fighting more than actual grappling. There was the highly influential "Irish" Danny McShain, a talented light heavyweight wrestler who helped to popularize the use of outside objects like folding chairs, as well as brawling outside the ring itself. He was joined by frequent rival and fellow hardcore pioneer Wild Bull Curry, known for his bushy eyebrows as much as for biting, gouging, and chair-swinging. The matches between McShain and Curry that took place in Ed McLemore's Texas territory in the 1950s are still considered early benchmarks of the hardcore style.

Getting Color

Another practice popularized in the 1950s by McShain, Curry, and others was something called "blading," or "gigging." Seen as barbaric by some, but merely a tool to increase ticket sales by others, blading arose from the desire to add blood to the proceedings. For many years one of the industry's most closely guarded secrets, it involves minor self-mutilation to make it appear as if a competitor is drawing his opponent's blood. Typically, a wrestler will bring a small razor blade or just a fragment of a blade into the ring with him, usually hidden in the athletic tape of the wrists or hands, or sometimes in the trunks. Other times, the referee may have the blade, and discretely pass it along to the wrestler at the appointed time. The wrestler will then use it to nick himself, typically on the forehead but sometimes other places like the arm, in order to produce blood, or "color."

The blood shed in this way is usually not a tremendous amount, but mixed with sweat it can look deceptively excessive, as if the performer were "wearing a crimson mask" (a euphemism coined by legendary announcer Gordon Solie), and taken from the tiny capillaries of the forehead, it results in a sufficient amount from a non-essential area of the body. Sometimes, performers will even consume coffee or aspirin before a match to thin the blood, adding to the illusion. Over time, frequent bladers are known to develop thick, brittle scar tissue on their forehead, and some—such as Dusty Rhodes and Ric Flair—developed so much that they no longer even required a sharp object, just a forceful poke, in order to get color.

By blading, promoters and performers seek to add to the "realism" of their matches, as well as provide a suitable level of escalation in brutality that indicates the intensity of a particular match or feud. It also can't be denied that the practice was designed to appeal to the outright bloodlust of some fans. It proliferated in the 1960s and '70s, particularly in the South. Certain performers, including Fred Blassie, the vicious "Madman from the Sudan" Abdullah the Butcher, brawling pioneer Bruiser Brody, and others, were especially known for the practice. But no one was more associated with outrageous bloodletting, as well as wild brawling in general, than Ed Farhat, known to wrestling fans as The Sheik. Under the guise of an incoherent maniac from the Middle East, he cut a swathe through opponents starting in the 1950s and stretching over the course of more than four decades.

Red Equals Green

During that time, the brawling, proto-"hardcore" style continued to gain traction. In Memphis, Jerry "The King" Lawler battled Terry Funk, a former NWA World Heavyweight Champion who fully embraced the hardcore ethos, in a wild "empty arena" match, and brawls outside the ring and into the stands became common in that territory. Carlos Colon's WWC in Puerto Rico upped the bloodshed more than ever, and also introduced elements like fire and barbed wire. In The Sheik's home territory of Detroit, he battled the likes of Bobo Brazil and Mark Lewin in matches that would set the standard for extreme action. Jim Crockett's NWA promotion offered attractions like scaffold matches, in which performers battled on a platform high above the ring, with the object being to knock off your opponents.

Meanwhile, across the Pacific in Japan, the year 1989 saw the birth of the world's first organization specializing in the hardcore style of working, which the Japanese referred to as "garbage wrestling" (see Chapter 12). The brainchild of Japanese wrestler/promoter Atushi Onita, the company known as Frontier Martial Arts Wrestling gathered together all the gimmicks that were becoming commonplace in American wrestling, like blood, barbed wire and weapons, and spotlighted them to create a product of unprecedented brutality, adding new wrinkles like explosives in order to up the ante even further. Crossing the line of simulated combat, the working conditions of FMW got to the point of being legitimately unsafe for the performers involved. Nevertheless, the group enjoyed some success, and even inspired other groups like Wrestling International New Generations (W*ING) and the International Wrestling Association of Japan.

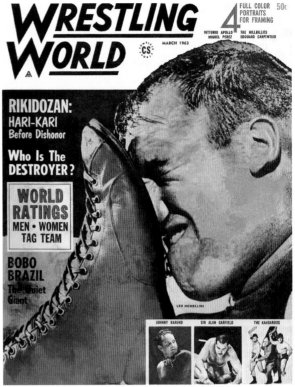

A rough-and-ready, brawling style of wrestling emerged during the 1950s and 1960s, aided by the sensationalistic content of the wrestling magazines of the day. *Author's collection*

The Revolution Is Televised

The concept of hardcore specialization at last found its way to the United States in the early 1990s, in the form of a Philadelphia-based organization which, although it never pushed the envelope as far as Japanese outfits like FMW, succeeded in bringing hardcore into the American mainstream, becoming a cult icon in the process. In 1992, Eastern Championship Wrestling seemed like just another Northeast independent promotion, rising from the ashes of Joel Goodhart's Tri-State Wrestling and featuring a mix of past-their-prime stars of the 1980s and up-and-coming indy workers.

"Todd Gordon and Bob Artese and Don E. Allen and Larry Winters were all part of Tri-State Wrestling, and after Joel Goodhart had closed up shop, there was a void there," explains ECW mainstay Brian "Blue Meanie" Heffron. "So they got together and tried to run some shows at local bars and cabarets. And eventually they landed TV. There's a sports channel here in Philly [and] they were desperate for programming, so Tod Gordon got a sweetheart deal to give them an hour a week. That's how ECW first got on TV, and it was the first major step in the growth of the product."

Under the control of founder Gordon, the company, a member of the struggling National Wrestling Alliance, took over not only Tri-State's former Philly circuit, but the circuit of the recently defunct National Wrestling Federation as well, covering Upstate New York and parts of Ohio. The company's home venue was a dingy, dilapidated bingo hall in South Philadelphia, with minimalist lighting and bleacher seating that recalled the down-and-dirty VFW Halls and armories of a previous generation. As humble as it was, the building would eventually gain worldwide notoriety as the ECW Arena.

"Philly always like the heels," says Heffron of the city that was home to the company. "I don't know what was in the water that made Philadelphians prefer the heels, but we like the ass-kickers. We like the guys who aren't afraid to get their knuckles busted, maybe get a scar on their face."

At the end of 1993, ECW head booker "Hot Stuff" Eddie Gilbert was replaced by Paul Heyman, who had been working as manager Paul E. Dangerously in WCW before parting ways and heading to Philadelphia at Gilbert's invitation. With the Heyman influence in place, things quickly began to change. Heyman had a creative vision to turn ECW into a whole lot

Heyman confers backstage with one of his infamous Atlas Security men during the height of ECW's 1990s glory days.

Robert Newsome/ Wikimedia

more than just another independent promotion, seeking to add a much-needed edge to the professional wrestling industry, comparing it to the way popular music had recently received a jolt to the system thanks to the grunge-rock revolution.

"Eddie was . . . booking the company, but it seemed like he was almost booking it as a goof, bringing his friends in, having fun and doing campy stuff," says Heffron. "Then Eddie brought in Paul, and Paul and Eddie were great friends. Tod was in a situation where he needed to move forward, but Eddie wasn't really getting the job done. It was an opportunity for Paul to be a booker, but he was between a rock and a hard place because he was replacing a friend. Eddie might have looked at it like Paul was trying to maneuver him out, but it was an opportunity. Paul had all these great ideas; he has a great mind."

Getting Extreme

Heyman's booking philosophy, as well as the new direction of ECW, was finally crystallized on August 27, 1994. Jim Crockett, former owner of the company that had become WCW, had joined forces with National Wrestling Alliance president Dennis Coralluzzo in an attempt to revive the once-proud NWA with a World Heavyweight Championship tournament, held under the auspices of one of the Alliance's leading current members, ECW. Scheduled to win the tournament and the title was Shane Douglas, the current ECW Heavyweight Champion. Chafing under the yoke of the NWA and looking to make a name for their company, Heyman and Gordon came up with their own secret plan. Under their orders, once Douglas won the NWA World title in the tournament final against 2 Cold Scorpio, he threw the historic championship belt to the mat and declared that he wanted no part of it. He declared that his ECW title was now a World Heavyweight Championship.

Crockett and Coralluzzo were outraged, but there was nothing they could do about it. The week of the incident, the company name was changed from Eastern Championship Wrestling to Extreme Championship Wrestling, and, according to plan, it was immediately the talk of the industry. Soon thereafter, Tod Gordon sold off his interest in the company to Paul Heyman, the man who had orchestrated so much of its new direction. Under his control, ECW would come to embody "hardcore"—in fact, it was there that the term was actually coined. Just as Heyman hoped, ECW became the punk rock of professional wrestling. Airing in local TV markets throughout the Philadelphia area, as well as on a late-night timeslot on the MSG Network that brought ECW into the homes of New Yorkers, the company started gaining a passionate underground fan base.

Under the ECW banner, "hardcore" meant much more than simply excessive violence and outrageous gimmick matches. "Hardcore" was a movement; a work ethic. It meant not insulting your audience. It meant presenting talent that worked their hearts out each night and did things no one in mainstream American wrestling was doing at the time. It meant making the fans a part of the show. It meant getting back to what had made pro wrestling so exciting and intense in the down-and-dirty days before it became glossy, neatly packaged family entertainment. The innovations that occurred during the company's mid-'90s heyday were many. Clever (and sometimes brutally honest) crowd chants became a staple, and many of them continue to this day in WWE rings and elsewhere. For the first time in wrestling history, fans were so into the action that they would actually chant the name of the promotion itself. Rules were virtually non-existent, with every match being presented for all intents and purposes as "no disqualification," with the referee there only to record the pinfall. Fans were encouraged to bring foreign objects for the wrestlers to use in their matches. The interview style was honest and in-your-face, with performers referencing their personal lives and other wrestling promotions.

Part of Heyman's genius lay in the ability to take talent and make them into more than they had ever been, emphasizing their strengths and hiding their weaknesses to manufacture stars at a much faster rate than either WCW or the WWF were doing at the time. He took a smiling, suspenders-wearing white-meat babyface named Tommy Dreamer and turned him into the face of hardcore, an intense everyman fighting for survival in extreme situations—a character said to be inspired by Bruce Willis's John McClane of the *Die Hard* series. He took Northeast indy mainstay The Tasmaniac, a squat performer using a savage gimmick, and transformed him into Taz, a feared and unstoppable wrecking machine. He took Scott Levy, known to mainstream fans only as the goofy Scotty Flamingo of WCW and the even goofier Johnny Polo of the WWF, and made him Raven, the sociopathic leader of a menacing cult.

And then there was the "homicidal, suicidal, genocidal" Sabu, the real-life nephew of The Sheik, who more than lived up to his uncle's notorious legacy. Heyman booked Sabu as ECW's special attraction, almost an equivalent to an Andre the Giant or Undertaker. Yet rather than immense size, it was his death-defying performance style that made him so unique. It included an unprecedented willingness to damage his own body for the sake of a great match, best exemplified by his propensity for putting his opponents through ringside tables. Although the practice dates as far back as a 1984 Memphis match between The Rock 'n' Roll Express and Lanny Poffo & Randy Savage, it was Sabu who popularized it to the degree that it is now a staple of nearly every major wrestling event. In WWE, it has reached new levels thanks to being incorporated into the traditional ladder match setup, resulting in the infamous "tables, ladders, and chairs" (TLC) match.

"Paul knew the guys he had had flaws or weaknesses that, if shown, you could see through them," explains ECW alum Dr. Tom Prichard. "So Paul knew he had to cover that up, and how to do sound bites. Also, Paul always said to drink the Kool-Aid and you'd be fine. Paul would pump up his crew. We were in the ECW Arena one night and he made this great speech and everyone was ready to go to battle and die if they had to. Paul would make these great motivational speeches, and lie if he needed to."

Hardcore Goes Mainstream

ECW was making major waves with its envelope-pushing storylines, emphasis on high-impact action, and overt sexuality. A genuine

Sabu strikes an iconic pose, c. 2009. *Chatsam/Wikimedia*

hardcore revolution was happening in professional wrestling, and the "Big Two" started to sit up and take notice. Before long, table spots were happening in both WCW and the WWF. Blading was en vogue, after being out of favor for years while mainstream wrestling courted young children as its primary audience. The fan base was growing tired of the increasingly bland and kid-oriented mainstream product, and discovering ECW's hardcore alternative in droves. So, in response, mainstream wrestling started to become just a little more hardcore.

Inevitably, Heyman soon discovered that his talent-rich roster was being raided, particularly by Eric Bischoff of WCW. Meanwhile, Vince McMahon of the WWF saw an even more beneficial approach: partnership. Ironically, as Heyman positioned his company as the ultimate counterculture, anti-authority organization, he began a secret working relationship with the biggest wrestling company of them all, staging inter-promotional angles, and even initiating a talent-exchange program. It was in his best interest, as ECW was on the verge of making the big move to pay-per-view, with its first such event, *Barely Legal*, set for April 1997. With a main event pitting ECW World Champion Taz against Sabu after a mind-blowing two years of buildup, the show was a resounding success. ECW was now playing with the big boys, and could legitimately lay claim to being the number-three wrestling company in North America.

The ECW influence continued to infiltrate the WWF and WCW, resulting in the national wrestling audience being exposed to the hardcore style like never before. Both WCW's nWo invasion and the WWF's Austin/McMahon storyline reflected the ECW sensibility, as did so much of what went into building the so-called "Attitude Era." Intense, long-form interviews with loads of insider references, which had once been the exclusive lynchpin of ECW programming and one of the major reasons fans tuned in, could now be found in WCW and the WWF as well, with performers spending nearly as much time talking as wrestling. The two major companies even instituted their very own Hardcore Championships in the late 1990s, officially acknowledging the form as a distinct subgenre within their own products.

ECW Implosion

Meanwhile, the growth of ECW itself continued with a deal to air a weekly Friday-night show on cable channel TNN, granting Heyman access to a national TV audience for the very first time. *ECW on TNN* premiered on August 27, 1999—exactly five years after Shane Douglas's history-making rejection of the NWA World Championship—but was beset with problems from the start. TNN immediately attempted to assert control over the promotion, seeking to tone down the very edginess that made Heyman's product so appealing. The relationship between ECW and the network was a rocky one, and when Vince McMahon made a deal in 2000 to switch the WWF's *Monday Night Raw* from the USA Network to TNN, the cable company was only too happy to drop Heyman in favor of the sports-entertainment juggernaut.

From that point on, the writing was on the wall. With the loss of national TV, ECW began bleeding money. Heyman wasn't above stretching the truth and performing some accounting acrobatics to keep his company above water, and these practices began alienating the talents who had believed in him for so long. The mainstreaming of hardcore had meant that fans could tune into the WWF and WCW to see the same stuff that used to be the main province of ECW—even if the mainstream version was nothing like the original, and even if most of those fans didn't realize where the style had originated. In April 2001, with most of the talent not being informed the company was dying, ECW declared bankruptcy.

The company that altered the landscape of the wrestling industry, the pioneering group that had put hardcore wrestling on the map, was unable to reap the rewards of the "extreme" renaissance it had ignited within the business, and fell victim to the cutthroat competition of the WWF and WCW's war for dominance. Within weeks, Heyman joined the WWF as a TV announcer and creative consultant, and the ECW brand and assets were purchased by Vince McMahon and absorbed into his company. The brand was then used in 2001 as part of a failed invasion storyline that also involved WCW, which McMahon had also purchased earlier in the year.

Life After Philadelphia

The watered-down WWF version of the ECW brand was a classic example of how the mainstream misinterpreted and mishandled the whole hardcore phenomenon. Missing the point that "hardcore" was an attitude more than anything else—or, perhaps more accurately, believing it would never appeal to a mainstream audience—the creative minds behind WCW and the WWF viewed it as not much more than over-the-top violence, gimmick matches, and outrageous props. Boiling it down to these elements, hardcore wrestling became a joke—a parody of itself that emphasized the ridiculousness of the proceedings more than anything else. What started as intense and gritty became cartoonish and laughable—the exact opposite of what Heyman envisioned "hardcore" to be.

In 2005, desiring to make the most of its ECW assets, WWE presented *One Night Stand*, a pay-per-view event held at the old ECW Arena and acting as a reunion of ECW talent. The show briefly resurrected the ECW look and feel, but by the time WWE fully re-launched the brand under the WWE umbrella in 2006, it was clear that the lesson was not learned. The product that aired on the SyFy Channel was nothing like the original ECW that had endeared itself to fans in the 1990s, but was rather WWE's toned-down interpretation of it. And since the company never took hardcore seriously, the new ECW seemed doomed from the start. It limped along for four years before WWE finally pulled the plug on the entire brand in 2010.

Professional wrestling today is a somewhat tamer product than it was during the mid- to late 1990s, particularly in WWE, leading some to refer to it as the "PG Era." The result of increasing corporate influence, as well as the political aspirations of principal co-owner Linda McMahon, WWE has clamped down on many of the hardcore influences that made the Attitude Era work. The hardcore title is a thing of the past, as is blading, which has, once again, gone underground. Nevertheless, the legacy of ECW, and of hardcore wrestling in general, continues to live on to a certain degree, both within WWE and throughout the industry. The last remnants of the ECW brand currently survive in the form of a yearly WWE pay-per-view event called *Extreme Rules*, which features hardcore-style gimmick matches and intense high-spots similar to those of ECW's heyday (minus the blood, of course).

Meanwhile, on the independent circuit, the ECW effect continues to be felt. In the 2000s, California-based Xtreme Pro Wrestling (run by porn producer Rob Black) and New Jersey–based Combat Zone Wrestling, carried on the hardcore tradition. CZW continues to operate to this day, and for a time even moved its base of operations to Philadelphia, running out of the former ECW Arena until the venue was finally closed down in 2012. Even former ECW headliner Tommy Dreamer, the face of hardcore itself, got into the act with House of Hardcore, a company founded in 2012, which professes to adhere to the true hardcore ethos, and has been presenting shows in New York, Pennsylvania, and California.

And so, hardcore wrestling is still alive and well, even if it has returned to the fringes of the professional wrestling business. Some might argue that such an extreme subgenre is best served in pro wrestling's underground, anyway. As for the niche fans who have supported it over the years and continue to believe in it, there is no question that that is how they prefer it.

Extreme Icons: The Renegades Who Personified ECW

Fans of hardcore wrestling will never forget the edgy cast of characters developed by Paul Heyman during his company's 1990s heyday.

- 911
- Axl Rotten
- Balls Mahoney
- Beulah McGillicutty
- The bWo (Stevie Richards, Blue Meanie, Nova)
- Cactus Jack
- The Dudley Boyz
- The Eliminators
- Francine
- Mikey Whipwreck
- New Jack
- The Pitbulls
- Public Enemy
- Raven
- Rob Van Dam
- Sabu
- The Sandman
- Shane Douglas
- Taz
- Tommy Dreamer

The Arabian Madman

For a dizzying, blood-soaked forty years, the noble Sheik was the living, breathing personification of what later came to be known as hardcore wrestling. Cutting a blazing trail through opponents far and wide and striking terror into the hearts of fans everywhere, he threw any semblance of actual wrestling to the wind and proved that outright violence, brutality, and bloodshed could be a drawing card in itself. Mayhem was his stock in trade, and nobody dealt it out like the gibberish-muttering maniac who bit, gouged, and stabbed his way to become one of the industry's greatest attractions.

Rather than the deserts of Syria from which he was billed during his career, he was born Edward George Farhat to Lebanese Catholic parents in Lansing, Michigan, on June 9, 1924, one of ten children. He would closely guard that identity throughout his life, beginning with his wrestling debut in 1949, when he first began to make waves under a completely fabricated alter ego, as one of the colorful cast of characters brought into Truman-era American living rooms, thanks to Fred Kohler's *Wrestling from the Marigold*, aired nationwide on the old DuMont Network. Initially known as The Sheik of Araby, he perfected a mysterious gimmick that came complete with traditional Arabic getup, as well as "praying to Mecca" on the mat before matches. It was all designed to infuriate fans, and it worked very well.

Also key to The Sheik's success was his aura of unpredictability and random violence. He never spoke, usually relying on obnoxious managers like Abdullah Farouk (a.k.a. "Grand Wizard" Ernie Roth) and Eddie "The Brain" Creatchman to do the talking for him. He seemed completely unstable in the ring, and as the years went on he became more and more prone to extreme acts of barbaric violence, assaulting opponents with chairs before the bell, throwing balls of fire generated by hidden flashpaper, and perpetually wielding a sharpened pencil. His matches were always guaranteed to feature bloodshed, both from his opponents and himself.

The act was such a sensation that it opened the doors for The Sheik to travel to just about anywhere he wanted and be a top star. He headlined throughout Texas, as well as in Los Angeles, where he battled "Classy" Freddie Blassie on numerous occasions. In the Northeast, he challenged WWWF World Champion Bruno Sammartino in bloodbaths at Madison Square Garden and the Boston Garden in the late 1960s, culminating in his being permanently banned from New York due to a crowd riot he incited at MSG. Such incidents were the norm wherever The Sheik plied his trade, but nowhere more so than in Detroit, the area that would become his "home turf."

In the early 1960s, Farhat purchased the Detroit wrestling territory from Jim Barnett, and remained secretly in control until it finally folded in 1980. The fans had no concept that the wild man who haunted their nightmares and savaged opponents on a regular basis in Cobo Arena was also the man in charge in the front office. Under his watch, Detroit in the 1960s and '70s became a hotbed for hardcore wrestling, with a reputation for the wildest action to be seen in North America. Sheik was the headliner, of course, regularly trading a version of the United States champion with fellow Michigan native and archrival Bobo Brazil in a feud that transcended eras, as well as territorial boundaries.

Decades before South Philly became the home of hardcore, the Motor City delivered a madcap brand of raucous action to its bloodthirsty blue-collar fans. And the action spilled over across the Great Lakes to Ontario, where Farhat was head booker for promoter Frank Tunney, and as The Sheik, enjoyed a five-year undefeated streak that included victories over the likes of Bruno Sammartino, Lou Thesz, Gene Kiniski, and Andre the Giant. His reign of terror continued until the Detroit territory finally closed down in 1980, due to what some have considered fan burnout after years of ceaseless, repetitive brutality.

In the 1980s and '90s, The Sheik soldiered on in the ring, enjoying particular success in Japan, where companies like FMW spotlighted hardcore wrestling and celebrated him as its pioneer. He had brief stints in both ECW and WCW alongside his real-life nephew and protégé Sabu, who successfully carried on his Arabian madman gimmick. Battling into his seventies, The Sheik finally retired in 1998 after suffering a heart attack in Tokyo. On January 18, 2003, heart failure brought to an end the life one of the industry's most feared villains and most important innovators.

The Hardcore Icon

Many of the legends of professional wrestling, men who achieved mainstream success in the business, have eschewed the hardcore style over the years for a number of reasons—perhaps preferring a more mat-based scientific approach, or perhaps believing it to be a bad way to do business. Nevertheless, there is one legitimate legend of the industry who has, above all others, not only embraced but influenced the hardcore style, helping it to gain wider acceptance along the way. A former holder of the NWA World Heavyweight Championship, a title with origins in wrestling's halcyon Golden Age, he has never been afraid to get his hands dirty—or bloody—and despite numerous so-called "retirement" matches, it seems he will never truly walk away from the business.

Terry Funk was born on June 30, 1944, in Hammond, Indiana, the son of rookie pro wrestler Dory Funk, Sr., and the younger brother of Dory Funk, Jr. After Dory Sr. finished his tour of duty in the South Pacific during World War II, the family soon relocated to Texas, where Terry's father not only became a major star, but also a top promoter when he took over the Amarillo wrestling territory with booker Karl "Doc" Sarpolis in 1955. As a result, Terry grew up around the business, and was a standout wrestler and football player during his years at West Texas State University.

He followed in his father's footsteps in 1965 when he made his debut working for his father's company. Just two years later, Sarpolis passed away and Terry and his older brother bought his share of the promotion, which they continued to run alongside their father, as well as long after he himself passed away in 1973 after suffering a heart attack during a brawl with other wrestlers at a post-show party.

Terry and Dory were headliners on the West Texas circuit, but also ventured far beyond its confines, performing for promoters throughout the country, as well as in Japan, where they became two of the country's most feared and despised foreign heels for many years. Along the way, the list of championships Terry accumulated is truly staggering: the United States Championship in Mid-Atlantic Championship Wrestling; the Americas Heavyweight Championship in L.A.'s Hollywood Wrestling; the Southwest Heavyweight Championship; the Missouri Heavyweight title for St. Louis promoter Sam Muchnick; and various tag-team championships with his brother in Georgia, California, and Texas.

Funk would also have an impressive run working for Eddie Graham in Florida, and it was there, on December 10, 1975, that he defeated Jack Brisco for the NWA World Heavyweight Championship, the most prestigious prize in the business. For fourteen months, he reigned supreme at the very top of the mat game, before finally losing the gold to former champion Harley Race in Toronto. The reign made Terry and Dory the only brothers to both hold the NWA World title, which was a testament not only to their respective ability but also to the respect their father had enjoyed during his lifetime.

From the beginning, Terry had always wrestled a more rough-and-tumble style than his more technically minded brother—a style typical of the brawling that was so popular in Southern rings. But as his career wore on, the more hard-core aspects became even more prominent. His legendary 1981 empty arena match in Memphis against Jerry Lawler had a major impact on the development of hardcore wrestling. He also brought his roughneck sensibilities to both the WWF and WCW during the 1980s, appearing at *WrestleMania 2* as well as challenging Ric Flair for the NWA World Championship in a wild series of bouts highlighted by a classic "I Quit" match at *Clash of the Champions IX* in 1989.

But it would be as part of ECW that Funk would experience the ultimate career renaissance. After first learning of the promotion while taking part in a 1994 WCW pay-per-view event in Philadelphia, he agreed to join up and lend his legendary name to the fledgling outfit. While there, he became a mentor to Tommy Dreamer, captured the ECW World Heavyweight title on two occasions, and engaged in all manner of increasingly insane and violent gimmick matches, perhaps most notably a barbed-wire match against Sabu in August 1997. The Funker was exposed to a whole new generation of rowdy fans, who embraced him as the "Hardcore Icon." Along the way, he succeeded in elevating ECW's status and making the careers of several performers.

In a perpetual state of semi-retirement, Terry Funk continues to amaze audiences with his fearlessness and his passion for the business. He has made twenty-first century appearances for WWE, WCW, TNA, Ring of Honor, and many other organizations, and was spotlighted in the groundbreaking wrestling documentary *Beyond the Mat*. A generation ago, he was termed "middle-aged and crazy." Little did we know back then that he was just getting warmed up.

20

Double-Cross!

The Monday Night War and Other Notorious Promotional Battles

It doesn't matter if people love you or hate you, as long as they feel strongly one way or the other. The worst place you can be is in the middle.

—Eric Bischoff

Professional wrestling is built around conflict; grudges, feuds, and rivalries make up the fuel that drives it forward as an engaging and profitable form of entertainment. Fans thrill to the intrigue and animosity that bursts forth from their TV and computer screens, cheering and jeering their favorites and getting caught up in the drama. Yet there is another level of drama, one that is not seen in any ring, to which the majority of fans have not been privy, especially before the rise of the Internet. After all, what we watch unfold on TV is, at the end of the day, scripted storyline, no matter how based in reality it may be. Behind the scenes, away from the cameras, lay the real conflicts—which very often can be just as intriguing as any angle, if not much more so.

Traditionally, this business has been a shady one, in which most feel they can never truly trust anyone—there's a reason that old-school locker-room etiquette demands that everyone look each other in the eye and shake hands, no matter how familiar they are with each other. Promoters have always battled over turf, and double-crosses are common occurrences throughout wrestling history. Very often, these battles have become super heated, with wrestlers inevitably getting pulled into the fray, either as pawns or as weapons. Whether they're fighting over talent, television ratings, or actual physical territory, promoters will seemingly do just about anything to protect and further their interests. And to those in the know who enjoy following this sort of backstage warfare, it can comprise the most fascinating "storylines" of all.

The Monday Night War

For modern-day fans, there is, of course, no better-known or well-chronicled promotional battle than the so-called "Monday Night War" that raged from 1995 to 2001 between the WWF and WCW, North America's two major pro wrestling organizations at the time. Covered exhaustively ever since, it has become a touchstone for an entire era, in which both companies fought for their very existence, and produced some of the greatest television moments and hottest stars ever seen in the process. Such battles had occurred many times in the past, but this was the first time in wrestling history that it was taking place on such a grand stage, over national television ratings.

It all started at the tail end of the summer of 1995, when WCW Executive Vice President Eric Bischoff took his plot to dethrone WWF Chairman Vince McMahon and turned it into an outright war. He did this by positioning his new, live, weekly program, *Monday Nitro*, in direct opposition to the WWF's flagship, live (every other week) program *Monday Night Raw*. Bischoff had already begun signing up former McMahon talent like Hulk Hogan, Lex Luger, and Randy Savage, and initiating his next step by getting the brass at Turner Broadcasting, owners of WCW at the time, to green-light a series that would run on Turner's channel TNT against USA Network's *Raw*, which already had two and a half years of momentum on its side.

The ensuing result was seen by many as payback of sorts for the numerous companies the WWF had muscled out of business during its national

Eric Bischoff led WCW to its most financially successful period during the mid- to late 1990s.   *daysofthundr46/Wikimedia*

expansion of the previous decade. For the first time, McMahon found himself not the predator, but the prey. Refusing to even acknowledge Bischoff, he publicly tagged Ted Turner as the enemy, and scrambled to develop a new generation of talent to help him combat the very real threat. *Nitro* had a corporation backing it with potentially limitless cash flow, made even more limitless by Turner's impending acquisition by media mega-giant Time-Warner, Inc. *Nitro* was live every single week; McMahon could not afford to do so with *Raw*. *Nitro* eventually ballooned to two hours, and then three. More stars made the exodus to WCW, eventually leading to a storyline in which former WWF performers were presented as "invading." McMahon tried to sue for copyright infringement, but it did little to stem the tide. Before long, WCW was beating the WWF's ratings for the very first time, and by 1996 had arguably edged it out as the world's most popular pro wrestling organization.

Wrestling fans of the era fondly remember the days of frantically switching back and forth between USA and TNT on Monday nights so as not to miss anything. In order to retain viewers, both promotions did their best to load their respective shows with as much action and as many dramatic twists as possible, including pay-per-view quality matches, title changes, heel/face turns, and shocking debuts on a weekly basis. Bischoff even made it a practice to reveal WWF results on his own show on nights when *Nitro* was live and *Raw* wasn't. For eighty-three straight weeks, *Nitro* led the ratings war, until slowly but surely McMahon began to turn things around with an edgier product and the white-hot Austin/McMahon storyline.

By the turn of the new century, WCW was in free fall and the clear-cut winner was all but assured. After struggling for their lives for years, the WWF pulled fully ahead on the steam of an exciting new crop of stars and fresher creative ideas. McMahon tried to buy his struggling competition outright and run it separately on TNT, but his own TV deal at the time prevented it due to conflict of interest. Finally, when new Time-Warner management came into power in 2001, they pulled the plug on the ailing property, canceling all WCW TV programming. The company went on the auction block, with Vince McMahon swooping in to pick up the pieces, outbidding none other than Eric Bischoff himself. After nearly six years, the Monday Night War was over, and the soon-to-be WWE reigned supreme over the wrestling industry.

But the Monday Night War was only one of a myriad of hard-fought promotional battles over the years. Wrestling promoters can be a contentious and opportunistic lot, and the history of the business is a history of turf wars and promotional conflicts galore. Here are just a handful of the many others . . .

Denatured Boy

In the early 1960s, Vincent J. McMahon and Toots Mondt were able to make their Capitol Wrestling (the future WWE) into one of the nation's major promotions due, in large part, to the drawing power of the colorful "Nature Boy" Buddy Rogers, whose services they had acquired from Columbus, Ohio, promoter Al Haft. Rogers was now the property of McMahon and Mondt, and, in 1961, they used their influence to broker a deal that saw Rogers crowned NWA World Heavyweight Champion, after defeating Pat O'Connor before a record-breaking Comiskey Park crowd, in a match they co-promoted with Chicago impresario Fred Kohler.

The National Wrestling Alliance was leery of the title change from the start, suspicious as they were of any member promoters who might try to monopolize the champion, rather than sharing him with the rest of the territories, as was the NWA agreement. Sure enough, McMahon and Mondt attempted to make Rogers nearly exclusive to Capitol, leaving promoters and bookers outside the Northeast high and dry. After a year and a half, the solution became clear: the NWA World title had to be taken off Rogers, and to do so, the Alliance called out of retirement former NWA champion Lou Thesz to pull it off.

Thesz was renowned for his "shooting" abilities, meaning he could legitimately defeat just about any opponent he wished if need be—unlike Rogers, who was pretty much just a performer rather than a genuine grappler. The Nature Boy and his backers attempted to duck Thesz as much as possible, but it was only a matter of time before the NWA painted them into a corner. The story goes that when Thesz finally got Rogers in the ring in Toronto's Maple Leaf Gardens, he walked over and whispered in his ear, "We can do this the easy way, or we can do it the hard way." Rogers chose the former.

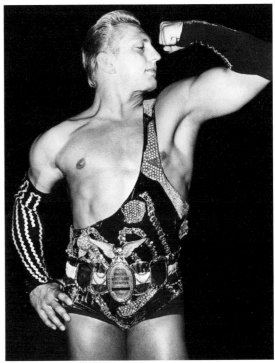

Prior to his world championship victory, Rogers had been billed throughout the 1950s as U.S. champion. *Jack Pfefer Collection, University of Notre Dame*

A "Big" Mistake

The Gold Dust Trio asserted its dominance over the wrestling business during the 1920s, an era when promotional disputes within the industry started becoming a factor as the industry became less about competitive sport and more about pre-arranged exhibitions. Manager Billy Sandow, booker Toots Mondt, and wrestler Ed "Strangler" Lewis made up the combine, with Lewis as its reigning World Heavyweight Champion. But there was another show in town vying for power, headed up by former world champion "Scissors King" Joe Stecher and his manager brother Tony, as well as New York promoter Jack Curley and St. Louis promoter Tom Packs.

It was bad for business for Lewis to remain champion for too long, as the trio liked to move the belt around to create drama. Their error, however, was in whom they chose to have the Strangler drop the belt to in Kansas City in 1925. An extremely popular football player from the University of Nebraska, Wayne "Big" Munn had only one problem: he couldn't wrestle a lick. A non-wrestler had never been champion before, but the trio took a chance and pulled the trigger. Little did they realize that one of Munn's future challengers, veteran Stanislaus Zbyszko, was now on the payroll of the Stecher outfit. Throwing the script out the window, Zbyszko upset the inexperienced Munn to become the new world champion, and promptly brought the title over to the Stechers, losing it to Joe per their arrangement the following month.

"It ended up [being] the biggest blunder in wrestling history, as Sandow lost control of the title when Munn got double-crossed," says noted wrestling historian Steve Yohe. "Losing control cost Sandow and Lewis the wrestling war with the Stecher/Curley/Packs group and the two joined the other side."

For three years, Stecher evaded the Gold Dust Trio and continued to reign as world champion, until finally agreeing to do business with Lewis in 1928 and dropping the title to him. The Zbyszko-Munn double-cross taught promoters a valuable lesson about keeping the world championship on individuals who actually knew how to wrestle, and it wouldn't be until the 1960s that this practice began to loosen up.

The Battle of Atlanta

A major power vacuum occurred in the Georgia area during the early 1970s that would permanently alter the course of one of the nation's major wrestling operations. For nearly thirty years, Georgia Championship Wrestling had been owned and operated by former wrestler Paul Jones, but toward the end of his life Jones handed over the day-to-day operations to his booker,

Ray Gunkel, also a top star in the promotion. Gunkel made some important decisions, including getting the company access to the brand new Omni Coliseum for its regular live events, as well as a Saturday-night TV timeslot on UHF station WTCG, owned by a local media upstart named Ted Turner.

However, Gunkel's untimely death of a heart attack during a 1972 match with Ox Baker sent matters into chaos. An aging Jones brought in Cowboy Bill Watts as booker and manager. A successful star of the 1960s, Watts was eager to get into the promotional end of the business. However, Ray Gunkel's widow, Ann, was angered by the maneuver, believing she would be getting her late husband's share of the company rather than Watts. Starting up her own company, All-South Wrestling Alliance, in opposition to Jones and Watts, she began luring away Georgia talent, and even secured her own timeslot on WTCG. (Rumors abounded that the beautiful former model had been romantically involved with Turner.)

Matters worsened until finally Jones brought in "troubleshooter" Jim Barnett, an itinerant promoter with a great deal of influence in the industry. Barnett began bringing the talent back, and worked to shut Ann Gunkel out of many key venues and local markets. By 1974, the short-lived All-South Wrestling Alliance was no more, and Barnett had assumed full control of Georgia Championship Wrestling. Two years later, WTCG became cable SuperStation TBS, making GCW the first wrestling promotion in twenty years to be broadcast nationwide.

A Matter of Trust

The mid-1930s was a time of absolute chaos within the pro wrestling business. A number of powerful promoters—men like Jack Curley and Toots Mondt in New York, Lou Daro in Los Angeles, Al Haft in Ohio, Tony Stecher in Minnesota, Tom Packs in St. Louis, and Paul Bowser in Boston—had joined forces to form what they called "The Trust," an early predecessor to the National Wrestling Alliance that sought to bring order and control talent. Their top draw was the extremely popular World Heavyweight Champion Jim Londos. But Londos had become such a success that he became difficult for the Trust to control, and so the paranoid promoters sought a new, more malleable and wet-behind-the-ears attraction that they could keep under their collective thumb.

Each promoter began establishing his own stars: Daro had Vincent Lopez, Mondt had Dean Detton, Packs had Orville Brown, Stecher had Bronko Nagurski. Bowser succeeded in maneuvering his man, an Irish discovery named Danno O'Mahoney, all the way into the top spot as the successor to Londos and new World Heavyweight Champion. O'Mahoney didn't know how to wrestle, but would be protected by willing "opponents" and enforcers (known as "policemen") like Ed "Strangler" Lewis, who discouraged any potential double-crosses.

But all bets were off when vengeful, disgruntled former Trust policeman Dick Shikat (who had reportedly been publicly beaten by Mondt in the lobby of Manhattan's Astor Hotel) went into business for himself during his match against O'Mahoney at Madison Square Garden on March 2, 1936, outwrestling and downright punishing the stunned Irishman to the point that referee George Bothner, under the watchful eye of the New York State Athletic Commission, had no choice but to award the title to Shikat. The German-born grappler then promptly put the title up for sale to the highest bidder, finally agreeing to lose to Ali Baba for promoter Nick Londos of Detroit. The whole dirty business was laid bare for the paying public, exposing O'Mahoney as a "phony" champion, and revealing the Machiavellian machinations of the business. The Trust crumbled apart, as reactionary promoters created their own world champions, isolated themselves in their local territories, and the business became more regionalized than ever before.

Texas Outlaw

Pro wrestling, as we have seen, can be a dirty business, but rarely has there ever been a dirtier and more hotly contested territorial war than what happened in the Lone Star State over a seventeen-month period between 1953 and 1954. Houston-based impresario Morris Siegel was the most influential NWA promoter in the South, and had been doing business for some time with Ed McLemore, the young upstart who ran the Dallas office. What McLemore also had going for him was television, presenting a regular show at the local Sportatorium. When Siegel started using his muscle to try and squeeze more TV revenue from his partner, things turned sour.

McLemore split from Siegel and seceded from the NWA, choosing to expand his own business into nearby towns like San Antonio and Corpus Christi. Siegel, who had fended off so-called "outlaw promoters" like Dizzy Davis with extreme prejudice in the past, became ruthless. He brought down the wrath of the NWA, installing a new Dallas promoter named Norman Clark to try and run McLemore out of business. It also helped that the entrenched Siegel had the Texas State Athletic Commission and Texas Labor Commission in his pocket, as well as reported mob ties. McLemore wouldn't relent, eventually even recruiting Siegel's own booker, Karl "Doc" Sarpolis. When the Dallas Sportatorium was burned to the ground on May 1, 1953, it was believed by many that Siegel was behind it, although nothing was ever proven.

McLemore proved a tenacious opponent, and eventually Siegel was forced to relent and work out a new partnership deal. McLemore would rejoin the NWA and agree to split Dallas profits 50/50 with Siegel. The Houston-Dallas partnership continued for many years, well after McLemore eventually sold off his interests to Texas legend Fritz Von Erich, the man who would transform the company into World Class Championship Wrestling.

A Savage Conflict

An "outlaw promotion" was one that had the audacity to run competition against the established NWA promoters who had staked claims to particular territories throughout North America. One particularly stubborn outlaw promotion was International Championship Wrestling, established in 1978 by 1950s and '60s mat star Angelo Poffo in Lexington, Kentucky. ICW was built around Poffo's two sons, Lanny Poffo and Randy Poffo (who wrestled as "Macho Man" Randy Savage), and quickly made in-roads in places like Tennessee, Georgia, Alabama, and Indiana. This naturally made the Poffos enemies of a whole lot of NWA promoters, including Jim Barnett, Jerry Jarrett, Nick Gulas, Dick the Bruiser, and Ron Fuller.

As they typically did in situations like this, the NWA members colluded to crush the offending party. Wrestler Ronnie Garvin would later testify to being instructed by Barnett to hurt Savage during a match, which he did, attacking him with a cinderblock. The NWA attempted to lure Angelo into coming to enemy territory to lose a televised match against NWA World Champion Harley Race, with the promise that it would lead to a series of title matches across the country, as a way of burying the hatchet. Poffo refused, believing the real intent was to use the TV footage to bury his reputation. Eventually, the Poffos would sue the NWA for its shady practices, dragging the whole ugly issue into court.

Lawler and Savage met in (and around) the ring for the first time in the Mid-South Coliseum on December 5, 1983. *Photo by* Pro Wrestling Illustrated

The fiercest battleground was Memphis, where ICW waged a brutal territorial war against Jerry Jarrett and Jerry Lawler's Continental Wrestling Association. The tipping point came in 1982, when Savage ran into CWA booker Bill Dundee in a local restaurant and called him out. The two wound up out in the parking lot, with Dundee attempting to pull a gun on the Macho Man, only to have Savage disarm him and use the blunt end of the weapon to break his jaw. Nevertheless, in the long run the Poffos were forced to cave in to their enemies when dwindling ticket sales put them out of business the following year. Taking advantage of the real-life animosity, the Poffos were brought into the CWA fold, with Savage and Lawler engaging in a red-hot in-ring rivalry that was promoted as the payoff to the long-running promotional war. That rivalry would help turn Savage into a national star.

The Original Montreal Screwjob

For many years, wrestling companies have employed names intended to give the impression of an actual governing body, when, in fact, the governing body is fictional and the appellation is merely a brand name for the product (à la "World Wrestling Federation"). This practice dates back to the late 1920s, when the very real governing body known as the National Wrestling Association, a division of the National Boxing Association, was formed, recognizing former Dartmouth footballer "Dynamite" Gus Sonnenberg as its world champion. When the original NWA stripped Sonnenberg, powerful promoter Paul Bowser swooped in and declared that he was still the champion—as recognized by his own "governing body," a fictional entity he called the American Wrestling Association (not to be confused with the later group of the same name).

Bowser had originally agreed for Sonnenberg to drop the AWA title to veteran Ed "Strangler" Lewis, but snubbed Lewis and had "Dynamite" lose the gold instead to another world-class grappler, Ed Don George. This was not a good idea, considering the Strangler's rep for being one of the industry's most legitimately dangerous men. When Lewis finally met the new champion in 1931 in what was supposed to be a run-of-the-mill successful title defense, he politely informed George that this was the night he would lose the championship—and there was nothing the champ could do about it. He played along, and Lewis walked away the four-time World Heavyweight Champion, much to Bowser's chagrin.

The AWA kingpin had revenge on his mind when he booked Lewis in a title defense against former Olympic gold medalist Henri DeGlane in Montreal three weeks later. Lewis's manager, Billy Sandow, sensed that a double-cross was in progress when the first fall ended with a fast count in favor of DeGlane—he protested so loudly that the Montreal Athletic

Commission removed him from ringside. When the parties returned to the ring for the second fall, matters got even more bizarre—DeGlane had bitten himself on the arm (or possibly had Bowser's enforcer Dan Koloff do the job) and tried to pass it off as the Strangler's handiwork in the ring. The referee disqualified the champion and awarded the title to DeGlane. Mob thugs flanked a gloating Bowser in the locker room to ensure that Lewis kept his distance. It's believed that fear of future double-crosses like this one led to the eventual universal agreement that championships cannot change hands on a disqualification.

The First McMahon-Crockett War

Vincent K. McMahon and Jim Crockett, Jr., would engage in a high-profile promotional battle during the mid- to late 1980s, but many fans may not realize that their respective fathers also battled each other a quarter-century earlier. As with many top stars in the McMahon organization over the years, 1950s headliner Antonino Rocca left on bad terms at the beginning of the 1960s, bitter over having seemingly been replaced by Buddy Rogers and Bruno Sammartino as the area's major attractions. He traveled south to the Carolinas, where he developed a solid working relationship with Mid-Atlantic head honcho Jim Crockett, Sr. In fact, Rocca even headlined the very first Crockett card at the legendary Greensboro Coliseum, the site that would become the home base of the Crockett organization.

Every promoter in the country had been looking for a way into the lucrative McMahon-controlled New York market, and with the vengeful Rocca on his side, Crockett had just the trick. Using one of New York's favorite performers, he was able to create a weekly Monday-night TV program that would air from Sunnyside Gardens in Queens, a stone's throw from the WWWF's Madison Square Garden stronghold. McMahon objected, as the show would be taking place at the same time as his Monday-night MSG events, but the State Athletic Commission allowed it since it was in a different borough of the city.

Fans who tuned in to *Wrestling with Antonino Rocca* were treated to a weekly main event featuring the flying Argentine, as well as a bevy of performers new to the market, many of them Crockett talent such as Gene Anderson, Rip Hawk & Swede Hanson, and George Becker. As novel an idea as it was, however, the show was not a success, and despite Rocca's appeal, the alien product was unable to build a loyal New York audience. Crockett retreated back to the Carolinas, McMahon continued his uncontested reign over the Big Apple, and Rocca would eventually mend fences and finish out his career with the WWWF as a TV announcer.

Stan Hansen 1, AWA World Title Belt 0

Traditionally, pro wrestling champions usually take temporary ownership of the title belts that they "win," carrying them around even away from the ring and being responsible for them until such time as they're called upon to lose them. That tradition benefited ornery veteran Stan "The Lariat" Hansen, who captured the AWA World Championship from Rick Martel on December 29, 1985, in New Jersey's Brendan Byrne Arena (the recently closed IZOD Center). Although an American, Hansen had been a top star for All-Japan Pro Wrestling promoter Giant Baba, and was granted the championship by AWA promoter Verne Gagne as a favor to Baba, just as he had done in the past for All-Japan stalwart Jumbo Tsuruta.

The problem arose when Gagne eventually ordered Hansen to drop the belt to a newly babyface Nick Bockwinkel six months later in the AWA's home town of Minneapolis. Hansen, still loyal to Baba, informed Gagne that he had already been booked by his boss on a tour of Japan as AWA World Champion, and wouldn't lose the title until he returned from the tour. He no-showed his title defense against Bockwinkel, and an incensed Gagne, who had already gone so far as to pre-tape TV interviews with Bockwinkel as the new champion, stripped Hansen and declared Nick the new titleholder by forfeiture.

The only problem was, Hansen still had the actual title belt, which he had taken with him to Japan. Displeased over the way the overbearing Gagne had attempted to bully him around, Hansen waited until he returned to the States, then ran over the prestigious title with his truck, and FedExed the broken fragments to Gagne in Minneapolis.

Vince's Growing Pains

They say you can't make an omelet without breaking some eggs, and that was certainly true during the WWF's national expansion of the 1980s, a time when Vince McMahon was crushing eggs left and right on his mission to create one red-and-yellow omelet stretching from coast to coast. Although he was successful in the end, it didn't always go smoothly, as stories abound of the many eruptions that occurred as regional promoters attempted to fight back against the tide:

- Jim Ross tells the tale of attending a secret meeting between various NWA promoters and, while in a men's room stall, accidentally overhearing several attendees discussing the possibility of actually bumping off the WWF kingpin, mafia style.

- Months before kicking off his expansion in earnest, McMahon would fly out to the Midwest to meet with AWA promoter Verne Gagne to negotiate the possibility of buying him out. When he was rebuffed, McMahon waited until Gagne and his son Greg had driven him back to the airport, then turned and menacingly remarked: "I don't negotiate." When the expansion occurred, it would be Gagne's organization especially that would see its talent pool decimated.

- When Jack and Jerry Brisco sold their majority shares in Georgia Championship Wrestling to McMahon in 1984, minority owner Ole Anderson was none too pleased, so when Vince and his wife, Linda, traveled down to Atlanta to officially take control of the TV studio from Anderson, they brought along their large business partner Gorilla Monsoon for protection. Unable to contain himself, the frustrated Anderson reportedly blurted out, "F— you Vince, and your wife, too!" Thankfully for Ole, however, things never got physical.

- Eventually run out of the Georgia territory after being rejected by the TV viewership, in a rare moment of defeat McMahon was forced to sell the coveted TBS timeslot to Mid-Atlantic promoter Jim Crockett, Jr. (in a play for national expansion himself), for $1 million. McMahon reportedly told Crockett, "You'll choke on that million"—and promptly used the money to fund the very first *WrestleMania*.

Hookers: The Most Feared Men in the Business

Prior to the 1920s, regardless of pro wrestling's "worked" nature, every single competitor who stepped into the ring was a formidably dangerous individual with genuine wrestling ability. They needed to be, lest they be taken advantage of by those who were. "It was different then from today, in that the performers were true wrestlers," explains Steve Yohe. "They were very tough guys. Most locals had very little chance against a major pro who worked the profession twenty-four hours a day and knew all the tricks."

Over the course of the '20s, "performers" were first introduced—athletes who could put on a good show, but weren't particularly skilled grapplers. The performers gradually took over during the 1930s, and by the 1940s they had all but dominated the business. It was no longer about "real" wrestling ability as much as it was about showmanship. Nevertheless, those who had the real skill were still very valuable.

As the business became more and more rigged, the "shooters" were those decreasing few who possessed genuine wrestling ability. Yet there was a higher level in the hierarchy—those who could not only "shoot," but who also possessed the ability to maim, cripple, even kill at will. These were the "hookers," so called because of their ability to "hook" their opponents with extremely dangerous submission holds that meant not only certain defeat, but also serious injury. In the past, when wrestling was merely a fixed sport, most successful wrestlers could be considered hookers, as the art of hooking had grown out of the carnival wrestling days. But, in later years, they became isolated specialists; unique individuals valued, feared, and respected by promoters and fellow wrestlers alike.

Promoters could rest assured that when a hooker was in the ring the outcome would go according to plan. Very often, promoters even kept one or two on the regular payroll—termed "policemen," they would be used to keep the talent in line, ensuring that no one got any bright ideas about deviating from the script, lest they find themselves getting "stretched" or bent into pretzels in the ring. Policemen might also be used to protect a top-drawing performer—if any wrestler outside the organization made a challenge, they would be forced to have to go through the policeman first before getting to the performer, a hurdle that usually nullified any such challenges. Conversely, certain rogue hookers might decide to "go into business for themselves," turning the outcome of a match to their own favor, and there would be little anyone could do once they set their mind to it (aside from consequently blackballing him, which often occurred).

If a promoter wanted to ensure that no one would double-cross his champion in the ring, his best move would be to put his title on a hooker, whom almost no one would be able to defeat in a legitimate contest. The performers who proliferated in the business as time went on usually had a high level of respect for the hookers—the latter may not usually be able to draw as much money as the former, but everyone knew who could thrash whom if it ever came down to it.

The role of the hooker has decreased steadily over the decades, as the business has developed more and more into overt entertainment and the value of legitimate toughness and wrestling ability became less and less. Very few wrestlers today could be classified as such, and those who can usually find a home in the world of MMA, where real grappling ability is prized.

Hookers of Note

- Ad Santel
- Bert Assirati
- Bill Miller
- Billy Robinson
- Brock Lesnar
- Dan "The Beast" Severn
- Danny Hodge
- Dory Funk, Sr.
- Ed "Strangler" Lewis
- George Tragos
- Hiro Matsuda
- John Pesek
- "Judo" Gene LeBell
- Karl Gotch
- Ken Shamrock
- Lou Thesz
- Ruffy Silverstein
- Stu Hart
- Toots Mondt
- William/Steven Regal

21

The Dark Side of the Business

Wrestling's Most Infamous Scandals and Controversies

Years ago, I used to enjoy traveling, the hotels, the restaurants, it was fun. I don't anymore. I want to be with my family. I get lonely for my wife, Nancy, for my children, but that's the sacrifice you make.
—Chris Benoit (as told to the author)

Any book of this nature would be doing a disservice to its readers by not giving them the whole story; by not delving into the not-so-pleasant aspects—the underbelly of the industry, if you will. For all its ability to thrill and entertain, this unique genre, beloved by so many, can also be a cold, dark, unforgiving world, filled with real-life violence, pain, and danger. It has ruined lives, and in many tragic cases, even ended them. For all the glitz and the glory, beneath the surface there is also sleaze and scandal. It is almost as if the business operates under its own private set of rules, separate from the morals and laws that govern society at large.

In such a traditionally closed and isolated world, it can be easy for misdeeds to flourish, protected by the secretive nature of the business, as well as the fact that most people in the mainstream have never taken wrestling seriously. It is as if because pro wrestling is "fake," then its problems must inherently not be real or worthy of attention. But although the action in the ring may be pretend, the people who take part in it are very real—human beings with all the weaknesses, vices, and flaws that go along with it. The history of the business is littered with stories of tragedy, wanton hostility, and wrongdoing. Here are just a few of them.

The Murder of Bruiser Brody

Frank Goodish was a family man from Detroit, Michigan, with a wife, Barbara, and an eight-year-old son, Geoffrey. To fans, he was the uncontrollable Bruiser Brody, a mammoth roughneck, an innovator of the brawling style, and a headliner for territories all over the world, including the WWWF, All-Japan, World Class, St. Louis, and Championship Wrestling from Florida. A very bright man who had the audacity to look out for his own interests rather than be easily manipulated by those in charge, he was also known for being notoriously uncooperative with promoters. An infamous cage match in Florida, in which he refused to work with Lex Luger and stopped "selling" for his opponent in mid-match, is a testament to this. But it was that same outspoken, strong-willed demeanor that may have also contributed to getting him killed.

By 1987, Brody was an international superstar, and had been drawing large crowds in Puerto Rico for promoters Carlos Colon and Victor Jovica of the World Wrestling Council. Some believe that, over time, he came to be the target of some resentment from local performers, bitter over an American coming in and "stealing" their paydays. One of these malcontents was Colon's booker Jose Gonzalez, who also wrestled as Invader I. On July 16, 1988, as he prepared for a match against Danny Spivey at Puerto Rico's Bayamon Loubriel Stadium, Brody was called into the showers by Gonzalez to "discuss business." Locker room eyewitnesses, among them American performers Tony Atlas and "Dirty" Dutch Mantell (later known as Zeb Colter in WWE), have indicated that Gonzalez then stabbed Goodish in the chest, piercing his lung.

It took nearly half an hour for an ambulance to arrive, during which time Goodish was hemorrhaging internally. Due to his immense size, the muscle-bound Atlas carried him to the vehicle, and rode with him to a nearby hospital as Goodish pleaded with him to tell his wife and child that he loved them. Police who arrived on the scene initially refused to take the situation seriously, believing it to be nothing more than a wild wrestling angle. Mantell has maintained that after Jovica failed to restrain him, Gonzalez went home and changed out of his bloody clothes, returning as if nothing had happened. Matters took an even more serious turn, however, when at 5:40 a.m. the next morning, Frank Goodish bled to death on the operating table.

Gonzalez was charged with first-degree murder, but the case was clouded by controversy. Many of the Puerto Rican wrestlers were afraid to step forward and endanger their jobs, and American wrestlers like Atlas and Mantell, who wanted to testify, were denied the opportunity. (Mantell claims he did not even receive his subpoena until after the trial was over.) Colon testified in defense of his head booker, and some even suspect that his powerful status in Puerto Rico may have influenced law enforcement officials as well. The charges were reduced to involuntary homicide; Gonzalez claimed self-defense, and, on January 26, 1989, was acquitted of all charges. He continued as a performer and booker in Puerto Rico for many years, even using the Brody murder on more than one occasion as fodder for wrestling angles.

The Rob Feinstein Bust

During the 1990s, Pennsylvania fan Rob Feinstein built quite an empire selling wrestling videotapes under the RFVideo banner. The only problem was that his tapes were generally bootlegged copies, and so when companies

Clasping his wrist and shouting his trademark "Huss!" Bruiser Brody exuded an in-ring insanity that belied Frank Goodish, the savvy businessman, in this photo taken in the early to mid-1980s.

Photo by Pro Wrestling Illustrated

like the WWF's TitanSports started taking legal action, Feinstein came up with the idea of starting his own pro wrestling promotion. This would give him all the original content he needed to support his lucrative home-video enterprise. And so, in 2002, he founded Ring of Honor along with former ECW booker Gabe Sapolsky. Feinstein could now handily market all the ROH videotapes and DVDs he wanted.

Everything went well for two years, until Feinstein found himself the target of a pedophile sting operation being run by a local NBC news affiliate in Philadelphia. When one of the news correspondents went online to pose as a fourteen-year-old boy in an online chatroom reputedly frequented by child molesters, he encountered none other than Feinstein, using an alias to disguise his identity. After establishing a rapport with the undercover reporter, Feinstein arranged a private meeting, believing the "boy's" parents to be away from home. When he arrived at the appointed place, he found not the expected fourteen-year-old child, but an NBC news crew, and quickly fled.

But the damage was done. The program segment, entitled "Perverted Justice," captured the whole thing on video, and it soon made major headlines throughout the industry. The lascivious transcripts of the online chat exchanges were made public, leaving no doubt as to the promoter's intent. Although no formal charges were ever made, Feinstein's reputation was irreparably damaged. He was forced to resign from Ring of Honor, the company he co-founded. Also, TNA Wrestling, which had been operating a talent-exchange program with ROH, severed all ties with the company. ROH was later purchased by the Sinclair Broadcast Group. Feinstein continues to sell pro wrestling DVDs and other merchandise through his own company.

Death in the Ring

Unlike its "sister" ring sports boxing and mixed martial arts, professional wrestling tends to be less physically dangerous in that the performers are not actively trying to harm one another. Nevertheless, accidents and unexpected occurrences do happen, and the list of athletes who have either died in a wrestling ring or from injuries received there is longer than one might imagine. It includes the likes of Iron Mike Dibiase (father of "Million Dollar Man" Ted Dibiase), *lucha libre* star Oro, super heavyweight Gary Albright, Japanese female wrestler Plum Mariko, Georgia wrestler/promoter Ray Gunkel, African-American fan favorite Luther Lindsay, *puroresu* legend Mitsuhara Misawa, and Stan Stasiak (the 1920s original, not the WWWF World Champion of the 1970s).

One of the worst early incidents of a wrestler dying as a result of a match dates back to the late nineteenth century, a time when many wrestling bouts were actually competitive affairs. Col. James Hiram McLaughlin, a Civil War vet and noted grappler, made it to the finals of a tournament for the Collar and Elbow Championship on March 10, 1870, in Detroit, facing Barney Smith, the favorite, in a brutal match. After throwing his opponent five times without the referee awarding him the victory (in those days falls were not yet decided by pinning), a frustrated McLaughlin went all out on his opponent, flipping him over his shoulder and sending him flying off the stage. Miller slammed his head into a guardrail and was knocked unconscious. The colonel was finally awarded the diamond-encrusted championship belt, the first such prize ever awarded in the sport.

Miller, meanwhile, never recovered from the head injury. The next morning he was found in his underwear, deliriously wandering the streets in the pouring rain. He was committed to a mental asylum, where he died shortly thereafter. Col. McLaughlin donated all his winnings from the match to Miller's widow as an apology, declaring, "I forgot I was so wicked strong." Incidents such as this one eventually led to ropes being used to keep participants in the ring.

The Tragedy of Owen Hart

Of all the deaths that have ever occurred in the ring, the most horrible of them all, and the one that resonates most with modern fans, was, ironically, the result of something that had nothing to do with the performance of the match itself, but took place before the bell even rang. No one who was watching the WWF's *Over the Edge* pay-per-view the fateful night of May 23, 1999, will ever forget the sight of a white-faced Jim Ross sitting ringside and somberly informing fans that Owen Hart had fallen to his death. In many ways, it was a grim culmination of many of the promotional excesses that went on during the Attitude Era.

An extremely talented performer beloved by fans and colleagues alike, Owen was the brother of former World Heavyweight Champion Bret "Hit Man" Hart, and had soldiered on in the company after the Hit Man's controversial departure a year and a half earlier. In the new, more cynical landscape of WWF TV, he had taken on the character of an over-the-top do-gooder superhero known as "The Blue Blazer" (a throw-back to a gimmick he had earnestly taken on earlier in his WWF career). As part of his *Over the Edge* match with The Godfather, and in keeping with the superhero shtick, he was supposed to be lowered into the ring from the rafters of Kansas City's Kemper Arena on a cable. Unfortunately, the clasp that was holding him gave way, causing Owen Hart to plummet seventy-eight feet, landing chest-first on the top rope.

The TV audience never saw the accident, as a video package was being shown at the time—but Ross's reaction was more than enough to alert everyone to the reality of what had happened. Some reports indicate that Hart died immediately, with others indicating his death occurred later that evening at a nearby hospital. Controversially, WWF Chairman Vince McMahon made the decision to go on with the show, stating it was what Owen would have wanted. The subsequent fallout included lawsuits from Owen's widow, Martha, and the polarizing effect on the Hart family—some siding with Martha, others siding with McMahon—that continued for years thereafter.

"It's hard to find a villain in that," says David Shoemaker, author of *Squared Circle: Life, Death and Professional Wrestling.* "It was part of the culture. WWF and WCW were in this real deadly game of one-upmanship, and in some ways it's amazing that the industry survived it, because they were pushing everything too far in every different direction. They were doing everything they could to innovate on the fly, and in almost any other instance of that it had been a huge negative for the business."

The Madison Square Garden Riot

Old-timers still talk about the night of November 19, 1957, when the most famous arena in the world was subject to the worst outburst of spectator violence in its 150-year history. It all took place during a presentation of the Capitol Wrestling Corporation, predecessor to WWE, and one of the first Garden shows put on by the McMahon family. The main event of the evening pitted number-one New York attraction Antonino Rocca and his partner, "The Flying Frenchman" Edouard Carpentier (holder of a disputed version of the World Heavyweight title), against hated villains Dick "The Bruiser" Afflis and Dr. Jerry Graham. Referee Danny Bartfield awarded the bout to Rocca and Carpentier on a disqualification due to outside interference, with just five minutes to curfew, and that's where things broke down.

A mêlée erupted after the bell between the two teams, and soon both Rocca and Graham were a bloody mess, in what may have been one of the earliest examples of blading ever seen in the Garden. Of course, the brawl was all part of the show, but that fact was lost on an audience that had been roiled to a fever pitch by the sight of real blood. It's said that about five hundred of the thirteen thousand fans on hand that night erupted into unbridled mutiny, fighting among each other and charging the ring to get their hands on the detested heels. Afflis was their main target, as terrifying cries of "Get the Bruiser!" rang out, and the panicked performer began tossing fans out of the ring *en masse*. Before long, a veritable army of more than sixty New York City police officers was dispatched to bring order. Trying to use his worshipped status to his advantage, Rocca stood on the top turnbuckle, earnestly pleading with fans in Spanish to halt the violence. When the smoke finally cleared, two policemen had been injured, three fans sent to jail, three hundred wooden chairs broken, and Dr. Graham's five-hundred dollar sequined robe stolen.

This had not been the first riot at the Garden, but it was by far the worst. The New York State Athletic Commission was not amused, and hauled all four performers in for a hearing. As a result, the four combatants were fined a grand total of $2,600, and Afflis, who had been the most involved in brawling with fans, was banned from Madison Square Garden for life. A ban on children under the age of fourteen was also put into place, and it stood for more than twenty years. Promoter Vincent J. McMahon was no doubt nervous about the incident, although he continued promoting shows at the

Garden, and, by 1960, he had gained exclusive control of wrestling at the venerated venue, a privilege that belongs to his family to this day.

The Mass Transit Incident

ECW could be a place full of bloodshed and violence, but nothing so crossed over into the realm of real-life brutality as on an untelevised house show at the Wonderland Ballroom in Revere, Massachusetts, on November 23, 1996. Eric Kulas, a seventeen-year-old wannabe wrestler, talked his way backstage, along with his father, Stephen, to convince ECW owner Paul Heyman to give him a shot in the ring. Lying about his age and his credentials (he claimed he was trained by Killer Kowalski), the inexperienced Kulas managed to get himself booked into a tag-team match against The Gangstas, New Jack, and Mustafa Saed, taking the place of absent performer Axl Rotten alongside partner D-Von Dudley.

Kulas was reportedly very difficult and demanding backstage, and when informed he would have to "get color" (or bleed), he asked New Jack to blade him, as he had never done it before. The ensuing match was captured on video via ECW's "Extreme Fan Cam" that was present during the event, and it shows Kulas being relentlessly double-teamed by The Gangstas, particularly New Jack, who assaulted the 350-pound rookie, performing as the Ralph Kramden–like "Mass Transit," with a toaster, crutches, and other foreign objects, using what appears to be real force intended to harm. Finally, New Jack bladed Kulas, but with far more severity than is customary, resulting in a dangerous amount of bleeding. Stephen Kulas can be seen pleading for his son from ringside, demanding that the match be stopped. As the young man is removed from ringside to a waiting ambulance, New Jack can be heard on the house microphone in a vicious, obscenity-laced tirade, declaring his apathy as to whether Kulas lives or dies, and his animosity toward white people in general.

Video of the ugly incident immediately began making the rounds, and led one of the major cable companies planning to carry ECW's first pay-per-view event, *Barely Legal*, to drop the show from its slate, only to have Heyman passionately persuade them to reinstate it, which they did. A lawsuit from the Kulas family against Jerome "New Jack" Young on charges of assault and battery inevitably followed, in which all the video footage was brought to light. During the proceedings, it was revealed that Kulas had lied about his age and his credentials, and also that he had asked New Jack to blade him prior to the match. The violence was ruled as part of the show, and Young, who later declared he had no remorse for what happened, was acquitted of all charges.

The Plane Ride from Hell

The tales of backstage brawls and wrestler misconduct on the road are legion, but none quite compare to what happened on a transatlantic flight involving an alarming number of inebriated WWF personalities on May 5, 2002. It would be the very last day that the company was known by the letters "WWF," with an official name change to "WWE" going into effect the following night on *Monday Night Raw*. And although the change had nothing to do with the infamous plane ride, it represented a bizarre sendoff to the industry's most widely recognized brand name.

After concluding a successful tour of the United Kingdom that culminated in the *Insurrextion* pay-per-view event in London's Wembley Arena, WWF talent, officials, and other employees boarded a plane to take them back to the United States. When the flight was delayed for well over an hour, a number of individuals apparently took advantage of the wait time by imbibing just a little too much alcohol. By the time the aircraft took off, it was filled with people whose judgment skills had been impaired, to say the least.

The stories that emerged from that notorious flight were numerous, and became more colorful with each retelling. There can be no doubt that a great deal of rowdy shenanigans took place. Ric Flair, for instance, was reported to have been parading the aisles in nothing but his ring robe, exposing himself to female flight attendants. Dustin "Goldust" Runnels took to the P. A. system to drunkenly serenade his ex-wife Terri, who was also on the plane. Booker Michael "P. S." Hayes allegedly got into an argument with John "Bradshaw" Layfield that resulted in Layfield decking the former Freebird. Adding insult to injury, reports indicated that the mischievous Sean "X-Pac" Waltman later cut off the back of Hayes's mullet haircut while he slept. Not to be outdone, Scott Hall and Curt Hennig took it upon themselves to spray shaving cream on several individuals aboard the plane, after which Hall passed out so deeply that concerned friends had to check to see if he had a pulse.

Hennig brought the insanity to a fever pitch when he allegedly challenged former NCAA Heavyweight Champion Brock Lesnar to an impromptu match in mid-flight to determine who was the better wrestler. Lesnar took Hennig down, with onlookers later declaring that the two nearly tumbled out the plane door. The struggle escalated until it had to be broken up by Triple H, trainer Fit Finley, and Lesnar's on-air manager Paul Heyman. As a result, Hennig was promptly fired from WWE, as was Scott Hall. (Lesnar was saved from repercussions, resulting as much from his position in major upcoming angles as from his lack of culpability for the fight.) Runnels was also let go once his contract expired the following year.

The Curse of the Von Erichs

In the annals of wrestling history, never was a family more beset with tragedy, and never has a name immediately conjured up more sorrow than that of the Von Erichs. Once the darlings of Texas, and beloved by fans far and wide, they crumbled apart amid ongoing family strife, drug addiction, depression, and suicide. To this day, they represent a cautionary tale regarding the extremes of what the pressures of the business can do, a heartbreaking story of dysfunction and loss.

Jack Adkisson was a former professional football player who had ascended to the upper echelons of the pro wrestling business as a performer under the name Fritz Von Erich. He and his wife, Doris, had six sons together, but would lose all but one of them. The first loss occurred in 1958, when their eldest child, Jack, Jr., was electrocuted in a puddle of water near their mobile home in Niagara Falls, New York, at the age of six. Not long after the tragedy, the family relocated to Dallas, where Fritz eventually became the owner, operator, and top star of the Dallas-based World Class Championship Wrestling. He would later build the entire promotion around his five surviving sons: David, Kevin, Kerry, Mike, and Chris.

The Von Erich boys were adored by World Class fans, and for a time during the early 1980s, the company was the hottest wrestling promotion in the country. Its TV programs aired throughout Texas, as well as in many other syndicated markets both nationally and internationally, including a unique deal in Israel that made World Class the most popular American wrestling in the Middle East. The biggest stars of the group were the three eldest sons, David, Kevin, and Kerry—all good-looking, athletic, and charismatic, they seemed to be destined for great things in the business. It was even rumored that David had been earmarked for the NWA World Heavyweight Championship.

But things took a horrific turn on February 10, 1984, when twenty-five-year-old David Von Erich was found dead in his hotel room while on a tour of Japan. The family announced that the official coroner's report listed the cause of death as acute gastroenteritis, but the report was never made public. Rumors have persisted for years (corroborated by both Ric Flair and Mick Foley in their respective biographies) that it was a cover-up for a drug overdose, and that fellow wrestler Bruiser Brody, first to discover David's body, had flushed the drugs down the toilet before the authorities arrived. The family and the fans were thrown into a state of shock, but Fritz made the controversial decision to use the death of his son as part of an angle to help further promote his surviving sons, refusing to break kayfabe in the media.

Fritz presented the *David Von Erich Memorial Parade of Champions* three months later at Texas Stadium, where Kerry Von Erich defeated Ric Flair to capture the NWA World Championship "for his brother." The angle helped Fritz draw more than fifty thousand fans to the show, setting a new all-time U.S. attendance record for wrestling. The event did nothing to change the fortunes of the Von Erich family, however. In 1985, Mike Von Erich suffered a serious shoulder injury while on a tour of Israel and, allegedly forced back into the ring by his father before it could properly heal, was diagnosed with toxic shock syndrome. Following this, he was never the same, and soon retired from the ring. Kerry, meanwhile, was in a near-fatal motorcycle accident in 1986 that eventually led doctors to amputate his right foot. He would secretly wear a prosthesis for the remainder of his career, and became addicted to painkillers.

On April 2, 1987, tragedy rocked the Von Erichs again when Mike Von Erich, dejected at the premature end to his career, overdosed on painkillers and died at the age of twenty-three. Youngest brother, Chris, was devastated by the loss, and was enlisted to begin wrestling to fill the void, despite lacking the size and athletic ability of his older siblings. By the end of 1988, World Class had fallen far from its former heights, with a dwindling fan base that had been demoralized by all the death and misfortune. Fritz Von Erich sold off the majority of the company to Memphis promoter Jerry Jarrett, which led to a lawsuit from eldest son Kevin, who had presumably expected to take over from his father. In 1990, Kerry left to work for the WWF, calling himself "The Texas Tornado."

On September 12, 1991, twenty-one-year-old Chris Von Erich, suffering from depression over the loss of Mike as well as his own doomed career, committed suicide on his parents' property by a self-inflicted gunshot wound, leaving behind a heartbreaking note. Ten months later, Doris and Fritz were divorced after forty-two years of marriage. Sadly, the family's tragedies were still not at an end. Kerry, ravaged by drug addiction, was arrested twice for cocaine possession, leading to his dismissal from the WWF. Believing his second arrest would result in major jail time, on February 18, 1993, Kerry Von Erich shot himself in the heart, on his parents' property just as his younger brother Chris had done, and died at the age of thirty-three.

Jack "Fritz Von Erich" Adkisson, patriarch of the seemingly cursed family, died of lung cancer on September 10, 1997, at the age of sixty-eight. His last surviving son, Kevin, wanting to get as far away from the traumatic memories of Texas as he could, moved to Hawaii along with his mother, Doris. He has remained there ever since, only very rarely returning to the States for special Von Erich tributes, including his family's 2009 induction to the WWE Hall of Fame, and the 2014 TNA event *Slammiversary*, in which his own sons, Marshall and Ross, made their national wrestling debut. The

Von Erich dynasty is now officially in its third generation; with any luck, they can finally reverse the misfortune that has haunted them for so long.

The Nancy Argentino Mystery

Jimmy "Superfly" Snuka is one of pro wrestling's most revered legends, and has entertained millions with his high-flying performances for years. And yet, there is a very dark cloud that has hovered over the Fijian superstar for more than three decades—a skeleton in his closet that doesn't seem to want to go away, emerging once again recently after an extended absence from the public eye. It involves the death, on May 10, 1983, of one Nancy Argentino, with whom Snuka (real name: James Reiher) had been romanti-

cally involved at the time. The case remained unresolved, and although Reiher has denied it many times and continues to do so, there are many who feel that he may have been responsible.

When police arrived on the scene at the George Washington Motor Lodge in Allentown, Pennsylvania, they reportedly found an uncontrollable, rampaging Superfly whom it took nine officers and several police dogs just to subdue. Argentino, found to be gravely hurt, was taken from the room and rushed to the hospital, where she died soon after from traumatic brain injuries. When questioned, Reiher would claim that the injuries resulted from an accidental fall she had suffered while they were taking a break on their way from the WWF TV tapings at Allentown's Agricultural Hall. However, as has been pointed out by investigative reporters such as Irv Muchnick, this account, which Reiher has stood by ever since, contradicts other

Snuka delivers the famous "Superfly Splash" to a prone "Playboy" Buddy Rose, in Madison Square Garden, on January 22, 1983.

Photo by Pro Wrestling Illustrated

versions he gave to several others at the time of the incident, including what he told the police when he first made the 911 call to report Argentino's condition.

The coroner immediately suspected foul play, deducing that the injuries seemed to have been the result of an attack consistent with "mate abuse," and recommended the case be treated as a murder. Autopsy reports released later also indicate that Argentino had suffered much more harm than just her head injury, including scratches and contusions over other parts of her body. But Muchnick and others maintain that police mishandled the investigation, eventually going along with Reiher's story and declining to pursue a murder charge. Muchnick even goes so far as to suggest a cover-up on the part of WWF owner Vince McMahon, who arrived on the scene and was present for part of Reiher's interrogation. The Superfly was McMahon's top attraction at the time, and it has been alleged that he may not have wanted anything to jeopardize this, particularly at a time when he was preparing to take his company national.

Dissatisfied with the apparent miscarriage of justice, Argentino's family brought a civil suit against Reiher, and also commissioned a private investigation. They would later even claim that the WWF offered them twenty-five-thousand dollars to drop it, which they refused. Eventually, they won the suit and Reiher was ordered to pay them five-hundred-thousand dollars, which he never did. In 2013, thirty years after the incident, the still-open case was brought up for review once again, and turned over to a grand jury for further investigation.

Steroids and Sexual Misconduct: The Tag Team That Almost Took Down the WWF

The early '90s was a rough time for Vince McMahon and TitanSports, the parent company of the WWF. Not only were TV ratings and arena attendance dwindling, but the organization was rocked with twin scandals that caused severe public relations damage and nearly brought the whole operation crashing down. They also exposed a lot of the unseemly and unethical things that were going on within the business to a much greater degree than the public was aware of at the time.

In 1991, longtime WWF ringside physician Dr. George Zahorian was arrested on charges of illegal distribution of anabolic steroids. When Zahorian revealed that among his clients were Vince McMahon and many of the performers who worked for him, the government came after the WWF chairman. The use of steroids in pro wrestling had been around for at least twenty years, and became more pronounced during the Hulkamania heyday of the '80s, when it seemed that all top stars needed to be abnormally muscular in order to receive a promotional push. For years, fans had been fairly certain this was going on, but when McMahon was brought up on charges it seemed to affirm the situation once and for all, revealing to what extent performance-enhancing drugs had become common.

Just as feds were closing in on McMahon for their impending steroid trial, matters got worse when a series of sex scandals broke simultaneously. Sensing that the company was in a weakened state, it seemed that those who had felt wronged in the past (or who had axes to grind) were coming out of the woodwork. Former WWF announcer Murray Hodgson alleged that McMahon's senior lieutenant Pat Patterson, who was openly homosexual, had made unwelcome advances toward him, and when he refused them, he was fired. Ring attendant Tom Cole declared something similar regarding senior road agent Terry Garvin. Cole also revealed that ring announcer Mel Phillips had recruited him and other underage boys to work on the ring crew, with the ulterior motive of making them targets of prurient sexual fetishes. Then, wrestler Barry Orton (uncle of current star Randy Orton) came forward to insist that both Garvin and Patterson had propositioned him as well. The implication in all cases was that McMahon and the WWF had known what was going on, and done nothing.

Patterson, Garvin, and Phillips all resigned amid the turmoil, and the WWF settled out of court with all parties. For a time, it looked as if the sex allegations might be included in the federal case against McMahon, but the government chose to maintain its focus on the steroid issue. The trial took place in June and July of 1994, and included testimony from none other than Terry "Hulk Hogan" Bollea, once McMahon's top star and one of the main performers accused of abusing steroids. In the end, the charges didn't stick, and on July 5, 1994, McMahon was acquitted. It was eventually also revealed that Murray Hodgson had been nothing more than a con man, his allegations against Patterson cynically made due to Hodgson's belief that Patterson's homosexuality would convince people they were true. Orton also announced later that he had exaggerated his claims with regards to Patterson, an error he deeply regretted. Patterson would be rehired, but Garvin and Phillips would never again work for the WWF.

"I remember when we were on *Donahue* at the time, and [Phil] Donahue said, 'Vince if you don't clean up this mess, you're not going be able to *give* your stuff away,'" says Dave Meltzer of the *Wrestling Observer* newsletter. "And Vince sort of shrugged it off, and I thought, that's not going to kill Vince's business, because people want to watch their wrestling. Even when they were getting all that bad publicity in early 1992, it's not like it stopped people from buying tickets. Things did go down terribly, but that was because Vince had his eye off the ball more than any of the other issues."

The company survived, but the whole mess had been a public-relations nightmare, the effects of which would be felt for years to come. The unhealthy steroid culture within the business had been laid bare, and there were rumblings of drug testing mandates with the increased public scrutiny. The superhero status of Hogan, Randy Savage, and others was demolished, as fans saw their idols made all too human. The sexual controversies torpedoed McMahon's attempt to position the WWF as wholesome family entertainment, exposing just how dysfunctional and deviant the underbelly of the wrestling industry could be. In order to bring his business back from the brink, McMahon would eventually have to abandon his family demographics for a time and produce an edgier, grittier product more in line with the image that had now been cultivated in the public eye.

Too Many, Too Soon

The life of a professional wrestler can be a very demanding one—demands from promoters to look a certain way, demands of an unforgiving schedule that require working while injured, demands of a rigorous lifestyle that cause some to party just as hard as they work. As a result, drug use has historically been common, whether those drugs be anabolic steroids, painkillers, or those of the recreational variety. But despite presentations to the contrary, pro wrestlers are flesh-and-blood human beings, and the human body is not meant to absorb the kind of punishment that many performers felt was necessary to put themselves through. The unfortunate but unavoidable consequence has been a rash of tragic, premature deaths that, particularly during the 1990s and early 2000s, seemed unrelenting.

Professional wrestlers began to die of drug-related causes as early as the 1980s, when the business was shocked by the loss of such athletes as Rick McGraw, Jay Youngblood, Gino Hernandez, Buzz Sawyer, and the Von Erichs. But that was just the tip of the iceberg. The dangerous lifestyle of the pro wrestler really began to take its toll after the drug and steroid culture had been in place for a number of years. Between the years 1994 and 2011, the height of this alarming trend, the industry lost a grievous amount of young performers. The list of notable pro wrestlers under the age of fifty who died during that period from causes related to illegal substances and/or depression, such as overdose, heart attack, and suicide, includes, but is not limited to:

- Art Barr
- Eddie Gilbert
- Big John Studd
- Jeep Swenson
- Brian Pillman
- Louie Spiccoli
- The Renegade
- Rick Rude

- Bobby Duncum, Jr.
- Terry Gordy
- Rhonda Singh
- Davey Boy Smith
- Rocco Rock
- Johnny Grunge
- Curt "Mr. Perfect" Hennig
- Road Warrior Hawk
- Crash Holly
- Hercules Hernandez
- The Big Boss Man
- Chris Candido
- Eddie Guerrero
- Bam Bam Bigelow
- Mike Awesome
- Sherri Martel
- Crush
- Umaga
- Chris Kanyon
- Lance Cade
- Luna Vachon

"I'm deeply interested in the juxtaposition of how these superheroes are actually mere mortals, and I think that's a powerful thing to the average fan, too, because it is presented as mythology," says David Shoemaker. "John Cena can break his leg and come back in two months. The concept of him dying is just unimaginable. To be these superheroes, guys are self-medicating like crazy. It's not nearly the problem that it once was, but it's nothing new to talk about the daily grind of cocaine, painkillers, booze, and then driving 300 miles in a tiny car to wrestle a match. That's no way to live your life."

Not even WWE was immune to the epidemic, as two top-level performers, Brian Pillman and Eddie Guerrero, were found dead in their hotel rooms, mere hours before major WWE events. Those two deaths in particular brought a great deal of attention and sympathy from fans, due to the high profile of the talent involved. In any other field of sport or entertainment, such a shocking amount of loss of life would be enough to spark a serious investigation, or at least draw the attention of the mainstream media and public. But with pro wrestling suffering from the stigma that it does, it seems the public's derision for the business breeds a certain kind of apathy.

"It's easy enough to shrug off because it's a 'fake' industry," says Shoemaker. "If wrestling's 'fake,' [people think] they can't be culpable for someone overdosing and dying. Now in the modern world where everybody knows everything, where ESPN will comment on the untimely death of a wrestler, it's impossible to pretend this isn't going on."

Chris Benoit

None of the tragedies that have rocked the wrestling business has brought as much mainstream attention and caused such deep-seated shock and sadness as what occurred during the weekend of June 22, 2007, when Chris Benoit, a contract performer for WWE and one of the most admired pro

Prior to his unspeakable crimes, Benoit was highly regarded by wrestling purists for his consummate skill.   *Photo by Pro Wrestling Illustrated*

wrestlers of his time, murdered his wife, Nancy, and seven-year-old son, Daniel, and then committed suicide. Of all the many untimely wrestler deaths that have occurred in recent memory, none has been so indicative of the endemic problems within the industry itself.

Benoit had been suffering from severe depression stemming from the loss of his best friend, Eddie Guerrero, as well as possibly from severe brain trauma he had accumulated over the years due to repeated injuries to the head that were not properly treated (according to later autopsy reports). He was also taking testosterone, allegedly to combat the damaging effects of years of steroid abuse. These physical influences were combined with a severely stressful and combative home life—Nancy had filed for divorce and issued a restraining order against Chris four years earlier only to withdraw her suit, and it is also believed that young Daniel may have suffered from some form of autism that had put further stress on the marriage.

Over a three-day period in late June of 2007, Chris Benoit first bound and choked Nancy to death, then drugged his son before smothering him to death. Finally, Benoit took his own life, hanging himself from a weight machine inside the home. Cryptic text messages Benoit had sent just prior to his death had worried those closest to him, and when police arrived at his Atlanta home on Monday, June 25, they discovered the heartbreaking results of the wrestler's murderous rampage.

At first, the details were not fully revealed, with only Benoit's death being initially announced. WWE immediately held a tribute edition of *Monday Night Raw* in his memory, only to reverse gears later in the week when the full, horrible story was told. Since that moment, Benoit's name has never again been mentioned in WWE programming, with the company acting as if he never existed in order to best distance itself from the unspeakable acts of one of its greatest attractions.

"I thought the Benoit situation was going to force their hand on the [drug issues], and to a degree it did," says Dave Meltzer. "It's not like the '80s when everyone was all 'roided up. I always thought Vince wouldn't be able to promote to the same degree without that because that was sort of his M. O., but he did. The top guys still have good bodies, and it's not necessarily as popular, but he is promoting successfully with a legitimate drug policy, as legit as any drug policy is going to be these days."

To whatever degree today's WWE wellness policies work, their institution in the wake of public pressure following the Benoit incident at least give the sense that maybe change is possible after all when it comes to pro wrestling's culture of substance abuse. It's just a shame it took such a heinous atrocity.

22

In This Very Ring

Twenty-Five Matches That Have Defined the Business

The name on the marquee is "Wrestling."

—Ric Flair

W hen all is said and done, it has always come down to what gets done inside the squared circle. Now, more than ever, there is a lot more to the industry, of course, but at its very heart, professional wrestling is still about the presentation of simulated physical combat. When all the talking and ballyhoo is done, after the pyro smoke clears and the music dies down, pro wrestlers are expected to deliver in the ring with thrilling action. And like any other field of endeavor, there are those who have been better at it than others, rising above the pack as the individuals who could be counted on to deliver a compelling performance time and again. Over the years, wrestling fans have been witness to some incredible feats of athleticism, and matches that have stood the test of time as either the most historic, the most mind-blowing, or a little bit of both.

What constitutes a great wrestling match has certainly changed dramatically, as prior to about 1925 most pro wrestling matches looked more like amateur wrestling contests. But even since pro wrestling evolved into pure performance, the styles have changed drastically, as you would discover by comparing a match from the 1930s to a match from the 1950s, or a match from the 1960s to a match from the 1980s, or a match from the 1990s to a match from the present day. The criteria are in constant flux, which makes it difficult and rather ambiguous to determine any so-called "greatest of all time."

When putting together a list of this kind, it's also worth noting that certain matches are included on the basis of their actual quality as entertainment, while others may earn a spot due mainly to their importance. Furthermore, due to the unfortunate lack of film preservation of the vast majority of embryonic pro wrestling matches, certain of these legendary bouts cannot be seen by fans today, but are included on the basis of their reputation and their significance to wrestling history.

The Great Gama vs. Stanislaus Zbyszko

September 10, 1910
White City Stadium, London, England

In a time when many pro wrestling matches were still legitimate contests, there were few, if any, who were up to the challenge of one Ghulam Hussein of India, known as The Great Gama. After years of facing all comers in the East, and emerging victorious in over 200 bouts without a loss, Gama turned his formidable attentions to the West, traveling to Europe to challenge the likes of George Hackenschmidt and World Heavyweight Champion Frank Gotch. But nearly all the top athletes of the day refused to face the man, presumably because he sought a true competition, as opposed to the staged works they were mainly used to.

Eventually, Gama's challenge was accepted by the mighty Polish shooter Stanislaus Zbyszko, who battled the fearsome Indian before a rumored 100,000 spectators (the number has never been officially confirmed) in a match sponsored by the popular *John Bull* magazine, which had also put up a valuable championship belt for the occasion. True to his reputation, Gama punished Zbyszko something awful, forcing him to the mat and keeping him there for most of the two hours and forty-five minutes they struggled with each other. It's said that Zbyszko knew early on that Gama's strength was insurmountable, and clung to the mat to avoid a fall. Finally, with night approaching, the referee called a halt to the contest. It was declared that the two men would resume their match the following week, but a daunted Zbyszko thought better of it and never showed, causing *John Bull* magazine to award their belt to Gama the Great, who returned to India undefeated, adding the accolade to his extensive trophy collection.

Frank Gotch vs. George Hackenschmidt

September 4, 1911
Comiskey Park, Chicago, Illinois

Dubbed "The Match of the Century" by enthusiastic newspapermen, the long-awaited rematch between World Heavyweight Champion Frank Gotch and the man from whom he had won the title in 1908, "The Russian Lion" George Hackenschmidt, was the biggest professional sporting event in

Although film footage of Gotch/Hackenschmidt has not survived the passage of time, this rare postcard from 1911 has.   *Library of Congress*

American history up to that point, and is still regarded by sports historians as one of the major events of all time. In an age when mass media was in its infancy, the match captured the imagination of the nation, and sparked a wrestling renaissance, galvanizing the mainstream public in a way that perhaps no professional wrestling has done since.

Hackenschmidt accidentally injured his knee during training with sparring partner Dr. Benjamin Roller, and went into the match with a psychological disadvantage. Although some, like Gotch expert Mike Chapman, are convinced of the match's legitimacy, others have deemed it as one of pro wrestling's first high-profile "works." Sensing blood in the water, the champion immediately went after Hack's injured knee, pinning him for the first fall in under fifteen minutes. The second fall wouldn't even last half that time—Gotch trapped the Russian Lion in his feared toe-hold, threatening to further injure the knee, until Hackenschmidt rolled on his back, allowing himself to be pinned rather than risk it. Hack never set foot in a wrestling ring again, while Gotch continued his undisputed reign for two more years.

Joe Stecher vs. Ed "Strangler" Lewis

July 4, 1916
Gene Melady Stadium, Omaha, Nebraska

In the late 1910s, there was arguably no greater drawing card in the business than "Scissors King" Joe Stecher, who also happened to be its most credible grappler, following the retirement of Frank Gotch. With Stecher installed as the new World Heavyweight Champion, a major challenge arose from upstart Ed "Strangler" Lewis, a Wisconsin wrestler of considerable skill who had been gaining a lot of attention, even being called the uncrowned champion in certain circles. The rivalry between Stecher and Lewis would reach epic proportions, as typified by this particularly grueling Independence Day encounter, which lasted exactly five hours.

Unimaginably long by modern standards, the bout saw Lewis wrestle defensively almost the entire time. Some grappling enthusiasts were enthralled by the endeavor, while more casual spectators found themselves quite bored, angrily urging the challenger to mount an attack that never came. Nevertheless, the Strangler impressed many simply by being able to survive so long with the champion. Finally, referee Ed Smith halted the affair for fear that one or both men might pass out from exhaustion. In the aftermath, there was frustration in both men's promotional camps, and they couldn't come to terms on an immediate rematch. In later years, the animosity would grow stronger, as their in-ring rivalry turned into a bitter business rivalry as well.

Ed "Strangler" Lewis vs. Jim Londos

September 20, 1934
Wrigley Field, Chicago, Illinois

Toward the end of his career, another top wrestler with whom Ed Lewis butted heads behind the scenes was "The Golden Greek" Jim Londos, who by the 1930s had superseded the Strangler as the industry's hottest superstar and reigning World Heavyweight Champion. The Strangler's backers badmouthed Londos in the press, maneuvered to have him stripped of title recognition in certain states, and even positioned Lewis as an alternate world champion in opposition. After years of such contentious wrangling, the two men finally agreed to "do business," and the resulting match was the most highly anticipated since the Gotch-Hackenschmidt match of a generation prior. In some ways, this match even surpassed that 1911 encounter, setting new American records for attendance (35,275) and gate ($96,302). That first record would stand for twenty-seven years, while the second record stood for eighteen. In the end, Lewis agreed to do the honors in the middle of the ring for Londos, granting him the spotlight as the 1930s' premier grappler, while his own in-ring career wound down.

Lou Thesz vs. Baron Michele Leone

May 21, 1952
Gilmore Park, Los Angeles, California

As the National Wrestling Alliance's World Heavyweight Champion, Thesz went on a mission to establish the new title as the closest thing to an undisputed championship the business had seen in decades. To that end, he traveled the country in the late 1940s and early '50s, facing (and usually defeating) several world championship claimants. The most high-profile of these encounters was his match with the flamboyant Italian mat star Baron Michele Leone, recognized as World Heavyweight Champion on the West Coast by California promoter Cal Eaton and his matchmaker Johnny Doyle.

Thousands were turned away that day at Gilmore Park, and the sellout crowd generated a colossal gate of $103,277.75, the first gate in pro wrestling history to surpass $100,000—and in a business where it's all about the money, that was an achievement on par with winning an Olympic gold medal. Veteran wrestler and tough-guy actor Mike Mazurki served as special referee, and he was the man who eventually slapped the mat three times to award the third and deciding fall to Thesz as a result of a backdrop (a move invented by Thesz). The Baron had been dethroned, and Lou would reign as undisputed champion for years.

Lou Thesz vs. Rikidozan

October 6, 1957
Korakuen Stadium, Tokyo, Japan

In the Land of the Rising Sun, Lou Thesz earned the nickname *Tetsujin*, which means "Iron Man"—and this match was most certainly a major reason for this. The reigning NWA World Heavyweight Champion, Thesz traveled to Japan to face its most colossal star, and the holder of the Japanese Wrestling Association's Heavyweight title, Rikidozan. The buildup to the match was unlike anything the country had ever seen, and is considered a major turning point in the explosion of Japanese *puroresu* as an international pro wrestling phenomenon.

Both men had legitimate wrestling credentials, and made the bout as athletic and intense as possible, with Thesz playing the subtle American heel to Rikidozan's Japanese superhero. The attention of a nation turned to the encounter, which was televised across Japan to an 87.0 rating, completely unthinkable by modern TV-ratings standards, when the average Super Bowl pulls down about half that number. Thesz and Rikidozan wrestled to a one-hour draw in one of the most intense contests of the modern era, setting the stage for more epic encounters down the road.

Pat O'Connor vs. Buddy Rogers

June 30, 1961
Comiskey Park, Chicago, Illinois

Taking place almost exactly fifty years after the famous Gotch-Hackenschmidt rematch, and in the very same location, O'Connor vs. Rogers was another meeting dubbed "Match of the Century," and was arguably the most highly anticipated high-profile match ever held for the prestigious NWA World Heavyweight Championship. Of course, in that intervening half-century pro wrestling had gone from corrupted athletic competition to completely scripted entertain-

ment, but that didn't take away from the excitement or from fans' enjoyment—if anything, it may have increased it. The match was the result of the combined efforts of promoters throughout the country, including Chicago impresario Fred Kohler and his business associates Vince McMahon and Toots Mondt out of New York (both of whom had a vested interest in Rogers).

The storyline going in was that Rogers, the long-reigning United States champion, had finally been granted his big shot at the World title that had been held by Pat O'Connor since he had defeated Dick Hutton in St. Louis nearly two and a half years before. A typical babyface angle, this was unusual because Rogers was the heel until the moment he actually won the title at the conclusion of the match and sneered to the crowd, "To a nicer guy, it couldn't happen!" The win

New Zealander Pat O'Connor first captured the NWA World Heavyweight Championship in St. Louis in 1959. *Jack Pfefer Collection, University of Notre Dame* marked the first time the NWA World Championship had been bestowed on a heel. The match itself wound up setting a new U.S. attendance record, with 38,622 spectators on hand. The new record stood for twenty-three years.

John Tolos vs. "Classy" Freddie Blassie

August 27, 1971

L.A. Coliseum, Los Angeles, California

The *L.A. Coliseum Supershow* was an early professional wrestling supercard that many view as one of the first major forerunners to the modern concept of pay-per-view events, due primarily to it being the first show to be broadcast extensively via closed-circuit, allowing fans in other parts of the country, in remote locations such as theaters, to witness the action live. Presented by L.A. promoter Mike LeBell and his booker Jules Strongbow, the *Supershow* was headlined by a white-hot grudge match between NWA Americas' champion John Tolos and former champion "Classie" Freddie Blassie, the longtime California heel, who had recently turned beloved babyface.

In an angle expertly devised by LeBell and Strongbow, Blassie was awarded "Wrestler of the Year" the very next day after losing the Americas' title to Tolos. During the ceremony, a vindictive Tolos went to the ringside doctor's bag, removed what was purported to be Monsel's powder, an acidic solution used to stop bleeding cuts, and threw it in Blassie's eyes. Fans were told that Blassie had been permanently blinded and would never wrestle again. In

OLYMPIC AUDITORIUM
SOUVENIR PROGRAM 50¢
COLISEUM COLLECTORS COPY
Mrs. Aileen Eaton Sprts Presentation—Mike LeBell, Promoter; Jules Strongbow, Bout Supervisor.

This program is published by Champion Sports Publishing Corporation, the largest publishers of wrestling magazines and programs in the world, 351 Manville Road, Pleasantville, New York 10570. Bert Randolph Sugar, President; Norman H. Kietzer, Editor.

The August 27, 1971, Blassie/Tolos match set an all-time attendance record for wrestling in California, one that stood for an astounding forty-four years.

Author's collection

true babyface fashion, he slowly but surely began to prove doctors wrong by regaining his vision, and accosted Tolos during a match, requiring security to remove him from ringside. The match was finally made—not for the usual Olympic Auditorium, but the much larger Memorial Coliseum. In the end, Tolos was turned into such a bloody mess that the match was stopped and the decision awarded to the vindicated Blassie.

Pedro Morales vs. Bruno Sammartino

September 30, 1972
Shea Stadium, Flushing, New York

After nearly eight years on top as WWWF World Champion, Bruno Sammartino was granted a well-deserved break as Puerto Rican sensation Pedro Morales was given a chance to run with the belt. But although he was immensely popular, especially with New York's Latino community, Morales labored in Sammartino's shadow, and fans clamored for him to defend his crown against the legendary former champion once and for all. Nevertheless, promoter Vincent J. McMahon was reluctant to do so because of conventional booking wisdom that warned against programming two babyfaces against each other, for fear that one of the two would lose his steam. (This fear reportedly stems from a series of 1936 matches between world champion Danno O'Mahoney and Yvon Robert that had exactly that unfortunate effect on O'Mahoney.)

Finally, the match was made for New York's Shea Stadium, the largest venue the WWWF had ever run, in the first of a series of three cards that would be broadcast on closed-circuit TV from that location. Although pouring rain that day kept some fans away, the resulting 22,508 attendance figure and $140,923 gate were both the highest for a WWWF event up to that point in time. Hedging his bets at the last minute, McMahon chose not to book a winner, but rather had Bruno and Pedro battle to a hard-fought time limit draw.

Jack Brisco vs. Dory Funk, Jr.

January 29, 1974
Higashi-Yodogawa Gym, Osaka, Japan

To this day, "Brisco/Funk" is a combination of names spoken with awed reverence among historians and old-time fans, thanks to the wrestlers' epic in-ring war that raged through the 1970s over the NWA World Heavyweight Championship. Whether it was Funk defending against Brisco, or the other way around, the two men were sure to deliver with a grueling, highly athletic performance that helped to lend credibility to the "sport" of professional wrestling, especially at a time when it was more gimmicky and sensationalized than ever before.

By the time of their legendary sixty-minute draw in Japan, the two men had already faced each other in six high-profile title matches over the past four years, in top NWA territories like St. Louis, Florida, Mid-Atlantic, and Georgia Championship Wrestling. Now they took their act international, and put on a veritable wrestling clinic for the extremely knowledgeable fans of Giant Baba's All-Japan promotion. Taking one fall apiece in the two-out-of-three falls affair, the participants fought to the time limit, telling a great story in the ring along the way. Brisco emerged with his title intact, leading to two more titanic championship matches over the next two years.

Tiger Mask vs. The Dynamite Kid

August 30, 1982
Madison Square Garden, New York, New York

Traditionally, New York–area fans are a passionate and dedicated bunch, but they were unused to seeing very much in the way of fast-paced, high-workrate matches, instead being accustomed to the broader, low-impact, histrionic style of (W)WWF bouts from that era. What a culture shock it must have been for them to witness high-flying hooded Japanese Junior Heavyweight Champion Tiger Mask take on lightning-quick, hard-hitting Englishman The Dynamite Kid in a match that opened the eyes of a lot of American fans. The two had already met extensively over in Japan, but this was the first time they were getting a chance to shine in a major U.S. engagement, a benefit of the WWF's working agreement with Antonio Inoki's New Japan Pro Wrestling. It was a style WWF fans had never seen before, reminiscent of what would later become the norm as those fans began to expect a lot more from performers from an athletic standpoint. It may not have been the main event that night (Bob Backlund vs. Buddy Rose was), but it was a sign of things to come on the U.S. wrestling scene.

Harley Race vs. Ric Flair

November 24, 1983
Coliseum, Greensboro, North Carolina

In response to Vince McMahon's impending threats to go national with the WWF, Jim Crockett of Mid-Atlantic Championship Wrestling booked what would become the industry's first annual supercard, *Starrcade*. Predating pay-per-view by two years, *Starrcade* began as a closed-circuit event broadcast throughout Crockett's territory, and to headline his big event, he chose his golden boy, Ric Flair, to challenge NWA World Heavyweight Champion Harley Race inside a steel cage in the region's number-one venue, the Greensboro Coliseum.

With Gordon Solie and Bob Caudle calling the action, the event definitely had a weighty, "big-match" feel, and Race and Flair gave it their all to produce one of the most exciting NWA World title bouts ever presented. The culmination of a months-long angle dubbed "A Flair for the Gold," in which the Nature Boy fought to regain the title he had lost to Race despite the champion taking out a bounty on his upcoming opponent, the match delivered in spades, and in the end Flair became the first wrestler to win the NWA World Championship in a steel-cage

Flair is congratulated on regaining the NWA World Championship by future challenger Ricky Steamboat on November 24, 1983.

Photo by Pro Wrestling Illustrated

match. The WWF was destined to win the eventual promotional war, but it wouldn't be due to superior in-ring workers, as those belonged to Crockett.

The Iron Sheik vs. Hulk Hogan

January 23, 1984

Madison Square Garden, New York, New York

Meanwhile, up north, Vince McMahon officially inaugurated the new era of the WWF and made the clarion call to arms in his war for national expansion by crowning Hulk Hogan the new WWF World Heavyweight Champion with a win over The Iron Sheik in the WWF's home field of Madison Square Garden. The Sheik had defeated long-reigning champ Bob Backlund after a controversial submission finish the month before, but was only being used as a transitional titleholder to get the belt on Hogan (remember that prohibition against babyface vs. babyface matches). And while this five-minute affair may not have been anything to write home about from a technical wrestling standpoint, that didn't matter—it electrified the crowd, got Hogan over as the most popular performer in the business, and led to Vince McMahon's eventual global pro wrestling domination.

Hulk Hogan vs. Andre the Giant

March 29, 1987

Silverdome, Pontiac, Michigan

For modern-day wrestling fans, there is one match that stands above the rest as the biggest of them all, and it's hard to dispute its position as the single-most publicized and well-remembered encounter of the last fifty years at the very least. As with the Sheik match, and many Hogan matches for that matter, it was far from a scientific wrestling clinic, with the Hulkster relying more on his charisma and physique, and the aging Andre the Giant virtually immobile. Nevertheless, the immense hype surrounding the match, and the magnitude of the two larger-than-life personas that clashed in the ring that day in the Pontiac Silverdome more than earn this match its place in history.

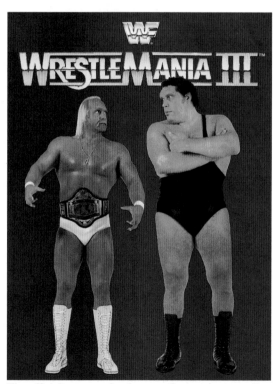

The official program for the most famous pro wrestling event of all time, held on March 29, 1987, in the Pontiac Silverdome. *Author's collection*

It was the main event of *WrestleMania III*, the event that finally fulfilled the promise Vince McMahon had made to himself four years earlier to make the WWF the biggest show in the wrestling business, and turn it into truly mainstream entertainment. In one of the most memorable angles of all time, career fan favorite Andre turned on Hogan, demanding a shot at the WWF World Championship Hogan had held for over three years. Their eventual matchup enthralled audiences around the world, as well as the record-shattering crowd that was assembled in the

Silverdome (WWF/E has maintained it was 93,173, although notable sources estimate the real number at closer to 80,000). Hogan's bodyslam and pin of the Giant was a watershed moment that remains burned in the collective unconscious of wrestling fans everywhere.

Randy "Macho Man" Savage vs. Ricky "The Dragon" Steamboat

March 29, 1987

Silverdome, Pontiac, Michigan

Hulk Hogan vs. Andre the Giant may have been the main event of *WrestleMania III*, but the match that stole the show pitted the Macho Man against the Dragon for the WWF Intercontinental Championship. Modern WWF fans typically will point to this particular encounter as the greatest of all time, and it certainly packs a great deal of action into a mere sixteen minutes from bell to bell. More than anything, it was the frequency of near-falls that made this one such a nail-biter, as well as the drama that had been building ever since the WWF shot an angle in which Savage famously "crushed" Steamboat's larynx with the timekeeper's bell some months before.

According to Steamboat, the match was choreographed down to the last detail, which was Savage's preferred way to work, and which may have been the reason it was so crisply performed. This was not common practice at the time, as most proficient wrestlers preferred to work with more of a loose match outline—however, Steamboat-Savage was a match ahead of its time, as that level of detailed choreography is closer to how bouts are put on today.

Ric Flair vs. Ricky "The Dragon" Steamboat

May 7, 1989

Municipal Auditorium, Nashville, Tennessee

As far as big-money matches of wrestling's modern era, it's hard to top this one in terms of pure athleticism, intensity, and ring psychology. Some call this the greatest pro wrestling match of all time, owing largely to the unbelievable stamina displayed by both performers. You had two absolute masters in there at the same time, who had become completely accustomed to each other as opponents after facing off in countless matches going back at least thirteen years. This particular match, at *Wrestle War '89*, was the culmination of WCW's hottest feud of the year, and the third of three stellar matchups Flair and Steamboat had put on in as many months. It's tough to choose among this one, their *Chi-Town Rumble* match from February in which Steamboat initially won the World Heavyweight title, and their first hour-long rematch from *Clash of the Champions* in April. In this blowoff match, Flair emerged triumphant over Steamboat to regain the title, then immediately turned babyface and launched into a brand new program with ringside judge Terry Funk.

Hulk Hogan vs. The Ultimate Warrior

April 1, 1990

Sky Dome, Toronto, Ontario

It was a battle of real-life superheroes, and the first time that the WWF had banked on a major main event pitting two babyfaces against each other since Sammartino and Morales some eighteen years earlier. And these weren't just any two babyfaces, but the two most popular performers in the entire industry: on the one side "The Immortal" Hulk Hogan, the WWF world champion and undisputed top dog for six years running, and on the other side a frenetic bodybuilder from Indiana named Jim Wellwig, who, as The Ultimate Warrior, had slowly been building a fan base over the course of two years until becoming the seeming heir apparent to Hogan's position as WWF's top star.

That certainly seemed the case when the Hulkster agreed to face the Warrior at *WrestleMania VI* in what was called "The Ultimate Challenge," a match that captured the imagination of fans who truly wondered who was the more powerful force in the WWF. With 67,678 screaming fans in attendance and a few million watching around the world on pay-per-view, Hogan and Warrior clashed in a battle of pure force, trading power moves back and forth until at last the Warrior triumphed, dealing Hogan his first clean pinfall loss in the WWF since his classic run had begun in 1984. It was quite an emotional moment, and although it wasn't quite the "passing of the torch" people expected, the two men shared something that night that will never be forgotten.

Shawn Michaels vs. Razor Ramon

March 20, 1994
Madison Square Garden, New York, New York

In today's WWE—and the entire landscape of American pro wrestling, really—the use of ladders inside the ring has become an accepted, common part of the show. Few fans will even raise an eyebrow at the thought of a ladder match, but they did back in 1994 when one was made between Intercontinental Champion Razor Ramon and former champion Shawn Michaels for the WWF's triumphant return to Madison Square Garden for the tenth installment of *WrestleMania*. In the storyline, Michaels had been stripped of the title only to return to action to find Ramon recognized as the champ—naturally, Michaels still considered himself the champion, and started parading around with his own title. Therefore, the rules of the ladder match stated that whoever could bring the ladder into the ring and then climb it to retrieve both I-C title belts—which had been suspended high above the ring—would officially be the undisputed titleholder.

Looking back at *WrestleMania X* now, this is the match that everyone talks about more than any other. Filled with insane high spots that were truly unique and groundbreaking for their time, the bout made a bona fide main-event star out of Shawn Michaels (despite the fact that he lost), and although the ladder match was not a new invention, this was the one that really added it to the lexicon of contemporary pro wrestling. Every ladder match since is compared to this one, and although the stakes have been raised over the years with such things as "tables, ladders, and chairs" (TLC) matches, this encounter will always be the originator.

Eddie Guerrero vs. Dean Malenko

August 26, 1995
ECW Arena, Philadelphia, Pennsylvania

It may not have taken place on a worldwide stage, and it wasn't even the main event of the ECW card on which it was presented, but this two-out-of-three-falls draw is a favorite of those fans who are particularly into workrate and enjoy intense chainwrestling. It became the talk of the industry shortly after it happened, as did the other matches in the series in which these two men engaged over the ECW Television Championship during the summer of 1995. In fact, it was these matches that landed them both contracts with WCW—which was also why this match was a farewell to the Land of Extreme, and an emotional one at that.

The match was a blinding display of incredible technical wrestling, and even though it was initially seen only by those lucky enough to be watching on ECW's network of Pennsylvania and New York–based UHF channels, it later became a cult classic among avid tape traders. Neither man would arguably ever again attain the same level of pure scientific prowess as what occurred this night at the ECW Arena, in a match that set the ultimate bar for technical grappling in America.

Bret "Hit Man" Hart vs. Stone Cold Steve Austin

March 23, 1997
Horizon, Rosemont, Illinois

Wrestling bookers and fans of great booking will mention something called the "double turn" in hushed tones. That's because it's so hard to pull off, but so great when done well. This is when the babyface and heel both switch sides simultaneously—and it happened during this gritty, bloody match that stole the show at *WrestleMania 13*. Stone Cold Steve Austin had been on the cusp of main-event superstardom, and this match put him there, courtesy of the amazing Hit Man, who had been flirting with heel status ever since cutting an extended bitter promo on *Monday Night Raw* two months prior.

The image of Stone Cold trapped in Hart's sharpshooter submission hold while wearing the proverbial crimson mask is what most remains with fans to this day, as he slowly won over the live crowd with his guts and stamina while they turned on the increasingly aggressive and sadistic Hit Man. This match also helped usher in the WWF's Attitude Era, being the first major bout put on by the company to feature blading in many years. Austin has gone on record calling this the finest match of his career, and with good reason.

Bret "Hit Man" Hart vs. Shawn Michaels

November 9, 1997
Molson Centre, Montreal, Quebec

In a business of screwjobs, the infamous "Montreal Screwjob" from the 1997 *Survivor Series* is the granddaddy of them all, changing as it did the course of pro wrestling history. Even putting its historical significance aside, the match itself was a truly great one—a textbook lesson in how to generate drama inside the ring. Maybe it was because Hart knew the reality of what was at stake that night, and the possibility of a double cross, but he put in the performance of a lifetime, and Michaels was right there with him. Given the backstage intrigue that took place earlier in the evening, it's a credit to both men that they were actually able to work together to such a degree.

Although the match featured a great deal of outside-the-ring action (presumably due to the fact that Hart was wary of being screwed over while inside the ropes), these two brilliant performers managed to make it work rather than having it devolve into typical garbage-wrestling chaos. Hart believed the finish would involve him escaping from a sharpshooter from Michaels, only to have outside interference from Triple H draw a disqualification. But once Michaels cinched in that sharpshooter and referee Earl

Hebner immediately called for the bell at the loud and expletive-laden request of Vince McMahon (seated ringside), the Hit Man knew the score. When the smoke cleared on one of the most hard-fought battles of the Monday Night War, Bret Hart had defected to WCW, Shawn Michaels was the new WWF World Champion, and Vince McMahon had set himself up to be wrestling's greatest heel.

Undertaker vs. Mankind

June 28, 1998
The Igloo, Pittsburgh, Pennsylvania

"As God is my witness, he is broken in half!" So screamed a nearly apoplectic Jim Ross from the announcer's table at ringside during one of many utterly insane bumps taken by Mick "Mankind" Foley during his legendary Hell in a Cell match against the Dead Man at the WWF's 1998 *King of the Ring*. This was only the second Hell in a Cell following 'Taker's initial one against Shawn Michaels some eight months earlier, but this is the one that is remembered as the greatest of them all, and the most indicative of the sheer brutality that can be unleashed in an encounter of this kind, in which the usual steel cage is enlarged to encase the ringside area and a roof is added to the structure. Ironically, although the point of pro wrestling performance has traditionally been to work as safely and harmlessly as possible while making it look like you were killing the other guy, the style of performers like Foley led to the contemporary philosophy in which many wrestlers are more than willing to legitimately put their bodies on the line for the sake of putting on a memorable match.

And memorable it was, as Foley bounced around the ring, fell through the roof to the mat below, and was tossed from the top through a ringside table, famously losing a tooth through his own nostril as a result of the impact. Foley's good friend Terry Funk could be seen looking genuinely concerned at his side as paramedics attempt to stretcher Foley out in a moment that seemed part shoot and part work. In the end, a new standard was set as far as the level of violence considered acceptable in mainstream American pro wrestling.

Stone Cold Steve Austin vs. The Rock

April 1, 2001
Reliant Astrodome, Houston, Texas

On three different occasions, the two greatest stars of the Attitude Era met in the main event of WWE's grandest stage, *WrestleMania*. And although it's tough to pick, their second matchup at *WrestleMania X-Seven* inside the world-famous Astrodome may have been the greatest of them all, topping off what is often regarded as the greatest *WrestleMania* of them all. Vince McMahon had just purchased his old rival WCW, and his company seemed to be on an all-time high going into the most ambitious event it had ever undertaken. It only made sense to have its two greatest attractions go one-on-one in the main event.

With 67,925 fans in attendance (the largest American crowd to witness a WWF event since *WrestleMania III*), Stone Cold defeated The Rock to regain the WWF World Heavyweight Championship, turning heel in the process by allying himself with former on-air archenemy Vince McMahon. Although the angle itself disappointed fans in the long run since they didn't wish to view Austin as a heel, the actual match was an appropriately explosive capper to what was arguably WWE's greatest pay-per-view event of all time.

Undertaker vs. CM Punk

April 7, 2013
MetLife Stadium, East Rutherford, New Jersey

One of the most exciting ongoing promotional angles in modern wrestling history was the Undertaker's *WrestleMania* undefeated streak, which lasted for twenty-one appearances. Because the Undertaker was not typically known to be a particularly athletic performer earlier in his career, his matches were often more about his sinister aura than they were about bell-to-bell mat action. Ironically, as he got older and became more interested in MMA fighting techniques, he worked to make his matches more compelling, particularly when he was defending his vaunted streak at *WrestleMania*. And bar none, the greatest of them all was the final match of the undefeated streak, his jaw-dropping encounter with CM Punk at *WrestleMania XXIX*.

Leading into the bout, Punk and his obnoxious manager Paul Heyman had been taunting 'Taker regarding the recent passing of his own former manager Bill "Paul Bearer" Moody. (Not even real-life death is beyond the auspices of a wrestling angle, although those close to Moody claimed he would have loved it.) Needless to say, come bell time, fans were beyond eager to see Undertaker deliver a sound thrashing to the brash young man who called himself "The Best in the World." Punk was already known for delivering matches that lived up to his audacious moniker, and he brought out the very best in the Dead Man, with a tense, marathon-like encounter that comprised the final victory in the fabled streak.

The Rock vs. John Cena

April 7, 2013
MetLife Stadium, East Rutherford, New Jersey

Not since The Rock had battled Hulk Hogan some eleven years prior at *WrestleMania X8* had there been such a match, pitting two icons of different generations against one another. But unlike the last time, when The Rock represented the current product, this time out he found himself in the role of the returning legend, taking on the industry's top-drawing current performer in Cena. This was the second year in a row in which the two men had faced off in the main event of *WrestleMania*, and it was known right after their first encounter that they'd be meeting again in a rematch the following year.

Previously at *WrestleMania XXVIII*, it was The Rock who was given the victory. But now, coming into MetLife Stadium as WWE World Champion, it was time for The Rock to do the honors for Cena. The live attendance that night was 80,676, making it very possibly the largest crowd ever to witness a pro wrestling event in the Western Hemisphere (depending on the validity of the *WrestleMania III* figure). With his victory, John Cena was able to further cement his status as the premier pro wrestler of his era.

Cena (right) redeemed himself from the previous year's defeat with a win over the People's Champion, April 7, 2013.   *Simon from United Kingdom/Wikimedia*

More Major Matches of Note

- Evan "Strangler" Lewis vs. Sorakichi Matsuda (1/28/1886)
- Frank Gotch vs. Stanislaus Zbyszko (6/1/1910)
- Earl Caddock vs. Joe Stecher (1/30/1920)
- Jim Londos vs. Man Mountain Dean (10/10/1934)
- Bruno Sammartino vs. Gorilla Monsoon (3/27/1967)
- Verne Gagne vs. Baron Von Raschke (8/14/1970)
- Bruno Sammartino vs. Ivan Koloff (1/18/1971)
- Terry Funk vs. Harley Race (2/6/1977)
- Harley Race vs. Superstar Billy Graham (1/25/1978)
- Bob Backlund vs. The Iron Sheik (12/26/1983)
- Ric Flair vs. Terry Taylor (6/1/1985)
- Ric Flair vs. Barry Windham (1/20/1987)
- Taz vs. Sabu (4/13/1997)
- The Rock vs. Hulk Hogan (3/17/2002)
- Kurt Angle vs. Brock Lesnar (3/30/2003)

23

The Gift of Gab

Wrestling's Most Terrific Talkers

With words we govern men.
—Benjamin Disraeli

I have wined and dined with kings and queens, and I've slept in alleys and ate pork and beans.
—Dusty Rhodes

Professional wrestling requires a unique skill set. Not only do you need to be in reasonably good physical shape and have the ability to deliver highly physical live performances several nights a week, you also need to have personality. Unlike sports in which achievement is measured strictly on the merits of athletic competition, pro wrestling is about image and charisma; about the ability to connect with an audience. If a baseball player hits forty homeruns a season, or a football player makes forty touchdown passes, he could have the personality of a tree stump and it really wouldn't matter. Not so in pro wrestling; a performer could pull off stellar matches every week, but if he lacks the ability to project his personality and speak charismatically and effectively, his marketability, and thus his potential for career success, is limited.

Some would even argue that the ability to speak well, or to possess "microphone skills" as it is often called, is even more important in the long run than wrestling performance. Certainly, over the years there have been many performers of somewhat limited physical talents who have become major stars based largely on their mic skills. Even in the best-case scenarios, a terrific in-ring performer is made all that much greater by the ability to deliver on the mic. To be sure, not all pro wrestlers are gifted in this area, and, in the past especially, wrestling managers were used as mouthpieces for those who couldn't (see Chapter 17). But now, more than ever, it is expected of top-flight performers, and is the key to making one a true total package.

The Wrestler as TV Character

It wasn't always this way. In the early decades of professional wrestling, the ability to work well in the ring, coupled with a good physical "look," was all that was needed for success. But television changed all that. With the advent of the new medium in the late 1940s, wrestlers suddenly found themselves under the bright lights and in front of the cameras with a mic thrust in their face, expected to emote verbally as well as physically. Those early days of TV were akin to the dawn of sound technology in the motion picture industry, when those silent movie stars who didn't have the pipes to make it in the talkies fell unceremoniously by the wayside. It was a brand new skill required of pro wrestlers, and it skewed the playing field even more so in the advantage of the performers, at the expense of the old-school no-nonsense grapplers and shooters. Wrestling suddenly needed as many "characters" as possible to fill the need for genuine TV stars.

Within the business, it's called "cutting a promo." A good wrestling promo accomplishes several things: it furthers the storyline; it gets a wrestler's character across; and it entices viewers to tune in to a show, or shell out their hard-earned cash for a ticket or a pay-per-view purchase. Many great promo men over the years have been hailed for their ability to "talk people into the arena." Recently, with the WWE Network and its business model based on monthly subscriptions, the importance of good promo skills in terms of selling tickets or PPV buys may have been slightly diminished within pro wrestling's major league, but it remains just as important for getting angles and gimmicks over as it ever was, if not more so.

In the old days, most performers who had the chops were given the leeway to wing it on the mic. As long as they hit the most important items (identifying their opponent, getting across storyline points, etc.) the specific verbiage was usually left up to them. Back then, the vast majority of promos were fairly short; usually no more than three or four minutes. Within the past couple of decades, however, that has largely changed. Storylines and characters are far more complex than ever, and therefore wrestling promos, especially within major companies like WWE and TNA, are now given a lot more time—sometimes as long (if not longer) than most matches. Because of this, many wrestlers' promos are very carefully scripted, necessitating performers to memorize numerous lines, like an actor in a live drama. Just as most matches are now more carefully choreographed than in the past, so are promos usually crafted by the creative team, down to the last letter.

There are generally considered to be two major types of talkers in wrestling: those who rely mainly on catchphrases usually intended to get an immediate crowd reaction or "pop," and those who prefer to speak more in an off-the-cuff, conversational tone, letting their personalities do the heavy lifting. Some particularly versatile promo men, such as Ric Flair, can combine both styles quite effectively. Given the contemporary slant toward scripted promos, the tendency is more in the catchphrase direction, and fans at live events have come to expect being able to talk along with their favorite catchphrases as a major part of the fun of attending a show.

The Art of the Promo

Mic skills are a major part of the entertainment package that is pro wrestling, and there are many fans that tune in just as much for what their favorite athletes will say on the stick as for what they will do once the bell rings. Just as there are many performers revered for their grappling skills, there have been those who are known for their ability to cut a promo. Here are twenty of the very best, men who could light an arena on fire with their words just as much as with their actions.

Count Billy Varga

One of the earliest unsung heroes of the wrestling promo, second-generation grappler Varga practically originated the gimmick of the "know-it-all" heel in the 1950s and early '60s, pontificating with big words and puffing himself up with cartoonish bravado. Popular primarily on the West Coast, his act inspired later promo masters such as AWA World Heavyweight Champion Nick Bockwinkel.

Catchphrase: "There is no wrestler that compares with me."

"Classy" Freddy Blassie

Before he was the managerial scourge of the 1970s and '80s, the self-professed "King of Men" was one of the industry's star attractions and most detested heels. This hatred was largely fueled by his gruff, over-confident, and often arrogantly indignant promos in which he would run down not only his opponents but the fans as well. This natural gift later served him well as the loudmouth representative of many a silent WWWF villain.

Catchphrase: "Listen, you pencil-necked geek!"

Harley Race

As with his in-ring work, there was nothing fancy or flamboyant about the eight-time NWA World Heavyweight Champion on the mic. With a voice that sounded like he gargled with razor blades, he could intimidate an opponent with just a word. He was a no-nonsense, meat-and-potatoes tough guy, and his interviews exuded that quality, with an effortlessness that gave him and his title instant credibility.

Catchphrase: (He didn't need one.)

Nick Bockwinkel

As his manager Bobby Heenan was fond of saying, Bockwinkel was the kind of a guy who, if you asked him what time it was, he'd tell you how to make a watch. Verbose, self-satisfied, and smug as the day is long, he was as cerebral a wrestler as they come, both inside the ring and out. During his time as AWA World Champion, he and Heenan made for perhaps the best wrestler/manager promos ever cut.

Catchphrase: "You cretinous humanoids!"

"The American Dream," live and in public, if you will.   *Photo by Terry Dart*

Dusty Rhodes

What Elvis was to rock 'n' roll, Big Dust was to pro wrestling, taking the inflections and intonations of African-American performers such as Thunderbolt Patterson and making them his own. The result was a babyface with the charisma of a Bible belt preacher who could galvanize a crowd like nobody before him, with a delivery that was as inspirational as it was thrilling. Fans identified with Rhodes as a fellow working man, and his promos went a long way toward achieving that.

Catchphrase: "Live and in public, if you will!"

Superstar Billy Graham

WWWF fans had never seen nor heard anything like Graham before. His jive talking and ability to seemingly speak in rhyme off the top of his head made him one of wrestling's first bona fide "cool heels." When paired against humble, soft-spoken babyfaces like Bruno Sammartino and Bob Backlund, he seemed like something from another planet—a flamboyant, self-aggrandizing egomaniac who was, as far as mic skills go, wrestling's answer to Muhammad Ali. As Graham himself admitted: "The first person that influenced me as far as my promos, my communication skills, was Ali. He was the absolute button that pushed me. He was so incredibly entertaining, that I started copying his stuff."

Catchphrase: "I'm the man of the hour, the man with the power, too sweet to be sour!"

Ric Flair

In the minds of many aficionados, Ric Flair represents the gold standard of wrestling promo artists. To hear him run off at the mouth about his abilities—a slow build from calm, cool, and collected to red-faced, bug-eyed bellowing—was to listen to the blueprint of what makes for an entertaining, effective wrestling interview. This, combined with the ability to back it up in the ring, is what makes Flair the choice of so many as the greatest of all time.

Catchphrase: "To be the man, you have to beat the man!"

Hulk Hogan

The Hulkster was all about charisma, and the chief way he expressed that charisma to his legions of Hulkamaniacs was through the microphone—which was typically held by "Mean" Gene Okerlund. "Well, you know somethin', 'Mean' Gene . . ." began many a pumped-up, sweaty, gesticulation-filled Hogan promo, in which he seemed to feed energy to his fans, and feed off that energy simultaneously.

Catchphrase: "Whatcha gonna do when Hulkamania runs wild on you?"

Michael "P. S." Hayes

When it came to The Fabulous Freebirds, Buddy Roberts was the veteran, Terry Gordy was the worker, and Michael Hayes was, without a doubt, the talker. Often acting as much as a manager as an active member of the team, Hayes had a style that was shaped by the same rock 'n' roll sensibility that formed the basis of what the Freebirds were all about. His ability to draw heat, especially during the trio's World Class feud with the Von Erichs, is legendary.

Piper was the high-water mark for wrestling promos during the 1980s.

Photo by Pro Wrestling Illustrated

Favorite putdown: "He's so slow, it takes him an hour and a half to watch *60 Minutes.*"

"Rowdy" Roddy Piper

Frenzied, frenetic, and frantic, Piper's promos were like smacks in the face, and his unpredictability was what gave him the edge. His way with words was highly influential in putting the WWF on the map in the mid-1980s during his war against the "Rock 'n' Wrestling Connection," and the company was so confident in his abilities that they gave him his own interview segment, Piper's Pit. Although not the first such segment, it was the first that really clicked, setting the standard for all to come.

Classic quote: "Just when they think they've got all the answers, I change the questions!"

Road Warrior Hawk

The Road Warriors are most known for their brutal, dominating ring work, but one-half of that legendary tag team, Mike "Hawk" Hegstrand, may have been one of the industry's most underrated talkers. Slightly deranged yet genuinely funny on the mic, he functioned for years as the spokesman for the duo, when that role wasn't being filled by their manager, Paul Ellering. Hawks's trademark delivery, intense and raspy, helped sell the team as the monsters they were.

Catchphrase: "Oh, what a rush!"

Randy "Macho Man" Savage

Without equal in his unique, over-the-top delivery, Savage created a promo style that was truly his own. He is perhaps best remembered today for his tense, paranoid interviews, delivered in that unmistakable gravelly voice that seemed to vacillate back and forth from restrained whispering to wild howling. Whether as a heel or face, he brought an extreme intensity to every promo, and made his character his own. As he once explained to me: "If you're trying to go out there and be something you're totally not like, unless you're the world's greatest actor, which I'm not, it's got to be something at least close to your natural persona. With me, I'm Randy Poffo, but it's kind of like Randy Poffo, but tripping that light fantastic."

Catchphrase: "Oooooh, yeah!"

Jake "The Snake" Roberts

Cold, calculating, and downright sinister, Jake the Snake stood out from the rest with his ability to get the job done without having to resort to the usual shouting and screaming customary in wrestling promos. Roberts was quite the opposite—calm and collected, he spoke in a menacing yet conversational tone that seemed to hint at an element of evil just beneath the surface. In a field hardly known for its subtlety, he was one of the most nuanced speakers of all time.

Catchphrase: "Trust me."

Arn Anderson

"Double A" filled the role of enforcer of The Four Horsemen, but he was much more than Ric Flair's lackey. During the Horsemen's 1980s heyday in the NWA/WCW, Anderson was one of the best promo guys in the entire company, perhaps second only to Flair himself. Together, they were the perfect counterparts; the Nature Boy's grandiosity was balanced by the Enforcer's measured, confident tones.

Classic Quote: "Adversity introduces a man to himself."

Mick Foley

Whether he was Cactus Jack, Mankind, or appearing under his actual birth name, Foley was a textbook example of how great promo skills could help to propel a performer into the upper echelons of the business. He did not have the greatest physique, and his in-ring style was based more on masochism than grappling technique, but when Foley got on the mic, you could be sure you were going to be listening with rapt attention.

Catchphrases: (as Mankind) "Have a nice day!"; (as Cactus Jack) "Bang! Bang!"

Stone Cold Steve Austin

There may have never been a top guy in WWE who was as naturally gifted on a microphone as the Texas Rattlesnake. First making waves in the company with his infamous "Austin 3:16" speech at the 1996 *King of the Ring*, Stone Cold had a reputation for delivering convincingly bad-ass interviews that seemed to be more like legitimate shoots, even if they weren't. Fans believed in Stone Cold Austin, due largely to his brash and authoritative promos.

Catchphrase: "And that's the bottom line, 'cause Stone Cold said so!"

The Rock

Although he was more the type who relied on an inventory of catchphrases, those catchphrases were so hilariously entertaining that they helped make The Rock one of the top WWF/E performers of the late '90s/early '00s, and one of the most famous pro wrestlers of all time. Whether he was laying the smackdown, threatening to stick his boot sideways up someone's candy ass, or challenging opponents to go one on one with the Great One, The Rock's promos were the highlight of any show.

Catchphrase: "If ya smell what The Rock is cookin'!"

Kurt Angle

One would think being a gold medalist in heavyweight freestyle wrestling at the 1996 Olympics would have been enough to make Angle a success in the WWF/E, but of course, pro wrestling requires a different set of skills. Proving his amazing versatility, Angle was able to enhance his unparalleled athletic credentials with a gimmick that played up his All-American wholesomeness, turning himself into an unbearably self-important "phony babyface." He remains one of the best "total packages" the business has ever seen.

Catchphrase: "It's true! It's true!"

CM Punk

Without question, Punk's most famous promo was the so-called "pipe bomb" he delivered live on *Monday Night Raw* in June of 2011, in which he sat on the entrance ramp and appeared to "shoot" on WWE, Vince McMahon, Triple H, and others (although the promo was indeed a planned part of the show). Known as the guy who would tell it like it is and wasn't afraid of offending anyone, his "worked-shoot" style interviews appealed to insider fans and casual fans alike.

Catchphrase: "I'm the best in the world."

The acid-tongued Punk at the January 20, 2012, edition of *SmackDown!* in Las Vegas, during his historic 434-day reign as WWE World Champion.
Steve Wright Jr./Wikimedia

Bray Wyatt

The new kid on the block, Wyatt (the real-life son of Mike "I.R.S." Rotunda) is a natural on the mic, and his enthralling promos are the key reason he has been able to get over as well as he has. Reportedly bucking the modern trend of scripted speeches, Wyatt comes up with most of his own stuff, and seems to have an innate rapport with the camera and with fans to a degree that is quite rare in the business.

Catchphrase: "Follow the buzzards."

24

Small Shows, Big Hearts

The Independent Wrestling Scene

I hate that term: Well, he's an "indy" guy. No, he's either good or he's not.
—John Cena

Following the downfall of the territorial system at the end of the 1980s, small-time promoters were forced to fend for themselves, and, as a result, a new phenomenon emerged in the business. All across North America, smaller "independent" wrestling organization began to take shape, giving rabid fans an entertaining local alternative to the big-time wrestling they saw on TV. Marked by young up-and-coming performers hungry to make an impression, as well as more than a few fading stars of the past hoping for one last chance at glory, the indy scene continues to thrive to this day.

Each week, far away from the bright lights, glitz, and glamour of the mainstream, independent wrestlers sweat and bleed before crowds of a few hundred (sometimes even fewer) in local VFW halls and high school gymnasiums, sometimes making less than what it takes to cover their travel expenses—if they're paid anything at all. And yet, in many cases, these indy performers put more of their heart and soul into their performance than anything you'll see on television—and their audiences often make up for what they lack in size with passion and knowledge. It can be a tough and unforgiving world, which sometimes leads to the "big time" and sometimes is just a continuing cycle of oblivion. For some, the reward can be an end in itself.

Defining Independent Wrestling

Any look at the independents necessitates asking the obvious question: Just what *is* an indy in the first place? What are the criteria? The answer is not as obvious as one might think. The first part of the answer is establishing just

Ontario's Leah von Dutch performs her "Flying Dutchman moonsault" on Ianna Titus during a June 2012 independent show.   *Tabercil/ Wikimedia*

what an indy is *not*: an indy is not the same as a territory. For one thing, an independent is an alternative to the mainstream, as opposed to wrestling territories, which in their day represented the major league of professional wrestling in their respective regions. The majority of healthy territories ran on an almost nightly basis, had ongoing storylines, weekly television, and usually paid their top performers enough to earn a decent living. In contrast, many indies are fly-by-night, operating under the vast shadow of national companies like TNA and, of course, the globally reaching WWE. With the exception of larger groups like Ring of Honor, most indies traditionally run a few dates per month, if that, and lack television exposure. As for pay, independent wrestlers know full well that the chances of making a lucrative living on the indy scene are slim indeed.

"To me, almost any company that's not WWE, is an indy, really," declares Brian "Blue Meanie" Heffron, who got his start in one of the industry's most successful indies, ECW. "If you're not offering someone a contract or giving them guaranteed employment for a certain amount of time, you're pretty much an indy. If they have you under contract, a year's worth of dates and financial security, that's a wrestling company. If not, you're an independent company."

The definition of an indy has changed over time, but by contemporary standards it can best be described as any pro wrestling promotion that is regional in nature as opposed to national, and lacks national television exposure. Also, although there are some notable exceptions, most independents do not have a regular talent roster under contract, and instead pay their talent on a per-night basis. They are often affiliated with a local training facility, and tend to run in venues far too small to be used by the major organizations. The majority of their business comes from live-event ticket sales, although in today's environment, many indies are able to generate revenue through marketing their own DVDs or even streaming content on the Internet.

"The definition of an independent promotion is generally one that runs in a local or tri-state type of area, and that restricts its action to a few different places," offers legendary pro wrestling journalist Bill Apter, who has been covering the indies for decades. "They're their own little companies, and they're not looking to compete with WWE or TNA."

Indy wrestling is also defined, to a certain extent, by an attitude. Although it's harder than ever for new performers to gain valuable experience due to the absence of a vital territorial system, many independent wrestlers, particularly the young, hungry ones looking to make a name for themselves, will put in an effort that far surpasses what they would seem to get back from it in a monetary sense. Today's indy wrestling boasts a bit of an anti-authority streak—these guys are not WWE, and they know it. More than that, they're proud of it. And the fans, responding to that attitude, often show a level of loyalty and devotion lacking in the much larger mainstream wrestling audience. They know they're going to get their money's worth, and will show appreciation for hard work.

That said, the indies can also be filled with chicanery, broken dreams, and just plain old bad business practices. For every scrappy indy group working hard to put out a respectable product, there are shady types looking to bilk what they can out of local audiences, advertising main events they know they can't deliver or performers they know won't even be on the card. There are also countless tales of wrestlers being taken advantage of by unscrupulous promoters—both green youngsters not yet wise to the business and hardened veterans down on their luck and desperate for the next payday. (This side of the business was portrayed in all its harshness in the 2008 Darren Aronofsky film *The Wrestler*.) Along with the freedom that comes from operating out of the view of the mainstream come the inescapable dangers associated with working this far off the radar, in a "Wild West" environment where it sometimes seems you can get away with almost anything.

The Origins of the Circuit

The concept of independent wrestling has its beginnings in the days of the territories, when certain smaller groups not affiliated with far-reaching outfits like the AWA, WWWF, or the NWA would attempt to run in opposition to the established companies, or in small markets where the big boys didn't bother to go. Often known as "outlaw promotions," these groups included Angelo Poffo's International Championship Wrestling in Kentucky, Lou Thesz's Universal Wrestling Alliance in Tennessee, Ann Gunkel's All-South Wrestling Alliance in Georgia, and Eddie Einhorn's ambitious International Wrestling Association. Each of these groups attempted to buck the territorial system, specifically earning the wrath of the NWA, which unofficially controlled most of the established territories throughout the country. These early outlaw promotions were independent in the truest sense of the word.

Back then, most wrestling promotions were expected to operate through a regional booking office and under the auspices of the state athletic commissions, which allowed the business to be monopolized by a select few. But things began to change dramatically in the 1980s, and the landscape became ripe for independent operators in a way it hadn't been. By the end of the decade, the vast majority of the territorial wrestling organizations had gone out of business, and two of them, WWF and WCW, had gone from regional to national companies. A landmark 1989 court case involving Vince McMahon led professional wrestling to be freed from the control of most state athletic commissions.

With the territories either gone or operating on a much larger scale, countless local promoters were left high and dry. However, the decimation of the NWA's power and the removal of state athletic commissions from the equation gave them the ability to strike out on their own and start opening up their own smaller promotions. There were no more territorial czars to stand in their way, and the lack of athletic commission supervision meant nearly anyone with a little money and a little vision could be a wrestling promoter, albeit on a small scale. Still, the death of territories also meant that there were no more regional booking offices to supply talent, and so those promoters had to be a little more resourceful in recruiting performers, mainly using either local unknowns looking to break into the business, or former national stars who were no longer working for a major promotion.

As a result of the changing landscape of the business, the beginning of the 1990s saw an explosion of independent wrestling, and the birth of the modern indy scene. Those early indies initially did their best to preserve the legacy and the feel of the territories, and many even managed to secure TV slots on local cable or UHF channels. There was the East Coast mainstay International World Class Championship Wrestling, run by former McMahon associate Angelo Savoldi and his family. Emerging from the ashes of World Class in Dallas was the Global Wrestling Federation, which enjoyed a daytime spot on ESPN and boasted future mainstream stars like Booker T,

John "Bradshaw" Layfield, and "The Patriot" Del Wilkes. Most passionate of all in his efforts to "bring back the territories" was Jim Cornette, who ran his Appalachian-based Smokey Mountain Wrestling with all the gusto of a classic Southern rasslin' outfit (and with the backing of rap music mogul Rick Rubin, of all people). The Memphis-based United States Wrestling Association, home of Jerry "The King" Lawler, found itself the lone survivor of the true old-school territories, operating in the '90s as a glorified indy.

Extreme Influences

At the time, the vibe of most indies was that of harmless, family entertainment. Most shows patterned their style after the mainstream in an attempt to appeal to fans of WCW and especially the WWF, and crowds were just as likely to feature the stereotypical hooting granny in the front row as the ubiquitous family of four out for a night of good, clean fun. That started to change thanks to the effect of the most ambitious, influential, and well-known indy of them all, the Philadelphia-based ECW (see Chapter 19 for a comprehensive look at this group).

By the late 1990s, the "ECW effect" was very apparent on the independent scene, with the majority of indies attempting to copy Paul Heyman's approach in the hopes that they might also experience some of his success. Suddenly, indy promotions were all about "extreme" action, presenting a product that featured ultra-violent hardcore-style matches, with adult-oriented angles. The little children and grandmothers were replaced by "smart" Internet fans, typically young adult males who often felt disenfranchised by what the mainstream companies had to offer, and wanted something edgier.

This development continued, eventually leading to its ultimate end point, the phenomenon known as backyard wrestling. Reaching its peak of popularity around the turn of the twenty-first century during pro wrestling's Attitude Era boom, backyard wrestling is a controversial and often dangerous practice seen by many as the lowest devolution of the wrestling business. Stripping pro wrestling of any trappings of its professional and regulated veneer, backyard wrestling is performed by individuals typically in their teens or early twenties, usually with little-to-no actual wrestling training.

Inspired by what they've seen in the increasingly hardcore world of the indies, backyard wrestlers created what can at best be described as a "pretend" wrestling environment, presented literally in backyards or other open outdoor spaces for informal gatherings of friends, with no proper supervision whatsoever. And although the environment may be "pretend," the performances are anything but, with an abundance of perilous stunts using fire, barbed wire, fluorescent tubes, and other weapons, as well as reckless blading and other ill-advised in-ring practices. Mainstream companies like WWE were troubled by the phenomenon, especially with how it might be linked in the public eye with their own increasingly violent product, and were quick to distance themselves from the world of backyard wrestling, employing a vigorous new "don't try this at home" public-service campaign.

The Indy Scene Today

In the years after the demise of ECW as an independent, and with backlash over backyard wrestling and its hazards, the independent circuit started to rein things in. The 2000s saw the indy scene really come into its own. The rise of the Internet made indies even more viable alternatives to the mainstream, giving them a conduit to reach an audience, and giving that audience a place to share their passions. No longer aping the territories, WWE, or even ECW, many indies worked to establish their own identity. Very often, a key element of that identity was a heightened level of workrate unlike anything fans would be likely to see in an average WWE or TNA ring, with performers pulling out all the stops, while at the same time not necessarily resorting to the hardcore tactics of a decade prior.

Fans saw the rise of indy stars—performers content to ply their trade on the circuit as an end in itself, rather than a route to WWE stardom (although that still happened for some of them). Also, many indies became breeding grounds for future mainstream stars, as independent promoters and bookers became interested in creating viable new talent for the future. Some of these, like Ohio's Heartland Wrestling Association, Kentucky's Ohio Valley Wrestling, and California's Ultimate Pro Wrestling, actually developed working relationships with WWE, acting as feeder systems for the industry's major league organization.

Although WWE now has its own in-house talent development system, the independent circuit is more than ever a proving ground for the performers of tomorrow, bustling with countless innovative promotions and seasoned wrestlers practicing their craft before appreciative crowds. Typical of the contemporary wave of independent wrestling is CHIKARA, a Pennsylvania-based group started in 2002 by indy darlings Mike Quackenbush and Reckless Youth. Defying the indy label, CHIKARA runs shows all over the country, and reaches a strong cult viewership through streaming video technologies like Internet pay-per-view, as well as home-video sales. With a product that blends elements of *lucha libre* and *puroresu* with a liberal dose of the absurd, CHIKARA is the avänt gärde of pro wrestling, putting on shows with tongue firmly in cheek, featuring performers with names like The Estonian Thunderfrog, Jervis Cottonbelly, and Blaster McMassive.

Also expanding beyond local boundaries is an organization known as Dragon Gate USA, an American extension of the Japanese group Dragon Gate that was established in the States in 2009 by former ECW and ROH booker Gabe Sapolsky. Taking a more serious approach, Dragon Gate USA shows its Japanese influence by presenting pro wrestling in a sports-like vein, with an emphasis on technical wrestling and clean finishes with minimal storyline silliness. Dragon Gate USA has a strong working relationship with extremely popular Northeast-based independent EVOLVE Wrestling, and has showcased the talents of such future WWE stars as Dean Ambrose, Daniel Bryan, and Cesaro (a.k.a. Jon Moxley, Bryan Danielson, and Claudio Castagnoli, respectively).

But perhaps no other independent group on the current scene has made quite the impact of Ring of Honor, which, just like ECW during the 1990s, has grown into what can accurately be described as the number-three wrestling promotion in North America, behind WWE and TNA. Unlike ECW, which imploded in under a decade, Ring of Honor has been going strong since 2002 and has the backing of a multi-million-dollar corporation. Like many independents these days, ROH has benefited from the proliferation of home-video technologies ranging from good old-fashioned DVDs to the exciting iPPV breakthrough that has allowed indy wrestling to bypass traditional TV routes to reach a worldwide audience.

Independent wrestling today has found an audience that, although it may be much smaller than the mainstream WWE audience, is arguably more passionate, more loyal, and more vocal about what it wants. With professional wrestling divided more sharply into the big-time and the small-time, when it seems that a company has to be on national television with loud music and pyro just to be taken seriously, it looked for a while like the more modest, grassroots independent approach didn't have a future in the grand scheme of things. But thanks to the tireless efforts of performers and the enterprising promoters who hire them, independent wrestling continues to thrive.

Make no mistake, the struggle with finding a wide audience is a very real one, and the mind-blowing production values fans have been conditioned to expect can sometimes make it difficult for indies to succeed. But for those fans who want something different from what they see each week on TV, and who are willing to support a product that puts substance ahead of style, there is an entire generation of talented athletes out there giving them their money's worth every night of the week.

Declaration of Independents

In addition to the ones mentioned in this chapter, some other important current indies (as of this writing) include:

- !Bang!: Founded by former NWA World Champion Dory Funk, Jr., this Florida-based promotion operates alongside the champ's Funking Conservatory training program.
- Combat Zone Wrestling: Based in New Jersey, CZW began in 1999 as a competitor of ECW, and continues to present its ultra-violent brand of hardcore wrestling to this day.
- East Coast Wrestling Association: Established by Jim Kettner in 1967 during the height of the territorial era, the Delaware-based ECWA is the longest-running indy in the country and boasts the annual Super 8 Tournament.
- House of Hardcore: This promotion, founded by ECW icon Tommy Dreamer in 2012, works to carry on the legacy and philosophy of ECW.
- Impact Pro Wrestling: Operating since 2003, IPW has been New Zealand's first major local promotion in decades.
- Juggalo Championship Wrestling: After stints in both WCW and the WWF, the Insane Clown Posse established their own indy league, which presents hardcore shows throughout the country, featuring live musical performances.
- Shine Wrestling: This female-only promotion out of Florida presents cards exclusively on Internet pay-per-view and features a developmental program headed by former WWE/WCW/ECW star Big Vito LoGrasso.
- Texas Wrestling Entertainment: Originally founded by former WWF World Champion Shawn Michaels during his initial retirement in the late '90s, TWE launched the career of Daniel Bryan, among many others.
- World League Wrestling: Founded by eight-time NWA World Champion Harley Race, the Missouri-based WLW is known for its slogan, "Shut Up and Wrestle!"
- World Xtreme Wrestling: Operated by Afa Anoa'i of The Wild Samoans (and uncle to current WWE star Roman Reigns), WXW is based in Florida, although it has presented shows all over the world.

Ring of Honor

It's not quite accurate to call Sinclair Broadcast Group's Ring of Honor Wrestling an independent, as the organization transcends many of the accepted definitions. It's either America's largest and most successful indy, or America's third-biggest professional wrestling company, behind only TNA Wrestling and the mighty WWE itself. With television exposure in various places all over the world, many performers under formal contract, a fully functioning front office with corporate ownership, and a recent foray into live pay-per-view cable distribution, ROH's streamlined, gimmick-light approach to wrestling is a breath of fresh air for many, and has launched the careers of many of the industry's top stars of the past decade.

"I despise that indy label," says announcer Kevin Kelly, the voice of ROH since 2010. "Ring of Honor is a wrestling company. We never worry about labels."

Ring of Honor can trace its origins back to the void left by the demise of ECW, which went bankrupt in 2001 and was promptly absorbed by the WWF. Wrestling video merchant Rob Feinstein, who had been selling ECW tapes and DVDs as his main source of revenue, decided the best thing to do after the company folded was to start up his own—a promotion whose shows he could market directly to customers as part of his home-video business. In this goal he was joined by someone else in need of a new career path, former ECW booker Gabe Sapolsky. On February 23, 2002, the company they called Ring of Honor opened its doors with a show in Philadelphia entitled *The Era of Honor Begins*.

In the beginning, ROH confined its operations to the Northeast, covering a region similar to that serviced by ECW in its heyday. The company received a shot in the arm thanks to a working agreement with TNA Wrestling, but things took a bleak turn in 2004 when co-founder Feinstein was forced to sell off his interests and resign in the wake of a sex scandal (see Chapter 21 for details). In the long run, however, this was a blessing in disguise for ROH, as ownership of the company shifted into the hands of longtime professional ticket broker Cary Silkin. Under Silkin's watchful eye, ROH would experience dramatic growth over the next few years.

First, with Feinstein out of the way, Silkin brought the whole home-video business in-house, and DVDs of its live events as well as shoot interviews became more popular than ever. The company stretched beyond its Northeastern home base, nurturing international relations with Japanese groups like Pro Wrestling Noah and Dragon Gate. By 2007, ROH performers were touring Japan regularly, and some of Japan's top stars were becoming champions in ROH. Silkin brokered a deal to bring ROH directly into the homes of fans with a series of pre-taped pay-per-view events to be carried on select cable networks. As the company's profile was raised and word spread, Silkin took his show on the road, bringing ROH to fans in parts of the country it had heretofore never been.

In just a few short years, ROH had attracted a strong cult following of Internet-savvy fans that responded to the company's exciting and unique product. Presenting pro wrestling in more of a sports context than WWE or TNA, ROH stressed clean finishes, solid technical wrestling, and athleticism over showmanship. It showcased a roster of performers who, much like the stars of ECW in years past, seemed a different breed from what fans were getting in mainstream wrestling: Former WCW prospect Adam Pearce, who also served for a time as ROH's head booker in place of Sapolsky; the charismatic Colt Cabana, longtime tag-team partner of CM Punk; indy icon Chris Hero, an import from the hardcore world of Combat Zone Wrestling; Internet favorite Kevin Steen, long considered one of the most underrated wrestlers in the world; the intense high-flyer Low Ki, one of the talents who first put ROH on the map; and the rough-and-tumble Englishman Nigel McGuiness, long-reigning ROH World Champion.

Ring of Honor earned a reputation as a proving ground for the superstars of tomorrow, and this can be observed in the sheer number of its performers who would later go on to great notoriety on a worldwide level. Among these is the aforementioned CM Punk, a future WWE World Champion who would co-opt his slogan "Best in the World" from his time in ROH; lightning-quick daredevil Bryan Danielson, who, as Daniel Bryan, would start his own fan movement as WWE's most inspirational underdog; Claudio Castagnoli, who would become WWE's own "Swiss Superman," Cesaro; and Austin Aries and Samoa Joe, whose accomplishments as world champions in TNA Wrestling were prefigured by dominant runs in ROH.

"I went in a snowstorm to the Hammerstein ballroom to see Ring of Honor, because it's pure wrestling," recalls longtime wrestling fan and promoter Evan Ginzburg. "Are they as charismatic? In most cases no, but I don't care because

Lead Ring of Honor commentator Kevin Kelly (left) interviews Nigel McGuiness in Chicago Ridge, Illinois, at the first ROH-TV taping under Sinclair ownership, August 13, 2011.
Steve Wright Jr./Wikimedia

I want to see *wrestling*. I want to see it treated as a sport, not as a circus. I used to see Bryan Danielson against Nigel McGuiness, and it was art."

With its buzz growing stronger than ever thanks to its stellar roster of talent, in 2009 Ring of Honor signed a two-year deal with HDNet Fights to produce its first weekly television program, to be carried in select markets. In 2011, at the conclusion of the deal, Silkin sold Ring of Honor to telecommunications company Sinclair Broadcast Group, operator of the largest number of local television stations in the United States. Sinclair immediately began airing *ROH Wrestling* on its multitude of syndicated CW and MyNetworkTV affiliates in select markets throughout America, giving the promotion more TV exposure than any other independent group in the country.

"The company wouldn't have lasted were it not for Cary Silkin," declares Kelly. "He funded it because he was passionate about it. There was enough good talent and enough creative juice to make sure it was really interesting to the fans. But the fans that really got into Ring of Honor in that period, they wouldn't have stuck around as long if it weren't for Cary Silkin. He funded it at a tremendous loss, until it was sold to Sinclair."

Although some critics feel that growth hasn't been as robust as expected under the auspices of media conglomerate Sinclair, ROH's 2014 entrance into the live pay-per-view television arena is a major step in the right direction. Even WWE has been forced to take notice of ROH of late, tipping its hat to the promotion on its website and in various documentaries touting the skills of the many current WWE performers who got their start there. Ring of Honor has come a long way since its humble beginnings as a Northeast indy, and looks to continue providing a unique brand of action to fans of great wrestling.

25

Calling the Action

Referees, Commentators, and Announcers

Remember: There are no small parts, only small actors.
—Constantin Stanislavski

It takes more than just the in-ring talent to make a compelling product. Whether we notice or not, there are key roles played by "civilians" at each event, and pro wrestling just wouldn't be the same without them. In this chapter, we shine a much-deserved light on the often-thankless parts played by those who almost never take a bow: referees, broadcast commentators, and ring announcers. Whether they're giving the illusion of "officiating" while accompanying the action in the ring, or selling it to the viewing audience for all they're worth, these folks always give it their all.

The Third Man in the Ring

They can suffer more boos and hisses than the worst of heels. Sometimes, they may be tossed around like ragdolls by men twice their size. They seem perpetually outpaced in a desperate attempt to bring order to chaos. Yet in the illusory world of wrestling, things are far from what they seem. The referee is just as much a part of the match as the wrestlers, and is in many ways the most important person between the ropes. The job of a great referee can almost go completely unnoticed. And, in fact, it's supposed to.

Although it seems obvious, it's worth pointing out that the most important thing to remember when trying to grasp the role of the modern pro wrestling referee is that he is not actually a referee. That is to say, he is not actually officiating a match, as there is no actual match to officiate, at least not in the literal sense. Rather, a pro wrestling match is a performance, and as in the case of the wrestlers, so is the referee a part of that performance. Contrary to the illusion generated by the code of kayfabe, pro wrestling does not actually have "rules" in the same sense that competitive sports have rules. The suggestion of rules exists to help tell the story, and is only real insofar as it serves that purpose. In this way, it is useful to imagine the wrestling ref as the equivalent of the boxing referees in *Rocky* (1976), or *Raging Bull* (1980), or the football referees in *Any Given Sunday* (1999). It's all a show, and the referee is an integral part of it.

The referee is there for several important reasons. From a fan perspective, he exists, of course, to help preserve the illusion of competition—to add legitimacy to the proceedings by giving them the trappings of sport. From a storyline perspective, the referee wears a couple of hats. Referees are infamous for missing much of the heels' cheating tactics, to the intense chagrin of the crowd. This is intentional, and helps generate crowd "heat," focusing the anger and outrage of the audience exactly where it needs to be: on the bad guys (as well as on the unfortunate ref). Conversely, the referee can help provide catharsis by eventually catching the heels in the act and penalizing them, or making a great call that gives the advantage, or even the victory, to the good guys. This results in the vindicated exultation of the crowd, and no great babyface triumph is ever complete without the image of the referee decisively raising the hand of the victor in the center of the ring. Although once a rarity, referees can also often be called upon to take a fall as part of the action. Known as a "ref bump"; this situation occurs when the referee is knocked down by a wrestler either "by accident" in the course of the match, or on purpose as retaliation for a perceived bad call. Taking bumps requires most modern referees to be a bit more athletic than some of their portly predecessors.

But from an insider perspective, the referee serves a purpose even more important. He is there to communicate with the wrestlers, guiding the match along in the process. He might be called upon to inform them when their allotted time is almost up and it's time to "go home" to the finish. He might relay messages from backstage regarding important spots in the match, or any last-minute changes to the script. He can also relay messages from the ring to the back, such as when a wrestler requires medical attention. In the old days, this called for intricate signals and hand gestures between the ref and backstage officials, but in the present day, referees are equipped with remote earpieces, allowing them to receive messages from the back with ease. In this way, the referee becomes the conduit with whom the promoters and bookers can communicate with the wrestlers during a match.

And, above all else, making the referee's job that much more difficult is the fact that he has to do all this without attracting too much attention to himself. A great referee blends into the background, asserting himself only when it serves the purpose of the match. After all, the fans should have their eyes on the wrestlers, not on the referee. A referee who tries to insert too much of his personality or get too histrionic in his mannerisms can derail a good match, distracting the audience and even throwing off the rhythm of the wrestlers. He must find the balance between fading into the background and establishing himself as the force of authority.

"The best referees are the ones the fans don't ever see," offers historian Scott Teal. "They're in the ring, they do their job, but unless they're part of the storyline, the fans shouldn't even know they're there."

The role of the referee has evolved just as the pro wrestling industry itself has evolved. In earlier years, when pro wrestling was treated more like a competitive sport, the referee was regarded as a legitimate official. In fact, in many states where there was an athletic commission in effect, the referees were not actually employees of the local wrestling organization, but were appointed by the commissions. That is not to say that referees were not in on the act, as they most certainly would need to be for any show to be a success. However, because wrestling promotions wanted to be treated like real sports in order to maintain kayfabe, it meant they needed to bow to the commissions and agree to take on the referees they were given. In those days, pro wrestling's true nature was not as out in the open as it is today, but it's safe to assume that athletic commissions were aware of it and typically chose to look the other way, content with maintaining the appearance that they were keeping everything on the level.

"In my day, the commission treated it like it was real, and so the referees weren't even in the same part of the building as the wrestlers," former Madison Square Garden referee Dick Kroll told me in a 2003 interview. "I'd get into the ring and know nothing about what was going to happen, and while I was giving instructions, I would ask who was going over. They'd say, 'I'm going over with a backbreaker,' or something like that, and that was the total input I would get. That was different in different parts of the country, but in New York that's what it was like. Then once it loosened up, I was able to be a part of the story. We'd have to watch the timekeeper; he'd put his pencil in his mouth, and that would mean there's five minutes left, and when he took the pencil out it was time to go home."

In professional wrestling's modern form, with athletic commissions relatively out of the picture and wrestling's nature an open secret, wrestling companies are permitted to operate as they see fit, and the referees have been completely brought into the fold as employees of the promotion. In this sense, the pretense of the legitimate official has been abandoned in favor of referees who are openly part of the show. Whereas in the past, promoters wouldn't want it known that the referees worked for them for fear that it would make their product appear rigged, these days major organizations like WWE and TNA are unconcerned with this detail, and make no attempt to hide the fact that their referees work for the promotion. It's a natural progression of the role of the referee, which finally allows them the freedom to do the job they'd been secretly doing for decades anyway.

Awesome Arbiters: Fifteen Refs Who Earned Their Stripes

- Bill Alfonso: A veteran of many of the major American wrestling territories of the 1980s, Alfonso got his start in the last days of Terry Funk's Amarillo promotion, later transitioned to Championship Wrestling from Florida, and worked high-profile stints for both WCW and the WWF. He later rose to even greater notoriety as a heel manager in ECW in the 1990s.

- Bronko Lubich: The Hungarian-born former wrestler pulled double duty in the Dallas–Ft. Worth area as both a head booker and head referee for Fritz Von Erich's World Class Championship Wrestling. Although notoriously slow in his three-counts, the stout old man is a sentimental favorite of many old-school fans.

- Charles Robinson: Also known as "Lil' Naitch" due to his resemblance to and admiration for Ric Flair, Robinson was a prominent WCW referee in the 1990s, who successfully made the transition to WWE when it took over WCW in 2001. He refereed Flair's WWE retirement match at *WrestleMania XXIV*.

- Danny Bartfield: A prominent boxer of the 1940s, Bartfield went on to become one of the top referees at Madison Square Garden from the 1950s through the 1970s. In a testament to the legitimacy afforded the business in an earlier age, Bartfield worked simultaneously as a boxing and wrestling referee.

- Dick Kroll: One of the primary Madison Square Garden referees for twenty-five years, Kroll was a (W)WWF fixture from the early '60s through the late '80s, refereeing many of the company's most historic matches, including Bruno Sammartino's shocking 1971 loss to Ivan Koloff, and Bob Backlund's equally shocking 1983 defeat at the hands of The Iron Sheik.

- Dick Woehrle: A tough-as-nails former middleweight fighter who reffed throughout the Northeast in the 1960s, '70s, and '80s, Woehrle was known for always being in shape and never taking any guff. Starting out as a boxing referee, he learned the business the hard way when the athletic commission assigned him as a wrestling ref one night without any notice. Working mainly in Pennsylvania, he is best remembered as the ref for the (W)WWF's weekly TV tapings in Hamburg and Allentown.

- Earl Hebner: The WWF/E's senior official from the late '80s through the mid-2000s, Hebner was involved in two major "screwjob" matches, the first being Hulk Hogan's loss to Andre the Giant on national TV in

1988 (which was part of a storyline), and the second being Bret Hart's loss to Shawn Michaels at the 1997 *Survivor Series* (which was not). His twin brother, Dave, has also worked as a referee.

- Ed Smith: At the turn of the twentieth century, when pro wrestling most resembled a major American sport, *Chicago American* sports editor Edward W. Smith was its most high-profile official. Among the matches he worked were both of the Frank Gotch / George Hackenschmidt encounters and Gotch's world championship defense against Yussif Mahmout, one of the Terrible Turks.

- George Bothner: Perhaps the greatest lightweight pro wrestler who ever lived, Bothner was a top-ranked competitor and a world champion around the turn of the twentieth century, who later became the top referee in the New York area during the 1920s and '30s. He can be seen refereeing the 1920 World title match between Joe Stecher and Earl Caddock, the earliest match to survive on film. Bothner also owned a renowned boxing and wrestling gym in Manhattan.

- Jerry Calhoun: Senior referee in the blood-and-guts Memphis promotion from the late '70s through the '80s, Calhoun was known for being quick and athletic, and also for taking a large amount of hellacious ref bumps—a staple of Memphis rasslin'.

- Joe Higuchi: The most renowned referee in the history of Japanese *puroresu*, Higuchi worked for Rikidozan's Japanese Wrestling Association in the 1960s, and for Giant Baba's All-Japan Wrestling from the 1970s through the '90s. Due to being fluent in English, he was frequently flown into the U.S. to officiate major NWA World title matches, and acted as a liaison for American wrestlers working in Japan.

- Johnny "Red Shoes" Dugan: After a career as a light-heavyweight wrestler in the 1930s and '40s, Dugan (real name: Ray Gedeon) became one of the most visible referees in the world thanks to his position as senior referee in the Los Angeles territory. During the 1960s and '70s he was a regular at L.A.'s Olympic Auditorium, known as much for his nimble agility as for his eponymous footwear.

- Mike Chioda: WWE's senior official following Hebner's departure for TNA in 2005, right up to the time of this book's publication. He was first brought into the company in 1989 by Gorilla Monsoon, whose son Joey Marella was also a referee.

- Nick Patrick: The son of masked wrestler "The Assassin" Jody Hamilton, Patrick's own in-ring career was cut short by injury, leading him to become a referee. He worked for Jim Crockett Promotions, later becoming senior official when that company transformed into WCW. He is best remembered as the "heel referee" for WCW's invading nWo faction. He also transitioned to WWE in the 2000s.

- Tommy Young: Considered by many the greatest pro wrestling referee of all time, Young was the main ref for the NWA's Mid-Atlantic territory in the 1970s and '80s, and was named NWA Referee of the Year on five occasions. The ref for countless NWA World Championship matches, he was known for leaping and sliding all over the ring to be in the right position for the three-count. His career was cut shot in 1989 by an injury suffered from a ref bump gone wrong.

Additional Worthies: Jack Doan, Jimmy Korderas, Teddy Long, Joey Marella, Danny Davis, Jim Molineaux, Jack Stanley, Gilberto Roman, "Judo" Jack Terry, John Bonello, Fred Atkins, Tim White, Mark Curtis, Chad Patton, Mickey Jay, Randy "Pee Wee" Anderson, Scott James/Armstrong, "Scrap Iron" George Gadaski, Sandy Scott, Scrappy McGowan, Paul Morton, and David Manning.

Bringing the Show Into Your Living Room

As with the many professional sports with which it paralleled itself, once pro wrestling began to be transmitted and recorded via the use of technology for the enjoyment of patrons not physically present for the matches, it necessitated the introduction of a new player in the performance: the broadcast commentator. Although there were those who called wrestling over the radio and provided voiceovers for film reels during the 1930s and '40s (legendary comedian Steve Allen among them), it wasn't until the arrival of television that the role of the broadcast commentator really took hold as an important part of the show.

If professional wrestling is all about storytelling, then perhaps there is no one who does more to enhance the performance going on in the ring than those who sit ringside and accompany the action with live commentary for the viewers at home. Great commentating is about playing up the strengths of the wrestlers and downplaying any perceived weaknesses in the performance. It's about providing some historical context when helpful, and emphasizing the important storyline points that give the match its gravitas, providing the viewer with a greater reason for caring about the proceedings. Wrestling broadcasters are responsible for naming many of pro wrestling's tried-and-true maneuvers on the fly, and can help to sell the action in a way that can add a heightened level of "realism" when done right.

"The play-by-play announcer is the helmsman of the ship," explains Ring of Honor lead commentator and former WWE commentator Kevin Kelly. "His job is to make sure the boat goes down the water straight. I liken it to the Chinese plate spinners. I'm directing with hand signals to my cohorts, I'm pointing at the cameras, I'm listening to the truck, I'm waiting to throw to a package, and the whole time I have to make sure I'm progressing everything forward, despite all the tumult around me. I have to make sure the story is effectively told. It's the chorus of the Greek tragedy—a bit of narration, conveying emotion if something is lacking."

Still practiced today (although to a lesser degree), another major aspect of the commentator's job is to "interview" the wrestlers, usually backstage or at ringside, acting as a conduit, of sorts, for the wrestler to "cut his promo." Usually setting the wrestler up with appropriate questions, the commentator's verbiage is kept to a minimum as he holds the microphone while the wrestler bellows, gloats, and otherwise spews forth angry, vengeful, or jubilant diatribes. The commentator is expected to react appropriately, while always making sure the wrestler takes center stage. This role has been minimized in recent years by the phenomenon of wrestlers cutting extended promos in the ring completely by themselves, thus eliminating the need for someone to set them up and hold the mic for them.

During the 1980s, a new wrinkle developed in the role of the ringside commentator, as promoters began to divide broadcasters into heels and babyfaces, just like the wrestlers whose matches they were calling. Adding more animation and conflict to the broadcast, play-by-play and color commentators began arguing back and forth, as one of them shamelessly backed the villains and the other tried to remain the even-keeled proponent of law and order in the ring. The heel/babyface announcer dynamic continues to this day.

As the role of the ringside commentator has evolved, it has come to include much more than merely describing what's going on in the ring for the viewers at home. Modern-day broadcasters like Michael Cole, John "Bradshaw" Leyfield and Jerry "The King" Lawler in WWE, and Mike Tenay

Jerry "The King" Lawler and Jim "J. R." Ross (here calling the action at *No Mercy 2007* in Rosemont, Illinois) were perhaps the most beloved team of announcers in the modern era.
Mshake3/Wikimedia

and Taz in TNA are expected to routinely plug merchandise, engage viewers via social media, and pitch additional services, such as the WWE Network and company websites. Combining all this with providing coherent, compelling accompaniment to the in-ring action makes the job of the pro wrestling broadcast commentator more challenging than ever.

Colorful Commentators: Twenty Broadcasters Who Roused from Ringside

- Bill Mercer: A prominent figure in the success of Fritz Von Erich's World Class Championship Wrestling, Mercer called wrestling in the Dallas area dating from the 1950s through the 1980s. Enjoying a successful career in sports broadcasting, he also called football and baseball, including stints with the Texas Rangers and the Chicago White Sox.
- Bobby "The Brain" Heenan: One of the greatest managers of all time, Heenan can also lay claim to being one of the greatest commentators of all time, particularly for his work in the WWF during the 1980s and early '90s. Perhaps the most genuinely funny commentator of them all, the self-professed "broadcast journalist" was the perfect foil for the blustery Gorilla Monsoon, and the two formed pro wrestling's equivalent of Abbott and Costello.
- Dick Lane: One of the first pro wrestling broadcasters heard when TV first took hold in the late 1940s, Lane continued right up through the early 1970s as the voice of wrestling on the West Coast, calling the action on KTLA from the Olympic Auditorium. He was known for naming many of wrestling's most common and popular holds, as well as his trademark catchphrase, "Whoa, Nellie!"
- Ed Whalen: One of the industry's most colorful broadcasters of all time, "Wailin'" Ed Whalen was the voice of Stu Hart's Stampede Wrestling out of Calgary, and one of Alberta's most beloved TV personalities. With his distinctively nasal delivery, he became an even bigger star than most of the wrestlers whose matches he would call.
- Gordon Solie: Known as the "Dean of Wrestling Announcers," Solie brought a big-match feel to the proceedings like nobody else. His gravelly delivery could be heard in both Championship Wrestling from Florida broadcasts, and on the nationally broadcast Georgia Championship Wrestling in the 1970s and '80s. With his sports-like style, he was even occasionally brought in for NWA World Championship matches in other areas, such as at *Starrcade '83*.
- Gorilla Monsoon: After retiring from the ring in 1981, Monsoon became one of the WWF's main TV broadcasters, a role he enjoyed for nearly fifteen years. An apologist for the babyfaces, he was known for his colorful

anatomical descriptions and for lambasting heels with insults like "snake in the grass," "Benedict Arnold," and "fountain of misinformation." He formed successful broadcast teams with both Jesse Ventura and Bobby Heenan, and was the voice of WWF pay-per-views for seven years.

- Jack Brickhouse: The voice of the Chicago Cubs during the 1950s, '60s, and '70s, Brickhouse was one of the country's most celebrated sportscasters, calling several World Series and the 1949 championship fight between Jersey Joe Walcott and Ezzard Charles. Between jobs, he was the voice of pro wrestling on the DuMont Network, and later became a regular broadcaster for the AWA's Chicago events. He came out of retirement in the 1980s for several major AWA shows.

- Jerry "The King" Lawler: He may be King of Memphis Wrestling, but as an announcer he's King of the One-Liners. A fixture on WWE television since the mid-1990s, Lawler is beloved by fans for his admittedly corny jokes and shameless admiration for the lovely WWE Divas. Although a heel announcer for many years, his beloved status eventually led to him being turned babyface.

- Jesse "The Body" Ventura: Perhaps the most acclaimed heel broadcaster of all time, the future governor of Minnesota joined Gorilla Monsoon and Vince McMahon for WWF pay-per-views and *Saturday Night's Main Event* telecasts. Claiming to call it like he saw it, Ventura defended the villains in a logical style that was hard to refute, and even praised the heroes when they earned it.

- Jim Ross: The most admired pro wrestling broadcaster of the past twenty-five years, "Good ol' J. R." was known for his irresistible intensity, homespun aphorisms, and his unsurpassed ability to instill a sense of passion in the broadcast. For the better part of a decade, he was the voice of WWE's *Monday Night Raw*, and got his start working for Bill Watts in the Mid-South area, followed by six years with WCW.

- Joey Styles: As much a part of ECW as any in-ring performer, Styles's exuberance sold the outrageousness and unpredictability of the ECW product, with his trademark exclamation, "Oh, my God!" He was also known for introducing many *lucha libre* and *puroresu* terms into the lexicon of American wrestling maneuvers.

- Kevin Kelly: The current voice of Ring of Honor, Kelly was also a member of the WWF/E's broadcast team from the mid-1990s through the early 2000s, working for a time as a broadcaster on *Monday Night Raw*. He's also remembered as a target of comical abuse during backstage interviews with The Rock.

- Lance Russell: The voice of Memphis wrestling from the 1960s through the 1990s, Russell's unmistakable Southern drawl accompanied countless matches fought by the likes of Jackie Fargo, Jerry Lawler, Bill

Dundee, and many others. Known for the calm, measured delivery that made him stand out from his colleagues, he was the lone voice of reason in one of the country's wildest territories.

- Lord Athol Layton: A successful wrestler of the 1950s and '60s, thanks to his articulate voice, the English-born Layton had an equally successful career as a broadcaster for promotions throughout Ontario, Michigan, Ohio, and upstate New York, most memorably The Sheik's Big Time Wrestling and Frank Tunney's Maple Leaf Wrestling. Standing six feet five inches and weighing 250 pounds, he was unusual in that he towered over many of the wrestlers, and wasn't afraid to drop the mic and mix it up if provoked.

- Mean Gene Okerlund: The ubiquitous man with the stick from the 1970s through the 1990s, first with the AWA, then the WWF, and finally WCW, Okerlund was known most of all for his interviews, as well as his ability to hype upcoming events. The stereotypical little balding announcer in a tux, he provided the perfect visual accompaniment to any wrestling promo, and was known for being the Howard Cosell to Hulk Hogan's Muhammad Ali for many years.

- Michael Cole: J. R.'s replacement as lead WWE announcer, Cole has been with the WWF/E since the mid-1990s. Known today as "The Voice of WWE," he heads up the broadcast team on both *Raw* and *SmackDown!*, as well as all WWE pay-per-view events.

- Mike Tenay: Alongside Taz, Tenay was TNA's lead announcer, calling the action on *Impact Wrestling* and all TNA pay-per-views. He is known for his expert understanding of the nuances of pro wrestling, providing a sports-like perspective. He is also an expert on Mexican *lucha libre*, and has used this passion to help get many *luchadores* over with American audiences. He was recently replaced on *Impact* by Josh Matthews.

- Ray Morgan: During the earliest days of Capitol Wrestling/WWWF in the 1950s and '60s, Morgan was the lead announcer, calling the action each week on *Heavyweight Wrestling* from the Capitol Arena in Washington, D.C. His dismissal led to the ascension of promoter Vincent J. McMahon's son, Vince McMahon "Junior," as the WWWF's lead TV broadcaster.

- Tony Schiavone: The voice of WCW's *Monday Nitro* during the height of the Monday Night War in the late '90s and early 2000s, Schiavone was known for his over-the-top hyperbole (with each broadcast being "the greatest in the history of our sport"). He got his start with Jim Crockett Promotions in the 1980s, transitioning from the Charlotte O's, a Crockett-owned minor league baseball team. He also worked briefly for the WWF, from 1989 to 1990.

- Vince McMahon: Known today as the chairman of WWE and the villainous Mr. McMahon on TV, Vince was for more than twenty-five years the voice of the company as a play-by-play announcer. With a more subdued and sober delivery in the 1970s, he later developed into a hoarse, yelling master of ballyhoo who supported the babyfaces with unflappable zeal.

Additional Worthies: Bob Caudle, "Chilly" Bill Cardille, Todd Pettengill, John "Bradshaw" Layfield, Taz, David Crockett, Pat Patterson, Billy Red Lyons, Lord Alfred Hayes, Sean Mooney, Jonathan Coachman, Josh Matthews, Todd Grisham, Eric Bischoff, Lee Marshall, Jeremy Borash, Don West, Doyle King, Boyd Pierce, and Renee Young.

Introducing Next, the Ring Announcers

Although they may not have as much to do as ringside broadcasters, the role of the ring announcer is one that dates back much further and is much more of a part of the live pro wrestling experience. On the surface, it seems like such a simple job: announce the names of the wrestlers before each match, and the winner at each match's conclusion. But the right ring announcer can add so much to the moment, whipping the crowd into a fever pitch, adding pomp, circumstance, and a sense of decorum. All with their own unique delivery or sense of theatricality, they bring flair to the proceedings and can make a ham 'n' egger seem like the most important wrestler in the world. And for most fans, hearing the voice of the announcer declaring their favorite as the winner, or better yet, the new champion, is nearly as thrilling as the victory itself.

In the beginning, before there was even a ring to announce in, the announcer indeed performed a relatively perfunctory role, simply informing the crowd as to who it was they were about see wrestle. However, starting with pro wrestling's transformation into a major American sporting event at the turn of the twentieth century, the increased spectacle required more grandiose personalities. Chief among these was Joe Humphries, the iconic Madison Square Garden ring announcer of the early twentieth century who pioneered much of what we now associate with the standard ring announcer of both boxing and wrestling. Following the example of Humphries and his West Coast counterpart Dan Tobey, ring announcers honed their skills to become consummate masters of ceremony, presiding over the night's action with authority and enthusiasm.

Back then, they used note cards to help them remember all the information they needed to relate, including names, weights, and home towns. But by the 1980s, with the desire for more polished TV broadcasts, ring announcers were expected to memorize everything, making their job an even more difficult one. Although in some ways a relic of the carnival-like atmosphere of pro wrestling's past, the ring announcer remains a vital part of the show. Traditionally a male role, in recent years major breakthroughs for women have taken place as both of the industry's major organizations, WWE and TNA, have utilized female ring announcers (Lilian Garcia and Christy Hemme, respectively).

In This Corner: Ten of Wrestling's Best Barkers

- Dan Tobey: What Joe Humphries was to New York, Tobey was to California, using his larger-than-life presence to add importance to events at Hollywood's Legion Stadium and the Olympic Auditorium for much of the first half of the twentieth century. He was famous for his exuberant, staccato delivery and hand gestures, eschewing the use of a microphone. A caricature of him can be seen in the 1950 Bugs Bunny cartoon, *Bunny Hugged.*

- "Friendly" Bob Freed: Each Thursday night in the 1950s and '60s, fans tuning in to Vincent J. McMahon's Capitol Wrestling from Washington, D.C. heard Bob Freed introducing some of the WWWF's earliest performers. A former USO master of ceremonies during World War II, he later became the ring announcer at Madison Square Garden, following the death of the legendary Johnny Addie.

- Gary Michael Cappetta: A throwback to the nasal announcers of decades past, Cappetta was the WWWF announcer for the *All-Star Wrestling* show and for the Philadelphia Spectrum during the 1970s and '80s, and later enjoyed a high-profile stint on WCW television during the 1990s.

- Howard Finkel: The best known and most revered among modern wrestling fans, Finkel was the WWF/E's top ring announcer from the late 1970s through the early 2000s, including a twenty-five-year run as Madison Square Garden announcer, following the retirement of Bob Freed. His booming voice (". . . and NEW champion!") was an integral part of the WWF/E product for many years. Retired from full-time announcing, Finkel currently works as a historical consultant to WWE.

- Harry Balough: Between the eras of Joe Humphries and Johnny Addie, Balough was the chief announcer for boxing and wrestling at Madison Square Garden for much of the 1930s and 1940s. Many of his New York–accented affectations—"Ladeez and gentlemen! The winnah and new champeen!"—later became stereotypical ring-announcer tropes.

- Jimmy Lennon: California's chief boxing and wrestling announcer following the retirement of Dan Tobey, Lennon was a fixture at the Los Angeles Olympic Auditorium during the 1950s through the '70s. Known for his unmistakable airy tenor voice, he was so respected by promoters

The Fink kicks off the festivities at Syracuse's Carrier Dome on December 30, 2009, for WWE's final show of the decade. *shstrng/Wikimedia*

due to his caché as a boxing announcer that he was sometimes brought in to other NWA territories for really big matches. He can even be seen as a ring announcer in the film *Rocky III*.

- Joe Humphries: The innovator of the role of the modern ring announcer, Humphries was the very first to add his own personality, delivering his announcements in a bold, theatrical voice rather than merely stating them conversationally. Beginning his career at the turn of the twentieth century, in the days before electronic amplification, Humphries didn't require a microphone. Known for waving his trademark boater hat to silence the crowd as he entered the ring, he was the chief announcer for New York boxing and wrestling until his retirement in the 1930s.

- Joe McHugh: Old-school WWWF fans remember the diminutive, bespectacled McHugh from weekly broadcasts of *Championship Wrestling*. He continued in his role until the WWF's national expansion in the mid-1980s, depriving fans in other parts of the country from ever hearing "I'm Joooooooeeee McHugh!"

- Johnny Addie: Boxing old-timers look back with fondness on the great Madison Square Garden barker of the 1950s and '60s, who called some of the sport's most historic encounters at that venue. Addie also covered wrestling at the Garden right up until his death, and became known for repeating the last name of wrestlers, a practice later imitated by the likes of Bob Freed and Joe McHugh.

- Tony Chimel: Starting out as a member of the WWF ring crew in the 1980s, Chimel got his start as an announcer in 1991, filling in for lead announcer Howard Finkel whenever necessary. He later became the weekly announcer for WWE's *SmackDown!*, and currently works as the announcer for WWE house shows, as well as the WWE Network program, *Main Event.*

Additional Worthies: Tom Miller, Lilian Garcia, Mike McGuirk, Justin Roberts, David Penzer, Joel Gertner, Bob Artese, Hugo Savinovitch, Mel Phillips, Jack Lee, Buddy Wagner, and Mark Lowrance.

26

The State of the Game

Professional Wrestling Today

Can you imagine the level of a mind that watches wrestling?
—Frederick (Max von Sydow), *Hannah and Her Sisters* (1986)

Although often referred to these days as "sports-entertainment" (to the chagrin of some and the confusion of others), pro wrestling is alive and well in the twenty-first century—in some ways thriving stronger than ever, and in others a decimated version of its former existence. It all depends on perspective, but whether one regards the changes that have occurred in the business as positives or negatives, it cannot be denied that it has transformed dramatically. Just as it always has, pro wrestling has changed into something utterly unique and different from what it was in earlier time periods. Not since a century ago, when the industry was defined by great individual matches rather than by a myriad of companies, has wrestling been so unified in the public eye. Never before has the structure of the business been so consolidated among so few power brokers. Today's pro wrestling is entertainment through and through, featuring performers who are multimedia superstars in ways that their predecessors could not have imagined.

For the first time in living memory, the professional wrestling industry is dominated by a single company: Vince McMahon's WWE. Not since the days of the Gold Dust Trio in the 1920s has a single organization had such widespread control, and not even the infamous trio enjoyed quite the stranglehold that WWE has enjoyed, and for so long. There have been other companies out there in recent years, most notably Dixie Carter's TNA Wrestling, but, by far, the lion's share of the market is dominated by McMahon. To the average individual, the terms "pro wrestling" and "WWE" are almost interchangeable. In addition to TNA, there is also a thriving independent circuit out there, but make no mistake about it: Vince McMahon has achieved the goal which he set out to accomplish back in the mid-1980s: he is the absolute master of his industry.

"Even though there's one company that owns most of the wrestling world, the state of the business today is fantastic," says Bill Apter, who has covered it for more than four decades. "No matter what country you go to, people know who these wrestlers are. China, India, anywhere. Everybody knows them."

Multimedia Madness

The structure of the professional wrestling business today makes it almost unrecognizable compared to what it was just a generation ago. Live-event ticket sales, once the backbone of the industry, are now a very minor source of revenue. Pro wrestling companies have diversified, branching out into many other areas to touch their fans in countless ways. Merchandizing, once thought of as ancillary, is central to the business model of companies like WWE and TNA. Fans today can purchase T-shirts, action figures, baseball caps, books, DVDs, and almost any other type of branded product one can imagine, emblazoned with the likenesses of their favorite performer or the logo of their favorite company. Licensees from companies all over the world clamber to land the account of a company like WWE, knowing that fans will buy almost anything with those instantly recognizable interlocking "W"s on it.

Television has been a tool of wrestling promoters for many decades, but today it is much more than that. Rather than just a method of getting viewers to attend live events or even to purchase pay-per-view shows, television is an end in itself. Companies live and die by the weekly ratings of their flagship shows—*Monday Night Raw* and *SmackDown!* in WWE's case, and *Impact Wrestling* in the case of TNA. The deals those companies strike with networks like USA and Destination America to carry their shows is incredibly big business.

When it comes to diversification, WWE has led the way. The company has its own record label, its own Hollywood film studio, consumer products division, home-video distributor, and more. Its website, as with the websites of most noted contemporary wrestling companies, features an entire section devoted just to selling its merchandise to the public, thus cutting out the middle man completely. A publicly traded company, today's WWE is a thoroughly corporate entity on a level that the old carny promoters couldn't have fathomed.

"It's become corporate, like everything else," offers Evan Ginzburg, life-long fan, longtime promoter, and co-producer of the 2008 film *The Wrestler*. "It was a blue-collar thing, and back when I was a kid it was three-to-six dollars for a ticket. You went every month to the Garden on a Monday night. Now it's become about how much merchandise they can sell. The blue-collar days are long gone. This is about selling T-shirts. . . . Ironically, there are wrestlers today doing things in the ring that the old-timers couldn't have dreamt of. It's just how they choose to present it. They turned it into a corporate product to sell toys and gimmicks."

The WWE Network

Another major source of revenue is pay-per-view television, the medium McMahon himself pioneered in the 1980s, and which took the place of ticket sales as the predominant way for fans to experience live events. However, although other companies like TNA and Ring of Honor continue to profit greatly from that technology, in the case of market leader WWE, things have changed. After nearly three decades of relying on the pay-per-view business as its bread and butter, Vince McMahon made a bold move reminiscent of his own leap from house shows to pay-per-views in the first place. On February 24, 2014, his company launched the WWE Network, a long-awaited streaming subscription platform

WWE is known for its annual *Tribute to the Troops* show for the U.S. Armed Forces. At the 2010 event, held at Fort Hood, Texas, Kane was one of the stars on hand.

Shamsuddin Muhammad/Wikimedia

through which fans can experience content on demand via their smart TVs, computers, tablets, and mobile devices.

"It certainly is potentially a game changer," says Dave Meltzer of the *Wrestling Observer* newsletter. "In the long run, it's the future. For the wrestling business, pay-per-view is going away."

Offering access to the company video archives that include all previous pay-per-view events, as well as old episodes of *Monday Night Raw* and *Saturday Night's Main Event*, the purchased footage of defunct companies like WCW, ECW, and World Class, as well as originally produced programming, the "over the top" service was met with enthusiasm by many die-hard fans. Most enticing of all to viewers on the fence about subscribing is the inclusion of every live monthly WWE pay-per-view event. Because of this offering, the very term "pay-per-view" has become outdated, as the primary way fans are now watching shows like *WrestleMania*, *SummerSlam*, and *Royal Rumble* is via the network. The trusted pay-per-view model that has served the company well since 1985 has been forsaken in favor of a service that is completely in-house, eliminating the cable and satellite operators with which WWE previously had to share profits.

Because of this, WWE's entire new business model has now been built around the network and the hopes for its success. It's all about growing a subscriber base, with compelling programming and ease of access. Upon its launch, the WWE Network was hailed as another master stroke from McMahon, and most fully expected it to transform the way many entertainment and sports companies provide content to their fans. However, following the initial fanfare, growth was not quite as robust as expected, with WWE hoping for a million subscribers by *WrestleMania XXX* but not reaching that number for nearly another year.

Cable companies retaliated against the introduction of the network, dropping WWE pay-per-view programming. With TV deals a major source of revenue, the company took a hit when NBCUniversal, the media conglomerate that airs *Raw* and *SmackDown!*, offered WWE a lower-than-expected contract renewal, believed to be the result of the perceived lack of exclusivity created by the subscription network. There is no denying that there have been some growing pains with the introduction of the new technology, and no one said it would be risk free. However, most insiders expect the WWE Network, in the long run, not only to succeed, but to alter the industry.

"Vince McMahon changed the business in terms of the territories, in terms of cable television, pay-per-view, and now the network," says Bill Apter. "This is going to set a precedent for other companies to do this, and I don't mean just wrestling companies."

A Changing Product for Changing Fans

Due in part to this changing business model, but also due to many other factors stretching back years, the product has also transformed drastically. Never before has the action been this fast and furious, as performers work a style that is more exciting and also more legitimately dangerous than at most points throughout wrestling history. At the same time, there is always a trade-off, and old-school fans will point to the decline of solid ring psychology and coherent storytelling that comes with amping up the action and speeding everything up to accommodate the contemporary attention span.

In addition, in-ring action shares the spotlight with so much more. The average high-level wrestling show features unprecedentedly high production values, with elaborate stages, state of the art sound and pyro, and HD cameras that make viewers feel almost like they are actually in the arena.

Today's style of wrestling can be very demanding on the body, as anyone who's ever been chokeslammed by The Big Show (in this case, Randy Orton) can attest. *miguel.discart/ Wikimedia*

Performers spend as much time on the mic as they do on the mat, and opening the show with an extended promo is now the norm. If there is one major take-away from the current pro wrestling product, it's that when it comes to "sports-entertainment," the "entertainment" aspect definitely takes precedent over the "sport."

The types of stories that are told have come a long way, as well. No longer are the simple babyface/heel grudges of years gone by enough to hold the attention of the modern fans. Angles are much more elaborate, and involve a great deal more nuance that requires many scripted vignettes to be incorporated into the show. Breaking the fourth wall, WWE and TNA commonly present backstage skits that stretch suspension of disbelief to the max—the camera is now omniscient, recording backstage interactions between wrestlers just as if they were a part of any other scripted dramatic TV series.

Crafting these stories is a battery of creative personnel that is light years beyond the old booking committees of years past. For its television shows, WWE utilizes a full creative team, also similar to what would be found on any other scripted dramatic TV series. Combining the insight of wrestling veterans like Dusty Rhodes and Michael Hayes with the entertainment industry know-how of experienced television writers, all overseen by Vince McMahon, his daughter Stephanie, and son-in-law Paul "Triple H" Levesque, it's a very modern system producing wrestling that is more a "television show" than ever before. When the bell rings, however, that's where the role of creative ends. Although the team decides who wins and loses, the actual nuts and bolts of the match is still something worked out by the performers with the guidance of producers (formerly known as road agents) that include retired wrestlers like David Finlay, Dean Malenko, and Jamie Noble, as well as Al Snow and Hector Guerrero in TNA.

In the post-Attitude Era environment, the creative forces in WWE have largely reined in the maturity level of much of the content, opting for a return to courting families and younger children as part of the fan base. Although the content is nowhere near as kiddie-oriented as it was during the Hulkamania and New Generation Eras of the late '80s through mid-'90s, it has caused many cynical fans to refer to the current climate as the "PG Era." Perhaps in retaliation, WWE itself has preferred to label it the "Reality Era," emphasizing the more realistic and less exaggerated tone for which they are currently aiming (although the accuracy of that claim is questionable at best).

When crafting the pro wrestling product of today, creative teams are keeping in mind the taste of today's very unique fan base. With wrestling's true nature an open secret for many years, an entirely new breed of fan has been cultivated, just as passionate as before but with a very different perspective—in fact, WWE has even branded them with their own name: the WWE Universe. While they may not all grasp the details of the way the business operates, the vast majority of today's fans do understand that what they're watching is completely scripted entertainment. And they watch it, first and foremost, to be entertained. They are, to a certain extent, in on the game, and thus expect the talent to put on a proper show for them. No longer buying into the drama in the same way they used to, they respond to what makes them gasp, what makes them laugh, what makes their jaws drop.

To wit, they aren't always watching to see who wins and loses as much as they are to see how the story progresses. It matters far less now how "tough" or "strong" a wrestler is perceived to be, just whether or not they can captivate their audience. They are aware of who is getting a promotional "push" and who is getting "buried," and root for their favorite performers to get that push in the same way that old-school fans rooted for their favorites to win matches. This meta-awareness causes the fans to put pressure on the ones making the creative decisions in ways old-school fans (who didn't realize that *anyone* was making creative decisions) ever did. The so-called Internet Wrestling Community (or IWC, for short) can be a formidable force in the current pro wrestling environment.

Part of the reason for this shift is the rise of mixed martial arts, which has evolved into a major professional sport in the twenty-first century. Presenting legitimate physical competition that incorporates boxing, wrestling, and many other fighting disciplines, MMA companies like the Ultimate Fighting Championship have, in some ways, taken things back full circle, to the days when pro wrestlers were not performers but actual combatants. With such a viewing option now available to fans, there is no question that the pro wrestling fan base has been affected. If fans want to see contests of toughness and athletic skill, they can turn to MMA. Those old-school wrestling fans who watched for that reason are now largely gone. In their place are fans who are interested purely in entertainment, plain and simple. The question of "who would beat whom?" is more irrelevant than ever.

"People don't really care if the world champion is a tough guy or not," says Dave Meltzer. "If they can entertain, no one cares if they are really good wrestlers or not. . . . Who wins and loses, while important, is viewed in a very different way. They still get mad, but before you would get mad at the heel. Now you get mad at the booker. Before, you wanted a guy to win the world championship because you were behind him, and because of the idea that he was winning something tangible. Now you get mad if the bookers don't put your guy in the big matches."

Major league wrestling has had to shift gears in order to meet the new expectations of its fans. A look at some of WWE's more recent main-eventers, including CM Punk and Daniel Bryan, bears this out. These were not performers who had the typical muscle-bound, superhero "look" that WWE typically goes for. Rather, they had charisma, intelligence, and a certain everyman quality that made fans relate to them exactly because they appear more down-to-earth. The extent to which the current fan is unimpressed by the traditional trappings of "toughness" or massive size was demonstrated in the way in which the WWE Universe rejected the return of the six-foot-six-inch, 278-pound, tanned and chiseled Batista, who was booked to be a babyface superstar at the start of 2014, only to be booed out of every arena in which he appeared and torn apart on social media by bored fans who much preferred the five-foot-eight-inch, 190-pound, bearded vegan Daniel Bryan.

"They know it's not real. They just want their favorite to win," adds Meltzer. "They have a huge influence, because if it was left up to the devices of the people running it, Bryan would've never gotten out of the mid-card, because he's not their kind of guy. The fans reacted in ways they didn't originally foresee, and they eventually learned how to work with that."

As a result of the conflict that can sometimes occur between creative writers and fans, in many ways the creative team itself can often draw more real-life heat from fans than any onscreen heel characters. Both WWE and TNA have been known to play into this for storyline purposes, including a 2014 angle in which real-life TNA president Dixie Carter was called to task by fan favorite Tommy Dreamer for not giving the fans what they want and only feeding her own ego.

Social Media Revolution

Fans are more influential than ever before, and a big reason for this is the rise of social media. Although initially suspicious of technology thanks to the all-exposing nature of the Internet, the business in recent years has fully embraced social media as the newest and most effective way to connect with fans. During a typical pro wrestling broadcast, fans are inundated with Twitter hashtags and top trends, and in this day and age, instead of being shown a performer's weight and home town on screen, viewers are shown their Twitter handles. Although there has been some conflict as to whether Twitter profiles should be in character or not, many performers have been savvy enough to use Twitter, Instagram, and other forms of social media to their advantage.

WWE, in particular, has harnessed the power of social media to make it a legitimate extension of the show, with individual Facebook pages for each of its performers, and angles that are actually continued and enhanced on Twitter. Combining the show with its own mobile app, WWE has created a whole "second-screen experience" for those willing and able to partake in it. Fans are actively encouraged to interact with the show using their mobile devices, even influencing it by making decisions via live polling. Fan interaction has indeed come a long way from the days of little old ladies whacking heels on the head with their purses as they came down the aisle.

Total Nonstop Action

As previously stated, the professional wrestling industry, particularly in North America, has been dominated in recent years by one company more thoroughly than at any other time in its history. But although WWE may be the biggest show around, it hasn't been the only show around. Starting in 2002, another company based out of Nashville, Tennessee, has provided WWE with the closest thing to direct competition within the wrestling business itself. It takes a lot for a pro wrestling company to be considered major league today, but with national cable TV coverage, working relationships with other organizations all over the globe, a roster of popular stars both homegrown and formerly of WWE, and a regular pay-per-view presence, Total Nonstop Action, otherwise known as TNA Wrestling, positioned itself as the number-two company in the United States.

Back in March 2001, former WWF and WCW wrestler Jeff Jarrett found himself out of a job. WCW had just been purchased by the WWF, and for the first time in modern pro wrestling history there was only one major company in North America. Due to a 1999 financial dispute with Vince McMahon, Jarrett was persona non grata in the WWF, so there didn't seem to be much future for him in a post-WCW world. That is, until he sat down with his father, former Memphis promoter Jerry Jarrett, as well as former WCW announcer and front-office employee Bob Ryder, and came up with the idea to start their own wrestling company.

The Opening Bell

With help from funding provided by healthcare corporation HealthSouth, the new company came into being in May 2002, and put on its first show the following month. The Jarretts brought in former WWF and WCW creative writer Vince Russo as head booker, and it was he who reportedly came up with the name Total Nonstop Action (primarily for the "TNA" play on words that would indicate the company's edgy, mature content). The organization would be affiliated with the National Wrestling Alliance—even though it was a shadow of its former self, the feeling was that the association of the NWA would help the group seem major league right off the bat. Without a regular TV deal, the idea was conceived to run low-priced weekly events on pay-per-view cable TV, from the company's home arena in Nashville, known as the TNA Asylum.

The weekly pay-per-view format wouldn't be the only thing that distinguished TNA from WWE. The company made waves through the innovative use of a six-sided ring, which set the product apart from a purely visual standpoint. Capitalizing on the wealth of young, agile performers on its roster, including the likes of "The Phenomenal" A. J. Styles, Low Ki, Amazing Red, Chris Sabin, and others, TNA set itself apart with the creation of the X Division, which emphasized high-flying, extreme-style action without limiting weight class, as other companies had done in the past.

When HealthSouth bailed on TNA due to financial difficulties, the company was saved by marketing executive Dixie Carter, who convinced her parents, owners of Dallas-based energy company Panda Energy

The tag team of Magnus & Desmond Wolfe at a July 2010 taping of *Impact* in Orlando, Florida.   *daysofthundr46/ Wikimedia*

International, to purchase a majority interest from the Jarretts. In 2003, Dixie Carter was named president of TNA, with the Jarretts remaining on as minority owners. Within a year, TNA had its first national television deal with Fox Sports, for a weekly show called *Impact*. The weekly pay-per-views were eliminated in favor of the monthly three-hour pay-per-view approach used by WWE. Suddenly, there were two wrestling companies on national television. When TNA jumped from Fox Sports to WWE's former home on SpikeTV in 2005, the company's profile was raised even higher.

Wrestling Matters

As much as WCW had done to distinguish itself from Vince McMahon's product in the past, TNA prided itself on more in-ring content, a wrestling-based product that stressed athleticism over entertainment. Nevertheless, their success at achieving that over the years has been questioned by some naysayers who have accused the company of trying too hard to emulate WWE with far less than that company's resources. Indeed, many former WWE headliners have enjoyed extended time in TNA; these include former WWE World Champions Jeff Hardy, Kurt Angle (who spent more time in TNA than he did in WWE), Ric Flair, and even WWE's living embodiment, Hulk Hogan, who served as on-air talent and behind-the-scenes consultant.

TNA parted ways with the NWA in 2007, preferring to carve its own unique identity instead. Amping up its competition with WWE, it even tried to go head-to-head by programming *Impact* on Monday nights against *Raw*. Following that short-lived experiment, TNA opted to return to its normal Thursday night timeslot, attempting to take *Impact* on the road to a different location each week, à la WWE's *Raw* and *SmackDown!*

Most recently, the company has struggled to maintain its position in the increasingly difficult landscape of major league pro wrestling. It was dealt a very serious blow in July 2014 when SpikeTV officially canceled *Impact*, pulling the plug on TNA's national TV exposure. Declining TV ratings and live attendance had resulted in declining revenue, which combined with the expenditures associated with touring and hiring expensive talent, led some to wonder about the future of America's number-two wrestling company. The weekly touring stopped, followed by a mass exodus of talent including Hogan, TNA perennials A. J. Styles and Christopher Daniels, and even Jeff Jarrett himself.

The very survival of TNA Wrestling was in jeopardy until November 2014 when the company made a deal with Discovery Communications that allowed *Impact* to move to the cable channel Destination America. Although a distant second-place to WWE, TNA has provided wrestling fans with a viable alternative, which is always a healthy thing for the business. To last for as long as it has is a testament to the willingness of the fan base to support more than one product. But in today's pro wrestling climate, national TV is crucial to staying in the game, and with reduced exposure on the much lower-profile Destination America, it will continue to be a challenge for TNA to remain an impact player in the wrestling business, rather than just another casualty.

Major Recent Stars

These performers have helped take pro wrestling into the twenty-first century, and have been the best and brightest in the business in recent years.

- A. J. Styles
- Austin Aries
- Bad News Barrett
- Batista
- The Bella Twins
- Bray Wyatt
- Brock Lesnar
- Cesaro
- CM Punk
- Daniel Bryan
- Dean Ambrose
- Jeff Hardy
- John Cena
- The Miz
- Paige
- Randy Orton
- Roman Reigns
- Samoa Joe
- Seth Rollins
- Sheamus

The Face of WWE

In the '50s it was Antonino Rocca. The '60s and '70s had Bruno Sammartino. The '80s boasted Hulk Hogan, and the '90s had Stone Cold Steve Austin. But since the mid-2000s, the number-one star in professional wrestling's number-one company, and the most high-profile performer in the entire business, has been John Cena. Although his decade-plus of WWE dominance has been a source of great polarization among the fan base, WWE has transformed Cena into the most dominant and decorated performer since the heyday of Austin and The Rock a generation ago. And unlike his predecessors, who came and went over the years as they made their way through other companies, thanks to the industry's transformed landscape, Cena has enjoyed a longer uninterrupted stay at the very top of WWE's main-event picture than nearly any other headliner in the company's history.

John Felix Anthony Cena, Jr., was born on April 23, 1977, in West Newbury, Massachusetts. Growing up in the 1980s, the young Cena became a die-hard WWF fan during the glory days of Hulkamania. He was further exposed to the business due to the fact that his father, John Cena, Sr., spent some time in the business as an announcer, manager, and promoter under the name Johnny Fabulous. Taking the route of his hero Hulk Hogan, in 1998 the twenty-one-year-old Cena headed out to California to embark on a bodybuilding career almost immediately after graduating from college with a degree in exercise physiology.

While working to support himself at a local Gold's Gym, Cena was urged to try out for Ultimate Pro Wrestling, California's top independent promotion at the time. Impressed with his ripped physique, UPW promoter Rick Bassman got Cena trained, and presented him as The Prototype, using a robotic gimmick reminiscent of The Terminator. At the time, UPW had a loose working relationship with the WWF, which helped Cena score a series of tryout matches that led to his being signed to a developmental deal in 2001.

After honing his craft for a year in the developmental system at Ohio Valley Wrestling, Cena was brought up to the main roster of the newly renamed WWE in June 2002, facing main-event star Kurt Angle in his first televised match. Although the youngster was initially quite popular as an underdog, he was quickly turned heel, using a white rapper gimmick that saw him portrayed as something close to pro wrestling's answer to Marky Mark. Although some elements of this character, including throwback jerseys, baseball caps, and other accoutrements, would remain throughout his career, Cena quickly developed beyond the limitations of the gimmick, and it soon became clear that WWE had its next potential main-event superstar on its hands.

After building momentum as one of the company's top faces, Cena was at last given the decisive push in 2005, capturing his first of an eventual fifteen WWE World Heavyweight Championships (as of this writing), with a win over John

"Bradshaw" Layfield at *WrestleMania 21* in Los Angeles. Along with the likes of Randy Orton and Batista, Cena became part of a new crop of WWE main-event performers late in the first decade of the 2000s. But it was abundantly clear that Cena was head and shoulders above the others; he is an attractive, clean-cut, well-spoken babyface champion who was soon being featured in motion pictures, on talk shows, and at countless charity events. John Cena had become the face of WWE.

Nevertheless, the ascendancy was not without its unique complications. Not long after Cena's push to the main event, a sizeable and vocal portion of the fan base began to reject the squeaky-clean, seemingly invincible hero, feeling he was being forced down their throats in place of edgier performers they felt were more talented and deserving. But with his strong appeal among women and especially small children, no other performer on the roster moved merchandise like Cena, whose T-shirts, baseball caps, wristbands, and just about anything else with his name on it became WWE's equivalent of printing money. The so-called "Cenation" responded positively to his inspirational mantras like "Hustle, Loyalty, Respect," "Rise Above Hate," and "Never Give Up." As a result, WWE continued to promote him as a babyface, leading to one of the most fascinating fan dynamics in wrestling history. At any given event, half the crowd can be heard chanting "Let's Go, Cena!" while the other half just as vociferously answers back, "Cena Sucks!"

Fan division notwithstanding, Cena's position as WWE's public ambassador is unquestionable, and was further solidified thanks to a pair of *WrestleMania* main events against The Rock in 2012 and 2013, in which he represented the embodiment of the modern WWE. Today it isn't uncommon for Cena to be referred to as the greatest WWE World Champion of all time, and after more than a decade at the top, he is beginning to ascend to the status of WWE legend/superstar emeritus, making way for a new generation of young main-eventers.

The Viper

If anyone can be said to possess the iconic look of a modern-day professional wrestler, it would be third-generation grappler Randy Orton, who has been a WWE main-event mainstay virtually since his official debut with the company in 2002. Along with John Cena, he has come to embody the contemporary era of the business. Once touted as the future of the industry, he has more than fulfilled that promise. And were it not for some personality conflicts and an infamous attitude that has gotten him into some hot water over the years, there are some who feel that wrestling's bad boy may have achieved even more.

Randall Keith Orton was born on April 1, 1980, in Knoxville, Tennessee, the son of "Cowboy" Bob Orton, Jr., a well-known heel performer from WWF's 1980s Hulkamania heyday. But that wasn't the limit to Randy's family legacy in the business: His grandfather, "Cowboy" Bob Orton, Sr., had been a top star of the 1950s and '60s, even main-eventing at Madison Square Garden in the early days of the WWWF. His uncle, Barry Orton, had been a WWF preliminary wrestler who made headlines in the early 1990s with allegations of maltreatment and sexual misconduct within the business.

It seemed Orton was destined for wrestling superstardom from the beginning, and despite the concerns of his famous father, he had set his sights on it from an early age, joining the wrestling squad while attending high school in suburban St. Louis. But before entering the business, the recently graduated Orton would make one major stop along the way, which would provide some hints as to the personal demeanor that would later come to haunt him. In 1998, he joined the U.S. Marine Corps, but ran into trouble when he repeatedly defied superior officers and went AWOL. Private First Class Orton was court-martialed, served thirty-eight days in military prison, and was dishonorably discharged from the service.

With the help of his father, Orton began to train for a career in the family business, and after a year on the St. Louis independent scene, he was signed to a WWF developmental contract in 2001. Distinguishing himself in WWF's feeder league Ohio Valley Wrestling alongside fellow future stars John Cena, Brock Lesnar, and Batista, Orton soon became one of a number of young athletes called up to the main roster during a time when the company had just rebranded itself as WWE and was looking for some fresh faces to build the company around.

Orton was highly regarded thanks to his impressive appearance and revered family history, and came in with high expectations in the spring of 2002. Although he had babyface looks, his cocky attitude soon tagged him as a natural heel, and he was teamed up with Batista, Triple H, and Ric Flair in the super-stable known as Evolution. It was there that Orton came into his own and began turning heads, as well as capturing virtually every title the company had to offer, including the World Heavyweight Championship, which he would eventually win (as of this writing) a dozen times. Later, WWE positioned him as the "Legend Killer," going through one former wrestling great after another as his heel heat grew and grew.

But with Orton's enormous and early success also came a certain amount of genuine hubris. Stories began to circulate of the youngster's difficulty backstage, and an immature attitude that included reported incidents of alleged harassment of female talent and drug use. These infractions led to suspensions and other disciplinary action, and many insiders feel that Orton's momentum as a star performer was damaged over time, preventing him from completely fulfilling the potential that many saw in him.

Despite all that, the so-called "Apex Predator" has nevertheless managed to etch his name among the all-time greats, achieving a level of success few can ever hope for, as a part of the most successful company in pro wrestling history. At the end of 2013, he unified WWE's two versions of the world championship, becoming the company's first undisputed champion in over a decade. Just as his father and grandfather before him, he has become one of the top stars of his era, a "Legend Killer" who became a legend.

The Juggernaut

In today's pro wrestling environment, there are a very limited number of places for new performers to hone their craft and prepare themselves for the big time. Therefore, in order to create the next generation of great talent and ensure that the business has a steady supply of quality athletes, companies like WWE have been compelled to make the process of developing new talent an in-house affair, cultivating a developmental system that can feed directly into their main roster. Right now, that system consists of NXT, a Florida-based program that has succeeded in grooming a whole crop of future main-eventers. But perhaps no NXT product is a greater WWE developmental success story than the second-generation powerhouse poised to become the next great pro wrestling superstar, Roman Reigns.

A member of one of the industry's most revered and populous families, he was born Leati Joseph Anoa'i on May 25, 1985, in Pensacola, Florida. His father, Leati Anoa'i, Sr., had competed as Sika, one-half of The Wild Samoans, one of the greatest tag teams of the 1970s and '80s. Also included in the incredible extended Samoan-American wrestling dynasty was his uncle, Wild Samoan Afa, his cousins Yokozuna, Rikishi, Samu, Umaga, The Usos, his brother Matt "Rosey" Anoa'i, and extended family members High Chief Peter Maivia and The Rock.

Before distinguishing himself in the ring, the gridiron was the first place that Anoa'i made a name for himself, becoming a first-team All-ACC defensive tackle at the Georgia Institute of Technology during his senior year, in 2006. He was signed by the Minnesota Vikings of the NFL in 2007, and later spent some time with the Jacksonville Jaguars and the CFL's Edmonton Eskimos. He played a single season as a defensive tackle, known for his overwhelming speed and power on the field—but an injury ended his football career prematurely, leading him to continue his family's legacy in the squared circle.

Unlike the majority of athletes who spend a little time cutting their teeth on the independent scene, Anoa'i went directly to WWE, starting his career as a completely homegrown talent in the developmental territory then known as Florida Championship Wrestling. Under the name Roman Leakee, he debuted on September 9, 2010, losing to Richie Steamboat, son of the legendary Ricky "The Dragon" Steamboat. While in FCW, he learned his craft alongside other future main roster talents like Antonio Cesaro, Bo Dallas, Husky Harris (a.k.a. Bray Wyatt) Big E. Langston, Alexander Rusev, Damien Sandow, and eventual teammates Dean Ambrose and Seth Rollins.

In 2012, FCW was rebranded as NXT, taking its name from the previous talent search series run by WWE. By that point, Roman was one of the group's most promising young performers. Finally, he got the big call from WWE creative, who renamed him Roman Reigns and teamed him up with Ambrose and Rollins as The Shield, an edgy group of renegades that incorporated aspects of real-life anti-authority renegades like Anonymous and Occupy Wall Street. The trio first appeared at the 2012 *Survivor Series* and were soon the talk of the WWE Universe, a radical, unpredictable heel unit intent on "exposing" what they considered hypocrisy and injustice in WWE.

Right from the beginning, Reigns distinguished himself as the most promising of the three very talented newcomers—a sleek enforcer who impressed fans with his lightning-fast power moves and intense charisma. He and Rollins enjoyed a five-month reign as WWE Tag Team Champions in 2013, which began with a win over Kane & Daniel Bryan at *Extreme Rules* in May. In two consecutive *WrestleManias*, The Shield bested three-man teams of WWE main-eventers, including Randy Orton, Sheamus & Big Show in 2013, and Kane & The New Age Outlaws in 2014. Reigns began to stand out as the most dominant of the group, setting a record for most *Survivor Series* eliminations (four) and most *Royal Rumble* eliminations (twelve). Right after *WrestleMania XXX*, overwhelming fan support led WWE creative to turn the group babyface, solidified with a barn-burner of a feud with Triple H's Evolution faction.

But it would take the implosion of The Shield itself for things to really heat up for Reigns. When Rollins turned on the group in June 2014, Reigns suddenly found himself one of the hottest singles performers in the entire business. With the support of the WWE Universe at an all-time high, WWE moved him into the World Heavyweight title picture, positioning him as the heir apparent to John Cena as the company's top star.

As of this writing, Roman Reigns is on the verge of greatness, a WWE mega-star in the making. He represents the new breed of pro wrestler, built from the ground up within a developmental system that prepared him for the role he enjoys today. The future is wide open for the second-generation force of nature, and his greatest achievements are still years ahead.

27

Shoots, Marks, Broadways, and Babyfaces

A Glossary of Insider Wrestling Terms

Even when I figured out what wrestling was, I was still a fan.
—John Carpenter

angle, *noun.* A storyline which progresses from week to week, month to month (or in rare cases, year to year) and serves to generate interest in wrestling matches. It usually involves two or more wrestlers who develop a rivalry and subsequently wrestle a match or series of matches.
example: One of the most successful angles of all time involved Vince McMahon playing an evil promoter who was constantly foiled by his rebellious employee, Stone Cold Steve Austin.

babyface, *noun.* A wrestler who is promoted by a company as "a good guy," someone for whom the fans can cheer. Often abbreviated as simply "face," the character is occasionally referred to as a "fan favorite." The definition has been challenged in recent years as wrestling's moral standards have become more ambiguous.

blade, *verb.* The practice of secretly cutting oneself with a hidden razor blade or other sharp object in order to give the appearance of having been injured during a match. This is done by performers to add an element of realism to a match, and is usually performed on the forehead or scalp.
example: Dusty Rhodes was well known for being willing to blade whenever asked.

blow up, *verb.* To be out of breath or completely exhausted, no longer able to perform efficiently.

example: The Ultimate Warrior had a reputation for blowing up early in matches.

booker, *noun.* Someone who plans out storylines and/or scripts interviews and matches. He helps decide the characters which will be played by the performers and who will wrestle whom. He also decides how the finishes of matches will play out, and pretty much controls everything you see on TV or in the arena.
example: WWE's bookers include Vince McMahon, Paul "Triple H" Levesque, and Stephanie McMahon Levesque.

booking, *noun.* Essentially, the "script," or the way in which a match, event, or storyline plays out.
example: Batista's return to WWE in 2014 was rejected by many fans due to questionable booking.

broadway, *noun.* A match that goes to a time-limit draw, traditionally lasting one hour, but occasionally of shorter, or even longer, duration.

bump, *noun.* Any blow, fall, etc., absorbed by a wrestler that makes it appear as though he is actually being hurt by his opponent. Bumps often involve a certain degree of risk and pain, and the more serious-looking ones are only performed by wrestlers who know how to handle them properly.
example: When a wrestler is bodyslammed, he is taking a bump.

verb. The act of taking a blow, fall, etc., in a match. A wrestler who takes these physical risks at the hands of an opponent is said to "bumping for" that opponent.

bury, *verb.* To ruin a wrestler's credibility with the fans by making him seem utterly unimportant, whether through the way he is described or the way he is portrayed. This is the opposite of a "push."
example: After an initially promising run that included winning WWE's *Money in the Bank* ladder match, Damien Sandow was buried by being turned into a bumbling comedy figure.

call, *verb.* The act performed by a wrestler indicating to his "opponent" what moves or actions will be performed. This takes place during the actual match and can consist of one wrestler whispering to the other or signaling in some other pre-arranged manner.
example: Shawn Michaels was known for being able to call a great match.

gimmick, *noun.* The meaning is pretty straightforward, except in wrestling the word is used specifically in reference to a gimmick used by a wrestler to create a character or further a storyline.

example: The Honky Tonk Man's gimmick was that he was an Elvis impersonator.

hardway, *adverb.* The way in which a blow is delivered, occurring through "real" physical contact as opposed to simulated actions. This is usually, but not always, the result of an accident.
example: When Ric Flair accidentally punched Bray Wyatt in the face at a 2014 Madison Square Garden live event, Wyatt bled hardway.

heat, *noun.* An enthusiastically negative reaction from a live crowd toward a heel. True heat involves fans responding to the storyline in a manner desired by the booker (i.e., booing the "bad guys"). However, if the negative reaction is not one that is desired and results in fan apathy, it is known as "bad heat." Heat can also refer to real-life animosity between wrestlers, usually occurring behind the scenes.

heel, *noun.* A wrestler promoted by a company as a "bad guy," "villain," or "rulebreaker," i.e., someone who elicits boos and other forms of derision from the spectators. As with babyfaces, the definition of proper heel behavior has blurred over time as concepts of good and evil have been redefined in popular culture.

hooker, *noun.* A wrestler who has enough knowledge of real wrestling holds that, if need be, he could legitimately put someone out of commission. Promoters have been known to put a hooker in the ring with a wrestler they wanted to punish. Hookers were also used by promoters as muscle when dealing with rival companies. Today, the hooker is all but extinct.

jabronie, *noun.* See **jobber.**

job, *verb.* When a wrestler loses a match, it is said that he was "jobbing to" his opponent. If a promoter instructs a wrestler to lose a match, he is "jobbing out" that individual.
example: Triple H jobbed to Daniel Bryan at *WrestleMania XXX*.

noun. The act of losing a match, it is often referred to as "doing a job."

jobber, *noun.* In order to make his opponents look good, this individual always loses by the match's conclusion. A jobber is sometimes referred to as a preliminary wrestler or a curtain-jerker.
example: Heath Slater is a known jobber.

juice, *noun.* A slang word for blood, it can also be a term for steroids.

verb. To bleed in a wrestling match (or to use steroids). The word's double meaning can be a source of confusion, in which case the context determines the meaning.

example: Ric Flair very often juiced (i.e., bled) in his matches. Hulk Hogan has admitted that he has juiced (i.e., used steroids) in the past.

kayfabe, *noun*. The all-important code of secrecy used by those in the business to shield the public from the so-called "tricks of the trade." By staying "within" kayfabe, wrestling personalities pretend that the matches are competitive and that the storylines are "real." To "break kayfabe" means to reveal the event's scripted nature. The sanctity of kayfabe has seriously eroded in recent years.

verb. To convince someone that something is "real" when it is actually simulated.
example: Are you kayfabing me?

mark, *noun*. A wrestling fan who believes that wrestling is a legitimate sport. It can also be reduced to mean someone who believes any particular aspect of wrestling is "real" when it actually isn't.

verb. When someone "plays along" (or is "marking out") even though they realize that what they're watching is a scripted performance.

mic work, *noun*. The term used to describe the level of adeptness at interviewing skills and conveying personality through use of the microphone.
example: The Rock consistently demonstrates his adeptness with mic work.

over, *adjective*. The ability a wrestler possesses to elicit the desired response from the spectators, whether that response be positive (for "good guys") or derisive (for "bad guys"); possessing the required intangibles that enable a wrestler to connect with an audience.
example: Following the breakup of The Shield in WWE, Roman Reigns got over as a singles star very quickly.

preposition. A performer who allows another wrestler to defeat him (or who makes him look good in any other way) is said to be "putting over" his fellow performer. The victorious wrestler is said to have "gone over" his opponent.
example: Legendary wrestlers sometimes put over the up-and-comers to help them attain a reputation in the industry.

pop, *noun*. A loud eruption of cheers from the crowd, whether it be in response to a particular wrestler, wrestling move, or the finish to a match.
example: Stone Cold Steve Austin usually elicited enormous pops from crowds.

verb. The act of an audience exploding into cheers.

potato, *noun.* A punch which is not pulled, thereby delivering real impact.

product, *noun.* The total sum of all aspects of a wrestling show, including matches, storylines, TV-production values, and the overall look and style of what a company presents as their "type" of pro wrestling.
example: ECW was known for having a very edgy product.

program, *noun.* A long-term plan devised by a promoter or booker that indicates what involvement a performer will have in upcoming storylines. (See also **angle**.)
example: John Cena is often placed in programs involving the WWE World Heavyweight Championship.

push, *noun.* An elevation in status which a wrestler receives through the efforts of effective promotion and marketing. Essentially, the promotion works to convince the fans that a particular performer is worth their attention. A push is usually designed along "good guy" (face push) or "bad guy" (heel push) lines.
example: After debuting in 2014, Rusev was given a tremendous heel push.

verb. You get the idea.

ring work, *noun.* A wrestler's actual in-ring athletic performance.
example: Cesaro is known for his great ring work.

rub, *noun.* An increase in attention devoted to a wrestler due to his association with an already well -established wrestler (or wrestlers).

run-in, *noun.* A scripted incident involving someone, usually a wrestler, literally "running in" and interrupting a match with the intent of "attacking" one of the competitors.

screwjob, *noun.* A) A particularly unsatisfying finish to a match, usually a disqualification or count-out; B) Any finish that is not definitive (e.g., a pinfall or a submission).
example: Promoters will sometimes plan a screwjob finish to try and build interest in a rematch.

sell, *verb.* To act as though something is legitimate when it is not; to make it appear that something pre-planned is actually "real." A wrestler who acts as though he is hurt during a match is "selling" his opponent's moves, and is said to be "selling for" the opponent.
example: When a wrestler winces in pain after being hit with a choreographed punch, he is "selling" the punch.

shoot, *noun*. Anything in wrestling which is genuine, whether it be a legitimately competitive match or an interview based on true events. A shoot can be a deviation from the planned outcome, or it can be planned.

> *verb.* Performing an action which is not part of the pre-arranged script. When used as a verb in the modern sense, it usually refers to words rather than actions.
> *example*: CM Punk had a reputation for shooting in interviews.

shooter, *noun*. A wrestler who legitimately knows how to wrestle, and can be called upon to do so, if necessary.

smart, *adjective*. A) Aware of the staged nature of wrestling; B) Hinting at actual behind-the-scenes machinations.

> *noun.* A fan with an "insider" perspective on wrestling; the opposite of a mark.
> *example*: *Monday Night Raw* sometimes features storylines designed to appeal to smarts.

spot: *noun*. A) Any particular segment of a match, whether it be a maneuver, exchange of maneuvers, or any other specific act which is part of the performance. This can include a special move for which a wrestler is known, or a series of moves especially worked out between two opposing wrestlers. B) "High spot"—a notable action highlight. C) "Calling the spots"—the dictation of which moves will be performed throughout the course of a match.

> *example*: The spots that Bret Hart was known for included the sharpshooter, and running chest-first into the turnbuckle.

squash, *noun*. A match during which a wrestler easily dominates and defeats his opponent.

> *verb.* To easily and quickly defeat an opponent.

stiff, *adjective*. A wrestling style or move which appears more "realistic" than usual, in which blows are thrown with greater impact and holds applied with more pressure than is seen in a typical choreographed match.

> *example*: Some performers, fearing serious injury, are hesitant to work with those whose style is considered stiff.

swerve, *noun*. A sudden twist in a storyline, resulting in an action contrary to what was expected; it is usually done to throw off smart fans that have access to wrestling information on the Internet.

> *example*: The fact that Mankind, and not Triple H, won the WWF World Championship at *SummerSlam '99* was a swerve.

tweener, *noun.* A performer who is not clearly established as a hero or a villain, but remains "on the fence." Usually this situation doesn't last long, and a tweener soon develops into either a "good guy" or "bad guy."

turn, *verb.* To switch one's identity from "good guy" to "bad guy" (heel turn) or vice versa (face turn).

> *noun.* The act of switching identities.
> *example*: Fans were shocked by Seth Rollins's heel turn in 2014.

work, *noun.* Anything in wrestling which is pre-arranged or scripted but presented as though it were real. This covers basically everything in wrestling, from the simulated matches to the fictional rivalries.
example: Undertaker and Kane are not really related; it is a work.

> *verb.* To wrestle (to work a match), or to convince the audience that something is real when it isn't (see Kayfabe).

worker, *noun.* A wrestler.

workrate, *noun.* The percentage of a match which consists of actual motion and action, as opposed to resting or stalling. This can also apply to a wrestler's typical performance.
example: Most *lucha libre* matches have a very high workrate.

Selected Bibliography

Books

Beekman, Scott. *Ringside: A History of Professional Wrestling in America.* Westport, CT: Praeger, 2006.

Billington, Tom, and Alison Coleman. *Wrestling Observer's Pure Dynamite: The Price You Pay for Wrestling Stardom.* Etobicoke, Ont.: Winding Stair Press, 2001.

Blassie, Fred, and Keith Elliot Greenberg. *"Classy" Freddie Blassie: Listen, You Pencil Neck Geeks.* New York: Pocket Books, 2003.

Hackett, Thomas. *Slaphappy: Pride, Prejudice & Professional Wrestling.* New York: Ecco, 2006.

Hornbaker, Tim. *National Wrestling Alliance: The Untold Story of the Monopoly That Strangled Professional Wresting.* Toronto, Ont.: ECW Press, 2007.

Jares, Joe. *Whatever Happened to Gorgeous George?* Englewood Cliffs, NJ: Prentice-Hall, 1974.

Lentz, Harris M. *Biographical Dictionary of Professional Wrestling.* Jefferson, NC: McFarland, 1997.

Mazer, Sharon. *Professional Wrestling Sport and Spectacle.* Jackson: University Press of Mississippi, 1998.

Morgan, Roberta. *Main Event: The World of Professional Wrestling.* New York: Dial Press, 1979.

Pope, Kristian, and Ray Whebbe. *The Encyclopedia of Professional Wrestling: 100 Years of History, Headlines & Hitmakers.* 2nd ed. Iola, WI: Krause, 2003.

Saks, Stu, ed. 2014 *Wrestling Almanac & Book of Facts.* London Publishing, 2014.

Sammartino, Bruno, and Bob Michelucci. *Bruno Sammartino: An Autobiography of Wrestling's Living Legend.* Pittsburgh, PA: Imagine, 1990.

Shields, Brian, and Kevin Sullivan. *WWE Encyclopedia: The Definitive Guide to WWE.* London: Dorling Kindersley, 2012.

Shoemaker, David. *The Squared Circle: Life, Death, and Professional Wrestling.* New York: Gotham Books, 2014.

Thesz, Lou, and Kit Bauman. *Hooker: An Authentic Wrestler's Adventures Inside the Bizarre World of Professional Wrestling.* Norfolk, VA: Self-published. 1998.

Wilson, Jim, and Weldon T. Johnson. *Choke Hold: Pro Wrestling's Real Mayhem Outside the Ring.* Bloomington, IN: Xlibris, 2003.

Periodicals

Meltzer, Dave. *The Wrestling Observer.* San Jose, CA.

Stern, Karl. *Pioneers of Wrestling.* Haleyville, AL: DragonKing Pro Wrestling Press, 2002.

Teal, Scott, Fred Hornby, et al. (eds.). *The History of Professional Wrestling: Madison Square Garden, 3.* Hendersonville, TN: 2000.

Websites

"1865 though 1902 Northeast results." Wrestling Observer/Figure Four Weekly. http://www.f4wonline.com/component/content/article/3193/.

1wrestlinglegends.com. http://www.1wrestlinglegends.com.

CANOE – SLAM! Sports – Wrestling. http://slam.canoe.ca/Slam/Wrestling.

CompleteWWE.com - Your #1 WWF & WWE History Resource. http://www.completewwe.com.

"InterMat Rewind: Gotch vs. Hackenschmidt." InterMat. http://intermatwrestle.com/articles/2904.

Kayfabe Memories. http://www.kayfabememories.com.

Legacy of Wrestling. http://www.legacyofwrestling.com.

Obsessed with Wrestling. http://www.obsessedwithwrestling.com.

PWI Online. http://www.pwi-online.com.

"Pro Wrestling." Bleacher Report. http://bleacherreport.com/pro-wrestling.

Professional Wrestling und Mixed Martial Arts. http://wwf4ever.de.

The History of WWE.com. http://www.thehistoryofwwe.com.

WrestlingClassics.com. http://wrestlingclassics.com.

Wrestling Lore. http://thewrestlingauthority.blog.ca.

Wrestling-Titles.com. http://www.wrestling-titles.com.

Wrestlingdata.com – The World's Largest Wrestling Database. http://wrestlingdata.com.

Index

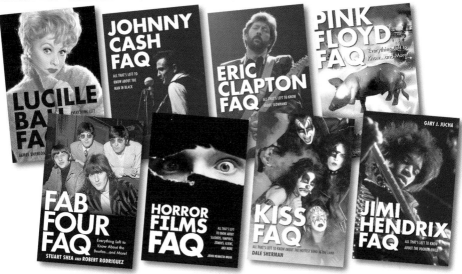